A PROJECT OF **SABR** SABRBOSTON

'75

THE RED SOX TEAM THAT SAVED BASEBALL

Edited by Bill Nowlin and Cecilia Tan

David Southwick, Project Coordinator

Library of Congress Cataloging-in-Publication Data

Edited by Bill Nowlin and Cecilia Tan. Foreword by Mark
Armour. Introduction by David C. Southwick.
Title entry: '75
Originally published: Rounder Books, 2005.
Includes bibliographical references.
Contents:
    ISBN 1-57940-127-9 (pbk.)
    1. Boston Red Sox (baseball team). 2. 1975 baseball
season. 3. Biography. I. Nowlin, Bill. II. Tan, Cecilia.
796357'092

2005934795

Player photographs and reproductions from the 1975 Boston Red Sox
yearbooks courtesy of the Boston Red Sox.

Red Sox memorabilia courtesy of Bob Donaldson.

Back cover photo courtesy of Bob Brady.

ISBN 1-57940-127-9

First printing, November 2005

Rounder Books
1 Camp Street
Cambridge, MA 02140

Designed by Glenn LeDoux

✂ CONTENTS ✂

❊⟨ CONTENTS ⟩❊

MEMORIES OF A SUMMER

by Mark Armour

Baseball was dying in 1975, or so many thought. The game was badly trailing pro football—a television ratings monster even in prime time—and was widely viewed as less hip, and less relevant, than its rival. The Oakland Athletics, admirable three-time champions between 1972 and 1974, dished up steady servings of 2–1 victories, which so stirred their fans that the team couldn't even sell out its home World Series games.

Among the storied seasons in Red Sox history, the 1975 team is often overlooked. Coming just eight years after the "Impossible Dream" and three years before the greatest Red Sox team many of us have ever seen stumbled and sputtered its way to a gut-wrenching denouement, the 1975 Red Sox sit in comparable obscurity. Sure, we all remember the classic World Series with the Reds, but what of the summer that led up to it? What of its players? What of its legacy?

For those of us in New England, the magic of 1975 was apparent early in the season. The failed comeback of Tony Conigliaro was a bump in the road, but the summer was filled with wonderful subplots and moments: the spectacular emergence of rookies Fred Lynn and Jim Rice, highlighted by Lynn's great night in Detroit; the dramatic return from injury of Carlton Fisk, the team's leader and best player; the double-header shutout of the Yankees by Bill Lee and Roger Moret in Shea Stadium; the daily human interest story of the beloved Luis Tiant and his family; and the biggest victory of the season, Tiant's September 16 blanking of the hard-charging Orioles ("Loo-EE . . . Loo-EE . . .").

The rest of the country caught on in October. The canonization of the 1975 World Series was not the retroactive doings of baseball's marketing department; it began while the games were still being played. By the middle of Tiant's five-hit masterpiece in the first game, the fans tuning in had become aware that they were watching something special. By the sixth game, the players were conversing about it on the field.

Darn the luck, the Reds won the World Series in seven games. This was a big disappointment, I grant, but losing a seven-game series to that great team was not remotely comparable to the crushing defeats that lay ahead for the faithful. The relationship between the team and its followers had not yet become bitter, as it would in 1978, or hostile, as it would after 1986.

Roger Angell, writing in the *New Yorker* after the 1975 season had ended, tried to capture what it all meant. His lead: "Tarry, delight, so seldom met. . . . The games have ended, the heroes are dispersed, and another summer has died late in Boston, but still one yearns for them and wishes them back, so great was their pleasure."

Hope sprung anew. We had just seen proof (as if proof were needed) that baseball could still be magical, could keep the country riveted for seven games, could leave us all wanting an eighth. In Boston, it was even better, since our team was suddenly awash in young, star players. Lynn and Rice, the freshman sensations, and Fisk, whose dancing Game Six image has become the season's symbol, were sure to be spending their Hall of Fame careers together in Boston, accompanied by several other good young players. No Red Sox team, it is fair to say, has ever looked to have a better future than this one did during that off-season. What could go wrong?

What first went wrong took place on December 23, just two months after the last out of the season, when baseball arbiter Peter Seitz, ruling in favor of the plaintiff in Andy Messersmith's grievance, effectively ended baseball's reserve clause. With the death of owner Tom Yawkey the following summer, the Red Sox dysfunctional management bungled their way through the early years of free agency, resulting in a series of painful contract squabbles, and eventually the bitter departures of Tiant, Fisk, and Lynn, among several others. The still-intact club exceeded its 1975 win total in both 1977 and 1978, but would never approach the innocent glory it provided us in the summer of 1975.

So 1975 was both a beginning and an end. Despite the predictions of doom by commissioner Bowie Kuhn and his reactionary owners, the *Messersmith* decision did not destroy baseball. The commissioner, and many pundits, underestimated the game—the renaissance forged by the Red Sox and Reds in 1975 would not be waylaid by a mere arbiter's ruling. But for the Red Sox and their fans, the glorious run of pennants never came, thwarted by the team's inability to properly adapt to the new order.

But when baseball is at its best, it compels us to live in the moment. As we all watched Bernie Carbo step in against Rawly Eastwick, down three runs in the eighth inning, we cared not what lay in the future. In that summer, and autumn, now 30 years distant, the moments provided by the players on this team thrilled a region.

I see them, still.

It was a cold, winter afternoon in January 2004 at Fenway Park. The Boston chapter of the Society for American Baseball Research (SABR) was holding its winter regional meeting at Fenway's Hall of Fame room. There were some research presentations and we heard from sportswriter Howard Bryant of the *Boston Herald* talking about his book *Shut Out*. I was glad to be able to introduce an idea for a chapter project that I hoped would not only promote participation in chapter activities, but would also benefit SABR's international BioProject Committee, which houses the largest collection of baseball biographies on the planet. The simple idea was to produce biographies of every player on the 1975 American League champion Boston Red Sox in time to celebrate their 30th anniversary the following year. Little did we know at the time that the fruits of our labor would result in this publication and a symposium to celebrate the collected research.

In 2002, our SABR chapter hosted the Society's 32nd annual convention and we organized *The Fenway Project*, which resulted in a book of that name being published in 2004. Researching the '75 Red Sox seemed like a good follow-up project and I was gratified with the initial response.

Several SABRBoston members were intrigued with the initiative and were supportive of the idea, volunteering to join the effort it took to ultimately put this collection together. We were approached by a wide variety of seasoned, experienced writers and editors; we were also pleased that a number of others wanted to participate, including a number of prospective authors who had never researched or written a piece of this nature before. The authors ranged from a high school student to retirees. All were motivated by a love of baseball and we achieved the goal of broad participation within the chapter. We were very impressed with the results. This was very much a chapter effort, and the extraordinary efforts of the contributing writers should be recognized. Over the course of the project, these writers successfully balanced their research and writing with the various demands of their personal lives, as they worked around such commitments as work, family, and foreign travel. One author even worked around his wedding and honeymoon to meet our deadlines! Authors were invariably generous with their time and spirit even as they responded to the sometimes detailed comments and questions occasioned by the various "peer review" readers who volunteered their time and talents, but posed numerous questions requiring follow-up research.

With all projects of this nature, there are several people to thank. You will meet the writers as you read on. The few who needed to be recognized here are the editors, Bill Nowlin and Cecilia Tan. Both are experienced writers and editors and added so much to this project to help it become a reality. SABRBoston chairman Seamus Kearney rooted for us from day one providing excellent moral support and SABRBoston secretary Paul Wendt for providing the ever-valuable electronic resource through a page on the SABRBoston web site to allow potential volunteers to learn about the project. Peer review readers included Mark Armour, Mark Kanter, Len Levin, Wayne McElreavy, and Mark Pattison. Bob Donaldson loaned us many

1975 season artifacts from his collection, and Debbie Matson of the Boston Red Sox offered photographs of the players from the team. The book was designed inside and out as a labor of love by talented chapter member Glenn LeDoux.

This is not a book about the 1975 season. Both Tom Adelman and Doug Hornig have written excellent histories of that exceptional year in Red Sox history. This is a book about the players on the 1975 team—every one of them. This is a collection of 37 biographies. The beauty of a biography is that it covers a subject's whole life, from beginning to end. These are not just baseball stories, but life stories. You will read how these 37 men arrived by various routes to constitute the 1975 team, put together one of the greatest seasons in Boston history, and then went their separate ways. You will read from A to Z (or at least to Y), from Kim Andrew's two 1975 at-bats to the veteran star Carl Yastrzemski. You will learn more about the regulars, the journeymen, and the "cup of coffee" players that carried the Red Sox to the pennant and right down to the ninth inning of Game Seven of the World Series.

You will learn about their beginnings, their childhoods and early baseball experiences. You will learn about their successes and tragedies, ups and downs. These are not just the stories of the ballplayers many of us rooted for 30 years ago, but the stories of three dozen baseball players. I think you will find many rewards in reading their stories, and on behalf of the SABR's Boston chapter, I wish you happy reading.

David C. Southwick
September 2005

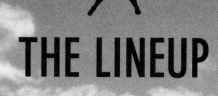

THE LINEUP

Photograph overleaf, L to R: Jim Rice, Fred Lynn, and Dwight Evans.

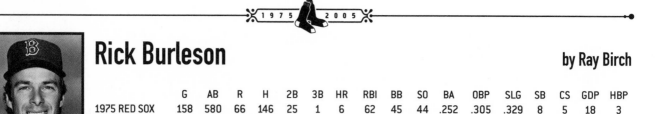
Rick Burleson

by Ray Birch

	G	AB	R	H	2B	3B	HR	RBI	BB	SO	BA	OBP	SLG	SB	CS	GDP	HBP
1975 RED SOX	158	580	66	146	25	1	6	62	45	44	.252	.305	.329	8	5	18	3

When reflecting on the career of Rick "The Rooster" Burleson, the fiery, intense shortstop of the Boston Red Sox, California Angels and Baltimore Orioles from 1974 to 1987, a quotation from former teammate Bill Lee perhaps sums it up best: "Some guys didn't like to lose, but Rick got angry if the score was even tied. He was very intense and had the greatest arm of any infielder I had ever seen." Burleson excelled as a Red Sox player for seven seasons, both at the plate and in the field. His participation in both the 1975 World Series and the 1978 playoff against the New York Yankees has secured his place in Boston Red Sox baseball lore. He was especially liked by Boston fans because of his burning desire to win and his constant hustle on the field.

Richard Paul Burleson was born on April 29, 1951 in Lynwood, California. He was selected by the Boston Red Sox in the first round of the 1970 amateur draft, with the fifth overall pick, during the January secondary phase. He played for the Winter Haven Red Sox in the Florida State League (Class A) in 1970, and split 1971 between two other Class A teams—the Greenville Red Sox (Western Carolinas League) and the Winston-Salem Red Sox (Carolina League). Rick moved up to the Pawtucket Red Sox in the Eastern League (Double A) for the 1972 season.[1] Burleson made the Eastern League All-Star team while at Pawtucket; the All-Star game was scheduled to be played on July 13, 1972 at Three Rivers Stadium, Pittsburgh, Pennsylvania but was rained out.[2]

In 1973 Burleson went to spring training with the Red Sox, but was optioned prior to the season to Pawtucket, the Red Sox Class Triple A farm club.[3] Burleson's manager at Pawtucket was Darrell Johnson, who became manager of the parent Red Sox in 1974, and one of his teammates was Cecil Cooper, a stalwart on the 1975 Red Sox World Series team. Burleson's fielding prowess, as a second baseman, was a vital part of teammate Dick Pole's seven inning no-hitter pitched on June 24 against the Peninsula Whips.[4] Burleson led the league in games played.

The Pawtucket club finished second to the Rochester Red Wings during the regular season, but in the playoffs they dispatched the Tidewater Tides and Charleston Charlies to win the International League championship Governors' Cup. This victory qualified them to meet the winner of the American Association championship, the Tulsa Oilers, for the Junior World Series title. In a best-of-seven series, the Pawtucket team defeated the Oilers to win the championship. In Game Two, Burleson drove in four runs with two singles and a two-run homer. In the third game, he had the game-winning hit, and in Games 4 and 5, he played a key role offensively.[5]

By spring training of 1974, it was apparent that Burleson was ready to make his move up to the parent club. Darrell Johnson, now the manager of the Red Sox, termed him "one winnin' sonavagun."[6] During the winter, Rick played in Venezuela for the veteran Luis Aparicio, who, along with Mario Guerrero, represented his main competition to win the starting shortstop job. In a prophetic moment before spring training, Burleson said "if they let me get the work in spring training, I'll be the shortstop." On March 26, Aparicio was released, reducing the competition to Burleson and Guerrero. It was announced that the two would alternate at shortstop and "get into 110 games apiece."[7] Guerrero won the job outright, though, while Burleson was sent to Pawtucket so that he would able to play every day.[8]

While at Pawtucket, Burleson played well enough to earn a call up to Boston. In his first game, May 4, the Rooster committed three errors in a 1–0 loss to Texas, tying an American League record for errors for a player in his major league debut.[9] Unfazed by his inauspicious debut, Rick followed up by hitting a three-run homer in the second game of a doubleheader against the Rangers the following night. After an injury to second baseman Doug Griffin, Burleson got more playing time, platooning with Dick McAuliffe at second. By mid-July, when Griffin returned, Johnson felt confident enough in the Rooster's .306 batting average to play Burleson full-time at shortstop.[10] By August, in the middle of a pennant race, Burleson had earned the admiration of teammates and coaches. Coach Don Zimmer remarked, "He hits pretty well because he hits like he plays. He's a little bulldog up there."[11]

The 1974 season ended in disappointment for the Red Sox, as they collapsed during the September pennant race. However, Burleson hit .284 for the

season, playing in 114 games, earning the club's rookie of the year award. He finished second to Bucky Dent for the shortstop nod on the Topps major league rookie All-Star team. Yet, despite his rookie success, it was felt by some people in the Boston organization that because of Burleson's average range at shortstop the Red Sox should deal for a veteran, established shortstop, such as Freddie Patek of the Kansas City Royals or Eddie Brinkman of the Detroit Tigers, and move Burleson to second base.[12]

As spring training of 1975 approached, Burleson expressed a desire to play shortstop, although he felt that as long as he played, he would be happy at short or second and batting anywhere in the lineup. By the end of May, though, Burleson was firmly in place as the Red Sox starting shortstop.[13] His fielding was consistently good, and he was learning how to play hitters better. As the 1975 season progressed, Burleson formed a slick-fielding double play combination with Denny Doyle, who was acquired from California to platoon at second base with Doug Griffin. In addition, his hitting earned him the second spot in the batting order.

The Red Sox clinched the American League East title by 4½ games over the Baltimore Orioles. In the ALCS, their opponents were the Oakland Athletics, the three-time defending world champions. The Athletics were the favorites and featured an All-Star batting order including Reggie Jackson and Joe Rudi and a pitching staff led by Vida Blue and Ken Holtzman, with Rollie Fingers in the bullpen. The Red Sox swept the Athletics in three games.

If the series against the Athletics had loomed as difficult for the Red Sox, then the World Series looked to present insurmountable odds. The Cincinnati Reds, also known as The Big Red Machine, came into the 1975 World Series as the overwhelming favorite, based upon their powerful lineup, with 108 wins and only 54 losses. After an extremely competitive World Series, the Red Sox lost to the Reds in seven games. The final batting line for Burleson in the 1975 World Series was 7-for-24, a .292 average, with a double and two runs batted in.

Good things seemed to be on the horizon for both Burleson and the Red Sox in 1976, as outfielders Fred Lynn and Jim Rice had established themselves as young sluggers. Yastrzemski, Evans and Petrocelli were returning veterans, and Burleson, Fisk, and Doyle gave the Red Sox a hustling, aggressive presence up the middle. Lynn, Fisk and Burleson all had contract disputes, however, heading into the season, which ended up as a disappointing one for the Red Sox, with manager Darrell Johnson being replaced at mid-season

by Don Zimmer, and the Yankees replacing them as AL East champions.

In 1977, the Red Sox presented a lineup that emphasized hitting the long ball. During a 10-game homestand in June, the Sox hit a major-league record 33 home runs.[14] Burleson had a 13-game hitting streak in April and May and, by the beginning of June, was hitting .325, as well as providing steady infield defense complimented by his rocket arm. This performance earned the Rooster a starting berth on the 1977 American League All-Star team, along with teammates Carlton Fisk and Carl Yastrzemski.[15]

The potent batting order returned for the 1978 season, but Burleson started slowly, and was hitting only .200 after 20 games. However, after getting on track, Burleson finished third in the shortstop voting for the American League All-Star team, and he was chosen as an alternate. An injury forced Burleson out of the Red Sox lineup until July 28, and a once seemingly insurmountable Red Sox lead of 10 games in the American League East had been reduced to 5½ games by the beginning of August. Burleson's worth to the team became apparent when he immediately went on a 16-game hitting streak upon his return.[16]

Still, the Red Sox led the Yankees by four games entering a September series at Fenway Park.[17] In the four-game set, the Bronx Bombers destroyed the Red Sox in all phases of the game, sweeping a series that became known as the Boston Massacre. In typical Burleson fashion after the debacle, he made no excuses saying that the Yankees were just better than the Red Sox and that it was now a 20-game race to the finish. The Red Sox and the Yankees finished in a tie for the American League East title to force a one-game playoff on October 2. Burleson was involved in a strange sequence in the ninth inning when, with the score 5–4 with one out, he walked. The next batter, Jerry Remy, then hit a line drive into right field. Yankee right fielder Lou Piniella positioned himself as if he would make the catch, which froze Burleson for a split second and kept him at second base. Piniella stabbed at the ball and guessed correctly. The next batter, Jim Rice, advanced Burleson to third with a fly ball, but he was stranded there when Carl Yastrzemski popped out to end the game.[18] Burleson batted .248 for the season in 145 games, and his absence during July may have been the difference that swung the balance towards the Yankees in the tight battle for the division title.

After a vigorous off-season training program with teammate Fred Lynn, Burleson and the Red Sox began 1979 with high hopes. The fiery side of

Burleson's personality was shown on May 16 when he was ejected and suspended for three games after he bumped an umpire while disputing a strike call. On June 4, Burleson hit the first grand slam home run of his major league career in a Red Sox win over the Rangers.[19] Despite a season which was disappointing for the Red Sox because of injuries and lack of key run production, Burleson again made the All-Star team for the American League. After the season, Burleson was also awarded a Gold Glove for his fielding prowess and also received the Thomas A. Yawkey Award as the team's most valuable player.[20]

Burleson arrived early to spring training in 1980, but soon began to suffer from a sore shoulder. Additionally, the contract he signed in 1976 after so much rancor was coming to an end. In May, his frustrations with the team in his contract negotiations became apparent; as he told the club to trade him and that he would not play without a contract in 1981. At the end of May, Burleson had a torrid batting streak, raising his average from .203 to .277 in one-month, batting in both the leadoff and second spots in the lineup. He had also played in every one of Boston's games through September 14 and led the league in putouts, assists, chances and double plays. He was quoted as saying that he would test the free agent market if the club did not sign him by the winter meetings.[21] Haywood Sullivan said that if he did not know that he could sign Burleson by World Series time, then he would trade him to avoid any more disruption to the team. The Sox were offering about $2.1 million over six years, while Burleson was asking for about twice that amount. Adding to the confusion in Boston was the fact that Lynn and Fisk were in similar contractual situations with management. Finally, on December 10, the Red Sox traded Burleson and Hobson to the California Angels for infielder Carney Lansford, pitcher Mark Clear, and outfielder Rick Miller. Prior to a grievance hearing regarding some contractual issues, Burleson agreed to a lucrative six-year, $4.65 million deal which made him the highest paid shortstop in baseball history.

Burleson got off to a great start in 1981. After a mid-season strike by the players' union, the Angels failed miserably in the so-called second season—at one point, losing 14 of 15 games. As usual, Burleson led by example, batting .291 after the strike, but despite the trades before the season, the Angels did not qualify for the playoffs. For his efforts, Burleson was named to *The Sporting News* American League All-Star team, batting .293 in 109 games, and also was named the Angels' Most Valuable Player for the season.

At the start of the 1982 season, Burleson suffered a rotator cuff injury to his right shoulder, ending his season and putting his career in jeopardy. Ironically, just days before his injury, the Rooster had set a record for the most assists by a shortstop in a game. After undergoing surgery, Burleson vowed that he would do all that he could to return. But, as of November, seven months after his surgery, he had yet to pick up a ball. Part of the problem was that some of his shoulder muscles had atrophied and needed to be strengthened.

Even the usually optimistic Burleson questioned whether or not he would be able to be in the 1983 Opening Day lineup. At the beginning of spring training, Burleson felt that he was throwing at "about 45 percent," and had every intention of being an integral part of the team, whether he was a starter or a utility player. New manager John McNamara expressed confidence in Burleson's return, noting that "if he's OK, he's our shortstop." Peter Gammons wrote, "One thing to remember. Never bet against Rick Burleson." Burleson went to Edmonton, the Angels' Triple A affiliate to get back into playing shape. The determination and perseverance of Burleson paid off handsomely, as he returned to the Angels' active roster and had two or more hits in each of his first seven games, while making only one error. Despite Burleson's heroics, the Angels floundered due to a combination of poor play and injuries. Although Burleson went back on the 15-day disabled list due to stiffness in his right shoulder, he batted .286 in 33 games.

Entering spring training in 1984, the jury was still out on how much Burleson could contribute to the Angels' cause. In order to compensate for his shoulder, Burleson tried to change his manner of playing, by positioning himself differently in order to reduce the lengths of his throws. The discovery of another tear in his right shoulder, however, dealt a serious blow to his comeback as a shortstop, although returning as a second baseman was still a possibility. He returned to the Angels' roster in September, but only to be used as a pinch-hitter and pinch-runner. Even in his limited role, Burleson proved to be feisty, criticizing management for failing to make moves that would keep the team in contention.

In the off-season, Burleson slipped and dislocated his shoulder while lifting weights, causing nerve damage in his arm, and costing him the entire 1985 season. Undaunted, Burleson continued his rehabilitation, trying to return and reward the patience that the Angels had shown in him. Working with Dr. Arthur Pappas, he progressed to a point where, in 1986, he attempted

in the final year of his six-year contract to come back as a second baseman. By March 9, he was able to play at second, attempting a relay throw from short center field in an exhibition game, with no ill effects. Burleson began the regular season hitting .358 in April, and played second, third and shortstop. Eventually, Dick Schofield, who had taken over as regular shortstop by 1984, returned to the lineup, taking Burleson out of the field and relegating him to designated hitter duties against lefthanders. Still, Burleson continued to make his presence known in the clubhouse and on the field when called upon, mostly as a late-inning substitute in the field. In the playoff series against his former team, the Red Sox, Burleson batted .273, hitting 3-for-11 while appearing in four games. Burleson's performance earned him the American League Comeback Player of the Year award for 1986.

Burleson became a free agent and signed with the Orioles on January 7, 1987, but was released on July 11 after playing 55 games at second base and seven games as a designated hitter. He'd batted just .209. It was the end of his 13 seasons of major league ball.

By 1989, Burleson had embarked upon a managerial career, becoming a part-time instructor in the Oakland Athletics system, a scout for the A's in 1990, and then, in 1991, full-time batting instructor under manager Tony LaRussa. After the 1991 season, he left the A's and took the batting coach job with the Red Sox under former teammate Butch Hobson. Former Red Sox manager Don Zimmer was third base coach, though Burleson replaced Zimmer there at midseason, when Zimmer became Hobson's bench coach. Burleson continued as third-base coach for the 1993 season.

Burleson was the Angels' third-base coach and base running instructor in 1995 and 1996. He made his managerial debut in 1997 with Seattle's Lancaster affiliate (California League), and the Jet Hawks went 75–66 in his inaugural season, improving to 78–62 in 1998, each year advancing to the league playoffs. Burleson joined the Dodgers' organization in 1999, leading San Bernardino to an 80–61 record and the California League Championship. He was promoted to Double A San Antonio (Texas) in 2000 and led the club to a 64–76 mark—the only sub-.500 record of his career. Burleson guided the Billings (Montana) Mustangs in 2001, 2002, and the first half of the 2003 season, where he compiled a 108–80 (.574) record, and helped the Mustangs to a pair of Pioneer League Championships (2001, 2003). He was promoted to manager of the Louisville River Bats for the second half of the 2003 season and the 2004 season. While, at

Louisville, Burleson gave an insight into his managerial philosophy in an interview with Rick Bozich of the *Louisville Courier-Journal*: "When a guy needs a kick in the butt, he's going to get it. And when he needs a pat on the back, he's going to get that, too." Burleson does not believe in an exceptional number of rules for his players, "except requiring them to be prepared and on time, avoiding mental mistakes, and playing hard." He was reassigned to the Billings Mustangs for the 2005 season.

Burleson's reputation as a hard-nosed, aggressive player can be supported statistically, especially in the years from 1975 to 1980, when he averaged over 150 games and over 600 at-bats per season. His clutch performances in 1975 against Oakland, batting .444, and Cincinnati, batting .292, provided the spark for the Red Sox that almost broke their long championship drought. But perhaps the greatest compliment that has been given to Rick Burleson came from teammate Jerry Remy, when Remy was asked to read the starting lineup some years later for a network broadcast. When he got to Burleson's name, he said, "Batting second, the heart and soul of the Boston Red Sox, Rick Burleson." To Red Sox fans of the 1970s, no better words could describe his contributions to those teams.

Cecil Cooper

by Eric Aron

	G	AB	R	H	2B	3B	HR	RBI	BB	SO	BA	OBP	SLG	SB	CS	GDP	HBP
1975 RED SOX	106	305	49	95	17	6	14	44	19	33	.311	.355	.544	1	4	3	3

Fitting his description in a June 1981 *Baseball Digest* cover story as "the Rodney Dangerfield of baseball," Cecil Cooper was a great player who didn't get the respect he deserved. An introverted Texan, Cecil Cooper remained in the shadows for much of his 17-year playing career. The left-handed first baseman spent his major league years with Boston and Milwaukee from 1971 to 1987, appearing in two World Series. "Coooop!"—as his fans would cheer when he stepped up to the plate—was a lifetime .298 hitter, two-time Gold Glove Winner, and five-time All-Star.

Cecil Cooper was born on December 20, 1949, in Brenham, Texas, a city with a population of 13,000 and located 70 miles northwest of Houston. Raised in nearby Independence, Cooper was the youngest of 13 children, seven boys and six girls. Cooper's mother Ocie died when he was just 10. His ball-playing father, Roy, worked with a nearby Department of Public Works. A 6'2" left hander, Cecil was taught baseball by his brothers John, Sylvester, and Jessie. John and Sylvester later played with the barnstorming Indianapolis Clowns of the Negro Leagues.[22] John was a pitcher while Sylvester was a catcher who, according to Cecil, once caught Satchel Paige. According to a 1980 *Sports Illustrated* story, Roy also played in the Negro Leagues.

Cooper followed his brothers, playing ball for three years at the all-black Pickard High School, transferring his senior year to the integrated Brenham High School. At Pickard High, he won two state championships under coach Henry Rogers. Intending to go to college after his graduation, Cecil was spotted by Boston Red Sox scout Dave Philley and was drafted in the sixth round of the 1968 amateur draft by the Red Sox. He opted to take courses at Blinn Junior College and Prairie View A&M during the offseason. Taken in the Rule 5 draft by the St. Louis Cardinals in November 1970, St. Louis returned Cooper to the Red Sox on April 5, 1971. He spent most of six full seasons in the minor leagues (in Jamestown, Greenville, Danville, Winston-Salem, Louisville, and Pawtucket), hitting .327 with 45 home runs and 304 RBI.

Cooper made his major league debut with the Red Sox on September 8, 1971, pinch-hitting for Roger Moret and grounding to second against Yankee pitcher Jack Aker. He got his first hit three days later, a pinch single off the Tigers' Joe Coleman. He hit .310 in 42 at-bats that month. Having hit .343 for Double A Pawtucket that season, it was thought that he had a shot at the starting job the next season.

Just prior to the start of the 1972 season, the Red Sox acquired Danny Cater from the Yankees and sent Cooper to Triple A Louisville. Another fine campaign in the minors produced a .315 average. Thanks to a league-leading 162 hits, Cooper returned to Boston in September, but garnered just four hits in 17 trips during the tight pennant race.

Despite the failure of Cater, Cooper again did not stick with the parent club in 1973, as the team elected to move Carl Yastrzemski back to first base the fill the hole. Cecil was sent to Pawtucket, now the Triple A affiliate, where he hit .293 with 15 home runs. This time he was recalled before the rosters expanded, first playing on August 24 and playing nearly full-time the rest of the season. In 30 games and 108 at-bats, Cooper hit .238 with his first three major league home runs. His first round tripper was struck on September 7 at Fenway Park, off the Tigers' Bob Miller.

In 1974, Cooper was the team's Opening Day first baseman, hitting third in the lineup. New manager Darrell Johnson used a lot of lineups, trying to divide playing time at first base, left field, and designated hitter amongst Cooper, Yastrzemski, Cater, Tommy Harper, and Bernie Carbo. Cooper ended up playing 74 games at first and 41 more at designated hitter, getting most of the starts when facing right-handed pitchers. He hit .275 in 414 at-bats.

Cooper did not have a good defensive reputation early in his career, which is why he spent a lot of time as a designated hitter. For 1975, the Red Sox had two new rookie outfielders (Jim Rice and Fred Lynn), plus the comebacking Tony Conigliaro, who initially won the DH job. The team had an awful lot of men trying to get a chance to play. At the end of May, Cooper was the odd man out, getting just six hits in 24 at-bats. He persevered, and by late June he was playing against all right-handed pitchers. He ended up hitting .311 with 14 home runs in 305 at-bats.

One of the team's hottest hitters from June through August, Cecil had a scary moment on September

7. The Red Sox were playing the second game of a doubleheader against the Milwaukee Brewers, when he was hit in the face by future teammate Bill Travers. Cecil had to be carried off on a stretcher and was bleeding from his nose and mouth. The incident hampered his performance the rest of the season. Then with Jim Rice's injury requiring Carl Yastrzemski to play left field, Cooper had first base to himself for most of the postseason. He was 4-for-11 in the playoffs but just 1-for-19 in the World Series.

Appearing in 123 games the following season, again splitting time between first base and designated hitter, Cooper hit a solid .282 with 15 homers and 78 RBI. After the 1976 season, manager Don Zimmer told Cooper told that he would become Boston's regular starting first baseman. This was not to be the case, as on December 6, 1976, Cooper was sent to the Milwaukee Brewers for two former Red Sox: first baseman George Scott and outfielder Bernie Carbo.

The trade was not particularly popular in either Boston or Milwaukee. In fact, Brewers owner Bud Selig was told by other AL East clubs that if you "keep making trades like that you will be in last place forever." In 1976, the Brewers finished dead last in their division with a record of 66–95. The extremely popular Scott had first played in a Red Sox uniform from 1966 to 1971 and had posted several good seasons for the Brewers. Alas, neither Scott nor Carbo ever again had the kind of success they had achieved in earlier seasons, while Cecil Cooper would become a legend in Milwaukee.

Cooper was a clutch contact hitter who could hit for both average and power. He kept putting up such solidly consistent numbers year after year that it was easy to overlook his achievements. In his first year in Milwaukee he hit .300, in his second year he hit .312, and in 1979 Cooper hit .308. Also in 1979, Cecil had a league-leading 44 doubles. Former Milwaukee player-coach Sal Bando once said of him, "Cecil Cooper can beat you with a home run or a flare to left or a bunt. And he can field his position. You have guys who can hit home runs and guys who can hit singles. But not many can do both. Cecil can."

Playing for a smaller market team in the Midwest allowed Cooper to thrive, and in 1980 he did just that. He hit better than .300 in every full month of the season finishing with a remarkable .352 average, 25 home runs, 219 hits, and an American League-leading 122 RBI. His season was largely overlooked because Royals third baseman by George Brett flirted with a .400 batting average, settling for .390. The unassuming Cooper said, "With Brett hitting close to .400 all year,

I didn't expect to get much publicity, and I didn't have any trouble living with that."

Coop was also part of a record game in 1980. On April 12, in an 18–1 Brewer rout of the Red Sox, he and Don Money connected for two grand slams in the same inning. This marked only the fourth time in major league history this feat has ever been accomplished. (There have been two since, most recently in 1999, when Fernando Tatis of the St. Cardinals hit both grand slams in one inning). In the late 1970s and early 1980s, the Brewers franchise was moving up in the standings, finishing with 93 wins in 1978 and 95 wins in 1979. In 1981, in a strike-shortened split season, the New York Yankees won the first half in the AL East while the Milwaukee Brewers finished first in the second half. This set the stage for a best-of-five game divisional playoff between the two clubs. Although the Yankees won the series in five games, it was the following year that the Brewers had the best season in franchise history. Cooper hit .320 with 12 home runs in the abbreviated campaign.

In 1982, first baseman Cooper was at the heart of the one of the era's great lineups, batting third behind Paul Molitor and Robin Yount, and in front of Ted Simmons, Gorman Thomas, and Charlie Moore. Cooper hit .313, with 32 home runs and 121 runs batted in. On October 3, 1982, in a game deciding the American League East championship, the Milwaukee Brewers defeated the Baltimore Orioles 10–2, closing out the season with a mark of 95–67. Their opponent in the ALCS was the western division champion California Angels.

The Brewers reached their first (and as of this writing, only) World Series as they eliminated the Angels in five games, becoming the first team in major league history to come back from a two-games-to-none deficit and win a best-of-five postseason series. In the decisive Game Five, Jim Gantner and Charlie Moore scored on Cooper's seventh-inning bases-loaded single. In a gesture reminiscent of former teammate Carlton Fisk, who waved his arms to keep the ball fair in Game Six of the '75 Series, Cooper motioned for the ball to get down. "I remember thinking, 'get down ball, get down.' The crowd was so loud I couldn't really hear myself saying anything, but I just wanted to keep waving so that ball would fall in there." He hit just 3-for-20 in the series.

The 1982 World Series was called the "Suds Series" because it pitted the two of America's largest beer cities against each other: Milwaukee and St. Louis. The National League champion St. Louis Cardinals featured first baseman Keith Hernandez and future

Hall of Fame shortstop Ozzie Smith. Cecil homered in a losing effort in Game Three, and his 8-for-28 record was not enough, as his team lost in seven games.

After the 1982 season, Cooper's teammate Robin Yount won the American League MVP award, and just as in 1980 when he lost to George Brett, Cecil finished fifth in the voting. Yount hit .331 with 29 home runs and 114 RBI. "Maybe, I'm the Lou Gehrig of my time," says Cooper, "always in the shadows of someone else. He's a pretty good role model, though."

While in Milwaukee, Cecil wrote a column for the Brewers' magazine, *What's Brewing?* He wrote about everything from his baseball experiences as a hitter and a first baseman to how kids could get autographs from their favorite players. In 1983, Cooper won baseball's coveted Roberto Clemente Award for his community service. Since 1970, the award has been given to players for their humanitarian service and initiatives. Cecil worked with Athletes for Youth, a Milwaukee-based inner city program teaching children about baseball, and was honorary chairman of both the Kidney Foundation of Wisconsin and the 1982 Food for Families Project. Bud Selig said of Cooper, "I think

Cecil does a lot more than any of us know. Cecil is shy. What he does, he prefers to do in anonymity."

Following his retirement in 1987, Coop was a player agent for CSMG International until 1996. He then worked as farm director for the Brewers as well as a scout. In 2002, Cooper returned to the dugout as bench coach for Milwaukee and got a chance to manage in the minor leagues for the Brewers' Triple A affiliate Indianapolis Indians. In two seasons, he posted a 130–156 record. In 2005, he took advantage of the opportunity to return to his native Texas where he currently serves as the bench coach for the Astros.

Cecil Cooper holds Brewers single season records in hits (219 in 1980) and RBI (126 in 1983). As a Brewer, he is ranked third all-time in batting (.302), hits (1,815), doubles (345), and home runs (201). He is second in RBI with 944. In his hometown of Brenham, Cecil had a field dedicated in his honor and a number retired at Brenham High School. In 2002, he was inducted into the Miller Park Walk of Fame. He lives in Katy, Texas with his wife Octavia and has three daughters: Kelly (born December 28, 1978, Brittany (born December 17, 1987), and Tori (born November 1, 1993).

Denny Doyle

by Herb Crehan

	G	AB	R	H	2B	3B	HR	RBI	BB	SO	BA	OBP	SLG	SB	CS	GDP	HBP
1975 RED SOX	89	310	64	82	21	3	4	36	14	11	.310	.339	.429	5	10	5	1

In mid-June 1975, the Boston Red Sox acquired veteran second baseman Denny Doyle from the California Angels to solidify the team's infield defense. But Denny Doyle did a lot more for the 1975 Red Sox than just shore up their defense.

Doyle batted a career-high .298 in 1975, batting .310 in 89 games with the Red Sox, and he put together a 22-game hitting streak that topped the American League that season. Most importantly, he brought a level of intensity and preparation that helped to bring the Red Sox within one game of their first World Championship in 57 years.

Interviewed recently in his Winter Haven, Florida home, Doyle still remembers every detail of joining the Red Sox on June 13, 1975. "I remember when I was first told about the deal. It was so exciting to go from a last-place team where I wasn't playing much, to a first place team where I would be a regular. I remember the writers covering the Angels asked for my reaction to the

move, and I told them I was disappointed. I said I was disappointed because I couldn't get an earlier flight to Kansas City to join the Red Sox."

Doyle, who was 31 years old when he joined the Red Sox, remembers meeting with Red Sox manager Darrell Johnson and his coaches before his first game with the team. "Darrell said to me, 'You are here for your defense. Anything you do with the bat is a plus.' Then he asked me where I liked to hit in the batting order. I told him that anywhere in the first nine was fine with me. You could almost hear a sigh of relief. It was the beginning of a great relationship and a wonderful year."

Robert Dennis Doyle was born on January 17, 1944, in Louisville, Kentucky. He grew up in the small town of Cave City, which is about 75 miles south of Louisville. He has fond memories of growing up in a warm family environment as part of a small, closely-knit community.

Sports were an important activity in the Doyle household. "My Dad was a good athlete but he had grown up working on his family's farm so he didn't get to pursue

an athletic career. I can remember playing catch with my dad in the backyard when I was probably three years old."

There is one moment with his father that stands out in Doyle's memory. "My Dad was kind of soft-spoken, and when he said something you paid attention. When I was about 10 or 11, he said, 'Son, if you are the first one there and the last to leave and you don't let anyone outwork you in between, you will do what you want to do and you will be successful.' I never forgot those words. That's what I did as a baseball player and that's what I still do today."

Denny Doyle played all sports at Caverna High School and he attracted plenty of interest from the professional baseball scouts. But when he graduated from high school his first love was basketball.

"I had chances to sign a professional baseball contract but they wanted to sign me as a pitcher and I didn't want to pitch," Doyle remembers. "And I had baseball scholarship offers from schools like Florida State and Arizona. But my dream at that time was to become the next Bob Cousy. Morehead State in Kentucky offered me a basketball scholarship and I took it."

By the end of his senior year at Morehead, Doyle had accepted the fact that his future was not in the NBA. But he was ready to pursue a career in professional baseball. His hopes were all but dashed when he wasn't drafted in the free agent amateur draft of 1965.

"That was the first year of the free agent draft for amateurs. Before that, all the clubs competed to sign prospects. Thousands of prospects were drafted, but I wasn't one of them. I was very disappointed," Doyle emphasizes, remembering that day forty long years ago.

"I stuck around Morehead State for summer school to pick up the few credits I needed for my degree. My baseball coach at Morehead approached me and asked me if I would help him out with a two-day Little League clinic he was giving in Ashland, Kentucky. I was still disappointed about not being drafted, but I told him I would help out.

"When we got there, Mel Clark, who was a long-time scout for the Philadelphia Phillies was there. He was surprised that I hadn't been drafted and he told me to bring my glove the next day and he would work me out. After our workout he called the Phillies and got permission to sign me. I may be the only former major leaguer who was signed from a Little League clinic," Doyle laughs.

It is less than 500 miles from Morehead, Kentucky, to Philadelphia. But Doyle's journey from Morehead State to Connie Mack Stadium encompassed stops in four cities, a coast-to-coast journey, and almost five years.

His odyssey began with the Phillies farm club in Spartanburg, South Carolina, where he led the league in hits and batted .308. In Spartanburg he teamed up with a shortstop who would be his double play partner for the next seven seasons. Spartanburg shortstop Larry Bowa would go on to play 16 seasons at the big league level and manage the San Diego Padres and Philadelphia Phillies for five and a half seasons.

Following a strong 1967 season with Tidewater in Portsmouth, Virginia, Doyle was promoted to Reading in the Eastern League. Reading, Pennsylvania was a short distance from Philadelphia, but at age 24 with two young children, Doyle was feeling a little discouraged.

"I had a good spring training in 1968, but I wasn't sure if I was on track for the big leagues. I talked to my manager Frank Lucchesi and he told me to hang in there. He said I was headed to Triple A the next season and the next stop was the big leagues."

Lucchesi proved to be as good as his word. The following season Doyle, Bowa and Lucchesi were all promoted to Eugene, Oregon, the Phillies top minor league club. At Eugene, Doyle led the Pacific Coast League in hits and was named both the league's Rookie of the Year and the Most Valuable Player.

Denny Doyle had the distinction of playing for the 1970 Philadelphia Phillies in their last year at ancient Shibe Park, which had been renamed Connie Mack Stadium. And he also played for the Phillies in their first year at Veterans Stadium in 1971. Best of all, he played both seasons as their regular second baseman. Connie Mack Stadium was showing its age, but Doyle remembers the well-manicured infield. "The stadium wasn't much but they still took care of the infield. It reminded me of Fenway that way."

In 1972, San Diego Padres pitcher Steve Arlin had a no-hitter in progress when Denny Doyle stepped to the plate with two outs in the ninth inning. Padres manager Don Zimmer pulled in his third baseman to guard against the possible bunt. Doyle placed a ball right over the third baseman's head and Arlin's date with destiny was over.

Denny spent four solid seasons with the Philadelphia Phillies. As Christmas 1973 approached, the Doyles were comfortably settled in their Laurel Springs home in southern New Jersey. Then on December 6, Denny learned that he had been traded to the California Angels.

"That was tough," Doyle reflects. "We had three little girls and we were happy in the area. You know it can happen any time in baseball, but to get traded to the other coast in a new league. That was hard."

The next season with the Angels, Doyle played in a career-high 147 games, and batted a respectable .260. But the team finished a disappointing sixth in the AL West. Despite the musical chairs with the manager's seat, the Angels managed only 68 wins.

The 1975 Boston Red Sox were considered a contender in the American League East, but they were not the favorites. That honor went to the Baltimore Orioles who had captured the division the two previous years. And the New York Yankees, who had finished two games behind the Orioles the previous year, were more highly rated than the Red Sox.

The team had a poor April, finishing the month with a 7–9 record and a fifth-place position. But the Red Sox improved in May, and a 6–0 win over the California Angels on May 24 at Fenway Park put the team in first place in the Eastern Division. Boston's pitching was better than predicted, and the "Gold Dust Twins," Jim Rice and Fred Lynn, were off to a great start.

For Denny Doyle, who was in the visitors' clubhouse with the Angels that day, the season was off to a terrible start. He had lost his starting job at second base to a rookie from Somerset, Massachusetts by the name of Jerry Remy. "It was a tough time for me," Doyle recalls. "The Angels were playing very poorly and I was hardly playing. It was not a good situation."

The Boston Red Sox compiled a record of 16–9 for May and held on to first place in the East. The team continued to play well into June, and it became clear that they were a legitimate contender in their division. General Manager Dick O'Connell concluded that they needed an upgrade from the injury-prone Doug Griffin at second base in order to compete with the Orioles and Yankees. On June 14, the Red Sox acquired Denny Doyle from the California Angels.

"I remember walking into the lobby of the Red Sox hotel in Kansas City and Don Zimmer said to Darrell Johnson, 'I told you he would be here.' Apparently Darrell had speculated that I would take some time to look after personal business. I was so happy to be joining a winning team and getting a chance to play, there was no way I was going to miss a minute," Doyle laughs in memory.

And Denny Doyle didn't waste any time making an impact on his new team. He made a game-saving defensive play in his first game and hit a key home run in his second game. He has a clear memory of both games.

"In my first game there was a ball hit up the middle and I dove for it and came up with it. I threw the runner out from my knees." Asked if he remembers the home run, Doyle responds, "I only hit 16 home runs at the big league level so I remember them all. That one came on a hanging slider from Dennis Leonard. It was nice to contribute right away."

The Red Sox rattled off six straight wins after Doyle was inserted in the lineup, and he felt comfortable right away. "That was a great team and it was easier for me to hit being surrounded by great players. I was batting second with hitters like Yaz, Fisk, Lynn and Rice behind me. It made me a better hitter. They let me put the hit and run on myself, and there was one point where we made that work seven times in a row."

It took him a while to get used to the passion of the Red Sox fans. "I had heard about it, and I had read about it. But until you play in front of those fans day-after-day you don't realize how much they care about their team. Red Sox fans are just unbelievable."

On July 12, the last game before the All-Star break, Denny Doyle hit safely against the Texas Rangers in a 7–5 Red Sox win. That began a hitting streak that saw him hit safely in 22 games. During his streak the Red Sox won 17 times and lost only five times. Doyle tends to downplay this personal streak.

"It was nice, and I'm proud of it. But it doesn't really mean anything because we didn't reach our goal that season. If we had won the World Series then it would really be something to talk about."

The Red Sox maintained their hold on first place and played consistent winning baseball throughout August. When the team returned to Boston in early September after a disappointing road trip, Doyle was shocked to see a sports page headline that read CHOKE AGAIN!

"I went into the clubhouse the next day and I said to Pudge, 'Am I in the right city?' I showed him the headline and told him they couldn't be talking about us. He said, 'You'll get used to it. That's just how they are here.'"

A more pleasant memory for Doyle is the time he spent with Red Sox owner Tom Yawkey. "I was always in the clubhouse early and he was usually around, so we got to talk. What a gentleman. He was a 'man's man.' I really enjoyed him."

The Red Sox overcame the fears of the press and their fans, clinching the Eastern Division title with a 5–2 win over the Cleveland Indians on September 27. The team then prepared to meet the West Division winning Oakland Athletics in the American League Championship Series.

The Oakland Athletics had won three straight world championships, and after winning 98 games to lead the AL West they were heavily favored to defeat the Red Sox in the 1975 Championship Series. But Boston won the first two games in Fenway Park, and hung on for a 5–3 victory in Oakland to sweep the A's in three straight games.

Denny Doyle wasn't surprised by the team's "upset" of the defending World Champions. "We had a team that never thought we would lose. We went into every game expecting to win. The fans might have been surprised that we swept Oakland, but we weren't."

Doyle had three hits during the three-game series.

But his scouting report on Oakland pitcher Ken Holtzman may have been his biggest contribution. Holtzman, who had won 18 games for the A's, was the losing pitcher in games one and three.

"I watched him [Holtzman] when I thought we might face him in the playoffs. And I had faced him in the National League. I noticed that when he was going to throw a curve to a left-handed hitter, he flared his glove during his windup and delivery. I passed that on to Yaz, Lynn, Carbo, and Cooper. It helped all of us."

The 1975 World Series between the Boston Red Sox and the Cincinnati Reds ranks high among World Series classics. The teams split the first two games at Fenway Park, with the Red Sox winning the opener behind a Luis Tiant masterpiece, while the Reds came from behind to win Game Two by a 3–2 margin.

The Reds won Game Three at Riverfront Stadium in Cincinnati, but Luis Tiant threw 163 pitches for a 5–4 Game Four win to tie the Series. A 6–2 Reds win in Game Five brought the Red Sox home to Boston with their backs against the wall.

Game Six featured Carlton Fisk's dramatic twelfth inning home run that has become baseball's most watched video clip. But Denny Doyle was involved in a ninth-inning play that fans still discuss 30 years later. The score was tied 6–6 and the bases were loaded with no one out when Fred Lynn lifted a fly to short left field. When Reds left fielder George Foster made the catch, Doyle tagged up and attempted to score the winning run. He was thrown out at the plate and the stage was set for Fisk's subsequent game-winning home run. After the game, Zimmer told the press, "I was yelling 'no, no, no' and with the crowd noise he thought I was saying 'go, go, go.'"

Asked for his memory of the daring ninth-inning dash for victory, Doyle replies thoughtfully. "First, let me say that Don Zimmer was the best third base coach I ever had. He and I teamed up over the last months of the season, and we were able to run on a number of outfielders with weaker arms. In Game Six, I was the runner and it was up to me to pick up the third base coach's direction. I didn't do that. There really isn't anything more to say.

"Except when I see Pudge [Fisk], I tell him, 'You ought to thank me. If I had scored the winning run you wouldn't be nearly as famous.' It's almost as if it was meant to be."

After taking a 3–0 lead in Game Seven, the Red Sox eventually bowed to the Reds 4–3. In a World Series that included five future Hall of Fame players, Denny Doyle was the only player on either team to hit safely in all seven games.

Like the rest of his Red Sox teammates, Doyle was bitterly disappointed by the loss, but he was comforted by the Red Sox prospects for future success. "That was a great team," he emphasizes. "And we had a nucleus for years to come. We all thought we would get another chance in the World Series."

But the 1976 Boston Red Sox never regained the magic of the 1975 season. The team started poorly and manager Darrell Johnson was fired in mid-season. Third base coach Don Zimmer replaced Johnson, but failed to turn the team around. The Red Sox won only 83 games and finished a distant 15½ games behind the division-leading Yankees.

In 1977 the Red Sox improved to 97 wins, but tied for second in the East Division with the Baltimore Orioles. The New York Yankees topped the East and went on to beat the Los Angeles Dodgers for the World Championship. Denny Doyle had played capably as the starting second baseman in both years, but the Red Sox were determined to make some moves in the offseason.

When Denny Doyle reported to spring training in Winter Haven, Florida, for the 1978 season, there was a familiar face contending for the second base job. The Red Sox had acquired Jerry Remy from the California Angels the previous December. The Boston Red Sox released Denny Doyle on March 28, 1978.

Asked how it felt to lose his starting job to Jerry Remy twice, Denny Doyle replies, "The only feeling I have is wishing that he [Jerry] never had that knee injury. He had a nice career. But it would have been an even better career, and a longer career, if he had never been hurt."

"I was devastated when I was released by the Red Sox," Doyle acknowledges. "I wasn't sure what I was going to do. I knew I could teach high school science and I had some discussions about coaching in the minors. The only thing I knew for sure was that I wanted to start a baseball school with my brothers."

Doyle's twin brothers Brian and Blake were both also professional baseball players. Blake had been drafted by the Baltimore Orioles and was playing in the minor leagues. Brian was in his rookie year with the New York Yankees. The Doyle Baseball School caught its first break when Brian, playing in place of injured Yankees second baseman Willie Randolph, had a sensational World Series against the Los Angeles Dodgers.

"Brian went seven for sixteen, with a number of key hits, and just missed being named the Series MVP. During a telecast, announcer Joe Garagiola mentioned that the Doyle brothers were starting a baseball school in December. The timing couldn't have been better.

"When our first session started in Winter Haven, Florida, we had 150–175 youngsters at our camp. Never in my wildest dreams did I imagine that we would touch

over 750,000 youngsters, coaches, and parents over the next 27 years."

Doyle Baseball is still headquartered in Winter Haven, Florida, but its reach extends far beyond. "We have trained so many instructors in our approach, that at any time in the spring there might be 15 to 20 sessions going on around the country that are part of our program," Doyle emphasizes. "We have had major leaguers like Tim Wakefield, and former Red Sox player Jody Reed here."

Denny and Martha Carol Doyle are long-time residents of Winter Haven, and they have two granddaughters and two grandsons. "When I look back over the years, I remember how my wife had to be mother and father to our daughters, Melynn, Robin, and Marci during my playing career. I have been very lucky to have her."

When Denny Doyle looks back on his career with the Red Sox, he thinks first of the great players from those teams. "Luis Tiant was just a great pitcher, a great competitor. And I always enjoyed playing behind Bill Lee. He worked fast and he always had an idea of what he was trying to do.

"And we had a whole lineup of great hitters. We had quiet leaders like Yaz and Rico, and a not-so-quiet leader in Pudge Fisk. And Rick Burleson was one of the most competitive guys I ever played with. He and Larry Bowa [Phillies shortstop] were in a league of their own when it came to intensity."

But Doyle ranks the Red Sox fans right up there along with his memories of his teammates. "I remember one game when there was a long rain delay. When they started to play again, there were only a few thousand fans left. They made an announcement inviting the remaining fans to move down to the front row.

"Well, there were these three fans in the front row down the right field line who were really giving it to me. They just wouldn't let up. There was a pop fly beyond first base and I caught it on the run. But I didn't stop; I kept running straight at them. When I got there, I took the ball, gave it to the loudest one, and said, 'You guys are great.' Years later I got a note in the mail from the guy. He said, 'About 12 years ago you gave me a ball and I just want you to know that it is still sitting up on my mantle.'"

There is one memory of Red Sox fans that particularly stands out for Denny Doyle. "It was during the World Series and my whole family was in town. We went out to dinner together to a nice restaurant on Newbury Street after the game. When we got there the place was packed and I wasn't sure if we could get seated. But I knew the maitre d' and he took us right away. When he was leading us to our table everyone in the room got up and gave us a standing ovation. That's something I'll never forget."

Reflecting on his years with the Red Sox, Doyle offers, "You know, when I joined the Red Sox I was in my tenth year of professional baseball. I had played in the National League and the American League. But I never felt like I had played in the major leagues until I played for the Red Sox in front of those fans in Fenway Park. Red Sox fans are in a class all by themselves."

Portions of this article originally appeared in *Red Sox Magazine* and the permission of the Boston Red Sox to use this material is gratefully acknowledged.

ARLINGTON CO-OPERATIVE BANK

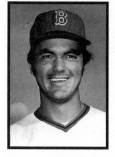

Dwight Evans

by Bill Nowlin

	G	AB	R	H	2B	3B	HR	RBI	BB	SO	BA	OBP	SLG	SB	CS	GDP	HBP
1975 RED SOX	128	412	61	113	24	6	13	56	47	60	.274	.353	.456	3	4	10	4

A member of the Red Sox Hall of Fame, Dwight Evans was voted Red Sox MVP four times by the Boston Baseball Writers. It's no stretch to agree with Herb Crehan, who wrote, "Dewey might be the most underrated player in the history of the Red Sox."

A three-time All-Star, Evans won eight Gold Gloves in the stretch running from 1976 through 1985. At one time or another, he led the American League in on-base percentage, OPS, runs, runs created, total bases, home runs, extra base hits, bases on balls, and times on base. He had a rifle of an arm, patrolling Fenway's capacious right field for 19 years from 1972 through 1990, and three times led the league in assists—but runners quickly learned not to try to score on Dwight Evans.

Born Dwight Michael Evans on November 3, 1951 in Santa Monica, California, his family moved to Hawaii when he was still an infant and he spent his early years living in Hawaii, mostly before Hawaii was granted statehood on August 21, 1959. Hawaii was built on beach culture, and Dwight did not get involved with baseball until the age of nine, when the family moved to the Los Angeles suburb of Northridge. He attributes his passion for the game to a Dodgers game his father took him to soon after they arrived in the area. Dwight joined Little League and both pitched and played third base, an all-star both at the Little League and Colt League levels. At Chatsworth High School, though, "I tried out for the junior varsity baseball team and I didn't even get a uniform." He was determined, though, and not only made the team his junior year but made All-Valley in the San Fernando Valley League. He won the league MVP award his senior year and found himself being scouted.

Boston Red Sox scout Joe Stephenson recommended Evans highly, and on June 5, 1969, the Red Sox selected Evans in the fifth round of the 1969 amateur draft. The 17-year-old Evans was assigned to the Jamestown, New York farm club. The Sox had so many people coming into Jamestown at that time that he had to wait a week to get a uniform and worked out in his sweatshirt and jeans. He got in 100 at-bats, though, and a .280 average, enough to be promoted to Greenville, South Carolina for the 1970 season. He kept advancing, spending 1971 with Winston-Salem, and made it to Triple A Louisville

for 1972. His was the classic trip up the ladder, one year at a time.

Evans told Herb Crehan that it was Louisville manager Darrell Johnson who made the difference when Dwight found himself outmatched at the Triple A level. "You are my right fielder whether you hit .100 or .300," Johnson told him, imbuing the 20-year-old with enough confidence to turn his season around. He hit .300—on the nose—with 17 HR and 95 RBI. Evans was named International League MVP for his 1972 season—and got a ticket to Boston, to join the big league club in the middle of a classic pennant race.

Dwight Evans played his first game for the Boston Red Sox on September 16, 1972, entering the game as a pinch runner for Reggie Smith in the bottom of the sixth in a game against the Indians at Fenway Park. He stayed in the game, playing right field. In his one at-bat, he made an out to the shortstop. It's an interesting tidbit that he batted out of order his first time up, but since he had made an out, the other team chose not to make a point of it. He got his first major league hit the very next day, pinch-hitting with two outs in the bottom of the ninth, in a game the Indians were winning with ease, 9–2. Evans singled to left. He added another hit the following day, starting in left field and going 1-for-3 with a single.

On September 20, Evans had a breakthrough day, playing left field in both games of a doubleheader against the visiting Orioles. Dwight was 2-for-4 in the first game, with a couple of singles. He was 2-for-4 in the second game as well, but the two hits were a seventh-inning triple off Mike Cuellar and an eighth-inning home run off Eddie Watt. In 57 September at-bats, Evans batted .263. He helped keep the Red Sox in the pennant race; this was the year they fell just a half-game short to the Tigers.

The following year, Dwight Evans was the regular right fielder most of the season, playing 113 games, 94 of them in right field. He was still finding himself in his first full season of major league ball, batting just .223 and with only 32 RBI, but he showed some power with 10 home runs, and made only one error all year long. 1974 featured another 10 homers, but a .281 average and Evans drove in 70 runs. His defense, and especially his throwing arm, was what kept him in the lineup.

In 1975, he had another good year playing a solid right field while Fred Lynn and Jim Rice joined him to form one of the all-time great outfields. Evans was involved in a league-leading eight double plays. Though he was subpar in the League Championship Series, Evans batted a strong .292 in the World Series and drove in five runs. His dramatic ninth-inning two-run home run tied up Game Three, a contest the Red Sox lost in the tenth. As always, Evans excelled on defense, and his catch of Joe Morgan's long fly ball in Game Six was one of the most spectacular in World Series play. After tracking down what looked like an extra-base hit, and snaring the ball, he fired to first base and doubled off Ken Griffey Sr. to retire the side.

The next season, Dewey hit .242 with 17 home runs in 146 games, and won his first Gold Glove award for his defensive play. In 1977 he battled a knee injury all year, spending much of the year on the disabled list. This was a shame, since he hit better than he ever had, finishing with 14 home runs and a .287 average in just 73 games.

The 1978 season saw the Red Sox leap out to a commanding lead, then give it all away in September. They fought back to tie the Yankees and force a single-game playoff for the pennant. Boston might have done better, but Dewey was a little woozy for the final month of the season, following an August 28 beaning. Even in the playoff game, he rode the bench, only coming in for a last-ditch ninth-inning pinch-hit role, in which he flied out to left field. It was his first appearance in a week. One wonders if a playoff game would have been needed had Evans been better able to contribute that final month. He hit .247 with a career-high 24 home runs on the season, but hit just .164 with one a home run in September.

After two more fairly typical seasons (21 HR, 58 RBI, .274 in 1979, and 18 HR, 60 RBI, .266 in 1980), Dwight Evans reached his 29th birthday with seven solid seasons under his belt. He was part of a great outfield, but clearly the third wheel amongst two of the better players in the game. His reputation was as a good hitter and a great right fielder. Beginning with the 1981 season, Evans underwent a remarkable offensive transformation, and was one of the best all-around players in the league for the next several years.

His first great season was 1981, unfortunately marred by a seven-week player strike. Besides his fourth Gold Glove award, Dewey hit a career high .296, and paced the league in home runs (22), walks, total bases, runs created, and OPS. Whereas he had always hit seventh or eighth under Don Zimmer, new manager

Ralph Houk recognized Evans' great on-base skills and hit him second in the order for all four years he managed him. He finished third in the balloting for Most Valuable Player. After playing in the shadow of his more famous teammates for several years, Evans was now the team's best player. Lynn and Carlton Fisk were gone, Carl Yastrzemski was nearing the end of the line, and Jim Rice would never again be the hitter he was in the late 1970s.

In 1982, Evans proved his resurgence was no fluke, hitting .292 with 32 home runs and 98 RBI, leading the league with a .402 on-base-percentage. After an off year in 1983 (22, 58, .238), he had another big year in 1984, slugging 32 home runs, driving in a career-high 104 runs (remarkable for someone hitting second in the batting order), leading the league in runs, runs created, and extra base hits. On June 28, 1984, Evans doubled, tripled, made three outs, then singled in the tenth, and lastly completed the cycle in style with a three-run walk-off homer in the bottom of the 11th off Edwin Nunez, for a 9–6 win over the Mariners.

The next two seasons were more of the same for Evans, hitting 29 and 26 home runs, and generally being among the league leaders in walks, on-base-percentage, and extra base hits. New manager John McNamara moved Evans to leadoff in 1985, though he eventually started hitting him sixth in 1986. Leading off the game for the Red Sox on Opening Day 1986, on April 7 at Tiger Stadium, Evans hit a home run on the first pitch of the entire major league season. The Red Sox made it again to the World Series in '86. Again, Evans' bat was quiet in the Division Series (.214), but just as in 1975, he ratcheted it up in the World Series, batting .308 with two homers and a team-best nine RBI. In Game Seven, Evans led off the top of the second with a solo home run, for the first run of the game.

Although the team struggled in 1987, it was another great season personally for Evans, with a .305 average (and a league-leading 106 walks), 34 HR, and 123 RBI. Despite a big drop-off from the team, Evans finished fourth in the MVP voting. Turning 36 after the season, Evans had two more fine seasons in 1988 and 1989. In 1987, he began playing first base quite a bit as the team had come up with a few young outfielders, and by 1989 he was often the designated hitter.

After the 1990 season, the Red Sox declined to re-sign Evans and granted his release on October 24. The Baltimore Orioles snapped him up on December 6 and he played in 101 games for Baltimore, batting .270 and acquitting himself well. Dewey received a tremendous ovation the first time the O's visited Fenway.

Evans would win the Gold Glove award in 1976, 1978, 1979, 1981, 1982, 1983, 1984, and 1985. Steady in the field, steady at the plate, Evans played 20 seasons in all, finishing with a .272 average, 385 home runs, and 1,384 RBI. Evans was, interestingly, a better hitter in the second half of his career than in the first half. A commonly-asked trivia question poses the query: Who hit more home runs in the American League than any other player during the 1980s? From 1980 through 1989, the answer was: Dwight Evans, with 256 homers in the decade-long stretch. He also led the league in extra base hits over the same period of time.

Playing 19 years with the Red Sox (only Yaz played in more games) enabled Dwight Evans to rank among team leaders in a number of batting categories. No Red Sox fielder approaches Evans in the number of Gold Gloves. The only major league outfielders with more are Willie Mays, Roberto Clemente, Al Kaline, and Ken Griffey Jr.—pretty good company.

After baseball, Evans worked for the White Sox in their minor league system for a few years, then hooked on with Colorado as major league hitting instructor in 1994. He was welcomed back to Boston in 2001, serving first as a roving instructor and then, in 2002, as hitting coach for the Boston Red Sox. Dewey is a frequent visitor to Red Sox functions and currently serves as a player development consultant for the team.

Carlton Fisk

by Brian Stevens

	G	AB	R	H	2B	3B	HR	RBI	BB	SO	BA	OBP	SLG	SB	CS	GDP	HBP
1975 RED SOX	79	263	47	87	14	4	10	52	27	32	.331	.395	.529	4	3	7	2

Born in Bellows Falls, Vermont, on December 26, 1947, Carlton Fisk embodies traditional New England values like pride, ruggedness, and individuality. That was what Boston Red Sox public relations director Dick Bresciani was trying to capture in 1997 when he wrote that Fisk was a "native of Vermont" on his original plaque for the Red Sox Hall of Fame. But the greatest baseball player ever born in Vermont—and the man responsible for perhaps the most dramatic moment in New England sports history—doesn't consider himself a Vermonter. Fisk grew up on the other side of the Connecticut River in Charlestown, New Hampshire, a town of less than 1,000 inhabitants—it just so happened that Bellows Falls had the nearest hospital. So in a display of traditional New England stubbornness, Fisk insisted that his plaque be re-cast (at a cost of $3,000 to the Red Sox) to delete the Vermont reference and reflect that he was raised in New Hampshire.

Fisk played American Legion baseball in Vermont for Post Five in the town of his birth, and for years a simple white sign with an "X" marked the spot at the Bellows Falls field where one of his blasts landed. In fact, in his first at-bat for Bellows Falls in 1965, Fisk crushed a home run at Cooperstown's Doubleday Field, the site where baseball was supposedly invented. In storybook fashion, he returned to Cooperstown in 2000 for induction into the National Baseball Hall of Fame.

Carlton Ernest Fisk inherited his extraordinary work ethic and athletic talent from his parents. His father, Cecil, worked for 13 years as an engineer in the tool-and-dye industry in Springfield, Vermont. A job like that would be enough for most people, but Cecil also worked the Fisk family farm. Often he dismounted from the tractor, raced to a local tennis match, soundly defeated his opponent, then returned to the farm to resume his chores. In addition to tennis, Cecil also was a superb basketball player. Carlton's mother, Leona, was famous in her own right as a champion candlepin bowler. Certainly the gene for coordination ran in the Fisk family.

The Fisks of Charlestown established an athletic dynasty. Carlton's older brother, Calvin, his younger brothers Conrad and Cedric, and his sisters, Janet and June, all exhibited unusual athletic prowess. In fact, the son who was destined for the Hall of Fame was not considered the most talented of the progeny. Carlton was chubby as a youngster, which is how and when he acquired his well-known nickname, Pudge. "If you saw him as an eighth grader, you would not believe he could accomplish the things he has," said Ralph Silva, his high school coach. But Carlton was strong, and Coach Silva honed that strength by implementing weight training long before it became commonplace.

Beginning in 1962, when Calvin and Carlton first played Charlestown High School sports together, and continuing through 1972, when June graduated from the newly-regionalized Fall Mountain School

District, the Fisks could be counted on to appear in postseason playoffs. Along with Calvin, Conrad, and younger brother Cedric, Carlton formed the nucleus of a dominant Charlestown presence in basketball, baseball, and soccer. Early on, though, Pudge's greatest accomplishments came on the hardwood. "Fisk could have made it in basketball," said Coach Silva. "He was that tough."

After developing his hoop talent in his grandfather's barn, Carlton went on to some legendary high school performances. In a 1963 regional playoff game at the Boston Garden, for example, he made such an impression in a victory over Winooski, Vermont, that Walter Brown, owner of the Celtics, leaned over to a local reporter and said, "You have got to tell me—who is that kid?" In 1965, playing against Hopkinton in the New Hampshire Class M semifinals, the 6'2" Fisk scored forty-two points and yanked down 39 rebounds—even though the opposition included players who were 6'10", 6'8", and 6'3". When he fouled out with a minute left, Fisk received a standing ovation from the Portsmouth crowd. Charlestown lost by two points, and an oft-told story is that after his son's memorable performance, Cecil Fisk's only comment was that Carlton had missed four free throws.

Cecil wasn't being harsh or overbearing—he simply understood that to excel as an athlete, mental toughness was essential. Cecil's philosophy on child-rearing was simple: "I expected them to do as well as they could, whatever they did." Cecil and Leona Fisk sat behind the bench during basketball games but never said a word to Coach Silva, never criticized his strategy and never let on if they disagreed with how their sons were handled. "No Hall of Famer ever had a better start than Fisk," said Bellows Falls American Legion coach Tim Ryan, "and it was because of his parents."

Because of the northern New England weather, Carlton Fisk's high school baseball career consisted of no more than 17 games a season. Before early-season practice he and his teammates often had to shovel off the Charlestown High School baseball field, which was shaded from direct sunlight. Sometimes the team simply practiced in the nearby Fisk cornfield. "I'd let them practice for as long as they wanted, long after we would have otherwise gone home," said Coach Silva. "Of course, they don't do that anymore."

Carlton demanded that practice be taken seriously; on one occasion he punched out a teammate for "goofing off." The competitive nature of those practices resulted in Carlton's first experience as a catcher. During batting practice, with Carlton manning third base and Calvin behind the plate, a foul pop drew both of their attention. With the entire team yelling "Fisk!" both attempted to make the catch, and the resulting collision made Calvin look like a hockey player (only one of the two teeth retrieved could be saved). Because the catcher's mask no longer fit over his swollen jaw, catching responsibilities fell to Carlton. (In typical Fisk fashion, Calvin played the next day, but in left field.)

Calvin, Carlton, and Conrad all pitched for the Charlestown team, which went 49–17 including playoff games during Carlton's high school career. One of those losses came in the Class M state championship against a strong team from Woodsville. Despite striking out 14, Carlton was a victim of his own aggressiveness. With one out and the winning run on third, the Woodsville batter laid down a perfect squeeze bunt that hugged the third-base line. Not hearing his teammates' cries of "Let it go foul!" Carlton leaped off the mound, picked up the ball and threw across his body, making an amazing play to nail the batter at first as the winning run scored.

Because of the short high school season, American Legion baseball takes on special importance in New England. Carlton played for Claremont in his first year of eligibility, but in 1965 he switched to Bellows Falls Post Five, the team that won the Vermont State Championship the previous year. In one game with Bellows Falls, so the story goes, Carlton was at the plate and behind in the count, fooled by two consecutive curveballs. When the catcher called for a fastball and was emphatically shaken off by the pitcher, the manager called time and approached the mound. "There's no way I'm throwing him a fastball," the hurler said. But the manager insisted that he throw what the catcher called for, and Fisk hit the next pitch (a fastball) on a line over the center-field fence.

Though he played in fewer than 100 games as an amateur, Fisk gained the attention of professional scouts. One thought he had potential but told Coach Ryan that his bat wasn't quick enough—his power was mostly to right field. Ryan's response was typically self-effacing: "He'll get better coaches in the minors who can teach him to hit to left." But despite his success in baseball (or, more accurately, his all-around athletic success, as he was named Charlestown High's most valuable player in soccer and basketball as well), Carlton accepted a basketball scholarship to the University of New Hampshire.

The decision to attend UNH was made easier by the presence in Durham of his older brother, Calvin, who was captain of the soccer team and an All-Yankee Conference sweeper. But soon Calvin was drafted by

both the Baltimore Orioles and the military. He was 25 by the time he returned from Vietnam, too old (according to the Baltimore front office) to embark on a career in professional baseball. Carlton's younger brother Conrad, considered the best pitcher of the Fisk clan, later signed with the Montreal Expos. He was undefeated and threw a no-hitter in the playoffs during his senior year of high school, but an arm injury ended his career prematurely. Cedric, whose scholastic batting average was higher than that of any of his older brothers, didn't pursue athletics beyond high school.

During the winter of 1965–1966, Carlton led the UNH freshman basketball team to an undefeated season. While at UNH he also met his future wife, Linda Foust, a native of Manchester, New Hampshire. Then, in January 1967, the Boston Red Sox drafted him in the first round. Fisk was at first suspicious, suspecting that he was the token New Englander the Red Sox had taken to pacify local fans. He ended up signing mainly because he realized "I could never be a six-foot-two power forward and play for the Celtics."

Carlton Fisk's baseball career almost came to an end at Waterloo, Iowa, Boston's entry-level team in the Class A Midwest League. Despite batting .338 with 12 home runs in 62 games, he was despondent. Pudge's letters home show that the source of most of his frustration was the team's losing record. The Waterloo Hawks finished 56–68, 26½ games behind the league-leading Cedar Rapids Cardinals. Losing was new and intolerable to Fisk.

But he persisted and in September 1969 the Red Sox called him up from Double A Pittsfield. The 21-year-old Fisk made his major league debut in the first game of a doubleheader against the Baltimore Orioles on September 18. His cup of coffee turned bitter—in two games he went 0-for-5 with two strikeouts—and Bill Liston wrote in the *Herald-Traveler*, "The word on Fisk is that he needs a year of Triple A ball, especially to enable him to handle breaking pitches with the bat."

That year of Triple A ball became one year with Double A Pawtucket in 1970 and another with Triple A Louisville in 1971, but Fisk remained upbeat and continued to improve. At Louisville his manager was Darrell Johnson, whom he credited for making him a major leaguer. "Johnson taught me to think about all the important facets of the catcher's role, the things that help pitchers in various ways and those that let your teammates know you want to win," he told an interviewer in 1973. Johnson also helped Fisk improve his hitting. "When I put the equipment on, my job is defense: to get the other team out, help the pitchers get the batters, help the fielders—to run the game," Fisk said. "Once I take the equipment off, however, I stop thinking defense and start thinking offense."

That new concentration resulted in a .263 average at Louisville, 34 points higher than his average the previous season at Pawtucket.

Despite his excellent play (.313 with two home runs) in 14 games with Boston at the end of the 1971 season, Carlton Fisk was only the third-string catcher for the Red Sox in 1972. The starter was Duane Josephson, who'd batted .245 with 10 home runs in '71 after coming to Boston in a trade with the White Sox. Bob Montgomery was the backup. But when Josephson was injured in the third game of the season and rival base runners were running at will on Montgomery, Fisk became a regular in Boston.

From the start, Carlton was a slugger. By June 13 the 24-year-old rookie had collected 32 hits, 20 for extra bases. His average was .278 and his slugging percentage was .574. His confidence rose with his slugging average, which stood at .628 by July 12. He was beginning to attract attention. "Fisk is rapidly gaining the reputation of being the Johnny Bench of the American League," wrote Larry Claflin. In July, Earl Weaver selected him to represent the American League in the All-Star Game in Atlanta. Fisk replaced Bill Freehan in the sixth inning and suddenly found himself playing against Hank Aaron and Willie Mays, whose bubble-gum cards he'd collected back in Charlestown.

For the 1972 season, Fisk caught 131 games and batted .293 with 22 home runs. His accomplishments earned him selection as the American League's Rookie of the Year, the first player ever to receive the honor by a unanimous vote. He also won the Gold Glove for AL catchers and finished fourth in balloting for the AL's Most Valuable Player Award. In a testament to the times, Pudge's salary reportedly rose from $18,000 to $30,000 which, according to Claflin, was "as big a pay raise as any player in the game."

The Red Sox had been searching for a quality receiver ever since the Birdie Tebbetts–Sammy White era of 1947 to 1959. In Fisk they finally had a tough, productive, intelligent, and dependable backstop. "If you play against him you hate him," said manager Eddie Kasko, "but if you play with him and want to win, you love him. He plays as if he were on the Crusades."

The dreaded sophomore jinx caught up to Carlton Fisk in the second half of the 1973 season. Batting .303 on June 23, he hit only .228 in July, .198 in August, and .186 in September. The extended slump was nothing compared to challenges soon to come. At Municipal

Stadium on June 28, 1974, the Red Sox and Indians were deadlocked at 1–1 with two outs in the bottom of the ninth inning when Cleveland's Leron Lee rounded third and crashed into the fully-extended Fisk, who was reaching for a high relay throw from Mario Guerrero. Pudge tore ligaments in his left knee. "My career was supposed to be over," he recalled. "I was supposed to walk with a limp and have chronic back problems the rest of my life."

But Fisk returned in 1975, and the long, lonely hours spent in rehabilitation made a lasting impression on him. Though for years the knee injury hampered his ability to throw out base-runners, he feels that it may have been a blessing. "In some ways, hurting my knee was one of the best things ever to happen to my off-season psyche," Fisk said while still an active player. "Now, everything I do is programmed toward getting ready to play baseball. Before, winter was just a time to have fun hacking around the basketball court." His obsession with conditioning was the secret to his 22-year career in the majors. Though injuries continued to plague him—in all he spent over five and one-half seasons on the disabled list—he always managed to return, allowing him to catch in 2,226 games, the most in major league history. "More than the home runs, it's the longevity that stands out as his greatest achievement," says high school coach Silva.

After coming back from the 1974 knee surgery, Fisk was hit by a pitched ball in spring training and broke his forearm. Returning to a standing ovation on June 23, 1975, Pudge hit .331 over the remainder of the season to lead the Red Sox to the AL East title. Fisk batted .417 against the Oakland A's in the League Championship Series, but his greatest heroics were yet to come.

Game Six of the 1975 World Series—a must-win game for the Boston Red Sox, down three games to two to the Cincinnati Reds—was a wild, seesaw affair. The Red Sox jumped out to a 3–0 lead on Fred Lynn's three-run homer in the first inning, but the Reds came back and took a 6–3 lead into the eighth, when Bernie Carbo's pinch-hit, three-run homer tied the game. In the ninth inning, the Red Sox failed to score despite loading the bases with no outs, and the game headed into extra innings with the score knotted at six.

It was 12:33 A.M. by the time Carlton Fisk stepped to the plate to lead off the bottom half of the 12th against Pat Darcy, the eighth Reds pitcher of the night. On Darcy's second pitch, Fisk lofted a high shot down the left field line. Millions of television viewers watched Fisk wave wildly as he made his way down the first-base line, willing the ball to stay fair. When it glanced off

the foul pole—a fair ball—John Kiley, the Fenway Park organist, launched into Handel's "Hallelujah Chorus" as the native Vermonter circled the bases in triumph. The home run touched off a celebration throughout the region—in Fisk's native Charlestown, church bells rang out in the early-morning stillness.

Many consider Fisk's game-winning blast the exclamation point on the greatest baseball game ever played. In Game Seven, however, Bill Lee couldn't hold on to another 3–0 lead, and the Reds took the series with a 4–3 victory. The Red Sox were once again denied their first World Series championship since 1918.

Fisk was named to the AL All-Star Team seven times during his tenure in Boston. During one pennant race when his team was battling the Red Sox, Baltimore Orioles manager Earl Weaver said, "The guy they'd hate to lose most, even more than Rice, is Fisk." In determining Fisk's importance, consider that in 1980 the Sox were 68–44 when he was behind the plate, 15–33 when he was not. Yet by 1981 Fisk was questioning whether the Red Sox front office really wanted him. Contract negotiations proceeded slowly, and then general manager Haywood Sullivan blundered by failing to mail his contract on time, rendering Fisk a free agent.

The Red Sox offered Fisk a guaranteed $2 million plus incentives. The perennially non-contending Chicago White Sox, for whom Fisk's acquisition would create instant credibility, offered $3.5 million. Nevertheless, the decision to leave Boston was difficult. After the Red Sox traded Rick Burleson, Butch Hobson, and Fred Lynn to the California Angels that winter, however, Fisk questioned Boston's commitment to winning. Conversely, the White Sox, with new owners Eddie Einhorn and Jerry Reinsdorf, were improving. Fisk decided to sign with Chicago.

In 1983 the White Sox made their first appearance in the postseason since 1959, and many credited Fisk's work with pitchers Britt Burns, LaMarr Hoyt and Richard Dotson as the key. Pudge averaged 125 games for Chicago through 1985, when he hit 37 home runs with 107 RBI. But that year his honeymoon with the White Sox front office ended with a bitter salary dispute, and subsequent re-signings in 1986, 1988, 1991, and 1993 were about as smooth as Vermont dirt roads during mud season.

At an age when most players are capable of nothing more than an occasional appearance at a fantasy camp or old-timers' game, Fisk continued his quest for personal goals. In August 1990, he hit his 349th home run as a catcher, setting a major league record. His son

Casey was there. "I had goose bumps when he hugged his boy at home plate," said White Sox manager Jeff Torborg. "That's a big emotional thing right there. It meant so much to those two and that family."

In 1993 Fisk caught his 2,226th game, surpassing Bob Boone as the all-time leader. Then, on June 28, the White Sox released him. The next day, Carlton and Linda Fisk sent a simple but heartfelt message to the Boston faithful. They hired a plane to tow a banner reading, IT ALL STARTED HERE. THANKS TO BOSTON FANS. PUDGE FISK. They sent a similar message across the sky over Comiskey Park.

Among the thirteen Hall-of-Fame catchers for whom numbers are available (complete statistics don't exist for Negro Leaguer Josh Gibson), Carlton Fisk ranks first in total games caught, at-bats, hits, runs scored and doubles, second in total home runs and putouts, third in RBI, and tied for fourth in fielding percentage. Fisk's 128 stolen bases for modern Hall-of-Fame catchers are second only to Ray Schalk's 176. He was an 11-time All-Star. The White Sox retired his number 72 in 1997, the same year he was elected to the Red Sox Hall of Fame. Fisk's election to the National Baseball Hall of Fame was almost a bygone conclusion, but it was made official in January 2000.

After some delay, Fisk provided the answer to a difficult question by announcing that he would wear a Red Sox cap into the Hall, even though he spent 13 years with the White Sox and only nine full seasons with the Red Sox. "I would like to say that this has always been my favorite hat, and I will be wearing this hat probably for the rest of my career," said the man who worked at the time as a special assistant to Red Sox general manager Dan Duquette. At that same press conference, Duquette told a surprised Fisk that the team had decided to retire his number 27. "I didn't think I met the criteria," said Fisk. "It gives me goose bumps to think about it. I didn't think it was at all possible." In the past, the Red Sox have stated that they will retire a number only for a player who is in the Hall, spent at least 10 years with the team, and finished his career in Boston. Duquette, by hiring Fisk, ensured that he was finishing his career with the Red Sox. In formal ceremonies during 2005, the left-field foul pole was officially named the Fisk Pole.

Fisk will always be remembered for his dramatic home run in the '75 Series, but the incident that best represents how he played the game came on an otherwise unmemorable night in 1989 when Deion Sanders, then a rookie with the New York Yankees, failed to run out an infield grounder. The next time "Neon Deion" came to the plate, the 42-year-old Fisk growled, "Listen to me, you #%*&. Next time run it out."

Even though Sanders played for the opposition—and the hated Yankees at that—he'd violated the Fisk Code of Baseball Ethics. Thou shalt hustle. Thou shalt run it out. To Fisk, the proper way to play the game was always important-with passion, preparation, hard work, integrity, and respect. He acquired those values on the farm in Charlestown, and they propelled him all the way to Cooperstown.

This biography was adapted from a previous work included in *Green Mountain Boys of Summer* (Tom Simon, ed., Shelburne, VT: New England Press, 2000).

Doug Griffin

by Ron Anderson

	G	AB	R	H	2B	3B	HR	RBI	BB	SO	BA	OBP	SLG	SB	CS	GDP	HBP
1975 RED SOX	100	287	21	69	6	0	1	29	18	29	.240	.288	.272	2	2	8	2

Doug Griffin's professional career spanned 13 years, beginning at Idaho Falls in 1965 and finishing with the Boston Red Sox in 1977. He spent eight seasons in the major leagues, seven of them with the Red Sox, and appeared briefly in the 1975 World Series.

Douglas Lee Griffin was born June 4, 1947 in South Gate, California. He was listed as an even six feet tall, and his playing weight was approximately 160 pounds.

He played high school ball at El Monte High School (California), graduating in 1965, where he had achieved honors in the All-Pacific League, All-Valley, and All-California Interscholastic Federation. He also lettered in basketball, football and track.

Doug was discovered by California Angels scout, Tufie Hashem.[23] He was drafted by the Angels in the 21st round of the 1965 amateur draft, and was assigned to Idaho Falls of the Pioneer League (Rookie League) where he played 31 games, batting .200. In 1966, Griffin

was sent to Davenport, Iowa, where he hit .276 with the Quad Cities Angels (Class A) of the Midwest League, and was named the league's All-Star second baseman.

For the next two years, he was in the Navy stationed at Pearl Harbor in the Submarine Service. While there, he played for military teams and the Honolulu Islanders, an amateur ball club of servicemen all-stars, which participated in the 1967 33rd annual National Baseball Congress World Series in Wichita, Kansas. Honolulu placed second to the Boulder Collegians, who won the series with a 5–3 victory over Griffin's club. Griffin received a first-team All-America selection, out of 520 players competing, by a board of major league scouts attending that series.

He returned to the Quad Cities team in 1969 playing in 60 games and batting .250. That same year, he advanced to Double A El Paso of the Texas League, where he hit .308.

Griffin was elevated to California's Triple A club, the Hawaii Islanders for the 1970 season. He had an excellent year in Hawaii batting .326 with 180 hits and slugging at a .437 pace. Griffin led the league with 35 stolen bases, and was named the Pacific Coast League All-Star second baseman, won the Topps PCL player of the month award in July 1970, and was named the league's 1970 Rookie of the Year. The 1970 Islanders team is still considered one of the greatest minor league teams of all time with a 98–48 won-loss record under the leadership of manager Chuck Tanner.[24] Spokane swept the best-of-seven PCL championship series in four games. Griffin had four hits in the series, and his two-run homer knocked in the only runs Hawaii scored in the final game.

Immediately following the PCL championship series, Griffin was called up to the parent club, making his major league debut for the Angels on September 11, 1970. Griffin's playing time alternated between second and third base, however, since he was competing with All-Star second baseman Sandy Alomar. He appeared in 18 games for the Angels, posting a .127 batting average with seven hits in 55 at-bats, but a very respectable .971 fielding percentage.

Among Doug Griffin's unique accomplishments, he participated in two minor league triple plays (Idaho Falls 1965 and Quad Cities 1966). He tied a Hawaii Islanders club record in 1970 scoring five runs in a game, and established a new Hawaii club consecutive hit streak record hitting safely in 28 straight games.

"Big-Dealing Bosox Counting on Griffin"[25] was the caption in the December 19, 1970 edition of *The Sporting News*, highlighting the arrival of Doug Griffin

in Boston. Red Sox GM Dick O'Connell made a block-buster trade with the California Angels on October 11, 1970 giving up Red Sox slugger and fan favorite Tony Conigliaro, catcher Gerry Moses, and pitcher Ray Jarvis for ace reliever Ken Tatum, outfielder Jarvis Tatum, and infielder Doug Griffin. The key acquisition for the Red Sox was Ken Tatum. Boston already had a solid second baseman in Mike Andrews—one of the 1967 "Impossible Dream" team—and gave no indication that they were ready to move Mike. In December, 1970, however, Boston made another surprising move, trading away Andrews and Luis Alvarado to the White Sox for Luis Aparicio. This opened up the second base spot, and set the stage for Doug Griffin.

Griffin was known for his glove and great speed, both factors that prompted the Red Sox to acquire him. His teammate, relief ace Ken Tatum, who came to the Red Sox with Griffin in the Tony Conigliaro trade, characterized Griffin this way: "He's not big, but he's a great competitor. He dives for balls, he can hit and run, and he will sacrifice himself to move along a base runner. He has very quick hands and he can make the double play."[26] Unfortunately, Griffin had more than his fair share of injuries, which without doubt served to shorten his career.

Griffin was an unknown before he set foot on Boston soil, with just 18 games of big league experience to his credit. The refrain around Boston from fans and writers alike was, "Doug Who? Where does he play?"[27] Griffin was the sleeper in the trade.

Red Sox management focused on Griffin's speed and his attributes as "a promising infielder," and the young second base prospect drew praise from manager Eddie Kasko who stated, "Our scouting reports on Griffin indicate that he has exceptional speed. We can use all the speed we can get."[28]

Griffin's emergence onto the Boston scene was nearly as surprising as the departure of Conigliaro, having greater residual impact on the club than the arrival of Ken Tatum. After the trade for Griffin, utility infielder Dick Schofield was promptly dealt, followed shortly by the trade of the popular Mike Andrews. With All-Star and future Hall of Famer Luis Aparicio on board, discussion quickly centered around the new double-play combination of Aparicio and Griffin. Interestingly, during the winter manager Eddie Kasko was quoted, "Our reports on the Griffin boy are excellent. He has excellent speed and they say he makes the double play very well. I plan to bat him second, behind Aparicio and in front of Yastrzemski."[29] Remarkably, this was Kasko's plan even though Griffin

was untested. One Boston sportswriter noted that the Red Sox double-play combination of Aparicio and Griffin was the lightest-weight in organized baseball. Each weighed 155 pounds. "The two of them just edge out Frank Howard," smirked one Red Sox fan.[30]

"Dude" and "Griff" were nicknames given Griffin by his Red Sox team-mates, though Luis Tiant called him "skeleton" because he was so thin and lightweight. What he lacked in size, though, Griffin made up for in agility, quickness, and speed, and he had a sure glove. His bat remained a question-mark, though, one that concerned the Red Sox brass. As spring training opened in Winter Haven in 1971, once again Red Sox management emphasized "defense and speed,"[31] in the words of manager Kasko. This approach was the brainchild of GM Dick O'Connell who sought to improve on the 1970 season which found the Sox finishing 21 games behind Baltimore. The die was cast: Doug Griffin was to be the starting second sacker on opening day.

An interesting twist to the Griffin rookie saga was announced by the Red Sox when spring training was barely underway; they named John Kennedy—the ""Super Sub""—to spell Griffin when necessary. "John will get a lot of work this spring at second, just in case Griffin can't do the job," Kasko stated.[32] Kennedy was acquired by Boston in 1970, and played in 43 games filling in for George Scott at third base. Kasko held him in very high regard. Griffin was untried, which left Kasko a bit unsettled. He needed a backup plan and Kennedy was it.

Luis Aparicio took Griffin under his wing both before and during spring training, which seemed to reflect an understanding he had with Red Sox management when they acquired L'il Looey.[33] He accepted the role with great enthusiasm as did Griffin. It was a great match.

Ted Williams made an observation about the Conigliaro–Andrews trades that brought Griffin and Aparicio to Boston; he said he could not remember a Red Sox team trading for defense at the expense of power. This was indeed innovative for Boston and maybe even risky. Confidence in the plan was suspect.[34] At the conclusion of spring training the Red Sox acquired power-hitting catcher Duane Josephson from the White Sox, with many expressions of enthusiasm from Sox management. Kasko reshuffled the batting order, moving Doug Griffin from the leadoff spot to eighth in the batting order. Griffin responded with four hits in that spot just prior to the team's departure from Florida.[35]

Griffin had a solid spring, living up to his reputation as a flashy fielder. The Red Sox were pleased to find he wielded a steady bat, too. The Sox were high on the rookie from California as the 1971 season opened. Sportswriter Larry Claflin reported in the May 15, 1971 edition of *The Sporting News*, that "Griffin is playing sensationally in the field, giving the Red Sox exactly what White Sox manager Chuck Tanner predicted for them last winter when he heard of the Griffin trade."[36] Griffin made only one error in his first 38 games of the season, but it was one that nearly cost the Sox the game. On the next play, however, he made a sensational maneuver as middle man on a double play eluding a sliding Joe Foy—who planned on upending Griffin—then throwing to first to end the game. The article goes on to say, "what impresses Red Sox players most about Griffin are his hands. He never seems to bobble a ball."[37]

Griffin was going strong in the spring of 1971. He combined brilliant fielding with a very respectable .261 average through May. Three times, he had three-hit games. Through the end of May, he made only two fielding errors in 209 chances. The Fenway Park crowd took an instant liking to the new young kid they called the "Dude." Pitcher Sonny Siebert was impressed noting that Griffin "made a difference" making more double plays, holding scores down and not giving opponents the extra out.[38]

Griffin was having such a good first half in his first year with the Red Sox that he received a credible number of votes by the players for their selections to the American League All-Star Team in a poll conducted by *The Sporting News*. He finished fifth in the players voting. Interestingly, Griffin received more votes than Sandy Alomar, who'd been the player in Griffin's way the year before with California. The player poll had no effect on the official selections that year, as the All-Star voting remained a fan privilege. Rod Carew was the fans' choice at second base. The player vote was nonetheless a mark of respect by Griffin's peers.

Continued good fortune was not in the cards for the oft-injured Red Sox second baseman. While he went out for catching a pop fly in short right field on June 28, Griffin's back went into spasms and he had to be helped from the field. Griffin had experienced similar trouble with his back in the past but never this seriously. Ironically this was the same game in which he hit his first major league home run. And, as was true at the time of most of his subsequent injuries, Griffin was playing very good baseball both at bat and in the field. Griffin was on the disabled list for nearly a month, from June 30 to July 27, missing 28 games.

The Red Sox were chasing the Orioles in 1971 but hitting was not their strong suit and that lack of offense kept them well behind the Baltimore club. Yastrzemski was having an off year and George Scott played hot and cold. Griffin was cited by the Boston brass as one of the few players who was hitting above expectations, this despite missing so many games due to injury.

Feuding among the players was unfortunately a factor in the slow demise of the Red Sox chances in 1971. Although it was felt this was not a principal factor in the team's collapse, it certainly damaged team symmetry and harmony. In the meantime, Griffin was hitting well after coming back from injury, though his back continued to bother him and required frequent treatments from trainer Buddy LeRoux.[39]

The Red Sox finished third in 1971, 18 games behind the AL East division-leading Baltimore Orioles. Griffin finished his season with a .244 batting average. Largely because of his slick fielding, Griffin became a candidate for AL Rookie of the Year, and placed fourth in the voting. Chris Chambliss of the Indians won the award, though the Boston baseball writers named Griffin the Red Sox rookie of the year.

1972 was a very good year for Doug Griffin. Once again he was placed on the All-Star ballot as a premier second baseman. He had a sensational spring both with the bat and in the field. "I have ceased to be amazed at the plays he makes. He did something spectacular every day,"[40] said manager Eddie Kasko. "He gets to balls I cannot believe he can reach,"[41] added Luis Aparicio. "He's positively uncanny at playing the hitters. When I saw him moving, I moved with him in right field, and you would be amazed how often Griffin moved the right way,"[42] said Reggie Smith.

But, hard luck would follow Doug Griffin in 1972, just as it had the year before. He was benched early in the season due to a slump, but came back strong, and was hitting well until early August when he was hit by a Gaylord Perry pitch that broke his hand. Griffin was on the disabled list from August 9 to September 1, missing 19 games. When he returned he had trouble gripping the bat, understandably affecting his hitting.

Griffin was granted the 1972 Gold Glove Award for his outstanding fielding. Despite the broken hand, by year's end he had improved his batting average to .260, and his 15 sacrifice hits tied him for third place in the league with three other players. In spite of turmoil in the clubhouse the Red Sox finished second, just a half a game behind the AL East's Detroit Tigers. If it had not been for the unbalanced schedule following the work stoppage at the start of the '72 season, the Red Sox might have played the same number of games as the Tigers. Had they played one more game, and won, they would have been tied for first place.

1973 was a year of promise for the Red Sox. They had a seasoned team returning, one bolstered by the pitching of Luis Tiant, Marty Pattin, John Curtis and Lynn McGlothen. The infield was an established one with Gold Glove winner Griffin, Luis Aparicio, Rico Petrocelli and Carl Yastrzemski. Griffin again appeared on the AL All-Star ballot, but back problems which cropped up during spring training plagued him throughout the year. On top of that, in May he was hit on the back of the hand by Billy Champion of the Brewers and suffered another fractured hand. Griffin served another stint on the disabled list from May 24 to July 13. It was a very unfortunate injury at a time when he was playing his best ball, batting .289 and only recently installed in the leadoff spot. His fielding had been superb.[43]

Griffin's second broken hand had a deleterious affect upon the 1973 Red Sox. Neither John Kennedy nor the new sub acquired from the Yankees, Mario Guerrero, had the fielding range or prowess to compare with Griffin. Worse, the fracture may have been intentional: it appeared to have been the product of a feud between the Red Sox and Brewers, principally involving Bill Lee of the Red Sox and the Brewers' Ellie Rodriguez. In this series at Fenway, when Griffin was reinjured, three Red Sox players were hit by pitches, Fisk (helmet), Cepeda (shoulder), and then Griffin. It nearly led to a brawl on the field.[44]

Injuries were taking their toll on Doug Griffin. It was becoming more a matter of how long might he last than how well might he play. After the 1973 season, Boston replaced Kasko with Darrell Johnson from their minor league system. They also dealt young outfielder Ben Oglivie for seasoned utility infielder Dick McAuliffe of the Tigers, in order to spell the oft-injured Doug Griffin at second. As Peter Gammons put it in the November 10, 1973 edition of The Sporting News, "McAuliffe will fill in at third and second, where a backup job often is needed since Doug Griffin usually gets hurt and has trouble with several right-handed pitchers."[45]

Griffin had played in 113 games for the 1973 Red Sox batting a respectable .255, and may have had his best season in the field making only six errors on 584 total chances, for a .990 fielding percentage, his best in the majors. He placed second to Bobby Grich of the Orioles for the AL Gold Glove award. Griffin ranked third in sacrifice hits with 13, and 10th in sacrifice flies with six. Boston finished second in the AL East again,

eight games behind the Baltimore Orioles.

Notably, on April 6, 1973 Griffin participated in the very first major league game featuring a designated hitter, against the New York Yankees. Ron Blomberg of the Yankees established baseball immortality by being the first DH. Griffin distinguished himself in that game with four hits, two RBI, and a stolen base.

Griffin longed for an injury-free 1974 season, and was off to a tremendous start, but he pulled a muscle. Petrocelli was also hurt. Though the year started with great hopes, manager Darrell Johnson was soon forced into constantly juggling lineups to replace injured players. On April 30, Griffin was beaned by a Nolan Ryan fastball knocking him unconscious. The beaning left him with a concussion and temporary hearing loss, and likely caused the premature end to Griffin's career.

Griffin had been playing exceptional baseball prior to the Nolan Ryan beaning. He had just come off on a tear, hitting safely in 15 consecutive games, and batting at a .347 clip.[46] The incident was a terrifying one, and it truly interrupted the rhythm of the surging Red Sox. "Griffin's injury was the most serious blow suffered by the Red Sox in the first month. It capped a period when they played as though possessed by disruptive devils," reported Peter Gammons in the May 18, 1974 edition of *The Sporting News*.[47] Griffin was on the DL for two full months from April 30 to July 1.

The Red Sox were again faced with questions regarding players and field positions following the Griffin injury. Rookie Rick Burleson, a shortstop, was asked to platoon at second base with veteran Dick McAuliffe in Griffin's absence. Before Griffin returned to action, catcher Carlton Fisk suffered a significant knee injury and was lost for the balance of the season.

Griffin returned to regular action in July. In his first game back, he got a double against Baltimore. The Orioles didn't treat him lightly: he was crunched at second base by a Don Baylor slide, and was brushed back by a Bob Reynolds pitch. He wasn't affected by the brush-back, he said. The following month, Griffin faced the man who put him on the DL, Nolan Ryan. Remarkably, Griffin got two hits off Ryan that day. But he may have lost a bit of his edge. Tim Horgan reported, "To his everlasting credit, he dug right in against the Angels' flamethrower as soon as he'd recuperated, but he never did regain the form that made him one of the few constants in the Red Sox infield."[48]

The Red Sox finished third in 1974, seven games behind division-leading Baltimore and five behind the Yankees, with an 84–78 record. Griffin played in only 93 games of the injury-plagued season, but played well,

batting .266, with another good year in the field.

During the off-season Darrell Johnson openly discussed possible trades involving several players including Griffin, but nothing materialized. Griffin was still suffering with back trouble and was heading for surgery, which made any trade talks involving him doubtful. Johnson had planned to move Burleson to second base and trade Griffin for a shortstop, but Griffin's back injury made him "untradeable," remarked GM Dick O'Connell.[49]

Various maneuvers were made by the Red Sox in the spring of 1975 to adjust for injuries. They continued to hope that highly-regarded shortstop Steve Dillard would overcome his own injuries and be able to play regularly. Mario Guerrero's name continued to come up, and Burleson appeared destined for second base. Griffin seemed not to have a place although the message was unclear. Manager Johnson was quoted by Tim Horgan of the *Boston Herald* in the March 3, 1975 edition, "I wish I could say Doug is still our second baseman. But I don't know myself where he stands. I've got to have a Burleson available. If Doug is all right, then it's simply a matter of who's the best man at the position."[50]

The Red Sox fueled the fire further, if not adding to the dilemma, by mentioning a newly-acquired player from the Baltimore farm system, Kim Andrew, as a possible replacement for Griffin. Player Personnel Director Haywood Sullivan, manager Johnson, and coach Don Zimmer were all very high on Andrew, a player more noted for his hitting than his fielding. As it developed, Andrew was used sparingly and never panned out for the Red Sox.[51]

When the 1975 season started Griffin owned the second base job. On June 14, however, the Red Sox purchased Denny Doyle, a journeyman infielder, from the California Angels. Manager Johnson platooned Griffin and Doyle most of the rest of the year. Doyle appeared in 89 games for the Red Sox during the regular season, Griffin 100. Doyle finished the year batting .310 with the Red Sox, Griffin .240. Johnson said of Doyle, "I knew he was a good player, but I never realized how good. He's simply uncanny at advancing runners."[52] Interestingly, after the platooning took effect, by mid season Griffin was hitting close to .300 and having his best year since 1973.[53]

But it was clear that Denny Doyle had become Darrell Johnson's man at second base, and by the division playoffs with Oakland, Doyle had a corner on the second base job. The irony was that 1975 was the first year Griffin avoided injury in his five full seasons with the club.

On August 31, 1975 Griffin was beaned again, this time by Oakland's Dick Bosman. Griffin experienced hearing and equilibrium problems, but recovered very quickly. This time he had been wearing an ear flap with his protective helmet.

Griffin did not play in the ALCS against the A's, and was not a factor in the 1975 World Series. He appeared only once as a pinch hitter for pitcher Jim Willoughby in the eighth inning of Game Five, and lined out to second base.

The following year, the infield was thought to be the only possible weakness. Surprisingly, Red Sox brass continued to talk about a Doyle–Griffin combination at second, but Johnson was settled on Doyle at that position in spite of his own, and management's representations to the contrary. Griffin was used sparingly in '76, platooning with Doyle and pinch-hitting. He finished the year batting .189 in just 127 at-bats.

By the fall of 1976 there was talk of both Griffin and Doyle being on the trading block. Griffin was rumored to be going to Detroit, but this never materialized, and springtime talk quieted down to a "'wait and see'" attitude with Red Sox brass. Don Zimmer, mid-season replacement for Darrell Johnson who was suddenly fired by the Red Sox on July 19, remained high on Denny Doyle describing him as "the finest hit-and-run man on the club."[54] But in the next breath Zimmer reported that the "battle for second and third base is wide open, with Doug Griffin and Denny Doyle seeking one spot and Rico Petrocelli challenging second-year man Butch Hobson for the other spot."[55]

Doug Griffin played in only five games of the 1977 season with six at-bats and no hits. He played his last major league game with the Red Sox on June 2, 1977. Almost three weeks later, on June 21, he was given his unconditional release.

Griffin did not continue a career in baseball following his release from the Red Sox. He worked briefly for his father in the construction trade in California in the late '70s, and performed the same kind of work in the '80s for Buddy LeRoux, who had a construction business in Winter Haven, Florida. Griffin is now retired and currently resides in Fresno, California. The Griffins have two children, Natalie and Chad, and four grandchildren.

One could assume that had it not been for the numerous injuries that plagued Doug Griffin throughout his major league career, he most likely would be remembered as one of the premier second basemen of his time. He had exceptional skills in the field, so much so that even when the Red Sox appeared to give up on him, he stuck with the team, because they could not find a replacement who could match his sure-handedness, range and quickness. Perhaps the ultimate compliment was summed up by Griffin's teammate, future Hall of Famer Carl Yastrzemski, when he said, "No second baseman we have had in my time with the Red Sox can go get the ball like Griffin."[56]

Fred Lynn

by Tom Nahigian

	G	AB	R	H	2B	3B	HR	RBI	BB	SO	BA	OBP	SLG	SB	CS	GDP	HBP
1975 RED SOX	145	528	103	175	47	7	21	105	62	90	.331	.401	.566	10	5	11	3

He arrived on the major league scene like a bolt of lightning through the evening sky. Fred Lynn played in his first game on September 5, 1974 and proceeded to smash major league pitching to the tune of a .419 batting average and a .698 slugging average over his first 15 games. He followed that up with one of the greatest rookie seasons of all time, leading the Red Sox to the World Series and earning the Rookie of the Year, Most Valuable Player, and Gold Glove awards for the 1975 season. Lynn was the first player to achieve this trifecta, an accomplishment matched by Ichiro Suzuki of the Seattle Mariners in 2001.

Fredric Michael Lynn was born on February 3, 1952, in Chicago, Illinois, to Fred and Marie Lynn. At age one his family moved to Southern California. He was an only child, and after his parents' divorce in 1965 he lived with his father, a textile service executive. Lynn grew up in the Lutheran Church and remains a Lutheran to this day. He has a United Nations heritage: English, French, Spanish, Native American, Norwegian, German, and Bohemian.

As a youngster, he loved sports and enjoyed playing football, basketball, baseball, marbles, and track. Despite being raised in the Los Angeles suburbs, Lynn was a Giants fan and not a Dodgers fan. He did not like the great-pitching, weak-hitting Dodgers, but the big bats of Giants sluggers Willie Mays and Willie McCovey.

His favorite players as a child were Mays and Roberto Clemente. He respected them as all-around players, with hitting ability, power, speed, defensive excellence, and a strong throwing arm.

He won batting titles in Little League, Pony League, and at El Monte High School. In high school, he lettered in baseball, football and basketball. While at El Monte, he became acquainted with Diane May Minkle, known as Dee Dee, a fellow student and a cheerleader. The two were married in February, 1974. The couple had two children, Jason Andrew born on March 16, 1978, and Jennifer Andrea on October 6, 1979. Fred and Dee Dee later divorced.

During his high school years, Lynn both pitched and played center field. In one game during his sophomore year, he pitched 13 innings. He could throw hard and also had good breaking stuff, but was a raw pitcher. No one worked with him on technique. As a junior he was 11–1 with a 1.01 ERA with many strikeouts. As a senior, he went 6–5 with a sub-1.00 ERA. In football, he kicked and returned punts and kickoffs.

Lynn wanted to be the first person in his family to attend college. The family told teams not to draft him, but that it would take a lot of money to prevent him from attending college. He was drafted by the New York Yankees in the third round of the 1970 baseball draft. He decided not to sign, and entered the University of Southern California on a football scholarship. As a freshman, he played with the varsity in both football and baseball. John McKay coached the USC football team and Rod Dedeaux was the baseball coach. Lynn was a teammate of future Pittsburgh Steelers star Lynn Swann. On the gridiron, he played wide receiver and defensive back, as well as kicker, punter, and returner of punts and kickoffs. Lynn says he played both offense and defense, and never came off the field. Although he enjoyed success as a football player, during his sophomore year, Lynn switched his scholarship over to baseball. Is it true that he never came off the field? This was a fantastic USC team, so if he really played nearly every play this would have been a huge national story. I never heard of him as a football player.

Lynn had met Dedeaux for the first time the summer after he graduated from high school. He played on an all-star baseball team of mostly high school seniors that played the USC varsity. Lynn faced future major leaguer Dave Kingman, a 6'6" pitcher at the time. Kingman was the hardest thrower he had ever faced up to that point, but Lynn walked on four pitches. After the game, Dedeaux approached Lynn. "I liked the way you hung in there." Dedeaux gave players confidence. He was a

good role model since Lynn was a shy youngster.

Lynn played for the USC varsity as a freshman, sophomore and junior and the team enjoyed three years of amazing success, going 54–13–1 in 1971, 50–13 in 1972, and 51–11 in 1973, winning the NCAA Baseball Championship each season. Lynn was an All-American in 1972. He was named MVP for the US All-Stars during a series in Japan. During his college career, he was a teammate of future major league players Steve Busby, Steve Kemp, and Roy Smalley Jr. He was a member of the 1971 Pan Am Team.

At first, Lynn majored in Business Administration, but he became bogged down as a junior and switched into Physical Education. If he couldn't be a baseball player, he wanted to teach. He also enjoyed history.

Lynn thought the Dodgers would take him with their first pick in the 1973 amateur draft, but the Dodgers drafted Ted Farr, a catcher out of Spokane, Washington. They were hoping Lynn would still be available in the second round. The Red Sox picked one slot ahead of the Dodgers that year and drafted him in the second round (the 28th pick overall—the Red Sox took Ted Cox with their first pick). Lynn signed with the Red Sox on July 9, 1973 by scout Joe Stephenson for $40,000. He was assigned to the Red Sox Double-A affiliate in Bristol, Connecticut where he played under manager Rac Slider. It was the first time he played on the East Coast. He started off strong, but tired as the summer wore on and ending up hitting .259 in 53 games as the team finished third in the American Division with a 62–77 record. It was at Bristol that he became teammates with Jim Rice. Lynn and Rice would remain with the Red Sox organization through 1980.

Lynn was promoted to Pawtucket, Rhode Island for the Triple-A playoffs, and both he and Rice helped the team win the Governor's Cup, defeating Tidewater three games to two and then Charleston, again three games to two, for the Junior World Series championship.

In 1974, Lynn started with Pawtucket and made the All-Star team, hitting .282 with 21 home runs and 19 doubles in 124 games. He finished tenth in the International League in batting average. Despite having Lynn and Triple Crown winner Jim Rice, the PawSox finished last, going 57–87, under future Red Sox skipper Joe Morgan.

Meanwhile, in Boston, the Red Sox hired Darrell Johnson as manager and held first place for 98 days. After August they struggled, winning 12 and losing 19, while the Baltimore Orioles and New York Yankees passed them in the standings, going 25–6 and 20–11, respectively. Rice was recalled in late August, and Lynn

was called up after the Triple-A season was over.

Although the season ended up in disappointment, the future seemed bright with a core of talented young players such as Jim Rice, Carlton Fisk, Rick Burleson, Cecil Cooper, Dwight Evans, Juan Beniquez, Rick Miller, and Fred Lynn.

The pain of the collapse of the 1974 team was erased by the joy of 1975, with the team being led by its two fine rookies. Lynn and Rice were known as the Gold Dust Twins. Rice had a fine rookie season, hitting .309 with 22 home runs and 102 RBI, but Lynn was even better, hitting .331 with 47 doubles, 21 home runs, 103 runs, and 105 RBI. He earned honors as American League MVP and Rookie of the Year and won a Gold Glove for fielding excellence. He led the league in runs, doubles, slugging average, OPS and runs created per 27 outs. He finished second in runs created and in batting average and fifth in on-base average.

It was not only his batting feats that drew attention, but also his wonderful fielding. Lynn was terrific diving forward, snaring line drives, and jumping to reach over fences and take home runs away from hitters. During his career, Lynn earned Gold Gloves four times.

In an interview with Jon Goode of Boston.com in 2004, Lynn reflected: "I am most proud of the Gold Gloves and really cherished those. I prided myself on defense. When I played basketball and football I always wanted to guard the toughest guy. When I played center field, I felt like I was guarding somebody and I didn't want any ball to fall in my area. I took it personally when balls would fall in and I didn't catch them."

Smooth and graceful, Lynn batted and threw left-handed. As a major leaguer, Lynn stood 6'1" and weighed 185 pounds. He was modest about his accomplishments. In the *1976 Complete Handbook of Baseball*, Lynn said: "One man doesn't make a team. All the awards are great, but they are secondary to winning. If we didn't win, none of these awards would mean anything."

During his magical season, Lynn staged a one-man assault on Tiger Stadium, on June 18, belting out three home runs (just missing a fourth), a triple and a single, driving in 10 runs in a 15–1 thrashing of the Tigers.

The Red Sox clinched the American League East on September 27. They faced the defending three-time champion Oakland Athletics in the American League Championship Series and swept the A's in three games. Lynn hit .364 in the series.

In the World Series, the Red Sox took on the Cincinnati Reds, winners of 108 games that season. Most baseball experts predicted the Reds would win easily, but the Red Sox battled hard and took the Reds to a seventh game. Many baseball fans consider that Series the greatest ever played. Five games were decided by a single run, two games went into extra innings, two games were decided in the ninth inning and in six of the seven games the winning team came from behind. The sixth game was perhaps the best World Series game ever played. Fred Lynn was the on-deck hitter when Carlton Fisk blasted his classic game-ending home run off Pat Darcy leading off the bottom of the 12th.

During that game, Lynn smashed a three-run homer in the first inning to give the Red Sox the lead. During a Reds rally in the top of the fifth inning, Lynn crashed into Fenway Park's then-unpadded wall in left center chasing a triple hit by Ken Griffey Sr. Fenway became silent, but Lynn remained in the game after receiving attention from Red Sox trainer Charlie Moss. In the World Series, Lynn played in all seven games, batting .280 with a double and home run, and five runs batted in, tying for most on the team. After the season, the Red Sox padded their outfield walls.

Expectations were high for the Red Sox in 1976, but the season was a disappointment. The league champions had added future Hall of Famer Ferguson Jenkins to the roster, but won just 83 games, finishing third in the American League East. Long-time owner Tom Yawkey lost a lengthy battle with cancer on July 9. A 10-game losing streak from April 29 through May 11, a poor season by starting pitcher Bill Lee, and a prolonged holdout by Lynn, Burleson, and Fisk all contributed to a lost season.

Red Sox manager Darrell Johnson was fired during the season and replaced with third base coach Don Zimmer. Lynn made the All-Star team, won his second Gold Glove and hit .314 with 32 doubles in 132 games, but the season was not fun for him. In the April 2, 1977 edition of *The Sporting News*, Lynn told Larry Whiteside of the *Boston Globe,* "For the first time in my life, baseball isn't fun. It was always easy to play a game. This is hard."

After Yawkey's death, the team was managed by a trust made up of his widow Jean Yawkey, James Curran, and Joseph LaCour. In August, Lynn, Burleson, and Fisk each agreed to five-year contracts. Owners and players signed a new Basic Agreement at the same time. Free agency for players was now possible. Later on, the team would fall into the hands of Mrs. Yawkey, former player personnel director Haywood Sullivan, and former Red Sox and Boston Celtics trainer Buddy LeRoux. This union would not be a happy one, and by 1981, Lynn, Burleson, and Fisk would no longer be Red Sox. One

wonders whether Tom Yawkey would have found a way to keep the three. In 1983, an acrimonious lawsuit took place. Sullivan and Jean Yawkey wanted to run the Red Sox as Tom Yawkey had and Buddy LeRoux always had his eye on the bottom line. Eventually, LeRoux sold his interest in the Red Sox and Sullivan ran the team for Mrs. Yawkey.

Lynn looked forward to the new season. "Last year is history and I'm not going to dwell on the past," he said. "I didn't sit back after 1975 and think about the past. I'm not going to sit back and do it with the 1976 season. It's history. People are going to say we're in it just for the money and nothing else. But that's not true. I really like the game. It's more than a job to me. It's a part of me and has been all my life. I'm happy that I came along when I did and am well paid. But with me, it's a matter of pride, not money. I enjoy the game."

He began that season on the disabled list, from March 24 through May 6, with torn ligaments in his left ankle. He ended up hitting .260 with 18 home runs and 76 runs batted in over 129 games. He made the All-Star team for the third time. The Red Sox swatted 213 home runs and improved to 97 wins and 64 losses, tied for second with the Orioles in the American League East.

In 1978, Lynn's ankle returned to health and he had a fine season. He played in 150 games, the most in his career, hitting .298 with 22 home runs and batted in 82 runs. He made the All-Star team for the fourth time and won his second Gold Glove. The Red Sox had a memorable season, jumping out to a big lead, slumping in September, bouncing back to win 99

games and tie the Yankees for the American League East Championship. The Yankees edged the Red Sox 5–4 in a one-game playoff in Fenway Park. Lynn singled and drove in a run.

Lynn spent the offseason strengthening himself on Nautilus machines. In 1979, he enjoyed perhaps his best season. He led the AL in hitting (.333), on-base average (.423), and slugging (.637). He also slugged a career-high 39 home runs, scored a career-high 116 runs, and had a career-high 122 runs batted in. He was named to the American League All-Star team for the fifth time and earned his third Gold Glove. He finished fourth in American League MVP voting. Those interested in statistical analysis will note that in the 1980 *Bill James Baseball Abstract*, Lynn had the highest value approximation method rating in the major leagues, earning 17 points. Under James's more recent Win Shares method, Lynn also led the majors with 34.

1980 was Lynn's last year with the Red Sox. In his farewell season, he hit .301 with a .383 on-base average and .480 slugging average. On May 13, he hit for the cycle against the Minnesota Twins. His season ended on August 28. He was batting against Oakland A's starter Steve McCatty when he fouled a ball off his foot, fracturing his right toe. He was named an All-Star for the sixth time and won his fourth and last Gold Glove.

Lynn was very successful hitting in Fenway Park. In his career, he hit .347 with a .420 on-base average and a .601 slugging average in 440 games and 1,581 at-bats.

The Red Sox were not willing to pay Fred Lynn what he felt he was worth, so on January 23, 1981, Lynn and

Steve Renko were both sent to the California Angels for Joe Rudi, Frank Tanana, and Jim Dorsey. Lynn enjoyed playing for the Red Sox and loved hitting in Fenway Park. In talking about Red Sox fans, he later said, "They supported you all the time. They were always there and let you know what they were feeling in the good side and the bad side, which was OK. As a player it keeps you on your toes. You don't ever come to Fenway with a complacent attitude. You come there to play otherwise they will let you know you are not living up to their expectations and I liked that."

A baseball strike wiped out the middle portion of the 1981 season. Lynn had to adjust to a new ballpark and struggled with a .219 batting average in 256 at-bats. This would be the lowest average in his career. He would, however, be named to the American League All-Star team for the seventh consecutive time.

1982 was a much better year for both Lynn and the Angels. With a veteran roster of All-Stars such as Rod Carew, Bobby Grich, Reggie Jackson and Don Baylor, the Angels won the American League West Division, winning 93 games. Lynn had a fine season, hitting .299 with a .374 on-base average and a .517 slugging average. He was an American League All-Star for the eighth consecutive time.

In the American League Championship Series, the Angels took on the Milwaukee Brewers in a best-of-five series. The Angels took the first two games, but the Brewers stormed back to take the next three games. It wasn't due to any lack of productivity by Fred Lynn. He was the hottest hitter in the series for either team, hitting .611, with 11 hits in 18 at-bats, two doubles, a homer, and five runs batted in. Lynn earned the distinction of being named Series MVP despite playing for the losing team.

In 1983, Lynn was named to the American League All-Star team for the ninth consecutive time. 1983 marked the 50th anniversary of the All-Star Game, and as it had been in 1933, it was held in Comiskey Park in Chicago. Lynn enjoyed a memorable game. In the third inning with Manny Trillo on third base, Rod Carew on second, and Robin Yount on first, Lynn stood in the batter's box against San Francisco Giants left-handed pitcher Atlee Hammaker. Lynn worked the count to 2–2, then drove a hanging slider into the right-field seats, the first grand slam in the history of the All-Star Game. The AL won the game 13–3, its first win since 1971. Lynn was named the game's Most Valuable Player.

During the regular season, Lynn hit .272 with 22 home runs and 74 runs batted in, a .352 on-base average and a .483 slugging average.

The next year, 1984, would be Lynn's last season with the Angels. Playing in 142 games, the most of his Angels career, Lynn hit .271, with 23 home runs, 79 runs batted in, a .366 on-base average and a .474 slugging average.

On November 8, 1984, Lynn was granted free agency, and signed with the Baltimore Orioles on December 11. He would play with the Orioles from 1985 to 1988. He hit 23 home runs in each season, from 1984 through 1987. He was a useful player, batting as high as .287 in 1986 with a .371 on-base average and a .499 slugging average. Injuries caused him to miss many games. The most games he played in a season for the Orioles was 124 in 1985.

In October 1986, Lynn married for the second time, this time to Natalie. The couple became acquainted while she was producing TV commercials in New Bedford, Massachusetts, and he was doing a Ford TV commercial at the same time.

On August 31, 1988, the Orioles traded Lynn to the Detroit Tigers for three players to be named later: Chris Hoiles, Cesar Mejia, and Robinson Garces. The Tigers were involved in a ferocious battle for the American League East crown, along with the Red Sox, Brewers, Blue Jays and Yankees. Lynn contributed seven home runs in 90 at-bats in 27 games for the Tigers, who ended up in second place, just one game behind the Red Sox.

In 1989, the bottom fell out for the Tigers as they dropped down to last place in the American League East, winning 59 games and losing 103. Lynn's batting average dropped to .241 with 11 home runs in 353 at-bats. The end of his fine career was drawing near.

Lynn was granted free agency on November 13, 1989 and he signed with the San Diego Padres on December 6. He would be returning to Southern California, and playing in the National League for the first time. Lynn got into 90 games for the Padres in 1990, making him a three-decade player. He batted .240 and hit six homers. He played his final major league game on October 3.

How good was Fred Lynn? At his best, he was as good as anyone, but injuries slowed his career down. There are seven skills in baseball: controlling the strike zone, hitting for power, hitting for average, offensive speed, fielding range, fielding reliability, and throwing ability. When healthy and at his best, Lynn did all these things well.

Lynn rates as the 17th-best center fielder of all time in *The New Bill James' Historical Baseball Abstract*. In Maury Allen's *Baseball's 100*, which came out in 1981, Lynn was rated as the 77th-best player of all time. I would disregard the Allen rating since it was just a few

years into Lynn's career. According to the 8th edition of *Total Baseball*, Lynn earned 280 win shares over his career and achieved 20.0 total player wins. According to the *STATS All-Time Major League Handbook*, Lynn created 6.09 runs per 27 outs, whereas an average player created 4.43 runs per 27 outs. In his major league career, Lynn played in 17 seasons, 1,969 games, 6,925 at-bats, with 306 home runs and 1,111 RBI, hit .283, a .360 on-base average, and a .484 slugging average. He played 1,584 games in center field during his career.

Lynn rates Fenway as his favorite baseball park to play in. Frank Tanana (before he hurt his arm) was the toughest pitcher for him to hit. His favorite pitchers to hit against were Bert Blyleven and Lerrin LaGrow.

During his post-baseball career, Lynn broadcast as a baseball analyst for ESPN from 1992 to 1995 and 1999 to 2000, for CBS TV in 1997–1998 and Fox TV in 1998. He was a consultant for Trinity Products–MLB Product

Line from 2002 to 2004. He also makes appearances at autograph shows. Lynn has been involved with Child Haven, a charity for disadvantaged children. He has donated some memorabilia to help raise funds for the organization. In 1994, Fred Lynn was inducted into the USC Hall of Fame. On November 14, 2002, he was inducted into the Red Sox Hall of Fame.

His hobbies are fishing, golf and tennis. His favorite food is cheeseburgers. He and his wife Natalie reside in Carlsbad, California.

In summing up his career, Lynn told authors Harvey and Frederic J. Frommer in *Growing Up Baseball*, "I wouldn't trade the time that I played for all the dollars you could make now. The country was just coming out of the Sixties. Everybody was having a pretty good time. There was not the media as we know it now. And a guy like me who was pretty introverted could just hide, play baseball, play with reckless abandon."

Rico Petrocelli

by R. R. Marshall

	G	AB	R	H	2B	3B	HR	RBI	BB	SO	BA	OBP	SLG	SB	CS	GDP	HBP
1975 RED SOX	115	402	31	96	15	1	7	59	41	66	.239	.310	.333	0	2	16	3

One of the most popular players to ever play for the Boston Red Sox, Rico Petrocelli will always be remembered for his familiar "Fenway Stroke" that sent many an opposing hurler's offerings into the net atop the Green Monster in left field. Although he was not physically imposing at 6'0", 175 lbs., he hit 210 lifetime home runs (including a then-league-record for shortstops—40 in 1969) and his career total of 773 RBI place him comfortably in the Red Sox top 10 in both categories. A two-time All-Star shortstop and veteran of two World Series with the Red Sox, Rico agreed to move to third base in 1971 to help fill a void in the Boston infield and enable the Red Sox to acquire shortstop Luis Aparicio. His 1976 season was his final one; Rico played in 1,553 regular-season and 17 postseason games in his 12-year career. He still holds the club fielding record for a season at two different positions in the infield, holding the third base record and effectively tied for the shortstop mark with Vern Stephens (1950) and Rick Burleson (1980).

Americo Peter (Rico) Petrocelli was born on June 27, 1943 in Brooklyn, New York, the youngest of seven children born to Attilio and Louise. His father and cousins ran a shop specializing in sharpening tools used

in the garment district. Rico developed his love for the game at an early age. At a time when there were three major league teams in New York, he was inspired by the great teams and players. As a youngster he was an avid Yankees fan, with his father taking him to both Yankee Stadium to see Mickey Mantle and the Bronx Bombers and to Ebbets Field to see the Brooklyn Dodgers.

Petrocelli started playing basketball at the age of six, but didn't play organized baseball until he was 12. By the time he started high school he was proficient at both sports, and would become an all-scholastic in both basketball and baseball at Sheepshead Bay High. When his family realized that he might have a chance at a professional career, he was allowed to concentrate on his athletic career full-time instead of getting a job to help support the family. His four older brothers all worked to bring in extra money, allowing him to pursue his dreams of becoming a pro baseball player. It was a sacrifice he has never forgotten.

A pitcher and a power-hitting outfielder in high school, he was considered a top prospect and a dozen scouts followed his progress his senior year. But while pitching in the city championship on an extremely cold day in 1961, he felt something snap in his right elbow. The scouts quickly disappeared until only four

(Cincinnati, Philadelphia, Baltimore, and Boston) remained. The Red Sox were the first team to invite him to a workout after the injury, a gesture which made a favorable impression. He and his family made the trip to Boston and after a successful workout, stellar Red Sox scout Bots Nekola (the same scout who signed Carl Yastrzemski three years earlier) signed him.

Rico started his professional career in 1962 with Winston-Salem, North Carolina in the Carolina League—batting .277 with 17 home runs and 80 RBI, but struggled in the field at his new position (shortstop), committing a league-high 48 errors. He was promoted to Reading in the Eastern League in 1963 and batted only .239, but he hit 19 homers and drove in 78 runs. The Red Sox brought him to Boston at the close of 1963, and the 20-year-old made his major league debut September 21 in the first game of a doubleheader against the Minnesota Twins at Fenway Park. In a portent of things to come in the future, Rico drove a Lee Stange offering off the fabled Green Monster for a double in his very first at-bat. The hit earned a standing ovation from the sparse crowd (only 6,469 in attendance) and would become one of his favorite memories.

By 1964, Petrocelli had been designated as one of the club's top prospects and was sent to the Red Sox Triple A affiliate in Seattle. He managed to hit only .231 and, homesick and depressed over his poor play, began to doubt his ability. At the suggestion of his teammate Billy Gardner he tried switch hitting, and when the Red Sox named him their starting shortstop at the start of the 1965 season he was encouraged to continue the experiment by then Red Sox manager Billy Herman with disastrous results—he hit only .174 through the first 20 games and the switch hitting experiment was then scrapped. Red Sox coach Pete Runnels suggested he use his natural ability to try to pull the ball more and take advantage of Fenway's inviting left-field wall. Rico would spend the rest of the season refining his "new" swing, steadily producing results. He hit his first major league home run June 20 against left hander Gary Peters of the White Sox, and ended with 13 for the season.

His balky right elbow hampered his throwing for most of his rookie year and the problem persisted into the 1966 season, eventually landing him on the disabled list for the first time in his career. To add insult to injury, Petrocelli was not a favorite of Herman. The "old-school" manager had little patience for his brooding and insecurities and made life miserable for the young Sox shortstop. The situation came to a head when Petrocelli left the team in the middle of a game to tend to a family emergency. Herman demanded he

be immediately suspended, but cooler heads in the Red Sox front office prevailed. Instead, he was fined the then-hefty amount of $1,000, but it did little to calm the conflict between manager and player. Things were finally resolved when Herman was fired in September, but even with his tormentor gone, Rico felt sure he would either be traded or sent back to the minors.

In 1967, new Red Sox manager Dick Williams took a different tack with Petrocelli. He brought long-time Red Sox minor league coach Eddie Popowski to Boston as the new third base coach and gave him the locker next to Petrocelli. The good-natured Popowski had managed Rico at both Winston Salem in 1962 and at Reading in 1963, and helped to build the young shortstop's self-esteem with daily pep talks. Williams also helped Petrocelli mature as a player by giving him the responsibility of being the leader of the club's young infield. Both moves resulted in giving him new-found confidence, and he blossomed as a player. He drove in the first run of the season with a single in the Red Sox 5–4 win over Chicago on Opening Day and later added a three-run homer for good measure. He earned the starting nod at shortstop for the American League in the All-Star Game, and finished with a solid all-around season batting .259 with 17 homers and 66 RBI.

Petrocelli was a central figure in the famous Red Sox–Yankees brawl at Yankee Stadium on the evening of June 21. Both benches cleared after the two longtime rivals exchanged beanballs. Then Petrocelli and Yankee first baseman Joe Pepitone got involved in some friendly verbal jousting. The two were friends who had grown up in Brooklyn together, but somehow things escalated quickly into a full-scale battle. It took a dozen Yankee Stadium security guards, including Petrocelli's brother David (who pulled Rico out from under a pile of Yankee players), to help restore order. The fight was recognized as a defining moment that helped to bring the '67 Red Sox together as a team. Boston fashioned a league-best 60–39 record from that point on, winning the pennant on the final day of the season after a 5–3 win over the Twins. It was Rico's catch of Rich Rollins' pop up that was the final out in Boston's "Impossible Dream" pennant race, a catch that would become one of the signature moments in the long history of the franchise.

Petrocelli had little success at the plate against the National League champion St. Louis Cardinals through the first five games of the 1967 World Series. Extremely run down by the long season, Petrocelli had a Vitamin B-12 shot prior to Game Six and proceeded to hit two home runs—a feat accomplished by only two other shortstops (Arky Vaughan and Alan Trammell) in a

World Series game. His second homer was one of three home runs hit by the Red Sox in the fourth inning, a World Series record that still stands. Although the Red Sox lost Game Seven to the Cardinals, the future seemed bright for both the Red Sox and Petrocelli.

The success of 1967 soon dissipated as a series of injuries doomed the defending American League champions to a fourth place finish in 1968. Petrocelli's batting average plummeted some 25 points as the chronic problem with his right elbow flared, causing him to miss 39 games. Rather than continuing to brood over his misfortune he took on a new positive attitude that winter. He changed his diet and gave up ice cream to help prevent the calcium deposits in his elbow from reforming. He also exercised his arms and wrists in the offseason. By the start of 1969 he felt stronger than at any time in his career, and the results were very evident. He began hitting home runs in bunches while hitting well over .300 for most of the first half of the season. He excelled in the field as well, threatening the record for consecutive games without an error by a shortstop by going 44 straight without a miscue. He would finish the season with a .981 fielding percentage, which remains the record for a Red Sox shortstop.

In July he was the overwhelming choice as the starting shortstop for the American League in the All-Star Game—his second such selection in three years. At the time he was hitting .309 with a remarkable 25 home runs. In the last year prior to the All-Star vote being returned to the fans, he earned more votes from his fellow players, managers, and coaches than any other player in the league. With the Red Sox out of contention since midsummer, his quest to break the American League record for home runs by a shortstop (39, by the Red Sox own Vern Stephens in 1949) became the big story in September. The record-breaker came on the evening of September 29 against the Washington Senators' Jim Shellenback at RFK Stadium. He finished the season with 40 homers and 97 RBI while hitting .297. His .589 slugging percentage was second only to Oakland's Reggie Jackson in the American League.

Rico showed that 1969 was no fluke when he came through with another solid season in 1970. He hit 29 homers and knocked in 103 runs, becoming the first Red Sox shortstop to crack the 100-RBI barrier since Stephens in 1950. He also played in a career-high 157 games, showing his injury problems were a thing of the past. Over the winter, Red Sox general manager Dick O'Connell told him the Red Sox had a deal on the table for future Hall of Fame shortstop Luis Aparicio, but in an ultimate show of respect O'Connell told him

he wouldn't make the deal unless Petrocelli would be comfortable moving to third base.

Rico readily endorsed the deal as being beneficial to the team and agreed to make the change. He reported early to spring training and worked for hours with former Red Sox All-Star third baseman Frank Malzone—the results were nothing short of amazing. Petrocelli set a major league record for third basemen with 77 straight games without an error. He also led the league in fielding percentage with a scintillating .976 mark (still the team record). He continued to produce on offense at a healthy clip, hitting 28 home runs and knocking in 89 runs while leading the team with what the Red Sox calculated as 12 game-winning hits. Between 1969 and 1971 his 97 home runs and 289 RBI were the most by any Red Sox player.

Although his power output dropped significantly in 1972 (only 15 home runs) he continued to drive in runs at a consistent pace, leading the Red Sox with 75 RBI despite hitting only .240. He was especially hot in August, hitting .344 with 23 RBI to help the Red Sox surge into contention for the division title—they would finish a scant one-half game behind Detroit. He also led the majors in grand slams with three. He would finish his career with a total of nine grand slams, good for second on the Red Sox all-time leader list behind only the great Ted Williams.

The injury problems that had plagued him early in his career returned with a vengeance in 1973. He missed the last 47 games of the season with chronic elbow problems, and his loss was keenly felt. Boston was only 2½ games behind division-leading Baltimore when he left the starting line up on August 12, but finished eight games off the pace. Off-season elbow surgery had him back and fit to start the 1974 season, but a series of new injuries set him back yet again. A nagging hamstring injury plagued him for most of the early part of the season, and then disaster struck September 15 when he was hit in the head by a pitch thrown by Milwaukee's Jim Slaton. The beaning shelved him for the rest of the season, and the Red Sox ended up squandering a 7½ game lead near the end of August—staggering home in third place. Despite his time on the disabled list he still tied for the team lead in home runs with 15 and finished second with 76 RBI.

Although Petrocelli was in the Opening Day lineup for the Red Sox at the start of the 1975 season, it was readily apparent that he was still suffering from the after-effects of the beaning. Although it was not public knowledge, he suffered from a severe inner ear imbalance that caused him a great deal of trouble with

his sense of balance. While he continued to perform at his usual high level in the field, he had difficulty gauging the ball as it left the pitcher's hand and his batting average dropped significantly. Despite his shortcomings at the plate, his leadership ability came to the forefront with a new group of young players that drove the Red Sox to their first pennant since 1967. With the red-hot Baltimore Orioles coming on strong in the season's final month Rico again demonstrated his ability to come through in the clutch. His solo homer off Baltimore ace Jim Palmer on the evening of September 16 accounted for the winning run in Boston's 2–0 shutout of the Orioles—a key victory that effectively put the Red Sox in firm control of the pennant race.

Thanks to medication that treated his inner ear imbalance, Petrocelli returned to his old form in time for the postseason. His seventh-inning homer off Oakland's relief ace Rollie Fingers in Game Two of the 1975 ALCS widened the lead in a one-run game and helped to propel the Red Sox to a three-game sweep of the defending champion A's. His stellar play continued in the World Series against Cincinnati, as he hit .308 and contributed some fine fielding plays at third base as Boston came within a run of winning their first World Series since 1918.

While Rico's play in the field continued to be above reproach, his lack of productivity at the plate became an issue in 1976. He began suffering reactions to the medication he was taking to correct his inner ear problems and he was forced to discontinue its use. The problems with his balance returned and severely hampered his ability at the plate. He hit a career-low .213 in 1976, and when Don Zimmer took over as manager shortly after the All-Star break he gave rookie Butch Hobson significant playing time at third. Rico was tried briefly at second base, but with little success. In a move that shocked New England, Petrocelli was

cut at the end of spring training in 1977, ending his 12-year playing career in Boston.

Out of baseball for the first time in his life he decided to remain close to the sports scene in Boston by writing a regular column in the *Boston Herald* that followed the progress of the Red Sox. He was also one of the early pioneers of the sports talk radio scene in Boston, co-hosting a show with Glenn Ordway. In 1979 he joined longtime Red Sox broadcaster Ken Coleman in the radio booth as the color commentator. On July 24 he had the privilege of calling former Red Sox teammate Carl Yastrzemski's 400th home run in a game against the Oakland A's at Fenway Park.

Petrocelli stayed only one year in the radio booth and after several years in the business world returned to uniform in 1986 as a manager for the Chicago White Sox Class A affiliate in Appleton, Wisconsin. He stayed in the White Sox organization a total of three years, eventually being promoted to manager of their Double A club in Birmingham, Alabama in the Southern League, but left to return home as the new Director of Sports Programs for the Jimmy Fund between 1989 and 1991.

His love for the game moved him to accept the manager position at the Red Sox Triple A affiliate in Pawtucket in 1992. That began a six-year stay for him in the Boston organization as a roving instructor. On September 7, 1997, Petrocelli was recognized for his outstanding Red Sox career as he and four other former players were inducted into the Red Sox Hall of Fame.

Since leaving baseball he runs his own private company, Petrocelli Marketing Group, based in Nashua, New Hampshire. He resides there with his wife of 40 years Elsie. They have four grown sons; Michael (39), twins James and Bill (38), and Danny (36). Rico remains active in the Boston sports scene as a frequent guest on Boston TV and radio sports programs.

Jim Rice

by Alex Edelman

	G	AB	R	H	2B	3B	HR	RBI	BB	SO	BA	OBP	SLG	SB	CS	GDP	HBP
1975 RED SOX	144	564	92	174	29	4	22	102	36	122	.309	.350	.491	10	5	19	4

James Edward Rice was born on Sunday, March 8, 1953, in Anderson, South Carolina, to Roger and Julia Rice. Residents of the town say that even as a lanky teenager, "Ed," as he was known to his friends, showed promise. He led his 1969 American Legion team to the State Finals. However, it was still a time of segregation in the south, and Rice, despite his promise, had to attend Westside High School—as opposed to the all-white T. L. Hanna High. Sometime before Rice's senior year, when integration was mandated, Anderson's district board drew lines to

decide who would attend what school. The resulting line was drawn so that the Rice household was included in the Hanna district. His engaging personality and gentle charm won over most of Hanna, and helped ease the racial tension that accompanied integration.

Rice's childhood hero was Westside alumnus and American Football League star George Webster, and Rice played football and basketball as well as baseball. In his senior year, Rice starred on Hanna's football team as an all-state kick returner, defensive back and wide receiver, and played in the North Carolina-South Carolina Shrine Bowl, leading South Carolina to victory. Baseball was by far his best sport, however, and when he was 18, the Boston Red Sox took him in the first round of the 1971 amateur entry draft (15th overall).[57]

After being drafted by the Red Sox, Jim played 60 games in 1971 for Class A Williamsport in the New York–Penn League at the tender age of 18. He hit .256 with five home runs. In 1972 he was sent to Winter Haven in the Florida State League, where he continued to improve his skills, garnering 17 homers in 130 games. In 1973, the Red Sox promoted him to Bristol in the Double-A Eastern League, where he quickly flourished, winning the league batting title with a .317 batting average. He hit 27 homers and drove in 93 runs. Later that year, he joined the Triple A Pawtucket Red Sox for the playoffs, and helped lead them to a Junior World Series championship over the American Association Tulsa team; in 10 playoff games, he hit .378 with four homers. The next year, 1974, Rice played with the PawSox for almost the whole year, where he won the International League's Triple Crown, Rookie of the Year, and MVP (.337, 25 HR, 93 RBI).[58]

The highly-prized prospect joined the parent Red Sox team for 24 games late in 1974, debuting on August 19. He hit his first major league homer on October 1, off Cleveland's Steve Kline. Rice batted .269 in 67 at-bats.

It took Rice a while to get settled in with the 1975 team. While fellow rookie Fred Lynn secured the center field job, the comebacking Tony Conigliaro was the Opening Day DH, a role earmarked for Rice. Tony's season fizzled quickly, and Rice had the job to himself within a few weeks. By July, he took over left field and held it the rest of the season. Jim hit .309 with 22 home runs and 102 RBI, and ended up second to Lynn for the Rookie of the Year award. Rice and Lynn were dubbed the "Gold Dust Twins" and formed what may have been the most productive rookie tandem of all time.

Hank Aaron was most impressed with the potential of the young slugger, and even speculated that Rice would go on to break his home run record.[59] But Rice's

season came to a premature end on September 21, in a 6–5 win over Detroit, when Tigers pitcher Vern Ruhle broke his left hand with a pitch, sidelining him for the rest of the season and forcing him to miss the World Series. To this day, many agree that with the offensive presence of their star left fielder, the Red Sox might well have won the grueling, seven-game World Series.

Recovering from his injury, Rice regressed a bit in 1976, hitting .282 with 25 home runs. In 1977, he became a full-fledged star, leading the league in total bases (382), home runs (39) and slugging percentage (.593). On August 13, 1978, he became the first Red Sox player since Ted Williams in 1939–1940 to total 20 homers, 20 doubles, and 10 triples in consecutive seasons. On August 29, in an 8–7 loss to Oakland, he had his first three-homer game (his second—and last— three-homer game would come exactly six years later on August 19, 1973).[60]

Jim Rice played his entire professional career with the Red Sox, but none of his seasons equaled the magic of 1978. He started the season on the right foot by hitting a game winning single in the 10th inning of the April 14 home opener,[61] and continued his torrid pace into October, when the Red Sox tragically lost to the New York Yankees in a devastating one-game playoff. It was a shame that one of the finest seasons in Red Sox history was overshadowed by the feeble swing of a weedy infielder. Rice's accomplishments were rewarded, though. He was voted the MVP award he so richly deserved, leading the majors in slugging percentage (.600), games (163), at-bats (677), hits (213), total bases (406), triples (15), home runs (46, the most for a Red Sox player since Jimmy Foxx hit 50 in 1938),[62] and RBI (139). He was the first American Leaguer to accumulate 400 total bases in a season since Joe DiMaggio in 1937.

In 1979, Rice had another big year, becoming the first player to have 35 homers (he had 39) and 200 hits (he had 201) for three consecutive seasons. Fans elected him, along with teammates Carl Yastrzemski and Fred Lynn, to start the All-Star Game.[63] It was an all-Red Sox outfield. Rice in particular was recognized as perhaps the best hitter in the game.

Rice had another hand injury in 1980, and suffered subpar seasons in '81 and '82 at least partially as a result. Nevertheless, in 1982, Rice had a day that is long remembered in Boston. He had a difficult relationship with the press, who presented him as a surly, unfriendly player. Jonathan Keane was a four-year old boy from Greenland, New Hampshire in 1982, and he would probably disagree with this assessment. On August 7,

Jonathan was attending one of his first Fenway games, sitting along the first base line in the field boxes, and watched as his favorite player, Red Sox infielder Dave Stapleton, stepped into the batter's box against Richard Dotson of the Chicago White Sox.[64]

Stapleton fouled a pitch sharply to the right, and the hard-hit ball cracked Jonathan in the head, cutting open his left temple and fracturing his skull. In a 1997 article, Arthur Pappas, a Red Sox team doctor for over 15 years, claimed he had never seen so much blood at Fenway. Rick Miller, who was near the on-deck circle, cried for Red Sox trainer Charlie Moss—but instead, Jim Rice, who didn't see anyone moving, instinctively leaped into the stands and picked up the unconscious toddler. Cradling Jonathan, Rice ran into the clubhouse, and brought him to Pappas in the trainer's room.[65]

In a 1997 article describing the incident, Pappas was quoted, "Time is very much a factor once you have that kind of a head injury and the subsequent swelling of the brain. That's why it's so important to get him to care so it can be dealt with. [Rice] certainly helped him very considerably." The supposedly unfriendly outfielder did something that many other Hall of Famers surely have not. He saved a young boy's life.

Jonathan Keane returned for Opening Day in 1983 to throw the ceremonial first pitch, and Rice's game returned as well, as he went on to lead the league in RBI (126) and home runs (39). He also won the Silver Slugger award and played spectacularly in his best year since 1979. And though the year of 1983 was not Rice's best, it provides more weight in the argument of whether Jim Rice should be a Hall Of Famer. SABR member Paul White of Shawnee, Kansas, one of Rice's most vocal supporters for election to the Hall of Fame, wrote in a 2001 article that there were a few reasons offered by sportswriters for Rice not to be admitted to the Hall. Chief among them is that Rice was one-dimensional.[66] In his article, White quotes Jayson Stark of ESPN.com, explaining why he did not vote for Rice in 2000. Stark's main argument was that Rice was one-dimensional, citing Rice's lack of Gold Gloves.[67] To counter Stark's claim, White offered the published opinion of Hall of Fame baseball writer Peter Gammons, who wrote in *Beyond the Sixth Game*:

[In 1983, Rice] probably should have won a Gold Glove for fielding excellence. Dwight Evans, who had the worst defensive year of his career, won one instead, proving clearly the value of a reputation."[68]

Rice had typically fine years in 1984 (28 HR, 122 RBI, .280) and 1985 (27, 103, .291), garnering All-Star honors each year. In 1986, his last big season, he hit .324, with 20 home runs and 110 RBI. The Red Sox returned to the postseason, and Rice was their primary weapon in the middle of the lineup.

After missing the postseason in 1975, Rice was healthy this time. He hit just .161 with two home runs in the Red Sox playoff victory over the Angels, but one of the homers was a key three-run wallop in Game Seven in the League Championship Series. He hit .333 in the World Series loss to the Mets, his only fall classic.

Bothered by an injured elbow, Rice fell off in 1987 (13, 62, .277), and he had to have off-season knee surgery. These injuries and eyesight problems plagued Rice for the next two seasons, and hastened the rather sudden end to his career after the 1989 season.

Rice spent all 16 years of his big league career with the Boston Red Sox, playing his final game on August 3, 1989. He returned serve the organization when he was appointed hitting coach in 1995, and young hitters including Nomar Garciaparra, Trot Nixon, and Mo Vaughn benefited from his tutelage. Rice continued as Red Sox hitting coach until 2000.

A controversy rages about whether Rice's statistics merit Hall of Fame recognition, but arguments about Cooperstown aside, Rice's achievements have been acknowledged since his retirement from baseball. On November 1, 1995, he was inducted into the Red Sox Hall of Fame in its inaugural class. The Red Sox also display a row of silver bats, replicas of all the Silver Slugger awards ever won by Red Sox players. Two of those belong to Jim Rice. In 1999, *Sports Illustrated* saw fit to rate him as South Carolina's ninth best athlete of the 20th century. On February 18, 2001, Rice was inducted into the Ted Williams Hitters Hall of Fame.[69] Rice stayed as hitting coach until 2000 In the 1999 All-Star Game Celebrity Hitting Challenge at Fenway Park, Rice, an eight-time All-Star himself, thrilled the crowd by hitting balls both off and over the Green Monster.

Rice and his wife Corine reside in Andover, Mass., where they raised their children (Carissa, 22 and Chancey, 25) and have lived since 1975. Being from South Carolina, Rice would prefer to be in a warmer climate, but his family enjoys New England.[70]

Ironically, Rice has joined the ranks of the Boston sports media, and now counts some of those he used to war with among his colleagues and is able to show his more gregarious, friendly side as a baseball analyst for the New England Sports Network.

Carl Yastrzemski

by Herb Crehan and Bill Nowlin

	G	AB	R	H	2B	3B	HR	RBI	BB	SO	BA	OBP	SLG	SB	CS	GDP	HBP
1975 RED SOX	149	543	91	146	30	1	14	60	87	67	.269	.371	.405	8	4	14	2

Before the 1975 playoffs started, skipper Darrell Johnson asked Carl Yastrzemski if he could still play left field. Yaz, who had played 140 games at first base that season, responded, "In my sleep." He played with both eyes wide open, and his outstanding fielding in left field was a key to the Red Sox sweep of the reigning champion Oakland A's.

Born on August 22, 1939, in nearby Southampton, New York, Carl Michael Yastrzemski came of age in Bridgehampton, Long Island (population 3,000) where he often played alongside his father in local semi-pro games. Father Karol Yastrzemski (whose name had been Anglicized to Carl) and Yaz's uncle Tommy owned an inherited 70-acre potato farm, their work a "legacy from Poland, folks coming over here and doing what they knew from the old country."[71]

In his first of two autobiographies, Yaz wrote, "I'm told that when I was 18 months old my dad got me a tiny baseball bat, which I dragged around wherever I went, the way other babies drag blankets or favorite toys. I vaguely remember playing catch with him as a very small boy, but my first clear memory is hitting tennis balls in the backyard against his pitching after supper every night when I was about six. Later we played make-believe ball games between the Yankees and the Red Sox, my two favorite teams...."[72]

Yaz's dad loved baseball. He might have tried to make it in baseball himself, reportedly having offers from both the Dodgers and the Cardinals, but was "reluctant to leave the potato fields of Long Island to try baseball during the Great Depression."[73] Before Carl was born, Carl Yastrzemski Sr. actually formed a semipro baseball team, the Bridgehampton White Eagles; he played shortstop and managed the team. It was almost entirely a family team, with Carl Sr.'s four brothers on the team, as well as two brothers-in-law and three cousins. The team played on Sundays, and did so for years. By the time Carl himself was seven, he was the team's bat boy, his first "job" in baseball. He first played for the team at age 14—young for a semipro player. Even at age 40, Carl's father was still "the guts of the ball club, a good shortstop and the best hitter of the team."[74] His father played with drive and determination, but channeled his ambitions to play professional baseball into his son Carl. Still playing (and out-hitting his son) at

age 41, Carl's dad was doing it for his son. The younger Yaz wrote, "I could tell the only reason he played was on account of me, just as that had been the only reason he kept the White Eagles alive for so long."[75] From the very date Carl signed his first pro contract, the elder Yastrzemski never played again, but the memory lasted. "I loved his spirit and intensity when I played alongside him."[76]

Some of Carl's teammates with the Boston Red Sox saw the influence of Carl's father in his son's drive for success. Former Red Sox catcher Russ Gibson remembered one time early on: "Yaz and myself, and two other guys, shared an apartment in Raleigh [North Carolina] when his dad came for a visit. We were all just starting out, but Yaz was hitting about .390 at the time. We all went off to play golf while Yaz visited with his father. When we got back, all his things were gone. When I asked Yaz what had happened, he said, 'My dad thinks I'm distracted living with you guys. He's moved me into an apartment by myself.'"[77]

Carl's father was quite a man himself. In Yaz's words, though, "nothing ever topped the time he kicked the Yankees' scout out of our house while I shouted, 'Dad, what the heck are you doing?' But my father not only kicked him out but would never talk to him or the Yankees again."

While Yaz was still a senior in high school, the New York Yankees made a pitch. Though not allowed to sign Yastrzemski to an actual contract until after he graduated high school, Yankees scout Ray Garland was still welcomed into the household to talk hypothetically. He traded bonus numbers with Carl's father, writing $60,000 on a piece of paper at the dining room table. Carl's dad wrote out $100,000. Garland reacted dramatically, flipping his pencil in the air and hitting the ceiling as he exclaimed, "$100,000? Are you crazy? The Yankees will never pay that." The Yankees never got the opportunity, despite owner Dan Topping becoming involved. The elder Yaz told Garland, "Nobody throws a pencil in my house. Get the hell out and never come back." That was it for the New York Yankees.[78]

Yaz attracted a lot of attention playing ball on Long Island. His last couple of years in high school, he played semipro ball for Lake Ronkonkoma, a team based about 60 miles from home. His father played for this team, too, always after work on the farm was done. It was around this time that Carl's father began to boost

him as a hitter more than as a pitcher—oddly enough, Carl learned this at a major league tryout camp for the Braves, where Carl faced nine batters and struck out all nine. The younger Yaz had the chance to sign on with a major league team before he even got out of high school, but Carl's dad had his eyes set on a sizable bonus and was prepared to turn down offers he saw as inadequate. Come his senior year, Carl's dad told his high school coach that Carl would not be playing football that year—there was too great a risk of injury, and it might hamper his development as a baseball player.

Red Sox scout Frank "Bots" Nekola had kept his eye on Carl since he was a sophomore in high school. He never threw any pencils in the Yastrzemski household, but he wasn't coming up with $100,000, either, and so Carl's father sent his son off to college. They'd fielded full scholarship offers from a number of colleges, but chose Notre Dame, playing on a scholarship that was half baseball and half basketball. Yaz completed his freshman year, without playing on the varsity team, but then the offers got more serious, even exceeding $100,000. The Red Sox didn't make the largest offer, but the admiration of the local parish priest for Tom Yawkey counted for a lot, and Yaz's father wanted him playing for an East Coast team, not too far from home. Yaz signed with the Red Sox in November 1958 for a $108,000 bonus, and their agreement to cover the rest of his college education. Sox GM Joe Cronin then met Yaz for the first time—and saw a 5'11", 160-pound kid. He couldn't help himself, blurting out, "We're paying this kind of money for *this* guy?"[79] Carl went back to finish up the fall semester at Notre Dame; his father increased his weekly allowance from $2 to $3 a week.

The first of many spring training camps came in 1959 and Carl was assigned to the Raleigh Caps in the Carolina League, a Class B team. The team switched him from shortstop to second base. He was struggling at the plate until manager Ken Deal got him in the box and told him to move up on the plate so he wasn't lunging at balls on the outer half of the strike zone. He says he batted close to .400 for the rest of the year. After Raleigh's season was over, he was invited to come to Fenway Park, not to play ball but to look in on the ball club. Ted Williams greeted him and told him, "Don't let them screw around with your swing. Ever."

Yaz then went on to Minneapolis to join the Millers as they entered the American Association playoffs. Wayne McElreavy notes that, oddly, Yaz was ineligible and there was a protest, but no forfeit was forced. The first time he faced Triple A pitching, and he went 7-for-18 in the six games it took to win the title. And then he

traveled to Cuba to play the Havana Sugar Kings for the International League championship. Fidel Castro came to the ballpark, arriving by helicopter and landing near second base. The Sugar Kings won in the seventh game, but it was the last time (until the Baltimore Orioles played an exhibition game in 1999) that an American pro team played in Cuba.

In January 1960, Carl married Carol Casper. In February, they headed to Scottsdale so Carl could train with the big league ball club. Carl lockered right next to Ted Williams. Ted rarely spoke to him. The main thing Carl learned from 41-year-old Teddy Ballgame was how thoroughly he prepared himself to play. The Red Sox had Pete Runnels at second base (Runnels would win the batting title in 1960), so they sent Carl back to the minors for another year to train him to play left field and get ready to take over for Ted Williams after the 1960 season. Yastrzemski batted .339 for Minneapolis, just missing out on the title by three points, and began to show some skill in the outfield, recording 18 assists.

Ted Williams retired. Both the baton and the burden of replacing the great Williams was passed to Carl Michael Yastrzemski. Opening day 1961 was April 11 at Fenway Park, and Yastrzemski played left field and batted fifth. Replacing Ted Williams in left field and in the hearts of Boston Red Sox fans was a Herculean task for any player, let alone a 20-year-old with two years of professional baseball experience. Ted Williams was a larger-than-life figure on and off the field, and had played for the Red Sox since 1939. Yaz singled to left his first time up, but ended the day 1-for-5. His first and second homers came in back-to-back games on May 9 and 10, but all in all, he struggled at the plate. "I started off very slow. I actually think that was on account of Ted. I was trying to emulate him—be a home run hitter and not be myself: just an all-around player. I could never be a Ted Williams as far as hitting was concerned." When Yaz struggled, the Sox asked Ted to interrupt his fishing and come pay a visit. Williams complied, visited, and watched Yaz take extra batting practice. He told Yaz he had a great swing, and to just go out and use it. "I think what dawned on me was that there can be a great swing that is not a home run swing at the same time."[80]

Yaz batted .266 in his rookie year, with 11 homers and 80 RBI, a good first year once he'd gotten back on track. There was no sophomore slump: Yastrzemski boosted his totals to .296, with 19 homers (and 43 doubles) and 94 RBI. His third year, he made the All-Star team for the first time, and improved dramatically again, to win the American League batting championship with a .321 mark. He led the league in base hits, doubles,

and walks. All the while, Yastrzemski was improving in left field, honing the solid defensive play that he is remembered for today.

He continued to add to his totals, again making the All-Star team in 1965 and 1966. In 1965, he accomplished one of the rarest of hitting feats—Yaz hit for the cycle in the May 14 game, with an extra home run thrown in for good measure. Later that year, Yaz even faced Satchel Paige, who came back to pitch one last time at age 59. He threw three innings and gave up only one hit—to Carl Yastrzemski. Yaz's first six seasons in the major leagues had established him as one of the star players in the game. But his 1967 season would propel Carl Yastrzemski to a place among the elite players in the history of the game.

"One of the big differences in 1967," Yaz recalled, "is that I was able to work out the preceding winter. In earlier years, I was finishing up my college work. But I had completed my degree at Merrimack College so I had time to focus on my conditioning. I reported to spring training in great shape."[81]

By the time the 1967 All-Star Game rolled around, Yaz was among the top five in the American League in batting average, home runs, and runs batted in. The Red Sox were only six games out of first place at the All-Star break, and it was clear that the team had as good a shot at the American League pennant as anyone.

The 1967 Red Sox held New England fans spellbound all summer and into the fall, as they battled for first place in the most exciting pennant race in American League history. Their thrilling win over the Minnesota Twins on the last day of the season touched off one of the great celebrations in Boston history. While a different Red Sox hero seemed to emerge daily, the one constant was Yaz.

Former teammate George Scott remembers it this way, "Yaz hit 44 homers that year, and 43 of them meant something big for the team. It seemed like every time we needed a big play, the man stepped up and got it done." In the final 12 games of the season—crunch time—Carl Yastrzemski had 23 hits in 44 at-bats, driving in 16 runs and scoring 14. He hit 10 homers in his final 100 at-bats of 1967. He had 10 hits in his last 13 at-bats, and when it came to the last two games with the Twins—with the Sox needing to win both games to help avert a tie for the pennant—Yaz went 7-for-8 and drove in six runs.

Yaz was no slouch in the playoffs, either, batting an even .400 (10-for-25) with three home runs and five RBI in the World Series against the St. Louis Cardinals. The storybook season came to an end when

the St. Louis Cardinals won the World Series in Game Seven, but Carl Yastrzemski's place was indelibly etched in baseball folklore. Yaz came within one vote of a unanimous selection as the Most Valuable Player of the American League. He was selected by *Sports Illustrated* as the "1967 Sportsman of the Year" at year's end. And he achieved baseball's "Triple Crown," leading the American League in batting (.326), runs batted in (121), and home runs (44). In all the baseball seasons that have followed, no other player has been able to match his Triple Crown feat.

Yaz also led the league in hits (189), runs (112), total bases (360), and slugging percentage, not to mention on-base percentage. His on-base plus slugging (OPS) was 1.040. How did a Triple Crown winner who brought his team to the pennant miss the MVP by one vote? One voter cast his first-place ballot for Cesar Tovar of the Twins. Tovar batted .267, had six homers to Yaz's 44, and drove in 47 runs to Yaz's 121!

The next year, 1968, Yaz won his third batting title, with a .301 mark. This was, for sure, the Year of the Pitcher, and Yaz was the only batter in the league to crack .300, a full 10 points ahead of the second-best Danny Cater. Only four batters hit .285 or above.

Between 1965 and 1979, Yaz was named to 15 consecutive All-Star teams. The game he remembers best is the 1970 All-Star Game held in Riverfront Stadium in Cincinnati. Yaz had four hits, to go along with a run scored and a RBI, to earn him MVP honors that year. He and Ted Williams [1946] are the only two American Leaguers with four hits in an All-Star Game. Never one to focus on personal statistics, when asked about this record Yaz responded, "I never knew that before. To tell you the truth, I was so sick of losing to the National League that I didn't pay much attention to that stuff."

It is sometimes written that Yaz had a "career year" in 1967, but never again approached that standard. It should be noted that in 1970 he led the league in runs scored, on-base percentage, total bases, slugging average, and—when rounded—he was .0004 out of the lead for the batting title. When coupled with his all-time high of 23 stolen bases, you have a year that would have been a career year for almost any other player.

Those 23 stolen bases made him only the second player in Red Sox history to steal more than 20 bases *and* hit more than 20 home runs in a single season. Former All-Star outfielder Jackie Jensen was the first Red Sox player to achieve this combination in 1954, and Jensen duplicated this feat during the 1959 season. Only three other Red Sox players have achieved this

standard during the past 34 seasons.

In February 1971, Carl Yastrzemski signed a three-year contract that was reported to pay him $500,000 over the three seasons. At that time his contract was the largest in baseball history.

The year 1972 was a frustrating one. The season started late, due to struggles between players and owners. Teams agreed to simply play out the schedule without worrying whether one team played more games than another. As fate would have it, the Red Sox entered the final three games of the year playing the Tigers in Detroit. There was no chance of a playoff tie. The Tigers had a record of 84–69 going into the October 2 game, and the Red Sox were a marginally-better 84–68. Whichever team won two of the three games would win the pennant. The Tigers took a 1–0 lead in the first game, but Yaz doubled in the top of the third to tie it—and the Red Sox would have scored at least one more run (with Yaz safe at third with a triple) except that Luis Aparicio stumbled after rounding third and retreated to the bag where he met up with the oncoming Carl, who was called out. One never knows what might have been, but this was a pivotal play and the Red Sox lost the pennant by a half-game.

Yaz had a subpar year in 1975, batting just .269 with 14 homers and 60 RBI, but his play throughout the postseason reminded fans that he had always been at his best in clutch situations throughout his career. His stellar play in the field and at bat carried over from the American League Championship Series against Oakland (he was 5-for-11, with a home run and two RBI) to the World Series against the Cincinnati Reds. Although the Red Sox lost to the Reds in seven games in one of the greatest World Series ever played, Yaz had scored 11 runs, and batted .350 during the 10 postseason games. As in 1967, the Red Sox fell just short.

From 1976 to 1983, Carl Yastrzemski made the American League All-Star team six times. On July 14, 1977, he notched his 2,655th hit, moving past Ted Williams as the all-time Red Sox hit leader. In 1979, he became the first American Leaguer to accumulate more than 400 homers (he reached the plateau on July 24) *and* over 3,000 lifetime hits (his September 12 single off New York's Jim Beattie was number 3,000). Back on June 16, he'd banged out his 1,000th extra base hit.

On October 1, 1983, the next-to-the-last game of the season, 33,491 of the Fenway Faithful gathered to pay tribute to Carl Yastrzemski. The pre-game ceremony lasted for about an hour, and then came Yaz's turn to speak. After 23 years of never flinching in a pressure situation, Yaz broke down and cried when he stepped to the microphone.

Once he regained his composure, he asked for a moment of silence for his mother and for former Red Sox owner Tom Yawkey. After thanking his family and everyone connected with the Red Sox, he finished with the words, "New England, I love you."

Carl Yastrzemski had played in 3,308 major league ball games—the record until Pete Rose topped it the next year—and played for 23 years for one team: the Boston Red Sox.

In January of 1989, in his first year of eligibility, Carl Yastrzemski was elected to Baseball's Hall of Fame. His vote total that year was among the highest recorded in the history of the Hall of Fame. On August 6, 1989, the Red Sox retired his uniform number and it still hangs today, number 8, overlooking Fenway's outfield.

The baseball careers of Ted Williams and Carl Yastrzemski are inexorably linked. Their paths crossed directly for the last time when they were introduced before the 1999 All-Star Game at Fenway Park as two of the 100 greatest baseball players of the 20th century.

THE LINEUP: Notes

1. "Class A Reports." *The Sporting News* May 23, 1970: 48.
2. "Klein, Demeter Skipper Eastern All-Star Squads." *The Sporting News* July 22, 1972: 39. Regarding the rainout, see *The Sporting News* July 29, 1972: 51.
3. "Deals of the Week." *The Sporting News* April 7, 1973: 45.
4. Trobennan, Bill. "Pawtucket's Pole Speeds Progress With No-Hitter." *The Sporting News* July 7, 1973: 36.
5. ———. "Pawtucket Defeats Tulsa for Series Crown", *The Sporting News* October 6, 1973, p.29.
6. Gammons, Peter. "Hustling Burleson . . . New Red Sox SS?" *The Sporting News* March 2, 1974: 18.
7. ———. "Boston Massacre Throws Big Burden on Youth." *The Sporting News* April 13, 1974: 17.
8. ———. "Transplanted Beniquez: Bosox Surprise." *The Sporting News* April 20, 1974: 4.
9. "A.L. Flashes." *The Sporting News* May 25, 1974: 28.
10. Gammons, Peter. "Bosox Hitch Picnic Pants to Bernie's Belt." *The Sporting News* June 24, 1974: 7.
11. ———. "Rooster Giving Red Sox Plenty to Crow About." *The Sporting News* August 10, 1974: 23.
12. ———. "Burleson Sure of Playing, But Where?" *The Sporting News* February 22, 1975: 45. The Topps team designation appears in *The Sporting News* November 16, 1974.
13. ———. "Burleson Flicks On Stars in Bosox Eyes." *The Sporting News* May 31, 1975: 8.
14. "Boston Bomb Squad Makes Shambles of Homer Marks." *The Sporting News* July 2, 1977: 30.

15. Kahan, Oscar. "Record Vote for Carew, Garvey as All Stars." *The Sporting News* July 23, 1977: 47.

16. Whiteside, Larry. "Busiest Bosox Starter Torrez Loves Work." *The Sporting News*, August 26, 1978: 12.

17. ———. "Remy is Mr. Consistency for Rollicking Red Sox." *The Sporting News* September 2, 1978: 24.

18. Pepe, Phil. "Little Bucky is Yanks' Mr. Big in Clutch." *The Sporting News* October 14, 1978: 23.

19. Whiteside, Larry. "Red Sox Refuse to Worry After Yanks' Blanks." *The Sporting News* June 2, 1979: 19.

20. Giuliotti, Joe. "Bosox Collapse Dims Rice's Swat Feats." *The Sporting News* October 6, 1979: 9.

21. ———. "Burleson Dares Bosox: 'Go Ahead, Trade Me.'" *The Sporting News* May 31, 1980: 32.

22. "No Condolences, Please." *Sports Illustrated* September 22, 1980: 60, 63. This article claims that Cooper's family played for the Indianapolis Clowns, and Cecil himself stated as much in a June 2005 interview. The SABR Negro League Committee has found no record to support it.

23. Source: Doug and Nancy Griffin.

24. Weiss, Bill and Marshall Wright. "Team #38, 1970 Hawaii Islanders (98–48)." MinorLeagueBaseball.com, (63rd article in a series of the 100 greatest minor league teams).

25. Claflin, Larry. "Big-Dealing Bosox Counting On Griffin." *The Sporting News* December 19, 1970: 41.

26. ———. "'Be Patient!' Tatum Cautions Hub Fans." *The Sporting News* January 9, 1971: 52.

27. ———. "'Am I Next to Go?' Andrews Wonders." *The Sporting News* November 7, 1970: 47.

28. ———. "Red Sox Give Up Power For Strength In Bullpen." *The Sporting News* October 24, 1970: 13.

29. ———. "Big-Dealing Bosox Counting On Griffin." *The Sporting News* December 19, 1970: 41.

30. ———. "Leg Injury 'Nothing Serious,' Luis Tells Bosox." *The Sporting News* December 26, 1970: 53.

31. ———. "Will Deals Buttress Porous Defense?" *The Sporting News* February 27, 1971: 33.

32. Ciampa, Fred. "Red Sox Ticket John Kennedy for Super Sub Office." *The Sporting News* March 13, 1971: 51.

33. ———. "L'il Looey Big Man as Bosox Leader–Teacher." *The Sporting News* March 20, 1971: 47.

34. Claflin, Larry. "Slugger Yaz Praises Red Sox Defense." *The Sporting News* April 3, 1971: 26.

35. ———. "Bosox See Josephson Arrival As a Harbinger of Happy Days." *The Sporting News* April 17, 1971: 25.

36. ———. "Griffin Answers Red Sox Search At Second Base." *The Sporting News* May 15, 1971: 20.

37. Ibid.

38. "Defense Helps Red Sox, Slab Ace Siebert Notes." *The Sporting News* July 3, 1971: 25.

39. Claflin, Larry. "Reggie Most Potent Bosox Mauler." *The Sporting News* September 11, 1971: 14.

40. ———. "Red Sox Tout Doug Griffin As King of the Keystoners." *The Sporting News* April 15, 1972: 10.

41. Ibid.

42. Ibid.

43. ———. "Griffin Sidelined by Fractured Hand." *The Sporting News*, June 9, 1973: 27.

44. ———. "Lee Keeps Bosox On Their Toes as Puncher–Pitcher." *The Sporting News* June 16, 1973: 29.

45. Gammons, Peter. "Hub Shoppers Return Home With Half a Loaf." *The Sporting News* November 10, 1973: 39.

46. Horgan, Tim. "Red Sox, Griffin Have Backs to Wall." *Boston Herald* March 3, 1975.

47. Gammons, Peter. "Griffin Beaning Multiplies Stumbling Bosox Distress." *The Sporting News* May 18, 1974: 17.

48. Horgan, op. cit.

49. Gammons, Peter. "Griffin's Surgery Bars Bosox Deal." *The Sporting News* November 23, 1974: 57.

50. Horgan, op. cit.

51. Gammons, Peter. "Red Sox Find They Picked Real Prize in Kim Andrew." *The Sporting News* April 19, 1975: 19.

52. ———. "Super Glove Work Helps Red Sox Boost Lead." *The Sporting News* August 16, 1975: 11.

53. ———. "What Price Doyle? Red Sox, Angels Disagree," *The Sporting News*, August 23, 1975.

54. Whiteside, Larry; "Red Sox to Wait and Watch on Deals." *The Sporting News* March 5, 1977: 20.

55. ———. "Bill Lee's Unchanged—If Arm's Okay." *The Sporting News* March 19, 1977: 42.

56. Claflin, Larry. "Slugger Yaz Praises Red Sox Defense." *The Sporting News* April 3, 1971: 26.

57. "Jim Rice." *Jim Rice Statistics*. Baseball-Reference.com. Retrieved September 29, 2005 <http://www.baseball-reference.com/r/riceji01.shtml>.

58. *Jim Rice*. BaseballLibrary.com. Retrieved September 29, 2005 <http://www.baseballlibrary.com/baseballlibrary/ballplayers/R/Rice_Jim.stm>.

59. Goldberg, Jeff. "The Day Rice Made Contact: One of His Memorable Moves Was to Aid an Injured Young Fan." *Hartford Courant* August 7, 1997.

60. "August 1977." BaseballLibrary.com. Retrieved September 29, 2005 <http://www.baseballlibrary.com/baseballlibrary/chronology/1977AUGUST.stm>.

61. "April 1978." BaseballLibrary.com. Retrieved September 29, 2005 <http://www.baseballlibrary.com/baseballlibrary/chronology/1978APRIL.stm>.

62. *Red Sox Media Guide* 2003.

63. Ibid. Yaz was injured, however, and unable to make a start in the outfield; he was moved to first base instead, where also-injured Rod Carew was supposed to start. He was replaced in the outfield by Cecil Cooper.

64. Goldberg, op. cit.

65. Ibid.

66. White, Paul. "My 2002 Hall of Fame Ballot: Slot #4, Jim Rice." BaseballLibrary.com. Updated December 10, 2001. Retreived September 29, 2005. <http://www.baseballlibrary.com/baseballlibrary/submit/White_Paul9.stm>.

67. White quotes Stark as saying, "[H]e was a one-dimensional player whose career thundered to a halt just as he was on the verge of cementing his sure place in the Hall (only 31 homers, 162 RBI after age 34). And you essentially have to vote on him as a hitter only, because he DH-ed extensively. He gave you no speed, no Gold Gloves, no off-the-field 'character-and-integrity' points." This is from Stark's November 19, 2003 ESPN.com article "Stark: My Hall of Fame Ballot." <http://espn.go.com/classic/s/2001/0115/1016923.html>.

68. Gammons, Peter. *Beyond the Sixth Game*. Boston, MA: Houghton Mifflin, 1985.

69. Livingstone, Seth. "2001: A Year Like No Other." *USA Today* December 26, 2001.

70. Neff, Andrew. "Rice Enjoys TV Analyst Stint." *Bangor Daily News* April 1, 2005.

71. Yastrzemski, Carl, and Gerald Eskenazi, *Yaz: Baseball, the Wall, and Me.* New York: Doubleday, 1990: 7.

72. Yastrzemski, Carl, with Al Hirshberg. *Yaz.* New York: Viking Press, 1968: 37.

73. *Yaz* (1990): 1, 8.

74. *Yaz* (1968): 46.

75. Ibid., 50–51.

76. *Yaz* (1990): 11.

77. Personal interview with Herb Crehan, 1999.

78. *Yaz* (1990): 19–20.

79. Ibid., 39.

80. Prime, Jim and Bill Nowlin. *Ted Williams: The Pursuit of Perfection.* Champaign, IL: Sports Publishing: 102.

81. Personal interview with Herb Crehan, 1999.

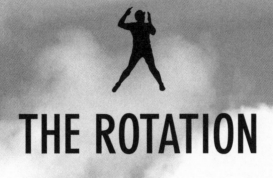

THE ROTATION

Photograph overleaf, L to R: Reggie Cleveland and Rick Wise.

Reggie Cleveland

by Maurice Bouchard

	G	ERA	W	L	SV	GS	GF	CG	SHO	IP	H	R	ER	BB	HR	SO	BFP
1975 RED SOX	31	4.43	13	9	0	20	6	3	1	170.2	173	90	84	52	19	78	724

He's the best I have,"[1] said Hall of Fame second baseman Red Schoendienst in 1973, when he was asked about Reggie Cleveland being traded to the Red Sox that winter. High praise, especially considering the Cardinals staff still included Bob Gibson. Boston GM Dick O'Connell called Cleveland "one of the best pitchers around."[2] In the winter of 1973, it was all upside for the 25-year-old Canadian, who had three solid major league seasons under his belt. Reggie Cleveland was poised to become a 20-game winner, if not the ace of a pitching staff, certainly a very valuable starter. Would he, could he, live up to the high praise and the equally high expectations?

On May 23, 1948, Reginald Leslie Cleveland was born in the small town of Swift Current, Saskatchewan, Canada. Swift Current, in the southwestern part of the province is situated 90 miles north of the Montana border, and 140 miles west of the provincial capital Regina, hard by the Swift Current Creek. It was a town of 6,000 or so when the future Canadian Baseball Hall of Famer was born to Gladys (Porter) and Bob Cleveland. It was the Porter side of the family that was athletic. Gladys played softball among other sports. Cleveland's grandfather, Leslie Porter, was scouted by professional baseball clubs but never signed because he could not be spared from the family farm.[3] Reggie Cleveland's father, Bob, was a ticket taker for the Canadian Pacific Railway but would soon rejoin the Royal Canadian Air Force (he had been a member during World War II) and move the family to the even smaller, more remote town of Cold Lake, Alberta near the Primrose Lake Air Weapons Range. But wherever the Air Force took him, Bob Cleveland would make sure there was organized baseball for his athletic son. The younger Cleveland played in small towns all over Alberta and Saskatchewan, usually playing with boys or men much older than he. In addition to baseball, Reggie Cleveland was a javelin champion who also lettered in curling and hockey for Beaver River High School, which is the Canadian Forces high school in Cold Lake.

It was baseball, however, where Cleveland was to make his career. After throwing a no-hitter for the Moose Jaw Phillies, Cleveland was discovered by Sam Shapiro, a diminutive carnival man and erstwhile "B-game" spring training umpire. While traveling with the carnival in 1965, Shapiro came upon the young right hander pitching in a semi-pro game and sent a telegram to his friend Red Schoendienst, then manager of the St. Louis Cardinals. Bill Sayles, Cardinal scout and former Red Sox pitcher, was dispatched to see Cleveland pitch, only to find he had worked a day earlier to help keep his team from being eliminated in a tournament. His next start was postponed by rain so Sayles asked Cleveland for a personal pitching demonstration, and Sayles was impressed enough to offer Cleveland a contract with a $500 bonus. Cleveland, on the other hand, was not impressed. Sayles raised the bonus to $1,000. Cleveland persisted and asked for more money, but Sayles demurred. Later, the 17-year-old Cleveland reconsidered, called Sayles and signed the contract.[4] Reggie Cleveland was a professional ball player.

In 1966 Reggie Cleveland started his career with the St. Petersburg Cardinals of the Class A Florida State League managed by one George Anderson (known as "Sparky").[5] Also in 1966, Cleveland appeared in 11 games for the Eugene (Oregon) Emeralds in the Class A Northwest League. It was back to St. Petersburg for two games to start the 1967 campaign. After recovering from an ankle injury, Cleveland was sent to the Northwest League again but this time to the Lewiston (Idaho) Broncs, where he led the league in games started with 19 and tied for the league lead in complete games with 11. The Lewiston team was managed by former big league pitcher Ray Hathaway. It is Hathaway (who would later become the Cardinals' pitching coach) along with Billy Muffett, who Reggie Cleveland credits with teaching him to pitch.[6] Cleveland was back in St. Petersburg once more for the 1968 campaign, this time compiling a 15–10 record over 27 starts and an ERA of 2.77, striking out 135 in 185 innings. After growing up on the frigid Canadian prairie, St. Petersburg must have seemed like paradise. In 1968, Cleveland married St. Petersburg resident Kathleen Kubicki. The couple, who took up residence in sunny St. Pete, would collaborate on three children, Michelle, Michael and Todd. The next year would be Cleveland's breakout year in the minors. He was 15–6 for the Arkansas Travelers (Double A Texas League) with an ERA of 3.39 over 23 starts. He tied for the league lead in complete games

with 13. Cleveland moved up to the Tulsa Oilers in the American Association (Triple A) for six games before making his major league debut.

On October 1, 1969, in the penultimate game in the 1969 schedule, the 6'1", 195-pound right-hander made his debut for St. Louis with a start against the Phillies in Busch Stadium. While Cleveland did not pitch well (four innings, seven hits, four earned runs) the Cardinals eventually won the game 6–5. Cleveland started the 1970 season in the minors but after posting a 12–8 in record in Tulsa, he was called up in August to the Cardinals. Cleveland got into 16 games, including one start, for the Red Birds but was 0–4 over that stretch. Despite his record, there was one appearance in Pittsburgh, on September 9, which showed he could succeed in the majors. Cleveland had been working with Schoendienst and Muffett on his mechanics. He had not been using his lower body effectively but was reluctant to make changes. Schoendienst and Muffett persisted, however, and through the use of movies, demonstrated his flawed delivery. Cleveland told *The Sporting News*' Neal Russo, "I certainly found out what I was doing wrong. I wasn't driving properly. When I corrected those things, I started to throw hard again and my control was a lot better. I had been doing things wrong like that all year and didn't realize it"[7] In the September 9 game, one in which the right-handed batting Reggie Cleveland got his first major league hit (off Dave Giusti), he pitched 3⅔ shutout innings, allowing just three hits while striking out four and walking no one. Cleveland was impressive enough to stay with the big club for the rest of the season, and, as it would turn out, to stay in the majors for good.

He started the 1971 season with St. Louis, and Cleveland would soon show he belonged in the Cardinals rotation with Bob Gibson, Steve Carlton, and Jerry Reuss. His first major league win came on April 20 against Juan Marichal. On paper it looked like a mismatch: Marichal, with his 206 major league victories, versus 22-year-old Reggie Cleveland still looking for his first one. On top of that, just nine days earlier, Cleveland had faced Marichal in St. Louis and had pitched poorly. He bounced back in his next start but was on the short end of a 2–1 loss against Al Downing and the Los Angeles Dodgers. "I was beginning to think I'd never win a game,"[8] said the Cardinals rookie whose major league record to that point in his career was 0–6. The Giants were in the midst of a nine-game winning streak when the Cardinals came to town. Thankfully, the game is not played on paper. Cleveland beat Marichal and the Giants 2–1 at Candlestick Park, giving up just the one

run over 7⅔ innings. Young Reggie was up to the task, striking out Dick Dietz twice with a total of five men on base. He also got George Foster and struck out pinch hitter Willie McCovey, too. Cleveland went on to win 11 more times in 1971 and was named National League Rookie Pitcher of the Year by *The Sporting News*.

The next year, Cleveland started like a Cy Young candidate. By the time he threw a complete game to beat the Braves 2–0 on July 13 (Cleveland had one RBI and Bernie Carbo the other), Cleveland was 11–4 with a 2.99 ERA. Unfortunately, he went 3–11 the rest of the way to finish 14–15 with a 3.94 ERA for the 75–81, fourth-place Cardinals. Not bad for a second-year man, but disappointing after the stellar start. The 1972 season could be viewed as a microcosm of Cleveland's career. He seemed to be in a constant cycle, with flashes of greatness followed by mediocrity or worse. He was frequently battling his waistline. His teammates gave him the nicknames "Double Cheeseburger" and "Snacks." Management and the press could not understand how he could gain weight during the season. While listed as 200 pounds, Cleveland would often carry 230 pounds or more to the mound. He was also, as he would later admit, battling the "major league lifestyle." He kept his problem well-hidden—as he would tell Dan Turner—because he was "such a good drunk."[9]

The following season would prove to be Cleveland's best year, at least statistically. He helped the 1973 Cardinals improve to a second-place finish at 81–81 with a 14–10 record, a 3.01 ERA and three shutouts. He struck out 122, while walking just 61 over 224 innings (his third consecutive year of pitching 220 innings or more). His 14 wins were second only to Rick Wise's 16 on the '73 Cardinals pitching staff. Repeating the pattern of the year before, Cleveland started hot. By the time he shut out the Expos and former teammate Mike Torrez 2–0 in Montreal on August 1, he had compiled a 12–5 record with a 2.94 ERA. After that Cleveland was 2–5. To be fair, Cardinals ace Bob Gibson had a lower ERA (2.77) but managed to lose 10 games as well in 1973. Cleveland was a rising star on the Cardinals staff and other teams were noticing.

On December 7, 1973, Reggie Cleveland was traded to the Boston Red Sox with Diego Segui and Terry Hughes for pitchers Lynn McGlothen, John Curtis, and Mike Garman. Red Sox General Manager Dick O'Connell was trying to acquire the 35-year-old Gaylord Perry from the Indians but could not get the deal done, and instead turned to the Cardinals. Reggie Cleveland, with his fastball, slider and curve, was the marquee player of the trade. After the 1973 season, O'Connell

completed what amounted to a 10-player deal with St. Louis, getting Rick Wise in a separate deal weeks earlier. After the trade for Cleveland, the Red Sox, who expected him to be a 20-game winner, thought they had "the best staff in baseball."[10]

Cleveland had pitched very well for St. Louis and fully expected to be in the starting rotation for the Red Sox in 1974. It was not to be, at least not at first. Cleveland came into camp overweight and with a bum left knee suffered in winter ball playing for Las Aguilas in Venezuela. Not surprisingly he had a sub-par spring and did not earn a spot in the starting rotation. Cleveland was the long man out of the bullpen and spot starter coming out of spring training. His poor spring and injury (later learned to be a torn meniscus[11]) carried over to the regular year. His first start may have been an omen of things to come. On April 15, Cleveland suffered a tough-luck 1–0 loss to Detroit. He struck out five, walked none, and allowed only three hits to the Tigers. Unfortunately for Cleveland, one of the hits was a Norm Cash home run in the fifth inning that sneaked around the right-field foul pole. The Red Sox batters, for their part, could not muster any offense against Boston native Joe Coleman who gave up only three singles. The Cleveland-Coleman pitching match-up occurred once again on July 26. Incredibly, Cleveland pitched 10⅓ innings, allowing only three hits and no earned runs, but still lost. An error by Boston third baseman Rico Petrocelli in the bottom of the 11th inning opened the door to a Jim Northrup game-winning single two batters later. Again, the Red Sox batters could do nothing with Joe Coleman who pitched 11 innings of four-hit ball. Four days later, Cleveland lost another matchup with Coleman. Reggie had a rather lackluster 1974 at 12–14 and it was not all the fault of poor offensive support. By early June, Cleveland's ERA was 6.30 though he finished with a 4.32 ERA as the Red Sox placed third behind the Orioles and the Yankees.

Cleveland was in the starting rotation along with Luis Tiant, Bill Lee, and Rick Wise to begin Boston's 1975 season. His first start (and win) of the year, April 12, was a memorable one. Cleveland pitched 12 innings allowing only two runs to the Orioles in a game the Sox eventually won in the 13th. The good times would not last, however. After losing to the Angels on May 25, Cleveland with his 3–3 record and 4.76 ERA was back in the bullpen. Except for one start in the second game of a doubleheader on July 6, he was out of the rotation until July 20. On June 29, the Red Sox beat the Yankees 3–2 to take back first place in the AL East. Late that night Cleveland was driving after midnight,

through Boston's Sumner Tunnel with his best friend from high school when he hit a puddle and rolled his car. Cleveland received 15 stitches around his right ear and eight in his mouth after being pulled, unconscious, from the wreckage.[12] In those simpler days before 24-hour sports channels, this DUI[13] incident went virtually unreported (there was a small story[14] in Toronto's *Globe and Mail*). Incredibly, Cleveland spent no time on the disabled list and pitched the next day (July 1).

While it would not have felt like it at the time, the July 6 loss to the Indians was the turning point in Reggie Cleveland's season. After that loss, he went 9–3 the rest of the year, lowering his ERA from 5.38 to 4.43. Even in defeat, he pitched well. For example, one of his three losses in the second-half came on August 8. Cleveland took a no-hitter into the seventh inning. With two outs in the seventh, Reggie Jackson hit a home run. A Billy Williams single in front of a Gene Tenace homer made it 3–2, A's. Oakland pitcher Ken Holtzman would make it stand up as Cleveland was handed a tough loss in this 99-minute game.

His start against the Yankees in Shea Stadium (Yankee Stadium was being renovated) on Saturday, July 26 was one of the most important of the year. Cleveland pitched 8⅔ innings allowing only two runs on five hits as Boston beat New York 4–2. This win set the stage for Boston's shutout sweep of the Yankees the next day, July 27, when Bill Lee beat Catfish Hunter 1–0 in game one and Roger Moret beat Tippy Martinez 6–0 in the nightcap, dropping the Yankees firmly into third place, 10 games behind Boston.

The Red Sox had some momentum to start the second half. In the last month of the season, the Sox were in a tough struggle with Baltimore for the AL East Division crown. When Bill Lee was ineffective due to elbow soreness in September, Cleveland stepped in and made a huge difference. Cleveland was 4–0 in September with a 2.21 ERA over 36⅔ innings (four starts and one five-shutout-innings relief appearance). He topped off his regular season with a complete game shutout of the Indians on September 26, lowering the Sox magic number to two. In that game, he faced only four batters over the minimum. He finished the season at 13–9 with a 4.42 ERA. It was the tale of two seasons again but this time Cleveland finished strongly after a mediocre start. The Red Sox finished first in the American League East, and Cleveland was an important part of their success. The Sox were five games over .500 (16–11) in September and Cleveland was four games over by himself. He had earned at least one post-season start.

Reggie Cleveland became the first Canadian-born pitcher to start a postseason game when he started the second game of the ALCS against Oakland on October 5, 1975. Cleveland did not get a decision (allowing 7 hits and 3 runs in 5 innings) but the Red Sox went on to win the game, 6–3. Boston won the next game as well, completing a sweep and dethroning the three-time reigning World Champions.

In the World Series, Reggie Cleveland would play his part and make a little more history. Cleveland first saw action in the third game on October 14 at Riverfront Stadium in Cincinnati. He came in to relieve Jim Burton in the bottom of the fifth with two outs, Ken Griffey Sr. on second and the Reds already ahead 5–1. Cleveland struck out Tony Perez to end the threat. The Red Sox scored a run in the top of the sixth and needed Cleveland to keep the Reds from doing further damage in the bottom of the frame. Cleveland did exactly what was required, pitching a scoreless sixth, by striking out Johnny Bench and then getting outs from George Foster and Dave Concepcion. It was an effective outing for Cleveland, who was removed for a pinch hitter in the top of the seventh. The Sox would come back to tie it in the ninth only to lose in the tenth.

In Game Five, Cleveland became the first Canadian-born pitcher to start a World Series game. Cleveland pitched well, shutting out the Reds through 3⅔ innings before surrendering a home run to slumping Tony Perez. The sixth inning would be Cleveland's undoing. After walking Joe Morgan, Cleveland induced the perfect double play ball from Bench (Morgan was still on first because Cleveland had thrown over to first 16 times during Bench's at-bat), but second baseman Denny Doyle did not see the grounder. Right fielder Evans fielded the ball and overthrew third, leaving runners at second and third with nobody out. Tony Perez was up next. Perez then drove the 1–2 pitch to deep left for his second homer of the night. The Reds would win the game 6–2.

Cleveland would make one more appearance in the 1975 World Series. On October 22, in the ninth inning of the seventh game, Cleveland was brought in to face Johnny Bench with Pete Rose on third and Joe Morgan on second after Jim Burton had given up a run to put the Reds on top 4–3. Cleveland walked Bench to load the bases. Next batter up was Game Five hero and new nemesis Tony Perez. This time Cleveland got Perez to fly out to end the threat, and was in line for the win if the Sox could score two runs in the bottom of the ninth. Alas, the Reds held on to their slim lead to win the game, and the series, 4–3.

The 1976 Red Sox looked to repeat as American League champions but could manage only third, more than 15 games behind first place New York. Cleveland, mostly a reliever now, finished 10–9 but with an ERA of 3.07, nearly a full run better than the league average. He pitched 170 innings and, incredibly, gave up only three home runs all year (all at Fenway Park).[15]

In 1977, the Red Sox won 97 games but finished in a tie for second with Baltimore. Cleveland's won-loss record improved to 11–8 but his ERA ballooned to 4.26. He pitched 190⅓ innings in 36 games with 27 starts and nine complete games. It the last year Cleveland would have more starts than relief appearances. He did have a couple of historic appearances. One notable start came on September 25, when Cleveland "scattered" 18 hits as he pitched a complete game and earned a victory against the Tigers in Detroit, 12–5.

The 1977 Red Sox had three young starters—Bob Stanley, Don Aase, and Mike Paxton—who needed work to mature. Reggie Cleveland volunteered to go to the bullpen to allow the Red Sox the flexibility of getting more starts for the three young guns.[16] It was a selfless thing to do. It was neither the first nor the last time that Cleveland, who Don Zimmer called "a real pro,"[17] put the team first.

At the start of the 1978 season, Boston had 11 pitchers and manager Don Zimmer wanted 10. Jim Wright, a 27-year-old rookie, was out of contract options and Cleveland was the odd man out. Cleveland's contract was purchased by the Texas Rangers on April 18 for $125,000.[18] Cleveland, for his part, was relieved. He told reporters, "Not knowing what was going to happen was driving me nuts. Now I know I have a chance to start. I'm very happy to go to Texas. It's a good ball club which can score runs and it's a good place to play."[19]

Cleveland was used exclusively in relief for the Rangers, appearing in 53 games. He got off to a slow start with the Rangers because he had not been used much by Boston. However, the turning point of his season came on April 28 against his former team. Cleveland pitched four solid innings, giving up only one unearned run, striking out three and walking none. He earned his first victory when Richie Zisk hit a two-run homer in the bottom of the 11th. Cleveland earned saves in his next three appearances, pitched in a non-save situation, then got another save, gaining self-confidence and the confidence of his manager. Cleveland ended the 1978 season at just 5–8 but with an impressive 3.08 ERA and 12 saves. He was the best reliever on the team and was named so by Rolaids in their relief pitching awards for the year.

Although successful in Texas, Reggie's stay would be a short one. The cash-strapped Brad Corbett traded Cleveland on December 15, 1978 to Milwaukee for Ed Farmer, Gary Holle, and $200,000.[20] Brewers GM Harry Dalton, who once thought Cleveland "too fat to pitch in the major leagues,"[21] had wanted Cleveland since at least the beginning of 1978. Dalton and the Brewers were high on Cleveland as a starter, at one point insisting he would pitch 200 innings for the team, but it was not to be. Cleveland, who had moved his family to Texas and bought into a farm there, was not thrilled to be traded. He let a bad attitude and his waistline both get out of hand. He had his worst year in the majors, 1–5 with a 6.71 ERA while pitching only 55 innings. Cleveland also had more walks than strikeouts for the first time in his career.

He came to spring training in 1980 with a new attitude and a new physique. A few of his teammates failed to recognize the new, svelte Reggie at the Brewers' Sun City, Arizona, spring training facility.[22] Cleveland reported a week early, after shedding 25 pounds in the off-season, and told manager George Bamberger, "You guys are going to be proud of me at the end of the season."[23] Cleveland pitched well in relief but still wanted to start. (Cleveland liked short relief. He once told *The Sporting News'* Tom Flaherty, "The idea is you go in with the game on the line. You either do it or you don't. I like that situation.") When his chance came June 16 in the second game of a double header against Detroit, he made the most of it. Cleveland had a one-hitter through 7⅔ innings before giving up home runs to Steve Kemp and Richie Hebner. Milwaukee won the game 5–3 with Cleveland getting the victory. In his next start, he shut out Oakland on six hits and then followed with a 5–2 complete game victory against California. On July 25, Cleveland won the 100th game of his career by beating Jim Palmer and the Orioles with a complete-game, four-hit shutout.[24] Cleveland was brilliant once again and, unexpectedly, leading the Brewers' staff. He finished the year at 11–9 with an impressive 3.73 ERA. He appeared in 45 games with 13 starts, five complete games and two shutouts. Again, he was recognized by Rolaids as the best reliever on his team.[25]

The next season, 1981, was a troubled one for baseball in general and for Reggie Cleveland in particular. For baseball, there was a two-month work stoppage in the middle of the season. Players received only about seven days' notice of the resumption of the season. Cleveland over-trained to get ready quickly and developed tendonitis in his right shoulder.[26] In addition, the "major league lifestyle" and family problems (Cleveland's family was still in Texas) were starting to catch up with him. He was pitching poorly and the worse he pitched, the more he drank. Eventually the 33-year-old Cleveland went to manager Buck Rodgers and said, "You've got a team in the playoffs [the Brewers were the second-half winners of the split season schedule], and you don't have any confidence in me and I don't have any confidence in me. Get somebody you're going to be able to use because I got to get out of here or I'm going to end up in the tank."[27] Cleveland played in his final game September 23, 1981, fittingly against the Red Sox. He pitched one-third of an inning, striking out 1975 World Series nemesis Tony Perez. After the strikeout, however, Gary Allenson hit a grand slam, Rick Miller doubled, and Cleveland was relieved by Jerry Augustine.

Reggie Cleveland's 13-year major league career spanned three decades with the birth of free agency right in the middle. He finished with 105 victories against 106 defeats,[28] appearing in 428 games, striking out 930. He won at least 10 games in seven straight years (from 1971 to 1977). At the time of his retirement, his 105 victories (Cleveland won another 53 games in the minors) were second only to Hall of Famer Ferguson Jenkins' 264 victories among Canadian-born pitchers (he has since been passed by Kirk McCaskill who has 106 major league victories). After his playing career, Cleveland moved to Calgary, Alberta with his second wife Charlene and their two children. Son John became a three-time Olympic swimmer for Canada ('88, '92 and '96) and son Todd played shortstop for the University of North Florida.[29] Always affable[30] Reggie Cleveland put his personality to work selling cars for Shaganappi Chevv-Olds in Calgary[31] and, later, selling real estate.[32] From 1991 to 1995, Cleveland worked for the Toronto Blue Jays as a pitching coach at their various minor league affiliates, from the instructional league in Florida, to St. Catharine's in the New York–Penn League to Hagerstown (MD) in the South Atlantic League.[33] Cleveland became a US citizen in 1980, and in 2005 was living in the Dallas, Texas area, selling luxury cars for Park Place Lexus. Reggie Cleveland was inducted into the Saskatchewan Baseball Hall of Fame and the Canadian Baseball Hall of Fame in 1986.

Bill Lee

by Jim Prime

	G	ERA	W	L	SV	GS	GF	CG	SHO	IP	H	R	ER	BB	HR	SO	BFP
1975 RED SOX	41	3.95	17	9	0	34	0	17	4	260	274	123	114	69	20	78	1093

As a major league ballplayer, William Francis Lee was as out of context as Condoleeza Rice in a mud-wrestling competition or Dennis Miller at a Three Stooges film festival. He was perhaps too smart for the room, too irreverent for the establishment, too hip for the jockocracy. He would have been more at home at a Warren Zevon concert or a Greenpeace convention.

Lee was one of those rare ballplayers whose off-field persona overshadowed his significant on-field performance. In baseball parlance, Lee is known as a "flake," a term that includes anyone who doesn't give pat answers to pat questions or dares to admit to reading a book without pictures. He was an original in a sport that often frowns on any show of originality. In fairness, Lee would have been an eccentric in almost any field he chose to pursue, but in baseball, he was considered positively certifiable. His often-outrageous statements and bizarre actions marked him as an oddity and ensured him a lasting reputation in the buttoned-down baseball world. They also earned him the nickname "Spaceman," a title he never fully embraced, arguing that his first priority was always Mother Earth. Nevertheless, Lee's record speaks for itself and places him in the company of some of the best pitchers in Red Sox history.

Boston being a city where blue collar and scholar co-exist, a city of stark contrasts, it is not surprising that he would be embraced by some and derided by others. When he called the city racist for the opposition to forced busing of black students to white schools, he alienated a conservative element in the city. But he won hardcore baseball fans over with his solid work ethic while on the mound.

William Francis Lee III was born in Burbank, California, on December 28, 1946, the son of William Francis Lee Jr. and Paula Theresa (Hunt) Lee. His baseball lineage is impeccable. His father had played sandlot ball and later fast-pitch softball. His grandfather, William F. Lee Sr., was a highly touted infielder in the 1900s in Los Angeles. His aunt, Annabelle Lee ("the best athlete in our family," according to Bill himself), was a star in the Women's Semi-Pro Hardball League in Chicago. She too was a southpaw, and played with the Minneapolis Millerettes, the Grand Rapids Chicks, and the Fort Wayne Daisies, in the All-American Girl's Professional Baseball League (AAGPBL). In 1944, Lee pitched a perfect game for the Daisies against the Kenosha Comets.

Bill Lee's own baseball apprenticeship took place at the University of Southern California where he came under the tutelage of highly respected coach Rod Dedeaux. As a member of the USC Trojans, he helped them capture the 1968 College World Series. Lee graduated from USC with a BA in geography, a degree both appropriate and useful in that he has become a roving ambassador for baseball throughout the world.

Immediately after graduation, Lee was selected by the Red Sox in the 22nd round of the free-agent draft (June 7, 1968). He was assigned to Waterloo (1–1, 1.33 ERA) of the Midwest league and then to Winston-Salem (3–3, 1.72 ERA) of the Carolina league.

Lee began the 1969 season with Pittsfield, racking up a 6–2 mark in 10 starts, with a 2.06 ERA. By late June, he was brought up to the big league club.

Lee's debut was a relief appearance on June 25, 1969, in the second game of a Fenway doubleheader against Cleveland. The Indians led 6–3 after three innings. Lee pitched the fourth through the seventh innings, giving up a run on four hits before being lifted for a pinch-hitter in the bottom of the seventh. After 19 relief stints, Lee earned a start late in the season, on September 30. The Senators beat him up and he suffered his third loss of the year, finishing the campaign 1–3, with a 4.50 ERA. The one win had come on September 20, when Lee threw 6⅔ innings of scoreless relief.

Early on, Lee started feeding zingers to the press. When he first came to Boston in 1969 and was given a tour of Fenway Park, he stared wide-eyed at the Green Monster and inquired, "Do they leave it there during the games?" Sports journalists throughout New England may have given silent thanks. The team could use a little color, and before too long Lee became the darling of the dailies. Over the years, reporters came to know that regardless of the on-field prospects of the Sox, this refreshing newcomer could provide them with lots of colorful copy. Lee rarely disappointed. He always seemed good for an original quote, not just some canned cliché.

In 1970, Bill opened the season with the big league ballclub and started five games, appeared in six others, and through the end of May ran up a record of 2–2, with a 4.62 ERA. His best game was a 2–1 win over Oakland on April 28 at Fenway. Then he had to switch uniforms. It was time to serve his country. Bill served in the U.S. Army Reserve, and was stationed at the Boston army base in South Boston. Though he dismisses the nature of the work ("the job was to get the donuts and free seats for the officers"), it is worth noting that the man so often portrayed as a rebel appeared not to have any apparent conflict with duly constituted authority. He rose to the rank of Spec. 5.

His duty done, Lee played his first full season in major league ball in 1971. All but three of his 47 appearances came in relief roles. He gave up 102 hits in 102 innings, posting an excellent 2.74 ERA. His won-loss record was 9–2. In 1972, Lee never started a game, again appearing 47 times and helping keep the Sox in the hunt right up to the final day when the team fell just a half-game short of capturing the pennant. Lee's record was 7–4, with a 3.20 ERA. He hit his only American League home run on the night of September 11 off Ray Lamb in Cleveland Stadium.

1973 was Bill Lee's breakout year. After four quality long-relief stints in April (totaling 18⅔ innings), and after several Red Sox starters struggled, Lee got his first start on May 1, and never left the rotation. He started 33 ballgames, and won 17 while losing 11. Only Luis Tiant won more (El Tiante was 20–13) but Lee lead the team's starters in ERA with a stellar 2.75. Lee was honored by being named to the American League All-Star squad, but did not appear in the game itself.

The year was notable in another way, too. Carlton Fisk became the team's player representative, with Lee as the alternate. This was remarkable for such young players, but both men arrived on the scene immediately willing to speak out for themselves and their teammates. This marked the start of a strong relationship between Fisk and Lee. The young take-charge catcher would often come out to the mound and get in Lee's face to get him to focus, or throw the right pitch. It was a very successful partnership for several years.

Lee won 17 games again in 1974 (17–11, with a 3.51 ERA), still the number-two man on the mound, behind 22-game winner Tiant. Both pitchers threw one-run games—but lost—in a frustrating Labor Day doubleheader at Memorial Stadium, Baltimore. Orioles pitchers Ross Grimsley and Mike Cuellar both threw 1–0 shutouts. The Sox finished the season just seven games out of first place, behind the Orioles.

Then came 1975. For the third year in a row, Lee won 17 games. His record was 17–9 (3.95 ERA), providing the team with an effective front three: Rick Wise won 19 and Tiant won 18. Lee remained a workhorse, tying for the team lead, throwing 260 innings (albeit down some 20 innings from '73 and '74) and was a major part of the pennant-winning Bosox ballclub.

Lee did not appear in the League Championship Series, which the Sox swept in three games behind starts by Tiant, Cleveland, and Wise. Bill started Game Two of the 1975 World Series. He held Cincinnati's Big Red Machine to just five hits and two runs over eight-plus innings, departing the game after Johnny Bench led off the ninth with a double. Dick Drago, on in relief, gave up two hits, giving the Reds a 3–2 lead. Red Sox batters went down 1-2-3 in the ninth, and Lee's great performance was wasted.

The day after Bernie Carbo and Carlton Fisk hit Game Six homers to keep the Series alive, Lee started Game Seven of the World Series. He pitched 6⅓ innings, shutting out the Reds through five until he gave up a prodigious two-run homer to Tony Perez on an ill-advised blooper pitch that Lee claims today "is still rising." He recalls the sequence of events that led up to the pitch and the resultant homer. "We were leading 3–0 in Game Seven of the World Series. The Reds had a runner at first in the sixth inning. For some reason, Zimmer waves Denny Doyle a few feet away from second base, making a double play impossible. Sure enough, Johnny Bench hits the ball to Burleson at short and Doyle is out of position to make the pivot. The ball goes by Yastrzemski and Bench is safe at second. I lost it and threw the blooper. Two-run homer. Someone should have come out and calmed me down. No one did. The next inning I get a blister and walk the leadoff man and he scores the tying run. The rest is history, but it should never have reached that point." Lee left with a 3–2 lead, but the Red Sox went on to lose the game and the World Series.

1976 was a disaster for Lee and the Red Sox. On May 20, Lee was trailing 1–0 to the Yankees at the Stadium when Lou Piniella and Graig Nettles struck for back-to-back singles. Otto Velez then singled to right, where Dwight Evans fielded the ball and eyed Piniella trying to score. Lou was thrown out by a country mile. A melee ensued in which Lee was blindsided by Nettles and fell awkwardly on his shoulder. He left the game crippled, unable to appear in another game until July 15. The Sox won the May 20 game but at great cost to their playoff hopes. "We won the battle, but lost the war of 1976," says Lee. To this day, Lee is bitter about Nettles'

perceived cheap shot. Recently, when he met the former Yankee at a baseball function, he says that the former All-Star third baseman didn't even bother to get out of his chair. "He hasn't aged at all well," commented Lee. "He looked like a duvet cover."

Lee's season hadn't started well. He was 0–3 with a 7.31 ERA at the time, and never really fully got back on track. He finished 5–7, with a disappointing 5.63 ERA.

The following year, 1977, Bill was used sparingly, only getting 16 starts. He posted another winning record, but it was just 9–5 (4.43 ERA) in 128 innings of work, far from the totals of 1973 through 1975 when he pitched more than twice as many innings each year.

In 1978, things seemed to turn around. Lee won his first four games, and was 10–3 in early July. There were underlying tensions, though, that racked the Red Sox. His relationship with management can only be described as tumultuous. A founding member of a Red Sox faction known as the Buffalo Heads, the sole existence of which seemed to be based on making Sox manager Don Zimmer's life miserable, Lee famously referred to Zimmer as "the gerbil" and openly questioned many of the strategic moves made by the beleaguered manager. "Zimmer wouldn't know a good pitcher if he came up and bit him in the ass," suggested Lee.

Lee enjoyed tweaking the powers that be and crafting controversial quotes. He once bragged about sprinkling marijuana on his organic buckwheat pancakes so that when he jogged to the ballpark he would be "impervious to bus fumes." He explained to the club doctor that a foreign object sighted on an X-ray of his foot was "an old Dewar's cap" that he had accidentally ingested. He angered the California Angels by suggesting that they could conduct their batting practice in the lobby of the fanciest hotel in town "and never chip a chandelier."

Lee was intensely loyal to his teammates and naively expected the same from management. When friends like Bernie Carbo (and later Rodney Scott with the Montreal Expos) were sold or traded, he took it personally and on two famous occasions conducted impromptu walkouts, further alienating himself from the baseball establishment and narrowing his job prospects. Carbo was traded by the Red Sox on June 15, 1978. Lee was so angry that he stomped out of the Sox clubhouse the following day, shouting "Today just cost us the pennant." (The team had a six-game lead at the time, and Carbo had only 47 at-bats.) He angrily announced that he was retiring from baseball. He was in a rough patch at the time, taking two losses while having 16 runs scored against him in the prior

three games (only six of them earned). A day later, Lee returned (sporting a T-shirt that read "Friendship first, competition second"). That surely didn't create a positive impression with Don Zimmer. When fined a day's pay of roughly $500 for the Carbo walkout, he asked if they could make it $1,500. "I'd like to have the whole weekend," he explained. Walking away from a first-place team, even for just a day, was a strong statement.

From July 15 through August 19, though, Lee seemed to fall apart, losing seven straight decisions. On closer inspection, though, one sees that in five of the seven losses, he gave up no more than three earned runs. The July 30 game was the most dispiriting defeat, a 2–1 complete-game loss to the Royals at Fenway Park. Zimmer's refusal to start Lee against the Yankees in September was a huge subplot in the collapse of the Red Sox. Lee appeared in two of the "Boston Massacre" games, but both times it was in relief. In the September 8 game, he threw seven innings in relief, allowing the Yankees just one earned run in a game New York won 13–2. On September 10, his last appearance of the season, Lee closed out the game with 2⅓ innings of scoreless relief; the Yankees won nonetheless, 7–4.

Lee was in the doghouse the rest of the season. One more win at any point along the way and the Red Sox never would have had to play New York in the infamous single-game playoff.

Before the year was out, he was sent packing. Lee was traded by the Red Sox to the Montreal Expos straight up for Stan Papi on December 7. Papi was a journeyman utility infielder with 88 games under his belt and 199 major league at-bats over three seasons. He had accumulated 46 hits (.231) and only one of them was for as many as three bases. It was an indignity that still rankles the proud competitor. When the trade was announced, Lee covered his disappointment with bravado, saying of the 1978 team, "Who wants to be with a team that will go down in history alongside the '64 Phillies and the '67 Arabs?"

Pitching for Montreal, reunited with Dick Williams (ironically the no-nonsense manager under whom he had first played for Boston a decade earlier in 1969), Lee regained his form and won 16 games against 10 losses. He was the ace of the staff, starting 33 games and throwing 222 innings, and posting an ERA with the Expos of 3.04. Montreal finished the season just two games behind the NL East-leading Phillies.

The next three years—the last ones of Bill's 14 years in the majors—were subpar ones. In 1980 and 1981 combined, Lee won 9 and lost 12, both years missing

considerable time mid-season. In 1980, he hurt his hip when he fell out of a building onto an iron fence. (Lee's version of the story is that he was out jogging, happened by a friend's apartment, and decided to surprise her by climbing up her building and tapping on her window.) In 1981, of course, he lost a great deal of playing time to the strike by major league ballplayers. Bill pitched very briefly in both the Division Series and the League Championship Series, getting a total of three outs without surrendering a run.

Lee left the majors for good in 1982 following the May 7, 1982 game, after one of a series of arguments with Montreal management. When friend Rodney Scott was released by the Expos on May 8, Bill Lee took another hike, walking out on the team. He never came back; he was himself released by the Expos on May 9. (Ironically, Scott signed on with the Yankees for a couple of months, but didn't last through August.)

Bill claims that he has been blackballed from major league baseball ever since. The years following Lee's departure from the majors can best be described as nomadic, ranging from independent baseball to senior league games both north and south of the border. At this writing, Lee still plays baseball and shows little sign of slowing down. Since leaving the major leagues, he has

been an effective, if somewhat unorthodox, ambassador for the game in such places as Cuba, China, the former Soviet Union, and small town Canada.

He's co-authored a pair of autobiographical books with Dick Lally, and offered an alternative look at a mythical Red Sox history with Jim Prime in *The Little Red (Sox) Book*.

When Lee left Boston after 10 seasons, he had accumulated 94 wins, third most by a Red Sox southpaw, behind only Mel Parnell and Lefty Grove. He ranks 13th overall in Sox pitching history. That's not bad when you consider the status of the pitchers ahead of him: guys like Cy Young, Roger Clemens, Pedro Martinez, Luis Tiant, and Smoky Joe Wood to name just a few.

Lee's Red Sox 94 wins came against 68 losses, and the three consecutive 17-win seasons came in a ballpark often considered a graveyard for left-handed pitchers. Lee relied on curves, sliders, finesse and guile to be effective—rather than an overpowering fastball. He called the fastball a "bully" pitch and preferred to out-think his opponents. Red Sox teammate Dennis Eckersley once claimed that he threw "steak" while Lee threw "salad." His overall major league win-loss record was 119–90, with a 3.62 ERA.

Lee derived considerable pleasure from the Red Sox victory in the 2004 World Series, and even more residual pleasure from the ALCS comeback over the team he hated most, the New York Yankees, the team he once termed "brownshirts" and "Nazis" and "thugs." Lee watched the games with his wife from a bar in Hawaii. Also present were a collection of Yankee fans that he claims shriveled up with each successive New York loss, "like testicles in a cold Nova Scotia spring." He couldn't resist adding the spurious news that George Steinbrenner planned to move the Yankees to the Philippines where they would play under the new name "The Manila Folders."

Like Yogi Berra and Casey Stengel before him, many of Lee's comments have made their way into the baseball vernacular and ensured his reputation for eccentricity.

Lee and wife Diana live in Craftsbury, Vermont. The Spaceman has two sons (Michael and Andy) and two daughters (Caitlin and Anna) from previous marriages. Aside from his continuing baseball saga, Lee also owns The Old Bat Company, which specializes in maple, ash, and yellow birch bats "from old growth forest."

Actor Woody Harrelson owns the movie rights to the Bill Lee story and it will be interesting to see who is cast in the title role. He'll have to be equal parts showman and athlete.

Roger Moret

by Seamus Kearney

	G	ERA	W	L	SV	GS	GF	CG	SHO	IP	H	R	ER	BB	HR	SO	BFP
1975 RED SOX	36	3.60	14	3	1	16	5	4	1	145	132	60	58	76	8	80	624

Roger Moret (born Rogelio Moret Torres) streaked across the skies of Red Sox Nation during the early 1970s like a comet with a stutter step: often brilliant but sometimes wild. Possessing obvious talent, he had some difficulty in harnessing it. Once established with the Boston Red Sox in 1973, he alternated two excellent seasons with a mediocre one. Still, he was able to compile an admirable cumulative ERA (3.43) and a 41–18 record with the Red Sox, ranking him among the best pitchers of the decade for the Bostons. Twice he led the American League in winning percentage. Then he went away from us, traded first by the Red Sox then, slowly and tragically, leaving baseball and sliding into the dark morass of mental illness.

Born in Guayama, Puerto Rico, on September 16, 1949, Moret's mound presence was that of a tall, slender, even spindly, left hander with a whip-like motion and a speedy fastball, mixed in with a decent curve and a good change-up.[34] He threw hard. Listed as 6'4" and 175 lbs, he says he was taller.[35]

Signed by the Red Sox out of high school as an amateur free agent in 1968 for a reported $8,000 bonus,[36] he spent his first season in the Class A minors with Winter Haven (Florida State League) in 1968 with a 6–6 record, improving in 1969 with Waterloo (Midwest League) to 12–6 in 25 games. His next three seasons alternated with the Red Sox and two levels of the minors, Pawtucket (Double A Eastern League) and Louisville (Triple A International League).[37] His 49–33 record in the minors revealed characteristics he would demonstrate in the majors: fewer hits allowed than innings pitched (7.94 per nine innings), more walks than usual (5.49 per nine innings), and a decent winning percentage (.598).

In the major leagues he logged a .635 career winning percentage in nine seasons derived from a 47–27 won/lost record with the Sox, Atlanta Braves, and Texas Rangers. In his three full years with the Red Sox (from 1973 to 1975), he fashioned a 36–15 record. Moret's Fenway Park record of 18–7 was one of the very best records ever for a Red Sox left hander.[38]

His first appearance with the Sox occurred as a September call-up in 1970, debuting in the major leagues on September 13 and pitching a perfect eighth inning in a 13–2 loss at Baltimore. In three games he posted a 1–0 record and an ERA of 3.24 in 8.1 innings. His first major league win occurred on his 21st birthday, against the Yankees on September 16, pitching four innings of shutout ball in relief of Sonny Siebert.[39]

His first prolonged stint with the Red Sox came in 1971 when he compiled a 4–3 record with a 2.92 ERA.[40] He had two stretches with the Sox that year, sandwiching a productive season with Pawtucket (11–8, 3.15 ERA). Strangely, the first seven games he appeared in were losses for the Sox, including two losses for himself. He garnered his first 1971 win, a complete game, on August 21 against the Angels in Anaheim. He finished the year with a run of 4–1 including a shutout and four complete game victories.

1972 proved to be a forgettable year for Roger who spent most of the season with Louisville. He made the parent club after spring training but left for Louisville when he pitched ineffectually in three games with the Sox, all losses. He didn't pitch for the Sox the rest of the year and had a middling (9–6 with a 4.54 ERA) stint with Louisville.[41]

The 1973 season is when Roger's stardom seemed assured. Starting the season in the bullpen, he earned a win against the Indians on April 22. That was the first of 11 straight wins reeled off while also recording three saves before finally losing to the Indians on September 16th. He had good success against the Yanks this year on the way to an American League-leading win percentage of .867 during a 13–2 season. He beat the Yanks three times, including a Fourth of July 1–0 shutout at the tail end of a Red Sox double header sweep of the New Yorkers at Yankee Stadium.[42]

Roger could not follow the success he had had in 1973, finishing 1974 with a 9–10 record and a 3.74 ERA. In the regular starting rotation during July and August, Moret amassed a 3–2 record with a 2.01 ERA that included an 11-inning complete game win against the Yankees on July 29. The highlight of his '74 season was a near no-hitter win with 12 strikeouts against the White Sox on August 21. Dick Allen hit a controversial infield single in the seventh inning for the only hit of the game. The win increased his record at the time to 7–5. Sox owner Tom Yawkey was so taken with Moret's performance that he gave him a new and improved

contract.[43] Unfortunately, after the near no-no, Roger finished the season on a 2–5 run.

Moret started 1975 in the bullpen picking up five wins and a save in relief and as a sometime starter before emerging as the fifth man in the rotation in late July. In fact, teammate Bill Lee thinks that the Red Sox really contended for the pennant when Moret entered the rotation. As a fifth starter, Moret's performance gave the other starting pitchers extra rest and the Sox "started winning left and right" according to Lee.[44]

Moret had two stints in the regular, five-man rotation, in which he pitched admirably—and often brilliantly. In a stretch of four starts, July 20—July 31, he collected three wins with one loss. One of his wins was again against the Yankees and contributed to their demise as a pennant contender. He pitched the second game of a doubleheader shutout sweep against them in their temporary home at Shea Stadium on July 27. The sweep effectively established the Sox as the team to beat in the American League East.[45]

In another period from August 11—September 15, Moret amassed six wins with two losses. In his September 6 victory over the Milwaukee Brewers, he benefited from 20 runs scored on 24 hits by the Red Sox, both American League season highs for the year. His 14–3 record at the end of the season earned him his second American League-leading pitching win percentage with a mark of .824.

The low point of Moret's 1975 season proved to be his strange trip back from New York City on the early morning of a scheduled start against the Orioles. He crashed his car into the back of a stalled truck on the highway. Somehow he avoided serious injury but did suffer cuts on his head that required a visit to a hospital.[46] X-rays proved negative but the Sox would not allow him to pitch. In fact, the team was not pleased with either the incident or the publicity and called him to task on his behavior. The incident probably contributed to doubt in the Sox front office about whether he could be a Red Sox pitcher of the future.

Though added to the 1975 Sox playoff roster, Moret saw little game duty during the playoffs, but the little he saw loomed important in the outcomes. He became the winning pitcher in the second game against the Oakland A's when he pitched one inning of scoreless relief in his only appearance during the Red Sox' three game series sweep. He came into the game in the sixth inning with the score tied, a man on first and no outs. He retired two batters, gave up a double and then induced the final out on a grounder to short. The Sox went ahead in the bottom half, making Moret the pitcher of record.

In the World Series against the Cincinnati Reds, he saw a little more action, and again at crucial times. He pitched five outs in 1⅔ innings of work, facing 10 batters, giving up two hits while relinquishing three bases on balls with only one strikeout. Unfortunately, for him and the Sox, in the Game Three of the World Series he gave up a hit to Joe Morgan in the 10th inning that scored the winning run, awarding a 2–1 edge in the Series to the Reds.

In Game Six, after starter Tiant surrendered a leadoff eighth-inning homer to Cesar Geronimo, Moret was brought in from the bullpen and set down the Reds 1-2-3. Cincinnati had a 6–3 lead. With Moret due up in the bottom of the eighth and two Red Sox on base, Bernie Carbo was sent up to pinch-hit. He hit a game-tying homer into the center-field bleachers.

In the decisive Game Seven of the Series, Moret relieved Bill Lee in the seventh inning with one out and a man on first. He faced four batters, getting one, walking one and giving up a run-scoring single to Pete Rose that tied the game. After Moret walked Joe Morgan, Sox manager Darrell Johnson called on Jim Willoughby to retire Johnny Bench. The Reds scored a run a couple of innings later, winning the game and the Series in the ninth.

His season and the Series over, Roger Moret would not appear in a Red Sox uniform again.

Years later in an interview with author Doug Hornig, Moret lamented that he didn't do well in the '75 World Series. However, he said he was upset that he was passed over for a starting pitching assignment in Game Three of the 1975 World Series. Moret still considered it his game to start, saying "I was ready. I could've beaten that team."[47]

During the offseason, on December 12, the Red Sox traded Moret to the Atlanta Braves for Tom House. Moret's record for the Sox far surpassed that of House and from all measurable appearances it seemed like, and probably was, an uneven trade for the Sox. The single reason why they let him go so cheaply most likely stemmed from the aftermath of his early morning car ride back from New York City.

His one season with the Braves in 1976 began his slow slide from the major leagues. He pitched just 77⅓ innings and his ERA ballooned to 5.00. Appearing in 27 games, only 12 of them starts, he posted a 3–5 record. It was the first season in the majors in which he gave up more hits than innings pitched.

In another December transaction, the Texas Rangers acquired Moret from the Braves on December 9 in a multi-player trade that brought Moret and four

others to the Texas team in exchange for power-hitting Jeff Burroughs and $250,000. Moret appeared to be a throw-in so the Braves could beef up their attack.

1977 proved to be a telling season for the slender left hander. With the Rangers he logged a 3–3 record with another decent ERA of 3.73 (league average 4.11) in 18 games, only eight of them starts. Unfortunately, surgery to repair a circulation problem in his pitching arm limited his season's contribution to the Rangers.[48]

Moret's 1978 season was a disaster. His contribution to the Rangers' season proved minimal, though he earned his first save that year with another successful outing against the Yankees: four innings of relief in a 5–2 victory over New York, giving up four hits and one earned run. But, for the year, he appeared in seven games, pitching only 14⅔ innings—and surrendering 23 hits, for an 0–1 record.

However, the real story for Moret in 1978 was his hospitalization at a psychiatric facility after his bizarre behavior on April 12 at Arlington Stadium. After some odd pre-game behavior, Roger Moret went into what was described as a catatonic state in front of his locker that reportedly lasted 90 minutes.[49] His teammates first kidded with him but as time went on the gravity of his

condition brought the team's medical staff. Attempts to awaken him failed. The Rangers staff sedated him and dispatched him to the Arlington Neuropsychiatric Center. By April 25, Roger's condition had improved and he was scheduled for release within a week.

His condition got better and he returned to the Rangers for several appearances in late May and the first half of June. His last appearance in the majors was a futile start against the Blue Jays at Arlington Stadium on June 16, 1978. He lasted a mere 1⅔ innings, giving up six hits and four earned runs. Regrettably, he lost his last game in the bigs.[50]

Roger made a couple of other comeback attempts. He was invited to spring training in 1979 with the Rangers and in 1980 with Cleveland but never again pitched in the majors.[51] In 1981 and 1982, Moret played in the Mexican League. In 1981, he pitched for Torreon, posting a 9–4 (2.42 ERA) record. In 1982, he split the season between Aquascalientes and Monclova with a combined 4–13, 4.40 ERA record.

Moret pitched for many years with the Santurce team in Puerto Rico until he was eligible for his major league pension. He now lives in Guayama, Puerto Rico near two family members.[52]

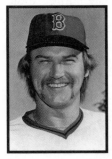

Dick Pole

by Bill Nowlin

	G	ERA	W	L	SV	GS	GF	CG	SHO	IP	H	R	ER	BB	HR	SO	BFP
1975 RED SOX	18	4.42	4	6	0	11	4	2	1	89.2	102	46	44	32	11	42	394

Richard Henry Pole was a 6'3", 200-lb. right-handed pitcher who first broke in with the Red Sox in 1973. Born October 13, 1950, in Trout Creek in Michigan's Upper Peninsula, he was one of the few Yoopers who worked a major league mound. Richard Henry Pole was signed as a free agent by the Boston Red Sox in 1969. He worked his way up through the minors fairly steadily, and when Ray Culp (2–6 at the time) experienced prolonged numbness in his hand, he was put on the disabled list and Pole was summoned to take his place. Pole debuted wearing number 45 for the Boston Red Sox.

After signing with the Sox, Pole was sent to Greenville in the Western Carolina League, posting a 13–10 record with a 3.18 ERA, leading the league in shutouts with three, and games started with 25. At season's end, he appeared in two games for Winter Haven in the Florida State League, losing both of them

despite giving up just two earned runs. He started with Winter Haven in 1970, moving on near the end of the year to Winston-Salem. In 1971, he spent the year with Pawtucket, then a Double A affiliate (8–7, 2.76 ERA). The following year, he made Triple A with Louisville. When the Sox established their Triple A team in Pawtucket, Pole returned for the 1973 season, going 12–9 and throwing a seven-inning 2–0 no-hitter against Peninsula on June 23. He led the International League with a 2.03 ERA and earned himself the call up to the big league club.

His first major league appearance was as starting pitcher the night of August 3 in a game against the Orioles at Memorial Stadium. It wasn't the best debut, as debuts go. He lasted only 3⅔ innings, giving up six earned runs on 10 hits, and taking the loss. He'd gotten his feet wet, though. His second start wasn't much better—3⅓ innings with four earned runs, but this game was decided in extra innings. Starting at home

on August 12, Pole got his first win in a major league uniform as Boston beat the Angels, 14–8. Pole had a strong start with just three runs in 5⅔ innings. He started some and relieved some, playing out the rest of the season with the Red Sox and compiling a 3–2 record, with an earned run average of 5.60. Before being called up, he had pitched well enough for Pawtucket to be named 1973 Most Valuable Pitcher in the International League.

The following year, 1974, Pole was called up from Pawtucket in late June. He filled in for a few weeks (June 22 through July 13), then went back to the minors until called up again at the start of September. His most impressive stint came on September 8 when Juan Marichal could get only one out in the first inning, tagged for four earned runs. Pole pitched for seven full innings, allowing just two more runs and keeping the Red Sox in the game against the Brewers. The Red Sox came from behind and won the game, 8–6, and Dick got the win. The win edged Boston into a tie for first place with the Yankees. In all, he put in 45 innings of work, mostly in relief, with a 1–1 record, and an improved 4.20 ERA.

Pole saw work in bunches in 1975, up at the start of the season, but out for virtually the month of May. He got in seven games in June, and the last was a June 30 game, a night game at Fenway Park against the Orioles, the first game of a twi-night doubleheader. He was pitching a brilliant game, shutting out the O's through eight innings on four hits. Going for the complete game shutout, Pole opened the ninth inning with a strikeout of Don Baylor. Then the Birds started hitting. Pinch-hitter Jim Northrup singled, and so did Brooks Robinson and Ken Singleton. That loaded the bases. There were still no runs scored. Next up was Tony Muser and he changed Dick Pole's life forever, driving a ball hard and right up the middle—a line drive right off Pole's face. It hit so hard that it ricocheted off his face and soared over Rico Petrocelli at third base. Muser was credited with a double, and two runs scored. But Dick Pole lay crumpled on the ground. His cheekbone was broken and his retina damaged as well. The final score was 5–2. Pole earned the win.

After missing two full months, he was reactivated on September 1 and got in four more starts in September, throwing three scoreless innings against the Yankees on September 1, winning a 3–1 game against the Orioles on September 4, and a game in relief on the 19th. Pole surrendered 11 home runs in just 89⅔ innings of play.

Pole's only post-season play came in Game Five of the 1975 World Series. Both the Reds and the Red Sox had two wins. After seven innings at Cincinnati's Riverfront Stadium, the Reds held a 5–1 lead, all charged to Sox starter Reggie Cleveland. Jim Willoughby threw two scoreless innings and Sox manager Darrell Johnson asked Pole to pitch the eighth. He faced two batters—Johnny Bench and Tony Perez—and walked them both. Johnson came out with the hook and brought in Diego Segui. On back-to-back sacrifice flies, Bench took third and then scored. Pole's postseason ERA is thus infinity, charged with one earned run in zero innings pitched. It could have been worse: Perez had already homered twice earlier in the game.

In 1976, Pole got more regular work, appearing in 31 games, starting 15 of them. He threw one complete game, on June 17 in Oakland. It was his first start after being bombed for six runs in the first inning six days earlier in Minnesota. He got an 8–3 win, up against A's starter Mike Torrez at the Oakland-Alameda County Coliseum. He also got his one and only major league at-bat. After seven full innings, the Red Sox had an 8–2 lead. First baseman Carl Yastrzemski was taken out of the game to give him a little rest, and Cecil Cooper took over at first base. Cooper had been the DH. With the move, the Sox lost the DH and Pole was put in Yaz's spot in the lineup. His one time in the batting order and he was batting cleanup in place of Carl Yastrzemski! Come the top of the ninth, and Dick led off. He put wood on the ball, grounding back to pitcher Stan Bahnsen, who threw him out at first. 0-for-1 lifetime.

As a fielder himself, Pole made only four errors— one each in the years 1974, 1975, 1976, and 1977. That he accumulated only 95 chances in his six seasons, though, left him with a modest .958 fielding average.

He gave of his better performances on May 22, 1976, facing the Yankees in New York. Pole started the game and pitched 8⅓ shutout innings, holding the Yankees to just four hits. He was tiring. Tom House came on in relief, and lost, 1–0, in the bottom of the 11th. His year-end ERA was a respectable enough 4.33.

After the 1976 season, it was expansion time with both the Toronto Blue Jays and Seattle Mariners entering the American League. Though he'd skippered the Red Sox to a pennant and into the seven-game World Series in 1975, manager Darrell Johnson hadn't lasted much more than half the '76 season. On July 19, Johnson was fired and replaced by Don Zimmer. But Johnson was retained as the first manager of the Mariners and when it came time for Seattle to pick in the November 5 expansion draft, Pole was one of the players not protected by the Red Sox. He was selected by Seattle as the seventh pick of the draft.

Pole began the 1977 season on the disabled list. His first appearance came in Boston on May 4, when he was brought in to relieve Stan Thomas, with Boston holding a 4–1 lead. Pole walked the first batter he faced, former batterymate Carlton Fisk. Dwight Evans bunted Fisk to second, and Fisk advanced to third on a wild pitch. Bernie Carbo walked and then Butch Hobson singled Fisk home. Pole got the next two batters, though, and the game was soon over, Seattle scoring just once in the top of the ninth.

Pole was a regular in the Mariners' rotation, starting 24 games. He ended the season with a 7–12 mark (the team was 64–98, but the Mariners were spared from being in the cellar since Oakland was 63–98). Pole's ERA was 5.15, but better than the 6.48 ERA (with a 4–11 record) he posted in his final year with Seattle (and in major league ball) in 1978. After the July 18, 1978, game, Pole never pitched in the majors again. He finished out the season with Seattle's Triple A affiliate, the San Jose Missions, but was 0–4 in the Pacific Coast League. He tried to make it back to the majors the following spring but was released by the Mariners on March 24, 1979.

In 1979, he played for Santo Domingo and Pittsburgh's Triple A club in Portland, Oregon. The next year, he played for Portland, and then Montgomery, the Tigers' Double A entry in the Southern League. The Montgomery team moved to Birmingham for 1981 and Pole played there at the start of the year, but spent most of the season with the Mexico City Tigers, posting a 5–2 mark. In 1982, Pole pitched for both Mexico City and the Nuevo Laredo teams in the Mexican League, but finally called it quits as a player, making a move to get into coaching. He spent five years in the Cubs system, working at Quad City, Pittsfield, and Iowa. Pole's first job as a major league coach came courtesy of Dusty Baker. The two had gotten to know each other while working in the Arizona Fall League, and when Baker was hired to manage the Chicago Cubs for the 1988 season, he asked Pole to be his pitching coach. Pole was hired in November 1987. Baker was quoted as saying, "I'd always wanted a left-handed pitching coach. The

more I was around him, the more I saw he thought like a left hander, though he's a righty. Left-handers usually throw less heat, there, they have to know how to pitch more, which is what it's all about. . . ." Right.

Pole was indeed thinking more. He said the years in Mexico had helped him in this regard, when he had begun to follow up on something Luis Tiant had told him in Boston. In 1999, he told the *Los Angeles Times*, "Luis Tiant always said I should throw changeups, but I was young and hard-headed and relied too much on my fastball. It didn't help then, but it helped me in my coaching life." Pole's more patient philosophy helped turn around the career of one of the Cubs' young pitchers, Greg Maddux. Just starting his second full year of play, Maddux came to training camp with a career 8–18 record and an ERA of over 5.50. With Pole as his pitching coach in 1988, Maddux posted a 3.18 ERA and won 18 games (18–8) and he credits Pole who, he says, "taught me how to throw pitches." In July 2005, after recording his 3,000th career strikeout, Maddux told Rick Gano of the Associated Press: "I remember when Dick Pole told me one day, 'Why don't you stop trying to strike guys out? Just try to get them out, and you'll probably strike out as many guys, if not more. He was right. I've always tried with two strikes just to make a pitch and get the guy out. You get a lot of strikeouts just on accident."

Pole served as pitching coach for the Cubs for four years, from 1988 to 1991, and when Dusty Baker was hired by the San Francisco Giants for the 1993 season, Pole followed Baker there as well, serving five more seasons as pitching coach (from 1993 to 1997). In 1998, he put on a Red Sox uniform for another year, serving as bullpen coach in Boston. He served as pitching coach for the Angels in 1999. When Indians pitching coach Phil Regan resigned after the Indians were pummeled for 44 runs in the final three games of the 1999 ALDS, Pole was hired by Cleveland for the 2000 season and served in that capacity for the 2000 and 2001 seasons. In 2002, Pole was pitching coach for the Montreal Expos. He's currently back with the Cubs, serving as bench coach since being hired in November 2002.

Luis Tiant

by Mark Armour

	G	ERA	W	L	SV	GS	GF	CG	SHO	IP	H	R	ER	BB	HR	SO	BFP
1975 RED SOX	35	4.02	18	14	0	35	0	18	2	260	262	126	116	72	25	142	1080

Luis Clemente Tiant y Vega was a colorful and charismatic right-handed pitcher who Hall of Famer Reggie Jackson once called "the Fred Astaire of baseball," won 229 games over parts of 19 seasons in the major leagues. His mid-career comeback, dramatic family reunion, and World Series heroics inspired a region, leaving him likely the most beloved man ever to play for the Boston Red Sox.

Tiant was born in Marianao, Cuba, the son of Luis and Isabel. His father, Luis Eleuterio Tiant, was a legendary left-handed pitcher, starring in the Cuban Leagues and the American Negro Leagues for 20 years. He was famous for a variety of outstanding pitches (including a spitball and a knuckleball), a tremendous pickoff move, and an exaggerated pirouette pitching motion. As late as 1947, at the age of 41, Luis put together a 10-0 record for the New York Cubans and pitched in the East-West All-Star Game. Monte Irvin claimed that the elder Tiant would have been a "great, great star" had he been able to play in the major leagues.

The younger Tiant was an only child, and grew up in a baseball-mad country. Luis was a star on various local youth teams, and as a 16-year-old played on an all-star club that traveled to Mexico City for an international tournament. His father did not encourage his making a career of the game, believing there was little chance of a black man being successful in baseball, but his mother was more supportive and carried the day.

After failing a tryout with the Havana team of the International League, Luis started his professional career in 1959, at age 18, for the Mexico City Tigers. His first year was quite poor (5-19, 5.92 ERA), but he followed this up with 17 wins in 1960 and 12 more the next year, after having been delayed for two months trying to leave his homeland. At the end of the 1961 season, the Cleveland Indians purchased his contract for $35,000.

During these three seasons, Luis spent his summers living in Mexico City, returning to Havana for the off-season to play winter ball and be with his family. In 1961, he met Maria, a native of Mexico City, at a ballpark—she was playing for her office softball team. After a short courtship Luis and Maria married in August 1961. At the close of the season they were planning to return to Luis' home in Marianao. Unfortunately, the political embarrassment and potential economic hardship of massive Cuban emigration led Fidel Castro's government to ban all outside travel. Upon the advice of his father, Luis did not return home to Cuba in 1961, not knowing when or if he would see his parents again.

Luis, being property of the Cleveland Indians in 1962, pitched for Charleston in the Eastern League and had a respectable year (7-8, 3.63) while adjusting to life in an English-speaking country. In 1963, for Burlington, he was likely the best pitcher in the Carolina League, finishing 14-9, including a no-hitter, with a 2.56 ERA, leading the league in complete games, strikeouts and shutouts. He was 23 years old, and presumably one of the prizes of the Cleveland farm system.

The following winter, Luis was not on the Indians' 40-man roster, but no team risked the $12,000 it would have taken to claim him. Despite a good spring in 1964, the Indians first sent him back to Burlington, but an injury to a pitcher on their Triple A (Pacific Coast League) Portland team brought Tiant to Oregon for the 1964 season. The Portland Beavers staff also included Sam McDowell, one of the more renowned young phenoms in baseball. McDowell was 20 years old, but had spent parts of the last three seasons with the Indians, and was clearly the star of the Portland team at the start of the season. Tiant was not in the rotation.

Luis picked up a relief win in Portland's first game, and another a week later. His first start was on May 3 in the Beavers' 15th game. McDowell, meanwhile, started hot and got hotter, pitching a one-hitter and no-hitter in consecutive starts in early May, before finally getting recalled on May 30 when his record had reached 8-0 with a 1.18 ERA, with 102 strikeouts in 76 innings.

Tiant quietly built up his own resume; at the time of McDowell's promotion, Luis was 7-0 with a 2.25 ERA. Saddled with lower expectations by the organization, Tiant was slower to get the attention of the Indians' brass. After finally losing 2-0 on June 5, Tiant won four more games to finish June with a 12-1 record. The Indians finally recalled him on July 17. Tiant finished 15-1 (a PCL record .938 winning percentage) with a 2.04 ERA, completing 13 of his 15 starts.

Tiant joined the Indians in New York on Saturday morning, July 18, and was asked by his manager, Birdie

RED SOX FANS ARE FAMILIAR WITH LUIS' GYRATIONS ON THE MOUND AND THE FACT HE HAS BEEN A 20-GAME WINNER TWO YEARS IN A ROW

LUIS ISN'T EXACTLY FOND OF AIRPLANES AND HIS SHRILL SCREAMS PIERCE THE SKY WITH EVERY BUMP

KAMIKAZE PILOT?

HEH HA!

HA... HA...

WHY YOU LAUGHIN' I HAVEN'T EVEN TOLD TH' JOKE YET!

LUIS TIANT!

THE FUN-LOVING CIGAR-SMOKING CUBAN HOPES TO HAVE ANOTHER 20 WIN SEASON AND IS ALSO HOPING TO VISIT HIS DAD IN CUBA NEXT WINTER WHOM HE HASN'T SEEN FOR MANY YEARS... RED SOX FOLLOWERS WILL BE ROOTING FOR HIM TO FULFILL HIS AMBITIONS

HE'S QUITE A GUY!

LUIS HAS THE INATE FACULTY OF KEEPING HIS TEAMMATES LOOSE BOTH IN THE DUGOUT AND CLUBHOUSE... BUT ON THE FIELD HE'S ALL BUSINESS

EDDIE GERMANO

Tebbetts, if he was ready to pitch. When advised that he was, Tebbetts told him he was pitching the next day against Whitey Ford. Tiant responded with a four-hit shutout, striking out 11. Luis finished 10–4 for the Tribe with a 2.83 ERA. His total line for 1964: a 25–5 record and 2.42 ERA in 264 innings.

Luis was afflicted with a sore pitching arm in 1965, finishing 11–11, and showed up the next spring having lost 20 pounds on the advice of his father. He started the 1966 season with three consecutive shutouts, a streak that ended in Baltimore when Frank Robinson hit a ball completely out of Memorial Stadium, the only time that was ever done. Luis hit a rough spell in May and June and spent the last half of the season in the bullpen, notching eight saves in 30 relief appearances. Despite only 16 starts, his five shutouts topped the American League. His ERA in 1966 and 1967 was more than adequate—2.79 and 2.74, respectively—but not enough to win more than 12 games each year.

In 1968, Tiant became a star, finishing 21–9 and posting a league-leading 1.60 ERA. Luis also led the league with nine shutouts, including four in succession (one short of the Doc White's 1904 record). He pitched his best game on July 3 in Cleveland when he recorded 19 strikeouts in 10 innings against the Twins. In the top of the tenth, the Twins got runners on second and

third with no one out and Luis struck out the side. The Indians finally pushed across a run in the bottom on the tenth to give Luis a 1–0 victory.

The following week, Luis started and lost the All-Star Game, giving the NL an unearned run in the first inning that turned out to be the only run of the game. After a 3–0 loss to Denny McLain in early September, McLain suggested: "Luis and I would each be fighting for 30 wins if he had our kind of hitting to go with his kind of pitching." (Catcher Bill Freehan took it a step further, insisting that Luis would be "going for 40 wins.") In the end, McLain finished 31–6 with a 1.96 ERA, and won the Cy Young and MVP Awards unanimously. Tiant ended his season with a one-hit, 11-strikeout masterpiece against the Yankees in New York.

The Indians finished 1969 with the worst record in the AL, and their worst winning percentage in 54 years. Luis fell to 9–20, and posted an ERA of 3.71. It was not really as bad as it seemed—changes to the strike zone and mound sent the league ERA up to 3.61. Nonetheless, Luis was an average American League pitcher, which was quite a step down from 1968.

In December of 1969, Tiant was traded to the Minnesota Twins in a six-player deal that brought Dean Chance and Graig Nettles to the Indians. In 1970 he won his first six decisions for a very strong Minnesota team, but left his sixth victory with a sore shoulder that had been bothering him since the spring. Luis went to see a specialist, who found a crack in a bone in his right shoulder and prescribed only rest. He sat down for just 10 weeks, and returned to lose three of four decisions in the final weeks of the 1970 season.

By spring training of 1971, Tiant claimed to be fully recovered, but soon pulled a muscle in his rib cage, missed two weeks, and was otherwise ineffective in only eight innings. On March 31 the Twins gave him his unconditional release. Calvin Griffith believed that Tiant was finished at age 30. Suitably devastated, Luis believed the move was intended only to save money.

The sole team willing to give him a shot was the Atlanta Braves, who signed him to a 30-day trial with their Triple A Richmond team. After limited work, the Braves were unwilling to promote him at the end of the trial period, so he signed with Louisville, the Red Sox Triple A affiliate. He pitched very well in 31 innings for Louisville—29 strikeouts and a 2.61 ERA—and was summoned to Boston on June 3.

He was not an immediate success. After his first appearance on June 11 resulted in five runs in only one inning, Cliff Keane wrote in the *Boston Globe*: "The latest investment by the Red Sox looked about as sound

as taking a bagful of money and throwing it off Pier 4 into the Atlantic." Tiant remained in the rotation, but he dropped his first six decisions. After one loss, Keane led a game story with, "Enough is enough."

Nonetheless, manager Eddie Kasko believed that Tiant could become a quality pitcher again. He shut out the Yankees for seven innings before losing 2–1 on a two-run home run to Roy White. He threw ten shutout innings, and 154 pitches, in his return to Minnesota, but did not figure in the decision. Kasko finally took him out of the rotation in early August. He was better in the bullpen—finishing 1–1 with a 1.80 ERA. After his four-month audition, many in the media were surprised he was still on the 40-man roster in the spring.

On March 22, 1972, the Red Sox traded Sparky Lyle to the Yankees for Danny Cater and Mario Guerrero, a trade that ranks among the worst that the Red Sox ever made, but which likely saved Luis' spot on the team. Kasko elected to keep him for the team's bullpen. By the end of July, Kasko's faith seemed to have been justified, as Luis was effective in a variety of roles—the occasional spot start, a ninth-inning save or a long relief stint. The team had floundered for the first half of the season, but a July hot streak had pulled them to within five games of first place at the start of August.

On August 5 at Fenway Park, Tiant started for just the seventh time and beat the Orioles. One week later in Baltimore, he beat the O's again, pitching six no-hit innings before settling for a three-hitter. After picking up a save in a relief appearance, he pitched a two-hitter in Chicago's Comiskey Park, losing a no-hitter with two outs in the eighth. After this game, on August 19, Kasko finally announced that Luis was in the rotation to stay.

Surprisingly, the Red Sox had climbed into a fierce four-team pennant race with the Yankees, Orioles and Tigers. Even more surprisingly, Luis Tiant had become their best player. Over a period of 10 starts, beginning with the game in Chicago, Luis racked up a record of 9–1 with six shutouts and a 0.96 ERA, all nine victories being complete games. He began with four straight shutouts, his streak of 40 scoreless innings ending during a four-hit victory over the Yankees at Fenway on September 8. After a loss in Yankee Stadium, Luis blanked the Indians back home on the 16th.

Before the second game of a twi-night doubleheader against the Orioles on September 20, the fans rose to their feet as Luis walked to the bullpen to warm up and gave him such an ovation that his teammates joined in. The crowd spent most of the evening chanting "Loo-Eee, Loo-Eee, Loo-Eee," as their hero recorded out after out. When he came up to bat in the bottom on the

eighth on his way to another shutout, the crowd again rose to give him an ovation that continued throughout his at-bat, during the break between innings, and throughout the entire top of the ninth. Larry Claflin, in the *Boston Herald* the next morning, wrote that he had never heard a sound like it at a game, unless it was "the last time Joe DiMaggio went to bat in Boston." Carl Yastrzemski, who had one of baseball's most famous Septembers only five years earlier, said "I've never heard anything like that in my life. But I'll tell you one thing: Tiant deserved every bit of it."

After clutch victories over both the Tigers and Orioles, Tiant lost his final start on October 3 in Tiger Stadium, a game that clinched the pennant for Detroit on the next to the last day of the season. Though he was essentially a relief pitcher for the first four months of the season, Luis finished 15–6 and won his second ERA title (1.91) and the Comeback Player of the Year award. By leading the Red Sox to an unexpected race for the pennant, Tiant won the hearts of the Red Sox fans. He would never lose them.

He capped his comeback by winning 20 for the second time in 1973, while the Red Sox again finished second. The next year Luis won his 20th by August 23 to give his team a seemingly safe seven-game lead. Unfortunately, the Red Sox went into a horrific team-wide batting slump that was responsible for a disastrous fade—they were 8–20 during one stretch—and finished in third place, eight games behind Baltimore. Considered an MVP candidate in August, Tiant won only two of his final seven decisions, although he continued to pitch well. In the four starts after his 20th victory, he lost 3–0, 1–0, and 2–0, and then had no decision in a game in which he gave up one run in nine innings. He finished 22–13 on the season with a league-leading seven shutouts.

Tiant was revered by his teammates in Boston, much as he had been in Cleveland and Minnesota. In 1968, Thomas Fitzpatrick written an article about Tiant in *Sport* entitled "The Most Popular Indian." When the Twins released Tiant, their longtime publicist Tom Mee called the scene in the locker room as Luis said goodbye to his teammates, "the most forlorn experience I've ever had in baseball."

The Red Sox had recently been a fractured team, but Luis kept his teammates laughing, largely by making fun of them and himself. He called Yastrzemski "Polacko," and Fisk "Frankenstein." After the 1972 season, Red Sox pitcher John Curtis wrote a newspaper story about trying to explain to his wife why he loved Luis Tiant. Dwight Evans would later say, "Unless

you've played with him, you can't understand what Luis means to a team."

Tiant's physical appearance was part of his charm. Red Smith once wrote that he looked like "Pancho Villa after a tough night of looting and burning." Boston writer Tim Horgan later suggested that Tiant's "visage belongs on Mt. Rushmore." A barrel-chested man who looked fatter than he really was, Tiant would often emerge from the shower with a cigar in his mouth, look at his naked body in the mirror and declare himself to be (in his exaggerated Spanish accent): "[a] good-lookeen sonofabeech."

Luis struggled for most of the 1975 season. While the Red Sox took over the division lead for good in late June, Luis was seen more and more as an aging (he was now 34) back-of-the-rotation starter. Luis may have had a reason for his struggles; his heart and mind were occupied with a long-overdue family reunion.

Though Luis' mother had traveled to Mexico City to visit Luis and his family in 1968 (his father was reportedly jailed to ensure her return), Luis had not seen his father in 14 years. A renowned jokester, his mood darkened when he thought of his homeland and his parents. In early 1975, he expressed himself to *Boston Herald* reporter Joe Fitzgerald: "How much longer? My father's seventy now and he's not well. Yet he still works in a garage down there, and here I am living like this, and I can't send him a dime for a cup of coffee. I listen to people in this country complain that they don't like this, they don't like that. I've got friends up here [fellow Cuban expatriates] whose parents have died and they couldn't go home to bury them. What can ever hurt like that? Now all the time, I think about my father dying and . . ." Luis spoke of his parents often, and had been led to believe many times over the years that a reunion could be arranged. When asked about his namesake, Luis would say, "I am nowhere near the pitcher my father was."

In May 1975, US Senator George McGovern (D-South Dakota) made an unofficial visit to Cuba to see Fidel Castro. While it was not the reason for his trip, he carried with him a letter from his Senate colleague, Edward Brooke III (R-Massachusetts), making a personal plea that Luis' parents be allowed to visit Luis in Boston. The letter suggested that "Luis' career as a major league pitcher is in its latter years" and "he is hopeful that his parents will be able to visit him during this current baseball season." The very next day, Castro approved the request and put the diplomatic wheels in motion for a visit.

After several delays and postponements, Isabel and the elder Luis touched down in Boston's Logan Airport on August 21. Their son, with his wife Maria, his three children, and dozens of reporters and cameramen, greeted them. As witnessed in homes all over New England, Luis embraced his father and shamelessly wept. Isabel told her son, "I'm so happy I don't care if I die now."

On August 26, the Red Sox arranged for Luis's parents to be introduced to the crowd and for his father to throw out a ceremonial first pitch. After a prolonged ovation, the 69-year-old Tiant, standing on the Fenway Park mound adorned in a brown suit and Red Sox cap, took off his coat and handed it to his son. He went into his full windup and fired a fastball to catcher Tim Blackwell—alas, low and away. Looking vaguely annoyed, he asked for the ball back. Once more he used his full windup, and floated a knuckleball across the heart of the plate. The fans roared as he left the field. His son later commented, "He told me he was ready to go four or five."

The younger Tiant was hit hard that night and again five days later. Whispers in the press box included the lament that it was a shame that his parents had not gotten here a year earlier, when Luis was still effective. Then, Luis took ten days off to rest his aching back.

On September 11, manager Darrell Johnson decided to give Luis one last chance to get it going, against the Tigers. The Red Sox lead, once as high as 8½ games, was now five. Luis responded with 7⅔ innings of no-hit ball before allowing a run and three hits. When asked about the bloop hit by Aurelio Rodriguez that ruined the no-hitter, Luis' father responded, "Don't talk about a lucky hit. The man hit the ball pretty good."

Luis' next start, on September 16, was the biggest game of the year and one of the legendary games in the history of Fenway Park. The hard charging Orioles, now 4½ games out, were in town and Jim Palmer faced Tiant. Many observers claim that there were well over 40,000 people in the park that night, several thousand over its official capacity. Predictably, Tiant pitched his first shutout of the year, a 2–0 five-hitter, and the crowd chanted all evening ("Loo-Eee, Loo-Eee, Loo-Eee"). Later in the month Tiant pitched another shutout in Cleveland, and the Sox won the pennant by 4½ games.

After these three remarkable performances, Tiant was the obvious choice to start the first game of the divisional playoffs. He three-hit the Athletics to start a Red Sox sweep. One week later, Luis began the 1975 World Series with a five-hit shutout of the Cincinnati Reds. In Game Four, in perhaps the quintessential performance of his career, Luis threw 163 pitches,

worked out of jams in nearly every inning, and recorded a complete game 5–4 win. He could not hold a 3–0 lead in Game Six, and was finally removed trailing 6–3 before Bernie Carbo and Carlton Fisk bailed him out with legendary home runs. Alas, the Red Sox lost the seventh game to the Reds the next evening.

The 1975 postseason marked the zenith of Tiant's career, as his family story, his charm and charisma, his unique pitching style, and, finally, his talent made him a national star. At age 34, he was said to have thrown six pitches—fastball, curve, slider, slow curve, palm ball, and knuckleball—from three different release points: over the top, three-quarters, and sidearm. His windup and motion seemed to vary on a whim. Roger Angell, writing in *The New Yorker*, once tried to put a name to each of his motions, including "Call the Osteopath," "Out of the Woodshed," and "The Runaway Taxi." It was said that over the course of a game Luis' deliveries allowed him to look each patron in the eye at least once.

With all of his loved ones nearby, Tiant won 21 games for a struggling Red Sox team in 1976. His parents never returned to Havana. They stayed with Luis for 15 months, until his father died of a lingering illness in December 1976. Two days later, while resting for the next day's memorial service, Luis' mother Isabel died in her chair, although she had not been ill. The two were buried together near Luis' home in Milton, Massachusetts.

After watching several of his teammates reap the rewards of the new free agency era, Luis had a protracted holdout in the spring of 1977. He came to terms, but managed only 12 and 13 wins the next two years. Tiant's relationship with the team's management was strained from this point forward.

After the Red Sox stunning slump late in the 1978 season, the Red Sox were 3½ games behind the Yankees with eight remaining. Prior to the subsequent contest in Toronto, Luis said, "If we lose today, it will be over my dead body. They'll have to leave me face down on the mound." He won, and the Red Sox went on to win their last eight games, including two more victories from Tiant on three days' rest. On the final day of the season, the Red Sox needed a win and a Yankee loss to force a playoff game. Catfish Hunter and the Yankees

lost in Cleveland and Tiant dazzled the Fenway crowd yet again with a two-hitter against the Blue Jays.

In the off-season, the Red Sox management offered the 38-year-old Tiant only a one-year contract, allowing Luis to sign with the New York Yankees for two years, plus a ten-year deal as a scout. Dwight Evans was devastated at management's ignorance of what Luis meant to the team. Carl Yastrzemski says he cried when he heard the news: "They tore out our heart and soul." Heart and soul aside, Tiant's September-October record for the Red Sox was 31–12. The Red Sox would not be in another pennant race for several years.

Luis won 13 games in 1979, including a 3–2 victory over the Red Sox in September, before falling to 8–9 in 1980. After the season, the Yankees released him. He signed with Pittsburgh in 1981, but spent most of the season with his old team in Portland. He excelled again for the Beavers—13–7, 3.82, including a no-hitter-but struggled with the Pirates and was released at the end of the season. He finished up his major league career with six games for the 1982 Angels, winning his final game (against the Red Sox) on August 17.

Tiant spent several years scouting for the Yankees in Mexico, always dreaming of a job with a major league team. He coached in the minor leagues for the Dodgers and White Sox in the 1990s before becoming head baseball coach for the Savannah (Georgia) College of Art and Design. He held the job for four years. For the 2002 season, he was hired by the Red Sox as pitching coach of their Class A team in nearby Lowell. Luis also is a part of the Red Sox Spanish broadcasting team.

Luis and Maria reside in the Boston area. They have raised three children: Luis Jr. (born in 1961), Isabel (1968) and Daniel (1974).

Luis Tiant was one of the most respected and revered players of his time, with his teammates, opponents, the media and his fans. His career was one of streaks, but his best streaks, in the pennant races of 1972, 1975, and 1978 and in the 1975 postseason, occurred when his team needed him most. He was believed to be finished in the middle of his career, but came back to have most of his best seasons and to become, for a few weeks in 1975, the center of the baseball world.

Rick Wise

by Bill Nowlin

	G	ERA	W	L	SV	GS	GF	CG	SHO	IP	H	R	ER	BB	HR	SO	BFP
1975 RED SOX	35	3.95	19	12	0	35	0	17	1	255.1	262	126	112	72	34	141	1091

Rick Wise won 188 major league ballgames, threw a no-hitter (and barely missed three or four others), and was the winning pitcher in what many still say was the greatest baseball game ever played, Game Six of the 1975 World Series.

He had a lot of support from his family growing up. His father was a high school history teacher, who took a teaching job in Oregon after World War II ended and moved the family from Michigan to the east side of Portland in 1948 or 1949. Rick was born on September 13, 1945, in Jackson, Michigan, but was raised in Portland. Rick's father had been a baseball pitcher under legendary coach Ray Fisher at the University of Michigan (where he'd faced Michigan State's Robin Roberts). He'd also played football behind Tom Harmon. He had quite a sports background, and both he and Rick's mother worked with their son as he developed as a ballplayer.

Rick had two brothers and two sisters. His youngest brother, Tom, played in the Astros organization. Tom Wise was about 10 years younger, and reached the Double-A level with Columbus of the Southern League in 1973 and 1974, but had surgery on both knees and progressed no further. He pitched some before entering pro ball, but was primarily a power-hitting third baseman/outfielder. Rick and his wife have two children and four grandchildren. None of them have pursued sports professionally.

Rick Wise began to rack up accomplishments early on. In 1958, while he was still 12 years old, his team went to the Little League World Series. Three years later, with more or less the same team, Wise went to the Babe Ruth World Series and pitched the second no-hitter in the history of that tournament. When he worked for the Red Sox in the 1975 World Series, it was his third Series.

Rick attended James Madison High School in Portland and helped lead the school to its first state championship in 1963. He excelled in other sports as well, and was all-city in football and basketball and all-city and all-state in baseball. He was just 17 when he graduated and was promptly signed to a major league contract by the Philadelphia Phillies. Scouts began to show interest from very early on; Rick believes that area

scouts began to take note from the time he'd played in the Little League World Series. As he got deeper into his high school years, he became more aware of scouts visiting the household and talking with his parents. As a minor, he never had much contact with the scouts themselves. There was no doubt what Rick wanted, though. "I knew I wanted to play pro ball. I knew at a very early age. I knew when I was in Little League that I wanted to play pro ball. Of course, my dad, being an educator, wanted to make sure I got an education. I had scholarship offers in all three sports, but I knew what I wanted to do from a very early age and it worked out just fine."

Glenn Elliott was the scout who signed the 17-year-old Wise to the Phillies, with a bonus of $12,000. Any bonus in excess of $8,000 made the recipient a "bonus baby" and the player had to be protected by the parent club the next year or become subject to a draft in which he could be lost. Rick played in Bakersfield during 1963 (6–3, with a 2.63 ERA and an impressive 98 strikeouts in 65 innings pitched) and then was brought up to the big league club the following year.

Rick spent the 1964 season with the Phillies, and they got him into 25 ballgames. He started eight games and finished with a 5–3 record, with an ERA of 4.04. Wise's second career start was quite an experience. It came June 21, 1964, in the second game of a doubleheader against the Mets at Shea Stadium. It was Father's Day and the day's first game saw Philadelphia's Jim Bunning throw a perfect game. Eighteen-year-old rookie Rick Wise had to follow that! He got the first four batters he faced, but when he walked Jesse Gonder, the 32,000-strong Shea Stadium crowd stood and gave the Mets a rousing ovation. "I couldn't figure out what all the commotion was about until I finally figured out it was their first baserunner in like 13 or 14 innings," Rick says. Wise threw the first six innings, allowing just three hits, and recording his first major league win. The total of only three hits in a doubleheader remains a league record.

The following year, 1965, the Phillies asked Wise to pitch in Triple A ball, with the club's Little Rock affiliate Arkansas Travelers, to polish his game. On his 20th birthday, Wise signed his Army papers and went into the Reserve, and his basic training at Fort Jackson, South

Carolina, took him most of the way through baseball's spring training. He played in Arkansas the full season of '65, and led the league in losses. The Phillies moved their Triple A club from Little Rock to San Diego, so Wise joined them there in 1966, got in playing shape and appeared in 12 games with San Diego before being recalled to the big league club in time for his first start of the season on June 2. Wise got in 22 games before the year was out, and appeared in 30 or more games each of the next seven seasons.

Wise's best year was 1971, his seventh season pitching for the Phillies. On June 23, Wise threw a no-hitter against the Reds at Cincinnati's Riverfront Stadium. The final score was 4–0, and Wise drove in three of the four runs with his two-run homer in the fifth and solo home run in the eighth. He's the only player in major league history to throw a no-hitter and hit two home runs in the same ballgame.

Wise holds a couple of other distinctions from 1971. On August 28, he again hit two home runs in a game— for the second time that year. On September 18, the Phillies hosted the Cubs at Veterans Stadium and Wise got off to a rocky start, surrendering a solo homer and a couple of base hits in the first inning, and a leadoff home run in the second. The Cubs had scored three times. The pitching coach paid a visit to the mound, and Wise says he told himself, "I better start getting things right here and locating my pitches better or I'm not going to be around long." Wise set down the next 32 Cubs he faced, all the way until Ron Santo singled in the top of the 12th. Wise won the game in 12.

In 1971, Wise won 17 games (the Phillies were a last-place team that lost 95 games). After the season, Wise was traded to the St. Louis Cardinals for Steve Carlton. Both players were in difficult contract talks with their respective teams. Wise was making $25,000 and was looking to John Quinn for more than a $10,000 raise after the season he'd had, and the many years of service to the Phillies. Carlton was having difficulties with Augie Busch in St. Louis. "We each got what we wanted from our new teams," Wise recalls, "But I loved Philadelphia. My family's from Philadelphia. My kids were born in Philadelphia. I didn't want to leave."

Leave he did, however, and he posted back-to-back 16-win seasons for the Cardinals in '72 and '73. Wise led St. Louis in wins, and had also been the starting and winning pitcher in the 1973 All-Star Game. But he was traded again, this time to the Boston Red Sox. In late October, Wise and Bernie Carbo were traded to Boston for Reggie Smith and Ken Tatum. "I was stunned when I got traded again," Wise confessed. "The Cardinals felt they needed hitting, and Boston apparently felt they needed pitching, so the trade was consummated."

Injury first struck in 1974. Wise is direct and not ambivalent about how it happened. "Darrell Johnson was the cause of that. [In] '74, I came over [to the Red Sox] and I was supposed to start the third game of the year behind the incumbents Tiant and Lee, in Milwaukee. We got the first two games in but it was very cold. So, Sunday I open up the blinds to go to the park and it was snowing. It snowed out the game, so we go home to Boston and the snow followed us. Snowed us out there. To make a long story short, when good weather finally gave us the opportunity to play, Darrell Johnson bypassed me and went back to Tiant and Lee. When I finally pitched . . . they traded for an All-Star pitcher, and it's the third game of the year. . . . I never figured that out . . . that's why they traded for me, to pitch. So finally it had been 12 days since I left spring training. I was pitching in Fenway, I think it was the backup Game of the Week, and it was a drizzly, dreary 37-, 38-degree day and I pitched a complete game, not having pitched in 12 days. I tore a triceps muscle and that basically ruined my whole season. I never could recover from it.

"It was my attitude to complete what I started. I had 138 complete games in my career so I knew what that was about. In retrospect, it wasn't too smart to pitch a complete game after not pitching for so long. I just kept pitching. That was my mentality." The injury pretty much made 1974 a lost season. There was some disappointment in coming to the American League, too. "I missed the hitting. I always figured I had an advantage over my opponent, because I could swing the bat pretty well." He had 15 career homers, despite playing six seasons in the AL where pitchers rarely pick up a bat.

The year after the injury, 1975, was exceptional. Wise led the team with 19 wins, one more than Tiant's 18 and two more than Lee's 17. At one point, he won six games in a row and nine decisions in a row as the Red Sox rolled toward the pennant. On July 2, he almost had himself another no-hitter, pitching 8⅔ innings of no-hit ball against Milwaukee. With two outs in the bottom of the ninth, Wise walked Bill Sharp and then gave up the first hit of the game—a home run to George Scott. Back in 1973, he'd also lost a shot at another no-hitter, in a game against the Reds when Joe Morgan singled with one out in the ninth. His first near no-hitter had come way back on August 8, 1968. The only play of the game scored a hit was a third-inning single by Bart Shirley, a three- or four-bouncer to Roberto Pena at

shortstop. Pena booted the ball, but the official scorer (a substitute "guest scorer" from San Diego) ruled it a hit, and wouldn't even change the ruling after Pena called upstairs to say, "You gotta change that. I should have had that easy. It should be an error."

Wise not only won 19 during the regular season in '75, but also won the clinching game of the American League Championship Series, beating the A's 5–3 in Oakland, holding them to six hits and two earned runs over 7⅓ innings. In the World Series, Darrell Johnson had Wise start Game Three, but the Big Red Machine got to him the second time through the order. Johnny Bench hit a two-run homer in the fourth, and both Dave Concepcion and Cesar Geronimo homered to lead off the fifth. After Jim Burton took over from Wise, the Red Sox eventually tied the game but the Reds won it in the bottom of the 10th after the controversial Ed Armbrister bunt. Wise had been tagged for five runs.

His only other appearance in World Series play got him a win. Wise was the fourth pitcher of the night in Game Six, and held the Reds scoreless (despite a couple of singles) in the top of the 12th. He never had to come out to throw the 13th, thanks to Carlton Fisk's home run leading off the bottom of the 12th.

Wise pitched well in '76 and '77, but it wasn't always cheerful in Red Sox clubhouse. There was a rift between manager Don Zimmer and a number of players like Bill Lee, Bernie Carbo, and Ferguson Jenkins. "We had our differences," Wise acknowledges diplomatically. "A lot of times it was Zimmer's way or no way." Nonetheless, Wise holds good memories. "I had my highest winning percentage of any of the teams that I was with when I was with the Red Sox and of course had an opportunity to get in the World Series. Those are the big things I remember most, my great teammates and the fun I had . . . how fun it is to play in Boston."

At the very end of spring training 1978, Wise was packaged in a six-player trade, sent to Cleveland with Ted Cox, Bo Diaz, and Mike Paxton for Dennis Eckersley and Fred Kendall. It was the second time Wise had been traded for a future Hall of Famer—first Carlton, then Eckersley. When he beat the Blue Jays on June 25, 1978, Wayne McElreavy points out, Wise became the first to defeat all 26 teams in existence prior to the 1993 expansion.1978 was a down year, but Wise was 15–10 in 1979. On July 3, 1979, Wise became the first pitcher to beat all 26 teams at least twice each, and before the season was over (with wins over the White Sox, Marines, and Blue Jays) he had recorded three or more wins against all 26 clubs, And then he was granted free agency by the Indians on November 1. Less than three weeks later, he hooked on with the San Diego Padres and finished his career with two seasons for San Diego, 1980 and 1981. In 1982, Wise appeared in just one game, coming in to throw the last two innings of the April 10 game against the Dodgers, but was released just six days later. There was a lot of turnover with the Padres, and manager Dick Williams wanted his own players. He shed most of the veterans. "My arm was still good," he says. Released when he was, after the rosters were set, he couldn't find another team to hook on with. "That was a pretty rude release. I'd never talked to any sportswriters. No one called me about my feelings. I just walked out of the stadium and that was it." He had a guaranteed contract with the Padres that paid him all the way through the 1984 season, so he took advantage of the unexpected time and spent the first summers with his family in 20 years.

After some time off, Wise felt himself becoming stagnant, so he sent out resumes. The Oakland A's offered him a position coaching Class A ball. He has now coached for 21 years. "I'll just say that I've coached at every level in the minor leagues, in affiliate ball and this is my sixth year in independent ball." In 2003 and 2004, Wise was pitching coach working with Butch Hobson and the Nashua Pride, and in 2005 became pitching coach for the brand-new Lancaster Barnstormers, in Pennsylvania. In August 2005, Rick enjoyed getting together for an autograph show that reunited most of the members of the 1975 Red Sox team.

THE ROTATION: Notes

1. Gammons, Peter. "Sox complete six-man trade with Cards." *Boston Globe* December 8, 1973: 20.
2. Ibid., 22.
3. Interview with Reggie Cleveland on August 8, 2005.
4. Smith, Red. "$20,000 Buys Many Cheeseburgers." *New York Times* October 17, 1975: 41.
5. August 4, 1990, interview with Reggie Cleveland by Dan Dinardo for the SABR Oral History Project. Transcribed by Joseph Hetrick.
6. August 8, 2005, interview with Reggie Cleveland.
7. Russo, Neal. "Reggie May Ease Card 'Pen Pains." *The Sporting News* October 24, 1970: 24.
8. ———. "Redbird Cleveland Chills Giants For First Win." *The Sporting News* May 8, 1971: 3.
9. Turner, Dan. *Heroes, Bums and Ordinary Men.* Toronto, ON: Doubleday Canada, 1988: 128.
10. Gammons, Peter. "'Best Staff in Baseball,' Bosox Beam." *The Sporting News* December 22, 1973: 36, 41.
11. August 8, 2005, interview with Reggie Cleveland.
12. Adelman, Tom. *The Long Ball.* Boston, MA: Back Bay–Little, Brown, 2003: 94.
13. 2005 interview.
14. Turner, 128.
15. Turner, 126.
16. Whiteside, Larry. "Aase, Paxton, and Stanley—Bosox' Trio of Hill Beauts." *The Sporting News* September 3, 1977: 8.
17. ———. "Red Sox Turn to Wright in Sale of Cleveland." *The Sporting News* May 6, 1978: 10.
18. Galloway, Randy. "Reggie Makes Mark in Ranger Relief." *The Sporting News*: June 10, 1978: 12. Also, *Boston Globe* April 19, 1978: 20. Curiously, on page 17 in the May 6, 1978 edition of *The Sporting News*, Galloway reports the selling price as $150,000.
19. Ryan. "Reggie (Almost)." *Boston Globe.*
20. Galloway, Randy. "Forgotten Jorgensen Strikes Ranger Fancy." *The Sporting News* March 31, 1979: 56.
21. Smith. "$20,000 . . . ," *New York Times* October 17, 1975: 41.
22. Flaherty, Tom. "Brews' Reggie—A New Look." *The Sporting News*: March 22, 1980: 42.
23. ———. "Reggie: From Joker to Ace." *The Sporting News* July 19, 1980: 37.
24. ———. "Travers Piles Up the Pluses." *The Sporting News*, August 16, 1980: 27.
25. Turner, 121.
26. Flaherty, Tom. "Bando Bows Out on a Happy Note." *The Sporting News* October 24, 1981: 36.
27. Turner, 129.
28. Cleveland disputes the official record. He claims it should be 106–106. See Turner, 130.
29. 2005 interview.
30. Ryan, 20.
31. Turner, 129.
32. 1990 interview.
33. 2005 interview.
34. "Roger Moret." Retrosheet.org. Retrieved September 29, 2005. <www.retrosheet.org/boxesetc/Pmorer101.htm>.
35. Hornig, Doug. *The Boys of October.* Chicago, IL: Contemporary Books, 2003: 211.
36. "Roger Moret." *Roger Moret Statistics.* Baseball-reference.com. Retreived September 29, 2005. <www.baseball-reference.com/m/moretro01.shtml>.
37. "Roger Moret." *Roger Moret Career Statistics.* TheBaseballCube.com. Retrieved September 29, 2005. <http://thebaseballcube.com/players/roger_moret.shtml>.
38. "Scoreboard, September 15, 1975." BaseballLibrary.com. Retrieved September 29, 2005 <http://www.baseballlibrary.com/baseballlibrary/chronology/1975SEPTEMBER.stm>.
39. *Events of Wednesday, September 16, 1970.* Retrosheet.org. Retrieved September 29, 2005. <www.retrosheet.org/boxesetc/09161970.htm>.
40. "Roger Moret." BaseballLibrary.com. Retrieved September 29, 2005. <http://www.baseballlibrary.com/baseballlibrary/ballplayers/M/Moret_Roger.stm>.
41. TheBaseballCube.com op. cit.
42. *Events of Wednesday, July 4, 1973.* Retrosheet.org. Retrieved September 29, 2005. <www.retrosheet.org/boxesetc/07041973.htm>.
43. "Scoreboard, August 21, 1974." BaseballLibrary.com. Retrieved September 29, 2005. <www.baseballlibrary.com/baseballlibrary/chronology/1974AUGUST.stm>.
44. Hornig, 116.
45. "Scoreboard, July 27, 1975." BaseballLibrary.com. Retrieved September 29, 2005. <www.baseballlibrary.com/baseballlibrary/chronology/1975JULY.stm>.
46. *New York Times* August 5, 1975: 33.
47. Hornig, 146.
48. *New York Times* April 25, 1978: 33.
49. Ibid.
50. *Events of Saturday, June 16, 1973.* Retrosheet.org. Retrieved September 29, 2005. <www.retrosheet.org/boxesetc/06161973.htm>.
51. Grossman, Leigh. *The Red Sox Fan Handbook.* Cambridge, MA: Rounder Books, 2005: 197.
52. Hornig, 211.

THE BULLPEN

Photograph overleaf: Dick Drago.

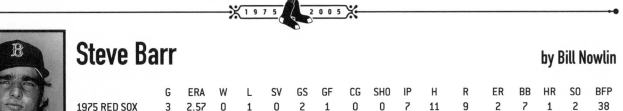
Steve Barr

by Bill Nowlin

	G	ERA	W	L	SV	GS	GF	CG	SHO	IP	H	R	ER	BB	HR	SO	BFP
1975 RED SOX	3	2.57	0	1	0	2	1	0	0	7	11	9	2	7	1	2	38

Pitcher Steve Barr debuted with the Red Sox on October 1, 1974. Born in St. Louis, Missouri, on September 8, 1951, Barr was signed fresh out of Carson High School in Carson, California, three months before he turned 18 by long-time Red Sox scout Joe Stephenson. He had been selected by the Sox in the seventh round of the 1969 amateur draft.

Barr worked his way up the Red Sox farm system, slowly at first, with a 0–4 record with Jamestown (New York–Penn League) in 1969, walking 30 batters in 28 innings pitched and posting an 8.36 ERA. In 1970 he pitched for Greenville in the Western Carolinas League, posting a 3–4 record in 15 games, and an ERA of 4.36; he was placed on the disabled list on June 26 with a season-ending injury. In 1971, after being suspended from the beginning of the season until July 9, he finished the season with Winter Haven (Florida State League) and appeared in 10 games (1–1, 6.00 ERA). Barr played in 19 games in 1972 with Winston-Salem (Carolina League), again with a losing record (8–9), but an improved 4.19 ERA. 1973 was split between Bristol (Eastern League, 7–10 with a 3.20 ERA) and Pawtucket (International League, 1–0 in three games, 5.79 ERA).

He played the 1974 season with Bristol again, putting up a very good 18–8 record, with a 2.45 ERA, leading the Eastern League in wins and earning himself a shot in the big leagues. Barr was summoned for his first start in the next-to-last game of the year in 1974, when Boston hosted the Cleveland Indians.

So it was that in game No.161, on October 1, manager Darrell Johnson gave the game ball to 23-year-old southpaw Steve Barr. Barr had earned pitcher-of-the-year status in the Eastern League under manager Stan Williams. That season over, the tall and large (6′4″, 200 lbs) left hander hadn't pitched for 36 days, so it wasn't surprising that he was a little rusty—not to mention possibly a little nervous. "He lost his composure," Johnson said after the game. Barr got through the first inning without trouble but walked Johnny Ellis to lead off the second inning. Ellis took second on a wild pitch that went into the seats. After inducing a grounder to third, Barr let up singles to Rusty Torres, Dave Duncan, and Luis Alvarado. Duncan's was an infield hit, and had Barr covered the bag, Duncan might have been out, though no error was assessed. He then walked Buddy Bell to load the bases and walked Duane Kuiper, forcing in a run. "What impressed me most," Johnson said, "is the fact that when we thought he was gone, he straightened himself out and came back." Frank Robinson was up with the bases loaded, but he didn't get much bat on the ball and Alvarado was forced out at the plate. Charlie Spikes then bounced back to Barr, who threw him out easily. Three runs on three hits and three walks, but he was out of the inning.

Barr settled down and threw a complete nine-inning game, giving up just three more hits and one more run, but Cleveland's Steve Kline fared worse and Boston scored seven times. Barr earned his first major league win, 7–4. In all, he struck out three and walked six. "He has the good fastball, the curve, a superb straight change," Johnson noted. "The question has been his composure and his ability to get the ball over the plate. I know this, he'll be given every opportunity next spring." Peter Gammons' game account in the *Boston Globe* was headlined, SOX ROOKIE HUMS A FEW BARRS OF 1975.[1]

Barr was back in 1975, but not at first. He opened the year in the minors, and was called up from Pawtucket on July 1 after Red Sox right hander Dick Pole was hit hard in the face by a June 30 line drive off the bat of Tony Muser. Pole's cheekbone was fractured and no one knew how long it might be before he could return to the rotation. Barr came in and threw the ninth inning in a July 1 loss to Baltimore. Flirting with danger, he gave up a single and walked three batters; he was very lucky to escape without giving up a run, thanks to a caught stealing, a popup to right, and Bobby Grich's grounder to short that ended the inning.

On July 5 in Cleveland, he had his next shot, but was bombed. Barr got through the first inning, but with one out in the bottom of the second, he surrendered a single to Charlie Spikes. He tried to hold the runner at first but his wild pickoff throw allowed Spikes to advance all the way to third. A sacrifice fly almost resulted in a double play at the plate, but Spikes was ruled safe. A single, an error by Denny Doyle, and a walk set up a grand slam to center field by Buddy Bell, and Jim Burton was brought in to relieve Barr. One and two-third innings resulted in six runs, only one of which was earned.

There was one more start in Steve Barr's Red Sox future. On July 10, Texas was in The Hub. The start lasted 4⅓ innings, in which Steve was touched up for three runs (one earned) on seven hits and two walks. He struck out two batters. After a double, a single, and a double in the fifth inning, Reggie Cleveland was called in to take Barr's place and protect the Red Sox' 7–3 lead. Cleveland just barely held on, giving up one run in the eighth and three more runs in the ninth, which tied the game 7–7. With two outs in the bottom of the ninth and nobody on, Doyle singled and advanced to second on a passed ball. Cecil Cooper, who'd come in to take over for Yaz at first base in the seventh, singled home Doyle with the winning run. Despite a 2.57 ERA on the season, Barr was sent south for more seasoning—south to Pawtucket, where he finished out the year.

After the 1975 season was over, the Red Sox made a move and sent both Barr and Juan Beniquez (and a player to be named later, who 25 days later proved to be Craig Skok) to the Texas Rangers for Ferguson Jenkins. With the Rangers in 1976, Barr had a chance to stretch out a little more, getting into 20 games. His first of 10 starts came on April 13, a complete game 3–1 win over the Athletics at Arlington Stadium. Steve was used intermittently throughout the season, ending up with a 2–6 record. There were a couple of tough luck losses

like the 3–2 defeat on May 16 at the hands of the same Athletics, but his 5.59 ERA betrays a failure to perform as hoped for. Barr threw 67⅔ innings, but surrendered 10 homers and 44 walks in that time. After the year was over, Barr was selected by the Seattle Mariners in the November 1976 expansion draft (54th pick overall), but 1976 proved to be his last season in major league ball.

At the end of spring training with the Mariners, Barr was assigned to Omaha (American Association) and went 4–8 with a 6.17 ERA in 17 games before Cleveland Indians Triple A affiliate in Toledo "obtained pitcher Steve Barr on loan from Seattle organization."[2] Wayne McElreavy points out that the story may be more unusual yet, in that Omaha was a Royals farm club. The Mariners, he says, used to share a number of minor league clubs. Barr's record with Toledo was 3–1 in eight games, with an even 4.00 ERA.

The *Los Angeles Times* of October 29, 1977 noted that Seattle had traded Barr to Cleveland for a player to be named later. Barr was invited to spring training in 1978 by the Indians, but spent the year with Cleveland's Triple A team in the Pacific Coast League in Portland, Oregon, going 11–7 in 28 games, with a 5.77 ERA.

Here our attempts to track Steve Barr's life ran out, and it proved impossible to catch up with Barr himself for an update on his life after '78.

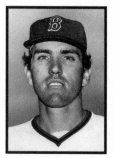

Jim Burton

by Les Masterson

	G	ERA	W	L	SV	GS	GF	CG	SHO	IP	H	R	ER	BB	HR	SO	BFP
1975 RED SOX	29	2.89	1	2	1	4	8	0	0	53	58	30	17	19	6	39	232

Perfect execution usually equals success in the game of baseball. For Jim Burton, one slider that dipped low and away sent him into the pantheon of World Series goats.

Jim Scott Burton was born to Hubert and Alyce Burton on Oct. 27, 1949 in Royal Oak, Michigan, a suburb 15 miles north of Detroit. Hubert Burton was a plant supervisor when his son Jim was born. He later owned a tool and dye business. Growing up in Michigan with two brothers, Burton enjoyed playing team sports, particularly baseball in the summer and hockey in the winter, as well as hunting and trapping. Burton developed his arm strength by pitching a lot when he was young, though it was not his plan to one day become a major league baseball player.

The young lefty won championships in Little

League, Youth League, and American Legion ball. When his Detroit Federation team won the All-American Baseball Association tournament in Johnston, Pennsylvania in 1969, Burton won recognition as the team's most valuable player.

Burton was awarded six letters in football and basketball while attending Rochester High School in Rochester Hills, Michigan. But scouts began to take notice of Burton's baseball ability and his hometown Detroit Tigers chose him with their 26th-round pick in the 1967 amateur draft. Still not envisioning a baseball career for himself, Burton declined the Tigers' offer and enrolled in the University of Michigan. While playing in Ann Arbor, Burton shattered records and advanced from a middle-round pick to the head of the class.

By the end of his college career, Burton struck out 288 batters in 228 innings, shattering the previous

record. He also tossed a no-hitter against the University of Wisconsin in 1971, the first one thrown by a Michigan pitcher in 88 years. He spent four years at the university and graduated in 1971.

One of the biggest winners in college baseball in his senior year with 19 victories, Burton was named to *The Sporting News'* All-American baseball team along with Ohio University's Mike Schmidt and Texas University's Burt Hooton. With his record-breaking college career coming to a close, Burton was a highly-regarded prospect. The Boston Red Sox chose the Michigan hurler in the first round (fifth overall) in the 1971 secondary draft.

Burton kicked off his professional career later that month pitching for Double A Pawtucket (then of the Eastern League), throwing a three-hitter against Quebec City in a 7–0 victory. He retired the first 15 batters before issuing his only walk of the game. Burton kept his no-hitter into the seventh inning. Burton became a feared pitcher in the Eastern League, shutting down offenses and being called "Pawtucket's prize southpaw" by *The Sporting News*.

His shutout streak stretched to 25 innings before Andy (Andre) Thornton of Reading hit a two-run home run off a hanging curve ball in the eighth inning to beat Burton and Pawtucket 3–1 on July 5. Burton was undeterred and continued blazing a scorching path through the league for a team that sat at the bottom of the standings. Burton finished the year 7–5. "I feel now like I'm starting to make progress," Burton told *The Sporting News.*

Burton remained in Pawtucket in 1972. He was the first Eastern League hurler to win 10 games and was rewarded in August with a call up to the International League Louisville Colonels. While Pawtucket struggled at the bottom of the league, the Louisville club was fighting for a pennant. In his first start, Burton shut down Syracuse as Dwight Evans slugged his sixth home run in a month to give the Colonels a 6–1 win.

Though Burton was playing for a better team, the improved talent in the International League slowed the 6'3" pitcher's progress. Burton was 2–4 with a 4.78 ERA and had five starts for Louisville, which topped the circuit. Following a stint in the Florida Instructional League, Burton's 1973 campaign further delayed his rise in the Red Sox system. He struggled with back injuries, compiling a 4–11 record with an ERA of more than five runs per nine innings. He also gave up more walks than strikeouts and hits than innings pitched.

After a slow start in 1974 with Pawtucket (now the team's Triple A affiliate), Burton resurrected his career,

throwing a two-hitter and striking out 18 against Charleston in June. In Pawtucket, Burton was known as much for his community service as for his slider. Before an August game against Syracuse, the Big Brothers Association of Rhode Island honored Burton, along with pitchers Craig Skok and Rick Kreuger and player-coach Tony Torchia. Frank Lanning, sports cartoonist for the *Providence Journal-Bulletin* said, "These young men are just passing through this community, but whatever their athletic future, their sense of civic responsibilities will make them assets wherever they live."

The Pawtucket team suffered from a bipolar offense—though it sported future superstars Fred Lynn and Jim Rice. The Triple A PawSox led the league in home runs, but finished sixth in runs out of eight teams. Burton's final record in 1974 did not impress, but his comeback in the second half placed him back into the major league club's future plans.

After pitching for Arecibo in Puerto Rico during the winter, Burton went to Red Sox spring training with a chance to make the 1975 team. The baseball fields of Winter Haven were an exciting place in the spring of '75. The two young rookies Rice and Lynn showed promise and the Sox already enjoyed an experienced team that had recently fallen just short of the pennant.

Though the team was loaded both with offensive pop and experienced starters, the Red Sox bullpen needed help and the big team watched their young arms closely. Burton's hope to make the team was quickly squelched when he was sent to the minor league camp in March. While playing for Joe Morgan in Pawtucket, Burton continued to advance. After six starts, he was among the league-leaders in ERA (1.24). His injury problems seemed behind him and he told *The Sporting News* in May that he was effectively using the corners of the plate. "If I make a mistake, I want it to be called a ball. I don't want to make mistakes over the plate," Burton said.

Burton's wildness, which was primarily responsible for keeping him out of the major leagues, seemed a thing of the past. He struck out more than double the amount of men he walked. While Burton prepared for his June 8 start against Tidewater, Boston reporters wrote about the young lefty in Pawtucket. His recall seemed imminent.

"Sure it was disappointing," Burton told *The Sporting News* about the wait. "But a lot of times things appear in the newspapers that don't quite work out that way, so I just began to accept it. But with the way I'm pitching, I'm sure I'll make it up there. It's just not going to happen that quickly."

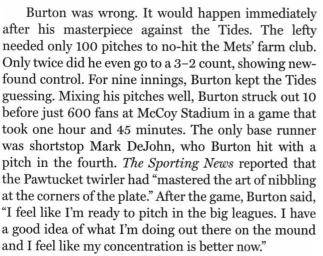

Burton was wrong. It would happen immediately after his masterpiece against the Tides. The lefty needed only 100 pitches to no-hit the Mets' farm club. Only twice did he even go to a 3–2 count, showing new-found control. For nine innings, Burton kept the Tides guessing. Mixing his pitches well, Burton struck out 10 before just 600 fans at McCoy Stadium in a game that took one hour and 45 minutes. The only base runner was shortstop Mark DeJohn, who Burton hit with a pitch in the fourth. *The Sporting News* reported that the Pawtucket twirler had "mastered the art of nibbling at the corners of the plate." After the game, Burton said, "I feel like I'm ready to pitch in the big leagues. I have a good idea of what I'm doing out there on the mound and I feel like my concentration is better now."

His success was not lost on Boston management, who called up Burton the next day to fortify its pitching corps. The Sox sent down infielder Buddy Hunter to make room for Burton. After a one-two-three appearance as a reliever against Texas at Fenway Park on June 10, manager Darrell Johnson gave Burton his first start of June 12. He excelled during a 9⅓-inning start against Detroit on the 16th. Taking on another lefty, Mickey Lolich, Burton surrendered only six hits and two runs in a game the Sox won 6–2 in 12 innings.

He was hammered in a June 23 start and didn't get out of the first inning. There was one more spot start in August, but Burton was otherwise used exclusively out of the bullpen the rest of the year. He shined as a reliever. In 25 relief appearances, his ERA was 2.38. His strikeout–walk ratio was almost three to one. He gave up more hits than innings pitched, but the young hurler wriggled out of trouble because of his newfound control and pitch selection.

Burton's teammates understood his importance, later voting him a full World Series share. He appeared on some ballots for *The Sporting News*' Rookie Pitcher of the Year.

After the Red Sox swept the powerhouse Oakland A's without Burton ever throwing a pitch in the American League Championship Series, the Bostons took on the Cincinnati Reds.

Burton would remain in the bullpen for the first two games in Boston and finally came in for Game Three, nearly a month after the last time he pitched. He threw to two batters, Ken Griffey and Joe Morgan, after relieving Rick Wise in the fifth. He walked Griffey and Joe Morgan hit a sacrifice fly. Griffey then stole second. With that, Johnson yanked the lefty for Reggie Cleveland, who faced Tony Perez. Burton would not contribute in Games Four or Five, nor the historic

Game Six, but the lefty reliever would pitch again in Game Seven.

With the game tied in the top of the ninth, and Jim Willoughby having been removed for a pinch-hitter in the bottom of the eighth, Johnson chose the only remaining lefty in the bullpen, Burton, rather than stopper Dick Drago. Drago had thrown three innings in Game Six. Johnson saw the left-handed Griffey and Cesar Geronimo, the first two hitters of the inning, and decided to play the lefty-versus-lefty percentage rather than going with Drago.

In Doug Hornig's book *The Boys of October*, Burton relayed his feelings warming up in the Fenway bullpen. "Warming up, my whole body went numb. It was surreal, like an out-of-body experience. In those days, they'd send a golf cart to bring you in, and when it came for me, I knew I couldn't ride in it. I had to trot in from the bullpen just to feel my feet on the ground. Otherwise, I might have floated away."

Burton's arm was stiff and sore from cold and inactivity. "I wasn't ready. I'd hardly pitched all the previous month. I was rusty. When I was warming up, I couldn't get loose. I could tell I didn't have anything," said Burton. The two batters he had faced in the third game represented his only work in the previous 33 days, since September 20.

Feeling nervous and rusty is not the prescription for success and Burton promptly walked the leadoff man, Griffey. Expecting a bunt and trying to keep Griffey close, Burton threw three times over to first. When he finally delivered to Geronimo, the center fielder sacrificed Griffey to second. Dan Driessen grounded to second for the second out, sending Griffey to third. With the switch-hitting Pete Rose next, Johnson visited the mound and advised Burton to keep the ball away from Charlie Hustle. Burton gave Rose a diet of curveballs that remained outside of the strike zone and the Red ran down to first base with a base on balls.

With runners on first and third and two outs, Burton's job did not get easier. Up stepped Joe Morgan, who would be named the 1975 National League Most Valuable Player. Morgan recalled in his book *Joe Morgan: A Life in Baseball* that he was working with Lew Fonseca on keeping his weight back as long as possible on breaking balls. Having Morgan on a 2–2 count, Burton and catcher Carlton Fisk decided on a late-breaking slider low and outside. The pitch was where Burton wanted it—a pitcher's pitch. Against most players, the young lefty would have walked off the mound to a raucous ovation, but he was taking on the National League MVP.

Morgan reached out with his bat, swiping at the sphere spinning down and away from him. "I knew I did not get good wood on the ball. I could feel the dead heaviness of the ball against the bat. I saw a blur of white heading toward center field and as I ran I watched it hit the ground," recalled Morgan in his autobiography.

Morgan told reporters after the game that he would not have hit the ball a couple of years earlier. Burton made his pitch and Morgan acknowledged the late-breaking slider was nasty, but that brought little consolation either to Burton or to Red Sox fans, who had waited nearly 60 years for a World Series title. The Reds had taken the lead and Johnson removed his young pitcher, who left the Fenway Park mound for the final time.

Speaking to reporters after the game, Burton tipped his cap to Morgan. "The pitch that Morgan hit was a very good pitch, a slider low and away, right where I wanted it. Give the man credit for hitting it. I don't think I could've made a better pitch. I can't say, 'Gosh, I shouldn't have thrown that pitch' or 'I should've thrown it to another location,'" said Burton.

In the high drama of the baseball clubhouse after the game, Burton placed his pitch and the ultimate result into perspective. "I'm not going around hanging my head about it. It's not like I killed a person," Burton told reporters.

Looking back nearly 30 years later, Burton still believed he made the right pitch. "It was the best slider I ever threw. A great pitch. I put everything I had into it. Everything. It was right at Morgan, and you can see him initially bailing out on it. . . . Then, when he realized it was going to be over the plate, he just kind of threw his bat at it," Burton told Hornig.

Though Burton's outing would be placed alongside other disappointing finishes for the Red Sox, the team publicly spoke in glowing terms about their 26-year-old rookie. "I know this," Ed Kenney, minor league director of the Red Sox, told *The Sporting News* after the 1975 World Series. "You haven't seen what Burton can do yet. He's a lot better than anyone gives him credit for."

There were trade rumors in the off-season involving Burton, but when spring came he was back in Winter Haven fighting for a job. Management figured Burton would either share left-handed duty out of the bullpen with Tom House or possibly fill the fifth-starter role.

While 21-year-old phenom Don Aase impressed, Burton struggled in Florida. *The Sporting News* reported Burton "can't seem to live down giving up the winning hit in the ninth inning of the World Series." His struggles would allow 20-year-old Rick Jones to fill the second left-hander slot in the bullpen, and Burton—who gave up 17 hits in three appearances—was assigned to Pawtucket.

Burton was surprised by the demotion. "The equipment manager at spring training took my stuff and put it into a cardboard box. I thought that epitomized me. One day you're a celebrity, the next day you're anonymous. One day you're in the majors—all first class—then you're here in the minors where it's sort of dog eat dog," Burton told the *Washington Post* in 1978.

His struggles continued in Pawtucket and reporters openly wondered if Burton was done. "Physically, I'm really OK. It's just a matter of some mechanical things that I have to get straightened out. Like on the curve ball, I have to get more in a groove on my release point. The trouble is that all this should be natural and I shouldn't really have to think about it. When you start thinking on the mound about exactly how you're throwing, then you get into trouble," he told *The Sporting News* in the May 15, 1976 issue. Burton led the International League in starts, but also struggled with his control, outpacing other hurlers in walks and runs while compiling a 5.59 ERA.

The following season, after pitching for Bayamon in Puerto Rico over the winter, Burton bounced back after being briefly sent to the Pawtucket bullpen because of wildness. He led the Pawtucket staff in innings, strikeouts and fewest hits allowed per nine innings. Down the stretch, he went 4–1 with a 1.54 ERA for Pawtucket as it raced to the International League title.

The Red Sox rewarded Burton with a call up to the big club in September. Nearly two years after his career-altering pitch to Morgan, Burton threw 2⅔ scoreless innings of relief against the Orioles in Baltimore on September 17, 1977.

Burton had clawed his way back to the majors, but his descent would not take nearly as long. He couldn't know that the brief stint against the Orioles would prove his final appearance in the majors. The Red Sox traded Burton to the New York Mets for infielder Leo Foster during the following spring training. Burton was going from a team with talent to one that floundered in the aftermath of the blockbuster trade that sent the franchise's best player, Tom Seaver, to the Reds.

The Mets sent Burton down to Tidewater, where he struggled with his control. He was then sent further down the ladder to Lynchburg in the Carolina League, the Mets' Class A affiliate. This was a new experience for Burton. As a highly-touted prospect seven years earlier, Burton bypassed Class A and started in Pawtucket fresh out of college.

Speaking to the *Washington Post* in 1978, Burton acknowledged that he was concerned about heading to Class A because he heard horror stories about players getting "buried down here." "It was hard to come here, but not as hard as people might think," he added. "It doesn't matter that it's A ball. What matters to me is how I'm throwing. I know what I have to do to pitch in the major leagues. I do feel I'm coming back. My confidence has been battered around a lot, and a lot of it is mental. It's something that I can regain. I don't think I'm that far from it."

Pitching in the low minors with guys who would never even have a sniff of the majors, Burton stood out—he was the guy who gave up the World Series-winning hit to Joe Morgan. Burton recalled warming up on the mound in Salem, Virginia while the public address announcer gave the crowd that day's trivia question, "What pitcher in uniform tonight lost the seventh game of the 1975 World Series?"

"You hope that people will have a little sensitivity. But you can't expect that. You can't crusade for that because nobody wants to listen. That's what being a professional is all about. You have to take the comments and the criticisms," Burton told the *Washington Post*.

Burton did get to pitch for a major league team again, but it was for the Mets in a 1978 exhibition game against the Tides. He went five innings and surrendered

eight hits and four earned runs. Tired of the elbow problems, Burton then hung up his cleats and returned to Michigan.

The transition from ballplayer to regular citizen was difficult for Burton, who spent four years trying to find his way after his pitching career. "A lot of athletes struggle with re-assimilating. And I did, too, in that my sense of identity and self-worth were tied up with athletic success," Burton told Hornig.

A friend told him about a possibility for a printing business in Charlotte, North Carolina. Intrigued by the idea of running his own business like his father, Burton moved south and found his place. "It wasn't until I began running my own business that the separation became permanent. It's so time-consuming that it finally forced the transition," Burton said.

In addition to spending time with his family, which includes three daughters, and running his business, Burton spends time traveling to Haiti for missionary work. He helped open a print shop for natives and prints educational materials for the schools.

His time in Haiti also provides him with a different perspective. Giving up a game-winning hit in the World Series isn't quite as important after one sees life in the third world. "You look back and you realize that baseball is such a small part of your life, when you think about it. There's so much that's more important."

Dick Drago

by Tom Harkins

	G	ERA	W	L	SV	GS	GF	CG	SHO	IP	H	R	ER	BB	HR	SO	BFP
1975 RED SOX	40	3.84	2	2	15	2	34	0	0	72.2	69	31	31	31	5	43	313

Some time in the 1975 season, pitcher Dick Drago stopped in a convenience store and was recognized by the counter clerk as a member of the Boston Red Sox. Not being familiar with Drago out of uniform the clerk asked the pitcher his name. Dick answered, "I'm Drago." To which the clerk responded, "Oh yeah, Drago Segui."[3]

That Dick Drago was mistaken for the older, Cuban-born, fellow reliever Diego Segui shows that Drago, while in Boston, played in the shadows of his more highly visible and more widely publicized teammates. Although never receiving the acclaim given to others, it is clear that he was a key player on his Red Sox teams; never was he more important than during the glory season of 1975.

Richard Anthony Drago was born in Toledo, Ohio on Monday, June 25, 1945. Of Italian-German descent, he had a typical middle-class upbringing in the medium-sized industrial city of his birth. His first baseball experiences were playing catch with his father. Of course he played local youth baseball, culminating in being named a Connie Mack all-star. At Woodward High School, Dick lettered in basketball and bowling as well as baseball. It was in baseball, however, that he truly excelled; his varsity record was 18–3, which included two no-hitters as a senior. Although he did receive some attention from scouts, Drago decided to accept a baseball scholarship to the University of Detroit. Although more known as a basketball or football school (the university dropped football in Drago's freshman year) it had recently produced a prominent baseball

pitcher for the White Sox: Dave DeBusschere. Better known as a pro basketball player, DeBusschere was an eight-time All-Star in the NBA.

After his freshman year, Detroit Tigers scout Herman Kander signed Drago to a professional contract. In 1965, he began the year at Daytona Beach in the Florida State League. After 14 appearances, and record of 4–7, he was promoted to Rocky Mount in the Carolina League. Unfortunately his midseason elevation did not meet with immediate success. Although suffering from errors behind him (one-third of the runs scored off him were unearned), he completed only three of eight starts while posting a 1–7 record.

In 1966, Drago returned to Rocky Mount and had a fine year, finishing 15–9, 1.79 ERA, with a league-leading seven shutouts. He was the winning pitcher in the Carolina League all-star game and, in the first game of a doubleheader versus Greensboro, he threw a seven-inning no-hitter (interestingly, his roommate, Darrell Clark, tossed another seven-inning no-no in the nightcap).

Drago was promoted to Montgomery (Southern League) for 1966 where he again won 15 games, this time leading the league. This earned him a promotion to Triple-A Toledo where he got in one game giving up two hits and one run in three innings.

In 1968, he spent the entire season pitching for the hometown Mud Hens and for the third year in a row won 15 games. He had 146 strikeouts, nine complete games, and a respectable 3.36 ERA. He was also named to, and pitched in the International League All-Star game. His continued success throughout the Detroit minor league system would suggest that a Tigers call-up loomed for 1969. Instead, the promising pitcher was selected by the brand new Kansas City Royals in the 1968 expansion draft.

For the Royals, Drago became the workhorse. During his five years in Kansas City, he averaged 32 starts, 10 complete games, and well over 200 innings pitched. His best year, and the only one in which he had a winning record with Kansas City, was 1971 when he posted a 17–11 record, completed 15 of 34 starts, and had an ERA under 3.00, and was selected as the Royals' Pitcher of the Year. One of his complete games in 1971 put him in the record books for fewest batters faced in a complete game. After retiring the first two batters in the first he gave up a solo homer to Frank Robinson and then set down the next 10 Orioles in order. After the Royals failed to score in top of the fifth, the skies opened up and after waiting it was declared over and Drago had lost the game 1-0. In 1973, his last year as

a Royal, his ERA exceeded 4.00 for the first time and he was outshone on the staff by Paul Splittorff. Later, Drago would say that Royals manager Jack McKeon quit on him that year. McKeon has denied this but it soon became clear that the Royals were ready to deal Drago in the offseason.[4]

On October 24, 1973 the Royals dealt Drago to the Red Sox for Marty Pattin, a 30-year-old right-handed starter who was two years older than Drago. Both players wanted and needed a change in scenery. Rookie Boston skipper Darrell Johnson used him in 1974: 33 games, 18 as a starter and 15 out of the bullpen. This dual role of starter–reliever was one he shared with Roger Moret. Drago said he favored starting but it was his relief work that made him a success in Boston.[5] Although his season ERA was 3.48, his relief ERA was a dominating 1.40. During the stretch run in which the Red Sox fell out of contention he pitched well but lost two games by scores of 3–1 and 2–1.

Over the offseason, the return from injury of veteran starter Rick Wise cemented Dick Drago's role in the bullpen for 1975. Wise led the team in victories and Drago emerged as the premier reliever. His 15 saves ranked fifth in the league and his 34 games finished placed him ninth. In the heat of the stretch drive beginning August 27, he pitched in 13 games, earning one win and eight saves. Darrell Johnson enthused that he was as important to Boston as the much more publicized Rollie Fingers was to Oakland.[6]

In the playoffs against Oakland Drago proved his worth, pitching 4⅔ innings in Games 2 and 3, earning saves in both. In Game Two at Fenway, Johnson sent for Drago after Moret walked the first batter in the top of the seventh. After Drago was announced, Oakland manager Al Dark countered with pinch-hitter Billy Williams. Williams, a lifetime .290 hitter and former NL batting champ, was not Drago's only concern as he prepared to pitch, because the batter whom Moret had walked was former Sox teammate, Tommy Harper, one of the best base stealers in the game. Nursing a one-run lead, Drago showed a lot interest in the runner leading off first. Drago began Williams' at-bat with three throws to first, making Harper dive back while Williams worked the count to 2–2. After one more toss to first, Drago struck Williams out with a high fast ball. Drago threw to first once more before pitching to the next batter, Billy North, before North lined the first pitch to center and Fred Lynn's throw to Cecil Cooper easily doubled up Harper. In a postgame interview Drago was asked how he was able to deal with the threat of Harper and still focus on the batters. He answered:

"That is what I get paid for."[7] The final two innings were much less stressful because his teammates got him an insurance run in both the seventh and eighth innings.

Moving to Oakland for Game Three, Drago came in to relieve the starter Wise with one out, two runs in, and two men on in the bottom of the eighth with the Red Sox holding a slim 5–3 lead. The pressure of the situation on the field was magnified by the frenzied Oakland fans whose unbridled exuberance caused a delay in the proceedings more than once. But it didn't faze Drago, whose one pitch to Joe Rudi was grounded to short for an inning-ending double play. Drago's ninth was not as easy. Once again he faced Williams who, on a 2–2 count, lined the ball off Drago's shin. The ball caromed to Cooper who tossed to the bloodied but alert pitcher covering first for a painful 1-3-1 putout. After the game *Boston Globe* reporter Peter Gammons commented on Drago's "bloody stocking" (the first reporting of a Red Sox pitcher's bloody sock in postseason play).[8] Gene Tenace popped to short for the second out. Drago then walked North on four pitches, bringing Johnson to the mound for a visit. Drago's wildness continued as Jim Holt worked the count to 3–0. Drago now bore down and after Holt fouled off one 3–2 count he grounded slowly to Doyle at second who threw to Cooper and the celebration began.

Drago also pitched in two of the seven games of the 1975 World Series. In Game Two, with the Red Sox leading 2–1 in the top of the ninth, Johnson summoned Drago to replace starter Bill Lee after Lee surrendered a first-pitch leadoff double to Johnny Bench. With the tying run on second, Drago got Tony Perez to ground out to short, but Bench advanced to third. George Foster flied to shallow left, no challenge for Carl Yastrzemski's arm. With two down, Dave Concepcion bounced a good pitch over Drago's head. Doyle fielded it, but couldn't make a play. Bench scored the tying run.

On the next pitch, Concepcion took off for second and despite Fisk's throw and Doyle's tag, the lead run was in scoring position. Ken Griffey fouled off two of Drago's fastballs before he lined a double to left scoring Concepcion. After Drago walked Cesar Geronimo intentionally, he got pitcher Rawly Eastwick to ground to second forcing Geronimo. After the Red Sox were retired in the bottom of the ninth, Drago suffered the loss and the series was tied 1–1.

After sitting out all three games in Cincinnati and waiting out three days of rain, Drago was next summoned into the sixth game with score tied to start the ninth inningDrago easily disposed of the three future Hall of Famers: Joe Morgan, Bench, and Perez.

Sitting in the dugout during the bottom of the ninth Drago, probably thought he was going to even his series record as the Red Sox loaded the bases with no outs. However, this situation just added to the drama of this legendary game as the Red Sox failed to score sending the game into extra innings.

In the 10th, Drago didn't have it as easy. After retiring Foster, Drago faced his Game Two nemesis Concepcion who singled and again stole second. Drago hitched up his belt and struck out Geronimo before pinch-hitter Dan Driessen flied out to Bernie Carbo in left. The Red Sox went down 1-2-3 and quickly Drago was back on the mound for his third inning of work. A cursory look at a scorebook for this inning would indicate a fairly routine three-batter, three-out inning: a hit by pitch, a force out, and a double play. However, it was anything but routine and required two outstanding plays by two Gold Glovers. After Drago nailed leadoff batter Pete Rose with a fastball, Griffey tried to sacrifice him to second but, but Fisk threw to second base to force Rose. On a 2–2 pitch, Morgan lined Drago's offering deep to right where Dwight Evans pulled Morgan's drive out of the first row of fans and instinctively threw quickly—if not accurately—towards first. Yaz fielded it and flipped to an alert and hustling Rick Burleson covering first to record the third out.[9] In the bottom of the 11th, Drago was pinch-hit for and, when the Red Sox didn't score, it ended his chance to win the greatest game in World Series history.

In the offseason, even championship teams try to better themselves. The Red Sox, however, made a move which didn't help them at all. On March 3, 1976 they sent Drago, their best reliever, to California, ostensibly, for three players who would never play an inning for Boston: John Balaz, Dick Sharon, and Dave Machemer. The term "ostensibly" is used because it was reported that Drago was sent to the Angels as "the player to be named later" for Denny Doyle (acquired the previous June). The Red Sox still sent minor league pitcher Chuck Ross to the Angels two days later to make everything look more legitimate. Drago pitched for the Angels for a year and a half. In 1976, he appeared in 43 games, all in relief, going 7–8 with a 4.42 ERA. 1976 also saw him throw a pitch which would make him the answer to a trivia question although no one knew it at them time. In June pitching against the Brewers in Milwaukee he surrendered a home run to Hank Aaron. As it turned out this was Hammering Hank's 755th and final roundtripper. The next season, he appeared in 13 games for the Angels with a record of 0–1, and a 3.00 ERA, before being traded on June 13 to the Orioles for

Dyar Miller. Drago pitched well for Baltimore appearing in 36 games and going 6–3.

After the 1977 season, Drago became a free agent and rejoined the Red Sox. He spent the next three years on teams that were never quite good enough to get into the postseason. During these three years he appeared in 133 games, mostly in relief, although in 1980 he did have a complete game. His composite record was 21–17 with 23 saves, and an ERA around 3.52.

One aspect of the game of baseball in which Drago excelled was in the role of bench jockey. Even as a relief pitcher, Drago would stay in the dugout until he had to go to the bullpen later in the game. He stayed in the dugout because it was the best place to watch the game and he liked to take every opportunity to study opposing players. This also provided him with a good location for getting on his opponents. Nothing was off-limits to the leather-lunged Drago if it irritated opponents and gave his team even the slightest edge.[11] Drago also did good work off the field, including many visits to see children in hospitals, bringing small gifts and signing autographs. In July, 1978, one of his hospital visits made the wire services and he cheered up a young patient by promising him a strikeout and tickets to the World Series.[12]

The most important game Drago appeared in during this second stint with Boston was on October 2, 1978—the infamous Bucky Dent playoff game. He came on in relief of Andy Hassler with two outs in the top of the ninth with Paul Blair on first. After keeping the speedy Blair close with three throws to first, he pitched to Thurman Munson who hit a grounder in the hole which third baseman Frank Duffy missed cutting off, but Burleson fielded it just forcing Blair at second.

Just before the 1981 season began, Drago was dealt to Seattle for Venezuelan righthander Manny Sarmiento, who would never pitch a game for the Red Sox. The deal upset Drago, who blasted the Red Sox for not releasing him so he could become a free agent.[13] For Seattle, he went 4–6 record with the highest ERA of his career; his 5.53 was more than one run above any previous season and almost two runs higher than his career mark. As disappointing as 1981 was for Drago, it became even more disappointing in that it was his last year. The Mariners released him on April 2, 1982.

The early years of his retirement from baseball were not kind to Dick Drago. Twice divorced, he was assessed significant child support payments and soon thereafter was assessed even more in tax payments, penalties, and interest because the IRS disallowed tax shelters he had claimed. This all came to a head in 1992 when

he was arrested in Florida and returned in custody to Massachusetts to face charges of failure to pay child support. Doug Hornig suggests that Massachusetts had decided to make an example of the ex-Sox player. His brother was able to post bond and he was released. As the trial was about to begin, Drago produced proof of payments, a settlement was reached, and he was allowed to return to Florida.[14]

This incident now behind him, Drago continued a successful business career in Florida. Today he lives in the Tampa area and is retired, although he enjoys online trading as a hobby. He also plays a lot of golf, shooting in the low eighties, and spends time with his children and grandchildren who live nearby. He has always retained his love for baseball and pitching, and played for the Orlando Sun Sox of the short-lived Senior league. More recently, he barnstormed across Canada with a team put together by his ex-Sox teammate, Bill Lee.

Although undergoing a successful triple bypass operation in 2004, he is in excellent health, only a few pounds over his playing weight. He still enjoys meeting with fans and participates in the Red Sox fantasy camps and cruises.[15] He enjoys visiting Boston whenever possible. "I came back with a friend for a visit in 2003. We got on the T and the driver hollered, 'Hey, Dragon! How are you doing?' My friend couldn't believe it. I hadn't pitched for the Red Sox in over 20 years and people still recognized me. I love Boston!"[16]

Despite the high profile of his post-baseball problems, Dick Drago should be remembered for what he was as a player: a good pitcher who worked very hard. He was never an All-Star or a Cy Young Award winner (he did receive some consideration for his 17-win season in 1971). A true measure of his quality of as a pitcher must look beyond his won–loss record and his ERA. To assess his worth one should see where he stood among his peers. Although he led the league only once in any category (nine double plays in 1971), he made the top ten 13 times in positive categories. In the pre-DH seasons of 1969 and 1970 he had 18 sacrifices. In his banner year as a starter, 1971, he was among the league leaders in walks per nine innings, shutouts, and strikeouts to walks ratio. As a reliever he was on the league leader boards in saves twice, games finished three times, and games played once. To be fair he also made the league's top 10 nine times in negative categories; all occurring when he was a young starter pitching a lot of innings for a less than mediocre expansion team. His top 10 finishers included: once each in home runs and earned runs allowed; twice in hits allowed and losses; and three times in hit batsmen.

Rick Kreuger

by Bill Nowlin

	G	ERA	W	L	SV	GS	GF	CG	SHO	IP	H	R	ER	BB	HR	SO	BFP
1975 RED SOX	2	4.50	0	0	0	0	1	0	0	4	3	2	2	1	0	1	16

Rick Kreuger grew up in a blue-collar suburb of Grand Rapids named Wyoming, Michigan. He was born—the youngest of four children—on November 3, 1948 to his mother Leona, a homemaker, and his father Bernard, an electrician at the large General Motors assembly plant at Grand Rapids. Bernie Kreuger, in Rick's words, knew "enough about baseball, just enough about pitching, that he told me a couple of things to do. They turned out to be very important things." One lesson was to "throw every ball at the knees. And the second one was to point my toe and look pretty." Bernie Kreuger knew that form counted when you pitch. He knew that rhythm was important and told Rick to "point your toe with your kicking leg and look pretty. It held me back, and allowed me to lean into the plate with my hip."

There was an alley beside the Kreuger house and Bernie would catch his son's pitches whenever he could, starting when Rick was around seven or eight years old. When Rick was old enough for Little League. Neither Rick's older brother Tommy nor their twin sisters played baseball. Rick had the desire, though, and they lived not far from the front gate for Lee Field, the facility for Lee High School. It was a walk across the street to play sandlot ball.

When it came time for high school, Rick made the varsity baseball team as a pitcher while still a sophomore (freshmen were not eligible) at Catholic Central, a Class A high school. He transferred back to Lee High, though, a much smaller school, where he should have been among the top talent—but the coach at Lee High already had his players in mind and would not let Rick join the pitching staff. He made him play the outfield and throw batting practice, but never so much as granted him a tryout on the mound. "I begged him all through my junior year, and he would not let me pitch. And, senior year came and I was begging him again. So finally, I just said to him well, can I just have the ball and I'll throw on my own against the screen, because my dad had taught me just take a piece of rag and put it up on the screen and throw at it. So I started doing that, and apparently the athletic director or the caretaker saw me and told the athletic director who told the coach, 'Give this kid a chance.' So he let me start

a game against another small school [laughs]. And I pitched a one-hitter for five innings and he still took me out. It even came down to the last game of the year, and we're beating the heck out of this team, so everyone was taking a turn at pitching. And I said, 'Let me throw, I want to throw.' 'Nah, you don't want to throw against these guys.' Ironically, when I finished there, I went to [Grand Rapids] junior college as a nobody. But the coach mistook me for a different Kreuger. There were two Bob Kreugers from large schools that had graduated, and both were pitchers and I signed up and he said, 'Kreuger, Kreuger aren't you a pitcher?' And I said, 'Yep', but I was left-handed. But anyhow, from there I became an All-American and I got a scholarship to Michigan State."

After Grand Rapids Junior College, Rick went on to Michigan State and started off well, though a basketball ankle injury robbed him of almost his full junior year. A Detroit Tigers scout based in Grand Rapids named Bob Sullivan urged the coach to give Kreuger a try as a pitcher. MSU was losing to Notre Dame by something like 7–0 and Rick came in and held them for four or five innings, while Michigan came from behind to win the game. Kreuger also helped with a home run. He got off to a tremendous start his senior year; he recalls, "No one even had a hit off me in the spring." After building a 4–0 record, he developed mononucleosis, playing a rainy, sleety game against Central Michigan and a few hours on the bus back and forth. Depleted by the disease, Rick ended the season with a 5–3 mark and the scouts were no longer hovering around. So Rick pitched for the local team, the Grand Rapids Sullivans (Bob Sullivan was owner-manager). The team had tremendous success, traveling to the 1971 National Amateur Championship in Wichita, Kansas. "We went to the national tournament and we won the national title. And, I beat Alaska in the final game. And actually I signed, just before I pitched that game."

A veteran area scout for the Red Sox named Maurice DeLoof signed Kreuger to the Red Sox in 1971 while he was just finishing up at Michigan State. The Sox sent him to their high rookie league in Greenville, South Carolina and he did very well. In 1972 he was to go to spring training and to play with Winston-Salem but suffered an injury in the offseason that almost

ended his career. In between seasons, he had gone back to Michigan State to begin work on a graduate degree. He was playing "tough-guy football" with his fraternity brothers—no equipment, no protective padding—and he had a head-on collision with another player. Both were knocked unconscious. In spring training, the radiant pain was still there and he was unable to pitch. Sent back home, a surgeon diagnosed a ruptured disc and cut him open to repair it. Rick figured his career was over and got a position teaching high school mathematics.

It was sometime in the middle of 1973 that he unexpectedly heard from the Red Sox again. A letter arrived, saying that if he thought he could still pitch to show up at Winston-Salem. School was over, so he reported to the Red Sox. Ironically, the manager there hadn't been expecting him and asked Rick, "What are you doing here?" Rick explained about the letter, and so manager Bill Slack said, "Wait a minute, I'm checking this out with [farm director] Ed Kenney." He called Boston, then told Rick, "All right, yeah, I'm supposed to let you on the team . . . but we're not paying you until you pitch." He pitched soon in enough, put into a game he won in relief. He was put in the next game, too, and would have won that one but for an error behind him. The manager gave Kreuger a start and he won three shutouts in a row, contending for the league's scoreless innings record. "He loves me now, but I told him I had to go back early because I was coaching the freshman football team, at high school." Rick pitched the first game of the playoffs, won it, and hopped in his already-packed car. Just then the manager came out and pleaded with him to pitch the second game, too, because the scheduled pitcher had a sore arm. Kreuger told him, "I'll tell you what. I can go put my uniform back on and start this game for you and go four or five innings." He left the game, with a lead, after five. He left, the team went on to win the playoffs, but the Red Sox were sore. "How could you leave us?" They told him, "You have to make it to spring training or forget it."

Rick took a chance, and left his teaching job, and reported in the spring of 1974, jumping to Triple A. Rick threw 155 innings, and was 6–8 but with a very good 2.92 ERA. There were more twists and turns to come in his unusual career. He was called up to Boston at the end of '74 but didn't appear in any games that year. Then, in 1975, he might have made the team out of spring training had it not been for a last-minute Tony Conigliaro home run. As Rick tells the story, it was the last day of the spring. He packed his bags and the clubhouse guys loaded them on the truck headed to Boston. Conigliaro was trying to mount a comeback, but it was "the last game or second to last game of spring, and he hit like .130, but he hit this home run, three-run homer or something. And so they tell me the last day as we're getting ready to pull out, 'Rick, we've decided to take Tony with us to Boston. You're going have to go, you know, back.' I was just devastated.

"Well, ironically, Darrell Johnson's daughter was chasing me around then, right. And I knew, those guys would say, 'Stay away from her. Stay away from her.' So I stayed away from her, and I even told her so. But that last day, I was so devastated. I was with the guys in Triple A, drinking it up and kind of having my pity party and she calls up and wants me to go off with her somewhere. So we do. Next thing I know she's writing and she's telling her mother all about me. And I didn't know this until I was brought up to Boston. And Mrs. Johnson said, 'Oh yeah you're Rick Kreuger, Dara's told us all about you.' Those guys said it was the kiss of death. So the next thing I know is that winter, Darrell Johnson takes my big league contract away from me."

He did get called up in 1975 but both he and Jim Burton were pitching very well for Pawtucket and there was a choice to be made between them. Each pitched a game in a three-day stretch. Kreuger pitched a nine-inning shutout in the first game. "And everybody's going, 'Kreug, you're going to the big leagues, man!'" Two days later, Burton threw a seven-inning no-hitter. Burton got the call in June.

Kreuger got called up eventually, in September, and debuted in a blowout game on September 6, 1975. By the time he took over for Roger Moret, the Red Sox had a comfortable 20–4 lead and one can guess that most of the 11,992 had already left County Stadium. Kreuger retired the side in the eighth, but gave up three hits and two runs in the ninth. He only appeared in one other game that year, September 28, and threw a perfect sixth and seventh inning against the Indians at Fenway. Dick Pole and Jim Willoughby weren't as good that day, and the Indians won, 11–4.

He didn't make the playoff roster, but did get a $250 check as a World Series share.

By 1976, Kreuger's troubles with Darrell Johnson were over. "The Red Sox had had enough of him. I don't know if it was because of his drinking or whatever else, but, anyways they got rid of him. As soon as they got rid of him, they gave my contract back to me."

Kreuger was stuck behind Bill Lee in the Red Sox system, but he played under Joe Morgan in Pawtucket until he got a call up to the big league club. The last night before he was to report, though, Morgan put him

in a game against Rochester and, while covering first base on a ground ball, his foot got caught in a little hole and as Rick puts it: "I sprained the crap out of my ankle." His first appearance with Boston in 1976 was in August. He was given a start on the 17th in the second game of a doubleheader at Comiskey Park. He was pulled in the fourth inning, with the Red Sox ahead 6–2. An inherited run scored after Pole came in. Kreuger got in seven other games, including three other starts, and wound up with a 4.06 ERA in 31 innings, with a 2–1 record. His best game was the September 21 night start against Milwaukee at Fenway. Rick had a no-hitter going into the seventh inning, but lost the 3–1 complete game, a three-hitter.

In 1977, Rick was back at Pawtucket once more, not making Boston out of spring training. This year, he only appeared in one big league game. It was August 26 and the Red Sox and the Twins were tied, 4–4, after seven innings at Fenway Park. Kreuger took over for Don Aase, to pitch the eighth. He threw four pitches and never recorded an out. With two strikes on Rod Carew, he threw the pitch he wanted but Carew flicked a flare over Hobson at third and made it to second base for a double. "Lyman Bostock comes up and I'm still thinking about Carew, and I throw the first pitch right down the chute." Bostock hit it to right field, where Jim Rice was playing that day. Rice fired the ball to the plate but with so much force it flew over the plate and into the backstop net. Zimmer called on Bill Campbell to come in. He got the first two batters, but then Mike Cubbage singled home Bostock, and Kreuger was charged with two earned runs in zero innings pitched, and quite properly tagged with the loss. Those were his four major league pitches in 1977, and his last four for the Red Sox.

Zimmer wasn't pleased. "He threw me in the bullpen after that, never to be heard from again." Ferguson Jenkins was banished to the bullpen, too. "Fergie was on such bad terms with Zimmer that he was actually sleeping out in the bullpen. He knew he was not going to pitch. So I started calling him 'Juan' and he started calling me 'Four Pitch,' because I only got four pitches in." Rick Kreuger was one of the Buffalo Heads, the group of Boston ballplayers that didn't get along well with manager Zimmer. "I was right in there with them."

Kreuger may have tweaked Zimmer a bit, too. Acting apparently on his own, he chose to warm up in the bullpen, and did so for 10 days in a row, hoping to get Zimmer's attention. He was "trying to get him to have to call me into his office or something, you know.

And he wouldn't say 'boo' to me. And the fans start saying, 'Hey Rick can we help you?' 'Yeah, put a sign out there that says "Kreuger Lives." So they put a sign out there, and by the 10th day, they say, well, 'Is there anything else we can do for you?' 'Yeah, add a word.' So they put a second sign that says, 'Kreuger Still Lives.'" The fan support likely didn't help Kreuger's cause, but it was probably a lost cause to begin with. "Zimmer was never Mr. Communication. I was a fun-loving left hander and not a blood and guts football player like he liked. Butch Hobson was perfect for Don Zimmer. Bill Lee and I were the complete opposites [of that]."

In spring training 1978, Rick says that Ted Williams approached him and asked him why he wasn't pitching in the big leagues. Kreuger told him that Zimmer seemed to have it in for him. "I became friends with Ted that spring. He would hit me fungoes and stuff. I think he took a liking to me and wanted to see if he could get me a break." He credits Ted for helping engineer a trade to the Indians in March 1978. The Red Sox got Frank Duffy in the exchange.

Kreuger appeared in six early-season games for the Indians, but he made his last major league appearance on May 7. Rick retired the only two batters he faced that day before being assigned to Portland in the Pacific Coast League, where he appeared in 37 games, carrying a 2.74 ERA.

In 1979, he signed out of spring training with Tokyo's Yomiuru Giants to play in Japan. He was 2–1 with a 4.66 ERA with the Giants, but it was a frustrating year, experiencing the oft-reported prejudice against gaijin (foreign) players in Japan, even finding his own catcher calling pitches that saw Kreuger throwing to a batter's strength instead of to his weakness. He stewed, and began to look like he might become a little controversial. "It felt strange being the center of prejudice," he recalls, but he had become a born-again Christian in the fall of 1977, during his last year with the Red Sox. "I made that commitment, but I had never been tested before." The strength he found in Christianity helped see him through a difficult time. Finally the team offered to pay his full salary if he would leave the team and go home. On one of his last nights there, one of the Giants' veteran pitchers invited Rick to his home and apologized to him privately. "And I said, Wow! I feel like I'm sane again."

After returning to the States, Felix Millan invited Kreuger to Puerto Rico and he played there with the Caguas Criollos. "Jim Bunning became the manager of the team; we finished second, but I had the best earned run average in the whole league. I got let go from that team because they wanted to bring Dennis Martinez

in for the playoffs." Bunning and Kreuger didn't click. "Him and I didn't hit off good. Any time I seemed to run into a blood and guts type manager who was overly serious, we just didn't communicate very well. They always thought that I was kind of goofing off, when it was just a style thing. I was more of a free spirit and they didn't like it. Don Zimmer was the same way. My manager Joe Morgan at Triple A, at first he was a little the same way, but then he got to know me and then he loved me."

The Cleveland Indians sent Rick a contract, inviting him to spring training with their Triple A affiliate, but Rick wasn't ready for a life of Triple A ball in the summer and working other jobs in the winter, so he walked away from baseball. He became a real estate broker and did well with that for a number of years, three years in residential real estate and 13 years in commercial. In 1996 and 1997, he served as head baseball coach at Cornerstone College, a Christian college, until they dropped their baseball program. When that position ended, Rick prayed for a day at his church, hoping for guidance on what he might do next, only to come home and get a call from a man who knew him from church. The man was starting a Little League team and offered Rick a job instructing the pitchers on the team. The local paper covered the story and from that grew a new sideline. In 1998, Rick founded Kreuger's Baseball School (www.kreugerbaseball.com) based right in Wyoming, Michigan. The school has worked with kids as young as seven years old all the way up to working with some pro players. For the past four years, he has been teaching eighth grade mathematics at a local school in Walker, Michigan, Walker Charter Academy.

Kreuger has done some missionary work, traveling to Russia and talked to children in orphanages and to soldiers. He has also gone on a couple of mission trips with former Cleveland Browns tackle Bill Glass. They visited prisons in Pittsburgh and Florida. "I'd throw baseballs and pitch them to the prisoners and then talk to them about faith. It was kind of fun. They would come out to bat off of me, but they wouldn't come out to listen to somebody on a soapbox. It was a different avenue to reach those prisoners."

Rick's daughter Sarah plays fast-pitch softball. "She has the best arm on her team," Rick asked in response to a question. "She threw five girls out at home plate from center field on her freshman team last year. And no girl has ever done that."

Rick Kreuger is content with his life, but there are concerns. He is one of a large number of former major league players who are excluded to one degree or another from the major league pension plan and he is one of 1,053 major league alumni pursuing a class action suit. (Details can be found at www.baseballpension.com.)

Rick still receives regular mailings from the Red Sox as part of their alumni program, and he occasionally comes across former teammates like Bill Lee. Some years ago, he joined Bill at the Senior World Series in Arizona, and almost won a game there one year, losing 1–0 in extra innings.

He enjoys watching the Detroit Tigers play, because he gets the local broadcasts and can better analyze the play, but he still follows the Red Sox most of all. "You become a Red Sox, and it's kind of like you're part of such a history there." With the Sox success in 2004, he was pleased, but there remains a wistfulness of sorts occasioned by the way things worked out in his own time with the Red Sox. "It's kind of bittersweet in the sense you were part of the team, and yet you were never allowed to be part of that team."

Diego Segui

by Joanne Hulbert

	G	ERA	W	L	SV	GS	GF	CG	SHO	IP	H	R	ER	BB	HR	SO	BFP
1975 RED SOX	33	4.82	2	5	6	1	24	1	0	71.0	71	41	38	43	10	45	316

On the evening of October 16, 1975, in the eighth inning of Game Five of the World Series, the Red Sox trailed the Reds, 5–1. In the bottom of the eighth, Dick Pole walked Johnny Bench and Tony Perez. Diego Segui, one of Boston's two Cuban pitchers, replaced him and inherited a tough situation with two men on, no outs, George Foster advancing to the plate, and a crowd of 50,000 not satisfied with the comfortable lead. Later, Dick Pole was asked what he thought about while out there during the few minutes of his World Series mound appearance. He said it was exactly what he didn't want to have happen, and he'd have to live with that memory.

No one asked Diego Segui about his own performance, about how Foster—a formidable hitter

during the regular season—hit a fly out to Dwight Evans, with Bench moving over to third and Perez waiting it out on first, how Dave Concepcion drove home Bench with his own fly to Evans, and Cesar Geronimo flew out to Fred Lynn to end the inning.

Yet there is little glory in it for the relief pitcher. Their brief mound appearances provide scant inspiration to reporters prowling for after-game stories. Diego Segui had traveled a long way in major league baseball before he found himself on the mound in his only World Series appearance, and yet there is a great story to be told about him.

Born August 17, 1937—or 1938 by other reports—in Holguin, Cuba, "la tierra de campeones," Diego Segui was first signed by the Cincinnati Reds as an amateur free agent early in 1958 after he was discovered by scout Al Zarilla while playing for Tucson's independent club. Released in April, Diego played for Tucson that year and was purchased at the end of September by the Kansas City Athletics. The next four seasons he pitched for minor league clubs and spent winters with teams around Central America and Venezuela, prompting concern that he would squander his pitching arm on meaningless games, instead of saving it for the major leagues. But he considered the off-season an opportunity to stay in shape. When Fidel Castro cancelled the Cuban Winter League season in 1961, players were confronted with a choice between returning to Cuba and joining amateur leagues or professional baseball outside their homeland. Among the notable players who did not return were Tony Oliva, Jose Cardenal, Cookie Rojas, and Frank Herrera.

In 1960, American players had been barred from playing in games in Havana because the Winter League had long attracted many major league prospects. Cuban sports commissioner Jose Llanura struck the final blow in 1961 when he announced that any Cuban player who failed to return to Cuba by the end of November would lose all his property and be required to have their 1962 contracts in order to receive a visa. Among those who chose to remain outside Cuba and pursue their major league aspirations were Luis Tiant with the Mexico City Tigers and Diego Segui, the ERA leader for Hawaii of the Pacific League.

Segui worked his way through the Athletics minor league system until the 1962 season when he joined the Kansas City Athletics, finishing 8–5 in 37 games. After three more years as a starting pitcher for a dreadful team, Segui was sold to the Washington Senators as the 1966 season got underway and was reacquired by the Athletics (for pitcher Jim Duckworth) on July 30

of the same season. At the time of the latter deal he was pitching in the minors, and he finished the season for Vancouver, the A's Pacific Coast League affiliate. He spent most of the 1967 and 1968 seasons with the Athletics, who moved to Oakland for the 1968 season.

Segui's best year on the mound was with the Seattle Pilots, the 1969 expansion team made famous by Jim Bouton in *Ball Four*. Finley had good reason to regret giving up Segui—believing the A's would have won the American League West division if he'd kept him on—as Segui was named Seattle's most valuable player. He spent most of the season trying to get him back. When the Pilots folded and the team moved on to Milwaukee, Segui returned to Oakland for the third time. Seattle would not forget him.

> Diego Pablo Segui
> You're not what you're s'posed to be
> Instead of the raves
> From the A's for your saves,
> It's your starts which have caused all the glee.
> —*The Sporting News*, August 15, 1970

The Athletics reacquired Segui (with Ray Oyler) for George Lauzerique and Ted Kubiak in December 1969. The A's intended to turn him into their primary right-handed reliever, but his fine performance earned him 19 starts among his 47 games pitched. His repertoire of pitches and mound quirks exasperated batters and umpires. He took his time, rubbed the ball between each pitch, and defended himself against allegations of using a spitball when he blew on his hands. He took leisurely strolls around the edge of the mound while blowing through his right fist, and re-arranged the dirt in front of the pitcher's rubber with his right foot. At times he paused between pitches by standing still, staring at the outfield while working on the ball, in deep contemplation as tension at home plate rose to an unnerving level. Joe Garagiola criticized his pitching performance before the 1975 World Series and described Segui's delivery as "like spreading ether over the ballpark," prompting the outraged pitcher to confront Garagiola before Game Five and attempt to get an apology out of him for the insult. His teams put up with his rituals as they valued his work ethic and variety of pitches. He never complained whether he was a reliever, a starter, or called in for only part of an inning. And he could throw a very decent forkball.

"It acts like a screwie," Segui attempted to explain. "It drops and sometimes acts like a screw-ball—sometimes."

He learned to throw the elusive forkball at a farm in Cuba, where a left-handed pitcher from a semi-pro team taught him to throw the traditional southpaw pitch. In a Cuban cow pasture he perfected his signature pitch, called the "tenedor." But was Segui's forkball truly a forkball? Or was it a Pedro Ramos "Cuban forkball," a pitch that was suspected to be a spitball? After all, the doubters hinted, he spent such a long time working over the ball before the windup. Such an accusation was vehemently denied by Diego.

"Definitely not!" he said, "maybe it reacts a little like a spitter, but it isn't."

After two-and-a-half fine seasons in Oakland, on June 7, 1972, the A's sent Segui to the Cardinals for future considerations. Segui played the next year and a half for St. Louis.

On December 7, 1973, the Red Sox traded pitcher John Curtis, Mike Garman, and Lynn McGlothen to St. Louis for Segui, Reggie Cleveland and Terry Hughes. The Red Sox were in dire need of some bullpen help, and asked those in the know around the National League who were the best right-handed relievers. Segui's name came up frequently enough to corroborate the scouting report from Haywood Sullivan and Frank Malzone.

Although many within the Red Sox organization looked forward to his arrival in the bullpen, Diego Segui wondered. As the MVP of the Pilots in 1969, an ERA leader in the American League in 1970, and owning respectable stats overall, why was he trade material year after year? In a March 1974 interview with *Boston Globe* reporter Clif Keane during spring training at Winter Haven, Segui said: "I sit and wonder each time that I have been traded, have I done something wrong? Did I not get along with the people? Why don't they like me, so that I have to go from one team to another so much? If you are confused about it, you can say that I am more confused than anyone else."

Segui pitched regularly early in the season with great success. By early June he developed calluses on two fingers of his throwing hand, causing a control problem that would nag him until late August. An epidemic of bumps, bruises and sore shoulders swept through Boston's bullpen forcing the starters into leading the league in complete games. In early September, he lost a couple of crucial games in late innings and ended up the season with a 6–8 record and 10 saves. Nevertheless, Darrell Johnson expressed confidence in Segui's ability to come back in 1975 in good condition.

Segui returned to the Boston roster for the 1975 season with his place in the bullpen assured. Confident that his pitching would be solid; there was no need to worry. Without comment nor complaint he resumed his role as a short reliever, willing to pitch whenever or wherever he was needed. When Luis Tiant's shoulder came up lame in July, Segui was ready to jump in as a starter, a role he had not played since May, 1972. It was July 29, and Diego lost a complete game, 4–0, to Milwaukee's Jim Colborn. "He [Segui] pitched a hell of a game," said Darrell Johnson. He gave up 10 hits, but struck out 11. Three solo home runs, two to Don Money and one to Darrell Porter, were the key blows.

Throughout the 1975 season, the Red Sox pitchers kept everyone on edge. Bill Lee and Diego Segui didn't want the paying customers to be bored, wrote Peter Gammons in the *Boston Globe*. Yet, the hitting, fielding and pitching brought the team to an American League pennant as well as the World Series, and Diego Segui made his one and only appearance on the mound at the World Series in the eighth inning of Game Five.

Just prior to the start of the 1976 season, Segui was released. He enjoyed the two years he played in Boston, according to Luis Tiant. "He is like a brother to me," he said. "We still call each other all the time, our wives are still very good friends."

He was not picked up by another major league team and instead signed with the Hawaii Islanders of the Pacific Coast League. In September, he was suspended by the club after a legal entanglement over money he claimed was owed him. When the newly-formed Seattle Mariners organized their roster, Segui's memorable year with the Pilots was recalled, and he not only made the team, but was anointed the Opening Day starter. On April 5, 1977, Segui faced the Angels with a crowd of over 57,000 in the Kingdome loudly applauding his return to Seattle. The win was not to be his, the Angels shut out the Mariners in their inaugural game, 7–0.

Over and over, Segui tried but could not get his pitches to sing again for him. His arm, that arm that he once called "the funniest one in the world" was not giving him much to smile about. He finished the 1977 season without a victory, but with seven defeats and an ERA of 5.69. He had some good moments that year, like when he struck out 10 Red Sox, a record that stayed on the Mariner's books for a long time. He tried so hard to make his famous forkball work, but it remained incorrigible, and his year with the Mariners had an unfortunate ending when he was released. After 20 years in professional baseball, he was without a job. He wanted to continue the work he had spent most of his life practicing, and since he had a family to provide for, he returned again to the minor leagues with the hope he could work his way back.

In 1978 he had a very successful year with Cordoba, Mexico, where, in his 21st year of professional pitching he achieved the first no-hitter of his long career and did it, no less, with a perfect game. Diego Segui would not have any more major league service, but there was another Segui working his way up. His second son, David, was showing interest and talent in baseball. He became a first baseman for the Baltimore Orioles in 1990. A part of Diego Segui had returned to major league baseball.

There are baseball players who earn fame from their statistics, for achieving great things on the field, and they can leave their mark upon sports history in any number of ways. Diego Segui has done so. Other players may be merely a footnote, or notable as an answer to some obscure baseball trivia question. Diego Segui can claim that as well. In 1984, when the crew of the space shuttle Discovery was circling Earth, the ground crew at the Johnson Space Center in Houston made baseball trivia a routine part of the program in order to keep the astronauts' minds sharp with something to ponder other than keeping the shuttle aloft. Reporters at NBC Sports in New York also had a hand in feeding questions to the shuttle crew, and they all sent questions they were sure would stump them. When the astronauts returned, they cornered George Abbey, director of the flight crew operations, their baseball trivia nemesis—and a native of Seattle—and challenged him with their own question. Who was the only man ever to play for both the Seattle Pilots and the Seattle Mariners?

"I told him it was Gorman Thomas," said Abbey. "In fact, I insisted that it was Gorman. But now I'm not so sure it wasn't Diego Segui."

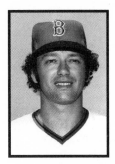

Jim Willoughby

by Jon Daly

	G	ERA	W	L	SV	GS	GF	CG	SHO	IP	H	R	ER	BB	HR	SO	BFP
1975 RED SOX	24	3.54	5	2	8	0	15	0	0	48.1	46	25	19	16	6	29	208

James Arthur Willoughby is best known for his contribution to the 1975 Boston Red Sox (including being pinch hit for in Game Seven of the World Series). Willoughby, a right-handed pitcher, also played for the San Francisco Giants and the Chicago White Sox.

"Willow," as he was often called, was born in Salinas, California, on January 31, 1949 (the same date as Fred Kendall, briefly his Bosox teammate in 1975). He has two younger sisters, Marcy and Beverly. Son of James Roger Willoughby, a noted scuba diver, and Marlene Dickison, he takes pride in having three-eighths Pottawatomi blood in addition to British ancestry. In fact, his great-aunt Mamie Echo Hawk served as the tribe's chief lobbyist for years in Washington. (A later Red Sox hurler, John Henry Johnson, also had some Pottawatomi blood.)

Willoughby was raised in the San Joaquin valley town of Gustine, California, but grew up a Yankees fan because his mother came from Mickey Mantle's home state of Oklahoma. As a youth, Willow also particularly admired Jim Thorpe and Satchel Paige.

Jim played both Little League and Colt baseball. While attending high school in Gustine, he played four years of varsity baseball and American Legion ball, two years of basketball, and had one year of track. Football was Jim's second-best sport. He played split end for two years. The University of California at Berkeley recruited him for football, but Jim was drafted out of Gustine High by the San Francisco Giants in the 11th round of the June 1967 draft, being picked right after "the Mad Hungarian," Al Hrabosky.

Jim faced a tough decision. Under NCAA rules at the time, he would forfeit his eligibility to play football for the Cal Golden Bears if he played baseball professionally. His family was of modest means and he wanted to attend college; a football scholarship would have afforded him the opportunity to do so. When Giants scout Dick Wilson offered him participation in the Professional Baseball Scholarship Program as part of his signing package, Jim signed with the San Francisco organization.

Willoughby pitched for Salt Lake, Fresno, Medford and Phoenix in the Giants' system all the while pursuing a degree in electrical engineering. As part of his scholarship plan, he spent the 1967–1968 off-season at Cal-Berkeley; he also took classes at Fresno State, Phoenix College and the College of San Mateo.

It was an interesting time to go to college in the Bay Area. Jim would sometimes drive his convertible with a roommate to Golden Gate Park and see bands such as Creedence Clearwater Revival, Jefferson Airplane, Big Brother and The Holding Company, and Country Joe and The Fish. Jim never finished his degree work; he remains a few credits shy of a bachelor's degree.

Willow was also a chess player—at one point, a rated member at the Burlingame Chess Club in California. During his baseball career, his opponents included fellow moundsman Steve Stone and sportscaster Dick Stockton. According to Peter Gammons, when Stockton was asked to compare Willoughby's chess-playing style to that of Boston Celtics guard Paul Westphal, Stockton replied, "Willoughby is a gambler. Westphal is very conservative."

For 1967, Jim was assigned to the Salt Lake City Giants in the Pioneer League, where he appeared in 17 games. Willoughby was still in school at the start of the 1968 season. After he finished his finals on a Friday, he got married to high school sweetheart Mary Ann Ryan on Saturday, started his honeymoon on Sunday, and got into a car accident on Monday. According to Jim in an email to the author, "I smacked my face on the windshield (I reported with two shiners!), but strained my pitching arm (both arms) by absorbing the impact with the steering wheel." He was assigned to Fresno for 1968, but he was ineffective, so he was demoted to Medford for most of the season.

In June 1969, again pitching for Fresno, Willoughby was named the player of the month for the California League. He was also named to the circuit's year-end All-Star squad. Unfortunately, he injured his right elbow that year with several weeks left in the season and had to pay a visit to Dr. Frank Jobe in Los Angeles. When the Giants knew he was healthy, they added him to the 40-man roster. But he wound up pitching for Phoenix in the Class Triple A Pacific Coast League in 1970 and led PCL pitchers in assists with 36. Willoughby had always been fascinated by spaceships—both the real and science fiction varieties—and got into model rocketry during his Phoenix years. After the season, Jim pitched in the autumn Arizona Instructional League. He returned to Phoenix in the Pacific Coast League in 1971, and made the Pacific Coast League All-Star squad that year with a 14–9 record. Best of all, he was called up to the parent San Francisco Giants on August 30.

It's a treat for any player when they first make the majors. In Doug Hornig's *The Boys of October*, Willoughby recalled arriving in the dugout for his first major league game. There were two coolers. One had water, but the other one had "red juice," a liquid amphetamine concoction. Willow tried to take a drink from the wrong cooler and was quickly chastised. "Red juice" was for veterans; not rookies. He appeared in two September games for San Francisco; the first was a three-inning start against Houston, which he lost.

1972 saw Willow's third tour of duty with Phoenix, but he was called up again to San Francisco August 3 when a sore shoulder placed "Sudden Sam" McDowell on the 21-day disabled list. Three days after his arrival, Jim extracted revenge on the Astros for that debut-start loss the year before by recording his first major league victory against them, a 6–2 Giants win in the nightcap of a doubleheader. Willoughby started 10 more games for San Francisco and finished the season with a 6–4 record and a very good 2.36 ERA. The Giants themselves finished the season in fifth place in the National League West Division, 17 games below .500.

Willow was a groundball pitcher who relied on a sinker and a slider and was more effective when he threw from a three-quarters arm slot or sidearm instead of throwing overhand. Willoughby used a slow curve roughly 10 percent of the time as well. He had what was described as a "herky jerky" motion. He had small hands for a pitcher, despite a 6′2″, 205-lb. frame.

During the off-season the Giants harbored high hopes for Willoughby in 1973 and penciled him into a five-man rotation along with Juan Marichal, McDowell, Tom Bradley and Ron Bryant. Obeying the new rule of Giants manager Charlie Fox, Willoughby shaved off the mustache he wore in 1972. Wearing number 42, Willoughby indeed began the season in the starting rotation, but by mid-May the Giants moved him to the bullpen. One of the problems Jim experienced with the Giants was that manager Fox and pitching coach Don McMahon tried to get him to throw harder; this caused him to throw more over the top. While Willoughby got more velocity, he lost movement on his pitches, making them flatter—and more hittable. Willoughby worked most of the rest of 1973 out of the bullpen, compiling a 4–5 record and a 4.68 ERA. Toward the end of the year, he studied motion pictures of his delivery and corrected it by dropping down more. "There's so much Cinderella in this game." Willoughby once said. "When I was going bad with the Giants and had changed my whole way of throwing, I had to get work. But when you're in the bullpen, you often aren't in the best throwing shape and the whole thing snowballs. One bad outing and you don't work for a couple of weeks, and when you get back, you're completely out of whack."

Willoughby pitched winter ball in Venezuela during the off-season with the Marcay club, managed by Giants scout Ozzie Virgil. Willow had wanted to go

to Venezuela the previous winter, but he'd worked a combined 250-plus innings between Phoenix and San Francisco. In 1973 he had pitched only 123 innings, and felt he needed more work. After finishing in Venezuela with an 8–7 record and an ERA under 3.00, Willoughby wanted another shot at the San Francisco starting rotation in 1974. According to the March 3, 1974 *New York Times*, Willoughby said, "They can have all that long relief stuff they want. After I fell out of the rotation last year, they tried me 'long' and during one spell I went 18 days without getting close to the mound." [Editor's note: from May 18 to June 3, he went 15 days without playing.]

But Willoughby got only four starts and 40 innings of work in San Francisco in 1974 (1–4, 4.61 ERA) before being outrighted to Phoenix once more. After the end of the season he was traded to St. Louis in a minor-league deal for infielder Tom Heintzelman. He expected to be invited to spring training with the Cardinals, but Jim wound up starting the season with the Tulsa Oilers in the American Association under manager Ken Boyer. This proved beneficial as minor-league pitching instructor Bob Milliken helped straighten out his delivery.

Willoughby was thrilled to meet one of his idols in Tulsa. Satchel Paige served both as a part-time pitching coach and a greeter at Oiler Field. Willow pitched well in Tulsa; well enough for Boston Red Sox general manager Dick O'Connell to select him July 4 as the "player to named later" to complete a springtime deal in which the Cardinals had received shortstop Mario Guerrero. Boston was on the way to its first pennant since the 1967 Impossible Dream season, but the Sox needed bullpen help. Dick Drago was having shoulder problems due to overwork and Dick Pole had recently been hit in the face by a Tony Muser line drive. Oilers manager Boyer recommended Jim Willoughby and, when executive scout Eddie Kasko visited Tulsa in 1975, he was impressed with the right hander.

Jim had never been a short man out of the bullpen before, but he took to it like a duck to water. In 24 appearances with 48⅓ innings pitched, Willoughby compiled 5 wins, 2 losses, 8 saves, and a 3.56 ERA. His first outing with the Red Sox was rocky, though. In the July 6 nightcap against Cleveland, he gave up a three-run homer to Oscar Gamble. Jim was fortunate in that Boston's bullpen was depleted at the time. They needed live arms and didn't have the option of burying him. He did not pitch in the American League Championship Series against Oakland, but he appeared in Games Three, Five, and Seven of the World Series against the Big Red Machine of Cincinnati. Willoughby was on

the mound in the 10th inning of Game Three when Ed Armbrister bunted and may have interfered with Carlton Fisk. In a controversial decision, the umpiring crew did not call Armbrister out for interference. This allowed Cesar Geronimo, who was on first, to advance to third and Armbrister to advance to second. Roger Moret, who intentionally walked Pete Rose to load the bases, replaced Willoughby. After Merv Rettenmund struck out, Joe Morgan hit a single over Fred Lynn's head to win the game for the Reds. After a mop-up assignment in Game Five, Willoughby was called on to put out a fire in the Game Seven. The score was tied 3–3 in the top of the seventh inning. The bases were loaded and there were two outs with Johnny Bench at the plate. Willoughby was able to induce Bench to pop up in foul territory to catcher Carlton Fisk. Willoughby then pitched a 1-2-3 eighth inning. In the bottom of the inning, though, with none on, two out and the score still tied, manager Darrell Johnson pulled Willoughby for a pinch hitter, the rusty Cecil Cooper. Cooper popped up to Pete Rose in foul territory.

Jim Burton, the rookie hurler who succeeded Willoughby, wound up giving up a run in the ninth and losing both the game and the Series. A story that has grown into a piece of urban folklore among Red Sox fans tells of a sportswriter going into a Boston area watering hole sometime after the World Series and encountering a solitary drinker mumbling to himself about Darrell Johnson, "He never should have hit for Willoughby." Peter Gammons is one who has spun that tale.

Johnson would not have had to pinch-hit for Willoughby had the designated hitter rule been in effect during the '75 Series. In fact, l'affaire Willoughby–Cooper–Burton may have led Major League Baseball toward adopting the designated hitter in the World Series in alternating years. This rule was in place until 1985, when it was modified so that the DH was always used in American League parks but not in National League parks.

In 1976, with Dick Drago being sent packing to California, Willoughby was the main short man out of the Boston bullpen for the whole season. While his record was an unfortunate 3–12, Willow pitched well. He recorded 10 saves and his ERA dropped to 2.82. The Red Sox failed to defend their American League East pennant and Darrell Johnson was replaced in midseason by third base coach Don Zimmer. As Willoughby's teammate Bill Lee has recounted, most notably in his book *The Wrong Stuff*, there was a culture clash between baseball lifer Zimmer and some of his players—a group of unconventional types

known as the Buffalo Heads whose number included Lee, Willoughby, Ferguson Jenkins, Rick Wise and Bernie Carbo. These young players came of age in the turbulent and countercultural 1960s and held a distinctly different worldview than that of Zimmer, a product of the Depression era. Zimmer rarely, if ever, drank and liked to spend his free time at the racetrack. The Buffalo Heads were more educated, were fans of rock music (which hadn't achieved the mainstream acceptance that it has today), and both drank and experimented with other drugs. Willoughby himself smoked pot and drank heavily, although he never took the mound drunk or stoned.

Willoughby was upset at the end of the 1976 season when outgoing assistant general manager John Claiborne admitted the Red Sox had private detectives tailing their players that season. But what really upset Willow was learning from a coach about the existence of written reports and learning that anyone with access to the locker room could have stumbled upon the reports.

1976 was the bicentennial of the United States' declaration of independence from Great Britain, but it also marked the independence of ballplayers from the reserve clause. It was the dawn of the age of free agency. In the offseason, the Red Sox signed Bill Campbell as their bullpen ace. Campbell had been with the Minnesota Twins and made it from Vietnam to a factory league to the majors. With Campbell on board, Willoughby's role was reduced. He spent time on the disabled list for the first time in the majors. On May 22, he slipped in the outfield during pre-game drills and broke his right ankle. He returned in August, but was less effective, posting a 4.91 ERA, his highest ever in the majors (not counting those four innings in 1971). Though the Red Sox finished just 2½ games behind the Yankees in an exciting pennant race, management cleaned house over the winter.

Before the first pitch was thrown in 1978, the Red Sox traded Fergie Jenkins to the Texas Rangers for John Poloni and cash, Rick Wise was traded with prospects to the Cleveland Indians in a deal that netted Dennis Eckersley, and Jim Willoughby was sold at the end of spring training to the White Sox for a figure barely over the waiver price. (Bernie Carbo was sold to Cleveland in mid-season, and Bill Lee, who staged a walkout after the Carbo sale, was traded to Montreal for Stan Papi, prompting graffiti artists in the Boston area to ask, "Who is Stan Papi?") According to Jim, he had never been officially informed by the Red Sox of his sale to Chicago. Peter Gammons of the *Boston Globe* was the one who broke the news to him.

The popular perception is that Don Zimmer broke up the Buffalo Heads because he didn't like those players. Zimmer was also perceived as not liking pitchers as a class due to the several beanings he received during his playing days. While there may have been some truth to this, there may have been other reasons that the Red Sox cleaned house.

Long time Red Sox owner Tom Yawkey passed away during the 1976 season. After his estate settled, the team was purchased by a partnership consisting of his widow, Jean R. Yawkey, former trainer Buddy LeRoux, and scouting director Haywood Sullivan. One result of this was the October 4, 1977, firing of general manager Dick O'Connell, whom Mrs. Yawkey disliked. Another was an attempt to maximize short-term profits at the expense of long-term success. LeRoux, for example, borrowed money to buy his stake in the team and needed profits from the Red Sox to cover his debt service. Plus, the ownership group received tax depreciation advantages for a limited number of years and looked to hold down expenses during that timeframe. The front office staff was slashed. Veteran players were let go in favor of players who were not eligible for salary arbitration and could approximate their production at a lower cost. While some were traded for other players, others were merely sold for cash to better the bottom line. In Jim Willoughby's particular case, he was a Buffalo Head pitcher, relatively expensive for a middle reliever, and a Dick O'Connell acquisition; so he had three strikes against him.

In any case, the curly-haired Willow joined Bill Veeck and Roland Hemond's 1978 White Sox squad. After winning 90 games in 1977, the Chisox proved disappointing, losing 90 in 1978. Willoughby started the season as the ace out of the bullpen, but as the season wore on he appeared less frequently as Lerrin LaGrow took that role. Frustrated with his lack of playing time, Jim asked the Chisox to play him or trade him. They obliged, sending him to the Cardinals once again for speedy outfielder John Scott on October 23.

The Cardinals released him March 30, 1979, and Willoughby signed on with Wichita in the Cubs system. His contract with Wichita allowed Jim to request his release if he wasn't called up to Chicago by the trading deadline. After the Cubs traded for Dick Tidrow, Willoughby asked for, and was granted, his release. He searched for another pitching job and found one in Portland, Oregon, the Pittsburgh Pirates Triple A affiliate. Jim eventually wound up getting summoned to the parent club as bullpen insurance, but never saw any action in a game. He did, however, receive a $250

World Series share from the "We Are Family" Bucs. Jim pitched the entire 1979 season with undiagnosed Type I diabetes; the type that usually strikes people much earlier than their late twenties. He was unaware of it until he went down to Venezuela to play winter ball and wound up in a diabetic coma. It was neither lengthy nor deep, but he was laid up in the hospital for a brief period of time. At this point, he retired from pitching. He said that he could have continued, but he was tired of the journeyman ballplayer's life.

After his baseball career, Willoughby did a stint in sports radio. He did a talk show in Waltham, Massachusetts, but he didn't care to invest the amount of time required to properly prepare for the broadcasts. In December 1980, he was named baseball coach at Suffolk University, but didn't last a whole season. He resigned in April after he was suspended for a bat-throwing incident during practice. He also explained that he found the politics at Suffolk worse than in any major league clubhouse that he experienced.

Willoughby moved back to his native California, where he worked construction until he got his contractor's license. Since then, he's been building houses on the western slope of the Sierra Nevadas.

Jim did get the opportunity to return to the pitcher's mound. In 1989 and 1990, he participated in the Senior Professional Baseball Association. First, he had a chance to reunite with some of the other Buffalo Heads with the Winter Haven Super Sox. Bill Lee was the player-manager, Fergie Jenkins was the pitching coach, and Bernie Carbo was a teammate. In 1990, Willoughby pitched for the San Bernardino Pride. It was the first time in his professional career that Jim

pitched since giving up alcohol; Willoughby, by his own admission, is a recovering alcoholic and stopped drinking in 1983. Because of this, Jim felt an affinity with one of his boyhood idols, Jim Thorpe, who, in addition to being a fellow Native American, also had a drinking problem.

Willoughby doesn't play chess much anymore, but he does spend time with one of his other hobbies: motorcycles. He acquired a fondness for motorcycles from his father, riding on the gas tank of his father's bike when he was a child. Jim and his third wife, Sandy, go on at least one long ride each summer.

Jim divorced Mary Ann Ryan in the late 1970s. She is the mother of his two sons, Trevor and Ryan. It was what Willoughby described as "a classic case of baseball divorce." He was married for six years to Boston-area attorney Cathy Cullen, but his problems with alcoholism ended that marriage. He has been married to Sandra Aubert since 1984.

Son Trevor played baseball for four years at California State-Fullerton. Ryan played basketball in high school but suffered from bad knee injuries.

In describing himself at his Web site (jimwilloughby. com), this is what Willoughby had to say: "I played professional baseball for 15 years spanning four decades. I drank enough, smoked enough, snorted enough stuff to kill me. I lost several dear friends like that. Yet, like one of my idols, Ozzie (Osbourne, not Nelson), I survived. Here I am today: 20 years of total sobriety thanks to my friends in AA. I am building houses, riding motorcycles, shooting guns, voting Republican. I'm happy, some say crazy. My buddy Bill Lee, The Spaceman, used to say it's better to be crazy than insane, I agree."

THE BULLPEN: Notes

1. *Boston Globe* October 2, 1974.
2. *The Sporting News* August 13, 1977: 34.
3. The author recalls the 'Drago Segui' anecdote in a Boston newspaper at the time but has been unable to locate the exact citation.
4. *Boston Herald* June 24, 1974.
5. Giuliotti, Joe. "Sox' Reliever Drago Rates Among Best in A.L." *Boston Herald* September 28, 1975.
6. Ibid.
7. *Boston Globe* October 6, 1975.
8. Drago's bloody stocking was reported by Peter Gammons, *Boston Globe* October 9, 1975.
9. Reds manager Sparky Anderson called Evans' catch the greatest he had ever seen. See "Evans Sensational Catch Balks Reds." *San Francisco Examiner* October 22, 1975, cited in Tom Adelman's *The Long Ball*, page 352.
10. Whiteside, Larry. "Lee Says Red Sox are Getting Rid of Critics." *Boston Globe* March 20, 1976.
11. Ribowsky, Mike. "Scoring from the Dugout." *TV Guide* May 3, 1980: 17.
12. "Drago pitches in for friend", *Boston Herald*, July 18, 1978.
13. Drago's reaction to this trade is found in an undocumented article dated April 9, 1981 found in the clipping file at the Hall of Fame.
14. Drago's story of his difficulties is characterized by Doug Hornig in his book *The Boys of October*, Chicago, IL: Contemporary Books, 2003: 93–97.
15. Interview with Dick Drago, October 1, 2005.
16. Crehan, Herb. "Dick Drago." *Red Sox Magazine* Sixth Edition (September) 2005.

H. F. Seaman

SPORTS EDITOR SAYS:

Red Sox Feel More Heat From Orioles

Sox end mini-slump, head into B... with a si...

SPORT...

Johnson

this 7-4 Red So... New York Y... night.

Boston tonight... and Sc... son... thi...

...gle to center. Cecil Cooper dou... ...led in another and Denny ...'s single got t... fourth

55-155-.555 off his night...Rick Mille... ble gum blowing Yanks Walt Willi... quarter of an inc... ...tion among m... ...sponsored by ...m comp... ...ner...as

Red Smith

...rope is tightening on the Boston Red ...ve pressed on when the ...to throw up th...

Smith

Just Maybe the Red Sox Are Real

It is foolhardy to suggest it this early, but maybe—maybe—those unlikely leaders of the American League ...t, the Boston Red Sox, are real. Quitting the snug safety ...Fenway Park last Tuesday night, they set out through ...Wild West filled with nameless, shapeless fears. Ahead ...many perils, but what they dreaded most was...

Cooper was ht by a breaking pitch thro... Brewer southpaw Billy Travers. X-Ra... negative, and it is expected Cooper w... play in a few days.

Reggie Cleveland won the ...relief help from Dick Drago ... Travers, who had h... ...the starter in Satu... ...n, 7-3. Ge... three hits in ...er, his ... ...ep ...

in Oakland, was a no-hit pitcher protecting a lead of 2-0 with two out in the seventh inning. Then Reggie Jackson hit his 28th home run. Billy Williams singled, Gene Ten-ace put a pitch out of sight, and it was Oakland's ball game, 3-2.

A defeat like that can leave a... ...than eight ...ung order, they ...ned Claude William ...was, Weeping Willie. Eight ...other characters were described ...the roster as pitchers, but their ...names sl...d on the Orioles, ...by the Yankees, but they left ...ly concerned because of the injury ...er, who was hit on the side of the

W Pitching

'Yaz' Old O Trick

It was the kind of trick that Joh...

Willie Keeler

Martin Hoping to Slow Bos

...in the stre... ...ht lengths in front a...

one Sox Milwaukee a three-run ...BI total to 89. Jim 22... homer, and three

Are AL Umpires Out For Earl?

...ct, stop to c... ...r last two ...even ri...

...Ori... ...the i... ...d ten of ...imore also ... n Fenway Par... ...or winning thei... ...on Baylor, Lee Ma... ...ht handed hitters can ... ... fence." ...er and Torrez are right ha... ...ball low and they can win th... ...every right to prevail in Men... ...s ago

Ame... Red Sox, thriving on pressur... Oriole aces ...gue

Mighty Yaz confident his Sox will stay up ...e]

Rice powers Bosox

HRs Pace Sox

THE BENCH

Photograph overleaf: Tony Conigliaro.

Kim Andrew

by Bill Nowlin

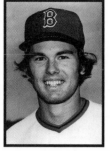

	G	AB	R	H	2B	3B	HR	RBI	BB	SO	BA	OBP	SLG	SB	CS	GDP	HBP
1975 RED SOX	2	2	0	1	0	0	0	0	0	0	.500	.500	.500	0	0	0	0

Kim Darrell Andrew, a lifetime .500 hitter in the major leagues and flawless in the field, had only a couple of sips of coffee early in the season with the pennant-winning 1975 Red Sox, but two years later found himself playing professional baseball in Italy.

Andrew was a Californian, born to Elbert L. Andrew and Frances Schandel Andrew in Glendale on November 14, 1953. His mother was a homemaker, raising Kim and his three sisters, one older and two younger. Early on, Kim's father had his own business, Andrew Signs, but he sold the company and went to work for the County of Los Angeles as a sign painter. After 15 years or so with the county, he went to work as an artist with one of the motion picture studios, working on sets and doing location work. One of his specialties was gold-leaf sign work.

With his father busy working to provide for the family, Kim's mother was more active encouraging her son in athletic pursuits. His father was more of an artist and his mother more the athlete in the family. She played a little softball and she tells Kim that from the time he was old enough to walk on both feet, he'd started picking up objects and throwing them. It was as an infielder, not a pitcher, though, that Kim made his mark. Even into the 21st century, Kim often spends more time watching a ballgame with his mother than even with his own two sons, Matt and Jason.

Andrew dates his beginnings in baseball to Mission Hills Little League at age nine. "I still remember my batting average my first year was .538," Andrew recalls. "From that point on, I excelled in each classification." He started out as a shortstop and played short right up through high school. When the Dodgers drafted him in 1971 they asked him to move to second base.

It was indeed the Dodgers who first showed interest in signing Andrew as a pro. He played shortstop for James Monroe High School in North Hills. The same school produced two other major leaguers, Craig Caskey and John Flinn. Caskey was a pitcher, who appeared in nine games for Montreal in 1973. He had a record of 0–0, and posted a 5.65 ERA in 14⅓ innings of work. Flinn was also a pitcher, who appeared briefly in three seasons with Baltimore and one with Milwaukee, finishing his career with a 5–2 mark and a 4.17 ERA. Though the Dodgers drafted him, Andrew did not sign with them and they elected not to redraft him in the winter draft. Kim played no ball that summer, but entered Valley Junior College in the fall. He played ball there and ended up with five hitting records, hitting over .470 by year's end. This attracted a visit from Orioles scout Ray Poitevint, who visited Kim's parents in the stands right after he'd hit a grand slam home run and asked, "Why is it Kim doesn't want to play professional baseball?" They looked at him in surprise and asked what he was talking about. Poitevint said Kim hadn't seemed interested in the Dodgers and the word was that he didn't want to play pro ball. The Dodgers had offered him only $5,000 to sign, and it hadn't been enough to secure him.

In truth, Andrew was a bit ambivalent. "I wasn't completely serious in signing with the scout when he came to the house here," Andrew explains. "In fact, I was interested in going into wildlife management, so I continued my education. Once I tried combining the scholastic side at the college level with pursuing my baseball endeavors after school, I found it was quite a challenge." Poitevint made a substantial enough offer and Andrew signed with the Orioles in 1972 as an amateur free agent just two or three weeks before the draft. Andrew still wonders what attention he might have attracted had he waited for the draft.

The Orioles assigned him to rookie A ball in Lewiston, Idaho. Andrew played well, hitting .325 and making the All-Star team. He had made the transition to second baseman, since the Orioles had the same sense that the Dodgers had expressed that second base would be his best position. Perhaps his legs weren't long enough (Andrew was 5'10" and 160 pounds), or he just didn't have the "look" to be a shortstop. He had the winter off, though he did get in a couple of workouts during the winter months under Poitevint's supervision, getting together with a number of other Southern Californians who were in the Orioles system. Kim stayed at home with his parents and worked a number of odd jobs, and took a few more courses in wildlife management. That field of work began to see some cutbacks, though, and he began to feel a bit more discouraged about prospects in the industry.

The following year, 1973, Andrew was assigned to

the Class A Miami Orioles in the Florida State League. He hit .336 with Miami, leading the league in hitting, and made both of the two All-Star teams that were selected. He also led all second basemen in fielding percentage, beginning to establish more of a reputation as a fielder as well.

In 1974, Andrew moved up the ladder to Double A, with an assignment to the Asheville (NC) Orioles in the Southern League. Once again, he was named an All-Star, this time placing second in the league in hitting, he recalls, with an average of .317. He wasn't protected, though. As he understands it, "after three years, if they don't invite you to the major league camp or whatever, then you're considered a free agent. That's when the Red Sox drafted my contract for $25,000, and brought me to the Red Sox spring training down in Winter Haven, Florida."

He went to spring training with the Red Sox and played in all 22 games, hitting .350 with just one error in the field. He shared "rookie of spring training" status with none other than Fred Lynn. "I like to say I forced Darrell Johnson to have to put me in the major leagues," he laughs.

Kim Andrew made the team out of spring training and appeared in two games early in the pennant-winning season of 1975. He managed to hit .500, but he got only two at-bats in the majors. The Sox had finished third the year before, not much over .500 themselves, playing to an 84–78 record. His debut game was April 16, 1975 in Yankee Stadium. Andrew came in to play second base in the ninth inning. Bob Heise, who'd been playing second moved over to third to take Rico Petrocelli's spot. Andrew neither batted nor had a fielding chance during his first game.

Kim Andrew's next appearance was in Boston on Patriots Day, Monday April 21, as Bill Rodgers won the Boston Marathon with a record 2:09:55. The Sox were hosting the Yankees this time, Dobson getting the start for New York. Bill Lee started for Boston, but got hammered for four runs in the top of the first and was charged with four more in the fourth. Boston was losing 11–0 after six. Doug Griffin had started the game and went 0-for-2, but then left after the sixth inning and Andrew took his place at second. Lou Piniella walked to lead off the New York seventh. Second up was Graig Nettles, who grounded into a force play, second to short (Andrew to Burleson). It was Kim Andrew's first fielding play.

Andrew's first at-bat in the major leagues came in the bottom of the inning. With one out, Burleson walked, but Andrew grounded to third, where Nettles

fielded the play and returned the favor, forcing Burleson at second. Andrew stood on Fenway's first base on the fielder's choice but didn't advance, as Heise hit into an inning-ending grounder to the pitcher.

Elliott Maddox lined out to Andrew in the top of the eighth, and Kim had his first major league putout. He was involved in no other fielding plays, but in the bottom of the ninth made his mark at the plate. The Sox were down 12–0 and at risk of being shut out before the holiday home crowd. Tim Blackwell, who'd come into the game to spell Bob Montgomery, led off the top of the ninth with a double to right. Rick Burleson grounded out to Nettles, but then Andrew singled to deep short. Blackwell held at second. Bob Heise followed with a single to left, scoring Blackwell, and moving Andrew to second base. Bernie Carbo hit into a double play to end the game. The Sox lost, 12–1, but Kim Andrew was batting .500—and that remains his lifetime average. With one putout and one assist, his lifetime fielding average was an unimpeachable 1.000.

Andrew never saw action in another major league game, though at the time he wouldn't have known that game was to be his last. Darrell Johnson told him, "You're not a bench player," and sent him down to Triple A Pawtucket so he could fine-tune his skills and play every day. After a couple of weeks in Pawtucket, playing under manager Joe Morgan, Andrew sprained his ankle pretty badly. He was sent down to Double A Bristol for a while, but returned to Pawtucket. "You feel like you're on a yo-yo string. It's a hard life, face it." Andrew was uncertain about his future. The big league club liked Denny Doyle a lot and he'd made his mark in the 1975 World Series. Andrew was more of a self-described "spray hitter, not a lot of power. Singles and doubles in the gap." In line with the times, team management wasn't very informative about the role they saw for him. Andrew confessed to some uncertainty: "At that point, I really didn't know what was going on. I'm not sure what they were thinking about me. . . . I talked to a couple of people, but at that stage and once you get up into Triple A, it's a business. You're on your own. And they didn't have agents in those days. You didn't have an attorney."

In 1976, Andrew played in 109 games for the Rhode Island Red Sox, batting .287. He began 1977 with Pawtucket (the team dropped the state's name in favor of resuming the city's name), appearing in 12 games before being sent to Rochester, where he batted .317 in 21 games—but felt he reached a point of no return.

Players had to look out for themselves, even if the uncertainty might undermine a player's determination in training. Andrew, who began his career with a bit of ambivalence, was now a bit adrift. He remembers his final stretch pro ball: "If you're in the minor leagues and you're not progressing . . . I told myself early in my career that if I'm not progressing, it's going to be a difficult row to hoe for me. It's easy to lie to a young 21-year-old kid, you know, which direction should I go, if this organization is not particularly keen on me at this time. What are my options? My last year that I was with the Red Sox, I started at Triple A and then they wanted to send me down, and I said, 'No.' I told them, I said, 'There's no way.' I wasn't going to [get demoted]."

He knew it was the end of the road. "There was no way I was going to play for the Boston Red Sox. That was my last year. I ended up getting picked up by the Orioles. Then they let me go after three or four weeks, and at that point, I was disillusioned. I went back in the mountains in North Carolina and did some fly-fishing. And during that period of time, believe it or not, Bill Veeck of the White Sox called and left me a message. He wanted me to play ball for him; he was really keen on me. He left this long message for me. I was sitting there with my fly-fishing pole and I had this beard, just back in mountains. I said to myself I had no idea anybody would be interested in me, but I also had [heard from] the Pirates and I had one other organization that had called and left a message. I thought for sure I was going to get pretty much blackballed because I had pretty much told one organization 'take a hike,' and then the Orioles dumped me, and I said to myself, that's probably it.

"I got disillusioned at that point and I was wondering if it was worth it. It's one thing to go through all that mentally, and it's another thing to have to physically throw everything together and go to another place and start all over again. It really takes a lot to stick with it. You really do find out how much you really do want it. And I think at that stage, I wasn't sure if I really wanted any more. With only two or three weeks left in the season after the call from Mr. Veeck and a couple of other organizations, I just said, you know what, I'm just riding out the rest of this season. Then I'll take the winter off and see what I want to do."

During the winter time (1977–1978), Andrew was approached to play professional baseball in Italy. He took up the offer and played the 1978 season for Bollate, a well-established ball club in Milano. The team played in a summer league, a season of 14 or 15 weeks, so Kim spent a summer playing teams in cities like Rimini, Florence, Rome, and Venice, before crowds ranging from 500 to 5,000.

Andrew recalls, "It was a pretty good experience, a cultural experience. I did my best to promote the game over there and at the same time make a few dollars. I think I led the whole league in hitting." The league fielded teams of varying talent—one maybe around Double A level, but another being perhaps no better than a good high school team. "It was not actually a big challenge for me, but I was able to play shortstop again and I loved it. I played so well over there that when I came back, I contacted a number of organizations, and the Pirates invited me to spring training from one of the letters that I wrote to the organizations. About two, two and a half weeks prior to me reporting, I slipped off a ladder and sprained my ankle. I figured at that point maybe that was kind of a sign: your baseball career is done. Officially. So I called it a career."

Kim returned to the United States and worked in sporting goods retail for a while, and then began working for the company he still works for in 2005: Federal Express. He has served the last 24 years as a freight driver for FedEx, marrying a year or two after his return and raising two boys. Both boys played baseball into their high school years, but neither pursued it further. Baseball still remains in Kim's blood, though. As of late summer 2005, he's contemplating taking early retirement at age 55 and then musing about trying to become a minor league batting coach.

Despite the way his career ended, in retrospect he sees opportunities perhaps missed. "I was watching a baseball game yesterday and there was a pitcher who'd been released three or four times. I said to myself, that's amazing. And he's pitching in the major leagues now. If I would have known that, I wouldn't have been so disillusioned back then, probably. I realize [now] there's always an organization that looks at you differently than the organization you're with."

He recalls several of the players with the Red Sox in those days, and felt particular affinity to Jack Baker, Don Aase, and Jim Burton. As a young rookie, he didn't have a lot of personal interaction with stars like Carl Yastrzemski. "I was the bottom man on the totem pole with that team and he had a lot of power, he had a lot of influence. I do believe he said a couple of things to me at one time or another, but I pretty much kept myself in line while I was with the team. Pretty much was there to do the job, if called upon."

Kim Andrew was remembered when it came time to distribute World Series shares, and received a check for $500. He hadn't expected a thing and was pleased to receive it; while with the team, he recalls making just $27,500.

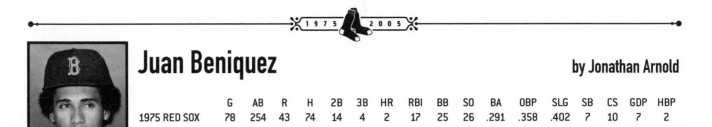

Juan Beniquez

by Jonathan Arnold

	G	AB	R	H	2B	3B	HR	RBI	BB	SO	BA	OBP	SLG	SB	CS	GDP	HBP
1975 RED SOX	78	254	43	74	14	4	2	17	25	26	.291	.358	.402	7	10	7	2

Juan Beniquez and Bob Heise were the principal utility men on the 1975 Red Sox team. Beniquez also served as designated hitter in 20 games, batting .291 in a total of 78 games. He went on to play for a total of eight different American League teams and holds the record for the most AL clubs played for. His career stretched for 17 seasons, until 1988, with 4,651 at bats and over 1,200 hits. He won a Gold Glove, hit three home runs in one game, and was part of Collusion III, where once again the owners were found to have conspired to keep player salaries down.

Juan Jose Beniquez Torres was born on May 13, 1950 in San Sebastian, Puerto Rico, and signed with the Red Sox at the tender age of 18. He made his major league debut as a shortstop only three years later, in the eighth inning on September 4, 1971, and grounded out in the ninth. But what a game he had the next day, in his first major league start, batting 3-for-4 with two doubles and driving in two runs as the Red Sox beat the Indians 8–1.

Beniquez was the regular shortstop for the rest of 1971, but he didn't make the team out of spring training in 1972. He was called up in June when starting shortstop Luis Aparicio was disabled due to a broken finger, and played daily until he set a modern major league record with two consecutive three-error games in July of 1972 (a total of seven for three consecutive games), after which he rode the bench for the rest of the season. He did play in the 1972 season finale that the Red Sox won, leaving them a scant half-game behind the division winning Detroit Tigers. One can only wonder what might have been if Beniquez had done a better job than Aparicio running the bases two days earlier, and thus scored the go-ahead run in the third inning on Yastrzemski's double in the deciding game?

Beniquez was slated as the Sox utility man for 1973, but Mario Guerrero's strong spring training won him the slot, and Beniquez was assigned to Pawtucket where he played at shortstop but was ultimately moved to the outfield. He spent the entire 1973 season at Pawtucket refining his outfield play. Though hitting only .298, he led the International League in batting.

Beniquez was Boston's 1975 Opening Day left fielder, and played in a total of 78 games, mostly in the outfield (44 games), but he also filled in at third base (14 games) and at DH (20 games). Despite his limited playing time, he was fifth on the team with seven stolen bases behind only Jim Rice and Fred Lynn who led the team with 10 each, and Carl Yastrzemski and Rick Burleson, who each had eight. Juan had a solid .291 batting average but a mediocre .760 OPS, reflecting his meager two home runs on the year.

Beniquez batted leadoff in all three games of the 1975 ALCS sweep against the Oakland Athletics, as the DH. He went 2-for-4, scoring one run and driving in another in Game One. He singled in Rick Burleson in the seventh, then proceeded to steal second, then third base; he scored after Billy North muffed Doyle's sacrifice fly. He ended up hitting .250 for the series.

In the World Series, he appeared in just three of the games, as there was no DH. He was a surprise starter for Game Four, leading off and playing left field, as Yaz moved to first and Cecil Cooper was benched. He managed one single in that game, but was held hitless in three at-bats in Game Five. His final appearance was as a pinch-hitter for Rick Miller, leading off the bottom of the ninth in Game Seven, when he flied out to right as the Sox failed to overtake the Reds for the final loss.

By now, Beniquez had acquired the tag of having an "attitude problem" and was dealt in November 1975, along with Steve Barr and a player to be named later (which proved to be Craig Skok) for Hall of Famer (and Buffalo Head) Fergie Jenkins. He played regularly for the only time in his career with Texas, virtually all of the games in the outfield. He was a prototypical "all glove, no hit" player, as he was rewarded with the Gold Glove for his centerfield play in 1977, but he hit only .269 with ten home runs and 26 stolen bases.

In the winter of 1978, he was part of a huge multi-player deal, in which Texas sent him, Mike Griffin, Paul Mirabella, and hot minor league lefthander Dave Righetti to the New York Yankees in exchange for Domingo Ramos, Mike Heath, Sparky Lyle, Larry McCall, Dave Rajsich, Greg Jemison, and cash. After appearing in only 62 games for the Yankees, he was dealt that winter to the Seattle Mariners. After one year and 70 games for the Mariners, he was granted free agency and signed with the Angels.

After two tough years in California (including

hitting a mere .181 in 1981), Juan found his hitting stroke again and proceeded to hit over .300 the next four years, the last of which was with the Orioles in 1986. During that single year in Baltimore, he had one of the more unlikely three-home run games, as he hit fully half of his six home runs on June 12, in a losing cause against the Yankees.

Beniquez finished up his career playing for Kansas City and then, finally, in Toronto. At the time of his retirement, he had the record for most AL teams played

for: eight. He was granted unrestricted free agency in 1988, after an arbitrator found the owners colluded against free agents in 1980 during the winter of 1980. Juan was one of seven players who were later awarded complete free agency to compensate for harm done him. However, this finding came much later, at the end of his career, and it was a little late for Juan. He decided to re-sign with the Blue Jays, but his career came to a finish when they released him on May 31, 1988, winding up an impressive 17 years in the major leagues.

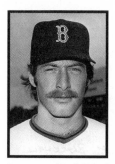

Tim Blackwell

by John Vorperian

	G	AB	R	H	2B	3B	HR	RBI	BB	SO	BA	OBP	SLG	SB	CS	GDP	HBP
1975 RED SOX	59	132	15	26	3	2	0	6	19	13	.197	.303	.250	0	0	3	1

Timothy Blackwell was a switch-hitting reserve catcher (with a .228 career batting average) who in 1980 had his best season at the plate, hitting .272 and catching full-time as a Chicago Cubbie. Blackwell grew up in San Diego and participated in Little League Baseball. A dual interscholastic sport star at Crawford High School, he was voted Most Valuable Player in both baseball and football. As a senior, he batted .392 in league games, hit .355 overall, and was declared the Hot Corner selection for the All-League First Team and the All-San Diego CIF second team. Upon high school graduation in 1970, Blackwell attended Grossmont Community College (El Cajon, California).

On June 4, 1970, the Boston Red Sox selected the infielder-catcher in the 13th round (304th overall) of the free-agent amateur entry draft. Red Sox scout Ray Boone signed the recruit. Blackwell was assigned to Jamestown (New York–Penn League). In 28 games, Blackwell batted .235, with 10 RBI, hitting three doubles and stealing one base.

Tim opened 1971 with Greenville (Class A, Western Carolinas League) and became a full-time catcher during that season. The next year he moved to Winston-Salem (Advanced A, Carolina League). In 1973, Blackwell was promoted to Double A Bristol (Eastern League) and batted a lifetime minor league career high .283. He also tied for the Eastern League lead in double plays by a catcher with 12. Next stop on the farm club express was Boston's Triple A squad, the Pawtucket Red Sox (International League).

At 1:00 A.M. on June 29 1974, Blackwell got a very early morning wake-up call in Norfolk, Virginia.

The 21-year old catcher learned that Carlton Fisk had injured his knee and was out for the season. Blackwell had 12 hours to get to Cleveland for a game against the Indians. "When Pawtucket Manager Joe Morgan told me about it, I was dazed," said Blackwell. "I never thought I would be going up to Boston this soon. After all, Carlton Fisk is one of the top catchers in the major leagues."[1] In fact, Pudge, a future Hall of Famer, topped Boston in home runs and RBI and was second to Red Sox captain Carl Yastrzemski with a .299 batting average and tied Petrocelli for the home run lead, when a collision at home plate terminated his year. Blackwell was so sure he would be staying put with Pawtucket that the young man had paid rent through August for his Cranston, Rhode Island apartment.

With Fisk now gone and Red Sox pennant hopes in the balance, the New England franchise's plan to fix the backstop gap was to have veteran Bob Montgomery alternate with the Triple A call-up.

So on July 3, 1974, before 27,730 in Fenway Park, Blackwell made his major league debut against the AL East Division rival Baltimore Orioles. He caught righthander Reggie Cleveland. In the bottom of the third, Blackwell singled in his first plate appearance, ending up on second base when O's third baseman Enos Cabell committed an error. He singled again in the bottom of the fourth. In the seventh, Blackwell grounded out to second, and in the ninth he flew out to center field flycatcher Paul Blair. The final score of the game was Baltimore 6, Boston 4.

In August 1974, Blackwell turned 22 and Dave Langworthy of *The Christian Science Monitor* wrote that for the Southern Californian, "sitting behind the

plate for the Red Sox is like playing catch with his baseball card collection. Luis Tiant and Juan Marichal, the two veteran righthanders who have accounted for over one-third of all victories in 1974, were both already started on major league careers when Tim was 11 years old. And the young catcher remembers asking for outfielder–designated hitter Tommy Harper's autograph when Harper played for the Padres in Blackwell's home town of San Diego." Harper never played for the Padres; perhaps the autograph was collected when Harper was visiting as a Cincinnati Red.

How did he feel about The Show? "Actually, handling pitchers in the majors is a little easier," Blackwell noted. "Most of them are veterans and they know what they can and can't do in situations. They usually stay with what works." Blackwell told Langworthy the big difference was the batters. "They're so much more aggressive than in the minors," he remarked, "It's unbelievable. They go after every pitch in the strike zone all out. As a catcher I have to be extra careful about things like where my target is. It's so easy to get burned."

Boston manager Darrell Johnson said, "I knew that Blackwell had the defensive fundamentals. He catches the ball well, he throws well, makes contact. He's never going to hit for big power, but he can hit for some average. What has impressed me most is the way he studies hitters and the game. He asks question after question. When he first got up here I might have to ask him about his calls on a couple of batters an inning. Now, it's maybe two for an entire game. And the fact that he throws so well has kept people from running on us."[2]

In sharing time behind the dish with vet Montgomery and having regular daily skull sessions with Red Sox skipper Johnson, a former catcher himself, Blackwell clubbed .246, eight RBI, and had a .971 fielding average for the year.

Fisk returned in 1975. As a reserve catcher with the American League pennant winners, Blackwell got into 59 games and raised his fielding average to .984, but batted just .197. These totals punched a return ticket to Rhode Island to play in the minors at the start of 1976.

On April 19, 1976, Tim was sold to the Philadelphia Phillies and sent to their Double A club in Reading (Eastern League). In addition to catching for Reading, he also played some outfield.

A little over a year later, on June 15, 1977, Blackwell and right hander Wayne Twitchell were traded by the Phils to the Montreal Expos for catcher Barry Foote and southpaw Dan Warthen. At the close of the season he had swung a dismal .091 in a mere 17 games. On January 14, 1978, Montreal released him.

Blackwell inked a contract with the Chicago Cubs a month later, on February 10. The Cubs assigned him to Double A Wichita (American Association), where he regained his form, batting .293 with 33 RBI. The 25-year-old was brought up to the parent club for the rest of 1978, and got 103 at-bats in 49 games, hitting at a .223 pace. But 1979 was a disappointing year. Tim accumulated 122 at-bats, but batted only .164.

In April 1980, emergency sirens went off for the Cubs. At the Cactus League's close and before Opening Day it was evident Chicago's first string catcher Barry Foote, down with back injuries, would be on the pine for some time. Cubs General Manager Bob Kennedy saw Blackwell as the obvious choice to replace Foote. Early on, under hitting coach Billy Williams' keen tutelage, Blackwell restructured his batting swing. "It's like starting from scratch," he said. He was prompted by bullpen coach Gene Clines to be more aggressive at the plate. "I can hear him [Clines] all the way from the bullpen. He could be in the upper deck and I'd hear him," Blackwell said.[3] Clines admitted that he was pretty loud, "I could be on Lake Shore Drive and you'd hear me." The 27-year-old Blackwell responded with a banner year, appearing in 103 games, with 320 at-bats. He swatted for a .272 average, with 30 RBI, and 16 doubles. With his glove, he led NL catchers in double plays with 16. In *The Sporting News* of August 30, 1980, Joe Goddard noted, "Blackwell put the ball on second base as no Cubs catcher has since Randy Hundley."

After working in another 58 games (.234 in 158 at-bats) with the Cubs, Blackwell was granted free agency on November 13, 1981. The San Diego native returned to the National League's Great White North outpost with a signed deal on January 14, 1982 with the Montreal Expos. In his final regular-season major league game on May 17, 1983, Blackwell was called upon to pinch-hit in the 14th inning. He flew out to right; (Montreal won the game, 3–2.) 14 days later, the 'Spos released him.

On June 20, 1983, Blackwell put his "John Hancock" on a California Angels contract. The Halos placed him for the rest of '83 baseball season at their Triple A affiliate Edmonton (Pacific Coast League).

After 1983, Blackwell still donned the stirrups, taking up coaching as a catching instructor and piloting minor league teams. In 1985, he managed the Clinton Giants (Midwest League), a San Francisco Giants Class A affiliate to a 71–69 record. For the Metropolitans organization, he steered the 1989 Pittsfield Mets (New York–Penn League) to the playoffs and garnered Manager of the Year hardware. In 1990, Blackwell

directed the Mets' Florida State League club, St. Lucie, to a 76–58 playoff qualifier record. Again in 1991, he managed Columbia (South Atlantic League) to a 86–54 overall finish and won the playoff championship.

Blackwell caught the eye of the independent leagues. In 1994 Mike Veeck's Saint Paul Saints (Northern League) hired him as their field chief. The '94 Saints were playoff champs. After two seasons in independent ball, Tim resumed managing in the affiliated minors with Baltimore, Colorado, and Milwaukee farm clubs.

In a June 2005 conversation at Shea Stadium now Houston Astros bench coach and fellow 1975 Red Sox teammate Cecil Cooper related how the Wisconsin based ball club got Blackwell. In 2002 Cooper was a special assistant to the Brewers' GM. Cooper wanted Blackwell in the Brew Crew establishment. Cooper's lobbying succeeded and Blackwell took the reins of Odgen (Pioneer League) and brought them to the 2002 playoffs. Blackwell managed the 2003 Brewers Class A affiliate High Desert (California League).

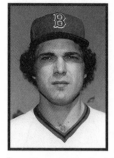

Bernie Carbo

by Andrew Blume

	G	AB	R	H	2B	3B	HR	RBI	BB	SO	BA	OBP	SLG	SB	CS	GDP	HBP
1975 RED SOX	107	319	64	82	21	3	15	50	83	69	.257	.409	.483	2	4	6	1

He was one of baseball's many free spirits whose habitual flakiness could drive management crazy, but Bernie Carbo's biggest legacy is hitting one of the all-time clutch homers in World Series history, and setting the stage for Carlton Fisk's even more memorable blast that ended Game Six of the 1975 World Series.

Bernardo Carbo was born on August 5, 1947 in Detroit, Michigan. During his sandlot days, he developed the opposite-field batting stroke which would serve him well in later years. Carbo often played pick-up games at Edward Hines Park in the Detroit suburb of Nankan Township. As the only left-handed batter in games where the teams were often short of players, any balls hit to right field were deemed automatic outs. Thus Carbo was forced to develop his hitting ability to left field. Carbo described his first Little League hit to Herb Crehan: "First time up I hit a ball that went between the outfielders. I slid into second base, I slid into third base, and then I slid into home plate for a home run."

The first major league amateur free agent draft was held in June 1965. Rick Monday was the first player selected in the draft. The first player drafted by the Cincinnati Reds in the first round was the 17-year-old Carbo, the 16th overall pick in the draft. To demonstrate what an inexact science the baseball draft is, the second round pick of the Reds was future Hall of Fame catcher Johnny Bench.

Carbo was slow to justify his selection as the first round pick. Carbo's temper, combined with his failure to take the game seriously enough, retarded his progress, while Bench took the fast track to the majors, making

his debut in 1967. Carbo's teammates labeled him "The Idiot," a title which would have probably made him feel right at home on the 2004 Red Sox. In 1965 at Tampa, Carbo hit a mere .218 with no homers and only 19 RBI. The following year, he demonstrated some pop in his bat at Peninsula with 15 homers, 57 RBI, and a .269 batting average.

In 1967 at Knoxville, his average took a tailspin to .201 with just two homers and 27 RBI. At Asheville the next year, Carbo was now known as "The Clown," but it was at this stop in the minors where he began to put it together. Carbo became the rehabilitation project of his manager George "Sparky" Anderson, who moved Carbo from third base to the outfield. Under Anderson's tutelage, Carbo's numbers improved to a .281 batting average, 20 homers and 66 RBI.

The next year in Indianapolis, Carbo played for another of his future big league skippers, Don Zimmer. Carbo hit .359 with 21 HR and 76 RBI at Indianapolis in 1969, and was named Minor League Player of the Year. He earned a call-up to the Reds, and made his debut on September 2. In an 8–2 loss to the Chicago Cubs at Crosley Field, Carbo pinch-hit for pitcher Dennis Ribant in the sixth inning against Ferguson Jenkins. Carbo was called out on strikes. He had two more plate appearances as a pinch-hitter, going hitless, and one appearance as a pinch-runner.

Carbo and manager Sparky Anderson were both promoted to the Reds in 1970. Anderson platooned Carbo with the right-handed-hitting Hal McRae in left field. Carbo was the starter on Opening Day, April 6, 1970, against the Montreal Expos at Crosley Field, hitting in the seven spot in the order. After grounding

out in his first plate appearance, Carbo homered off Joe Sparma for his first major league hit in the fourth inning. He later walked and singled in a 5–1 Reds victory. Carbo jokingly described the home run to Herb Crehan, as "the longest home run in baseball history. I hit it out of the park onto Route I-95. It landed in a truck and they found it in Florida, 1,300 miles away."

On April 21, 1970, Carbo had his first multi-homer game, swatting a pair against the Braves. On July 27, 1970, he drove in five runs against the Cardinals, a career-high in a game. He went on to enjoy a stellar rookie year for the Reds, hitting what would prove to be full-season career highs in all of the three major offensive statistics, batting .310 with an on-base percentage of .454, and slugging 21 homers while driving in 63 runs in 125 games. He was named *The Sporting News* National League Rookie of the Year but finished second in the BBWAA's Rookie of the Year ballot to Montreal pitcher Carl Morton, who was 18–11 for the last-place Expos.

The 1970 Reds, led by rookie manager Anderson, won 70 of their first 100 games on the way to winning the National League West title. In a three-game sweep of the Pirates in the NLCS, Carbo appeared in two games, going hitless in six at-bats. In a five-game World Series won by the Baltimore Orioles, Carbo extended his hitless skein, going 0-for-8 in four games. He did, however, manage to involve himself in a Game One controversy. In the sixth inning, with the score tied 3–3, Ty Cline hit a chopper in front of the plate. Plate umpire Ken Burkhart moved to call the ball fair as Carbo slid home, trying to score from third as catcher Elrod Hendricks attempted to tag him. Burkhart was spun to the ground, placing him with his back to the play as Hendricks tagged Carbo with an empty glove (the ball was in his bare hand). Burkhart incorrectly called Carbo out and left the score tied in a game that the Orioles would win 4–3.

After Carbo had begun to pay dividends in 1970 to the Reds for their first-round draft investment in him, he slipped in 1971. His batting average fell to .219 with five home runs and 20 RBI in 106 games. He had held out in spring training due to a contract dispute. Drug use began to take its toll on his body. "I was a drug addict and alcoholic for 28 years," Carbo told *The Sporting News'* Andy Clendennen in a 2001 interview. "I started drinking when I was about 16 or 17, started on marijuana when I was 21, did cocaine when I was 22 or 23, and got into crystal meth, Dexedrines, Benzedrines, Darvons, codeine. There wasn't much that I didn't do." A holdout again in spring training 1972, Carbo was

traded to the St. Louis Cardinals after hitting only .143 in 19 games. The trade for outfielder–first baseman Joe Hague took place on May 19, 1972. Carbo spent the balance of the 1972 and 1973 seasons with the Cardinals, hitting .258 in 99 games in 1972 and improving to .286 in 111 games in 1973.

On October 26, 1973, he was again traded, this time to the Boston Red Sox, along with pitcher Rick Wise, for Reggie Smith and Ken Tatum. Carbo had an awkward introduction to his new owner, Thomas Yawkey. As reported by Herb Crehan, "[r]ight after I joined the team I walked into the clubhouse and there was an older gentleman straightening things up. I gave him $20 and asked him to get me a cheeseburger and some french fries. When the clubhouse kid delivered the food, he asked me if I knew who I gave the $20 to I told him I didn't." It was Yawkey. Carbo appeared in 117 games in 1974 for a Red Sox squad that enjoyed a seven game lead in late August only to fade to third place at the end, seven games back of the division-winning Orioles. He hit .249 with a dozen round-trippers and 61 RBI, serving as both an outfielder and designated hitter. Following his mediocre 1974 season, Carbo became the first Red Sox player to file for salary arbitration against owner Yawkey and subsequently the first to lose.

During his first season in Boston, Carbo quickly became a favorite of both the fans and the press. His gift of gab made him the Kevin Millar of his time with the media. Scipio Spinks, a former Cardinals teammate, sent Carbo a stuffed gorilla dressed in a Cardinals uniform which Carbo traveled with and named "Mighty Joe Young."

During the magical 1975 season, Carbo was a key bench contributor for the Red Sox. He appeared in 107 games during the regular season, playing the outfield in 85 games and serving as the DH in 13. Although he hit only .257, he amassed an OBP of .409, drawing 83 walks. (Bill James, in *The New Bill James Historical Baseball Abstract*, lists Carbo as 19th-lifetime on the list of the highest rates of walks per 1,000 plate appearances.) He hit 15 home runs and drove in 50 runs. He had two-homer games in each of the first three months of the season, including a one-man show in the leadoff spot on May 18, 1975 when he went 3-for-4, banging out two homers and driving in all four runs in a 4–2 win over the Kansas City Royals at Fenway. On April 27, he homered off Lerrin LaGrow and Tom Walker in a 5–4 loss to the Tigers. On June 10, he took Ferguson Jenkins deep twice in an 8–3 loss to the Rangers.

While doing the job off the bench, Carbo continued to contribute to his developing reputation for eccentric

and sometimes oblivious behavior in Boston. During the June 26, 1975 game at Fenway, Carbo crashed into the right field wall, taking a homer away from the Yankees' Chris Chambliss, in the process dislodging a chaw of tobacco in his mouth. Carbo is reported to have held up the game for 10 minutes while he searched for the missing chaw and then popped the same into his mouth upon discovering it on the warning track.

With Carl Yastrzemski, Fred Lynn, and Dwight Evans manning the outfield, and Juan Beniquez in the DH spot for all three games of the Sox sweep of the three-time defending champion Oakland A's, Carbo failed to get up off the bench during the ALCS. His first postseason appearance came in Game Two of the World Series at Fenway. Pinch-hitting for Dick Drago, Carbo lined to left field in the ninth inning of a 3–2 loss which knotted the Series at a game apiece.

Carbo was again used in a pinch-hitting role in Game Three at Cincinnati's Riverfront Stadium and this time he delivered the first of his record-tying two pinch-hit homers in the same World Series. In the seventh inning, Carbo pinch-hit for Reggie Cleveland. His solo shot narrowed the Reds' lead to 5–3 and set the stage for Dwight Evans' game-tying homer in the ninth. The Sox would lose, 6–5, in 10 innings on a Joe Morgan single scoring Cesar Geronimo. Geronimo had advanced aided by the controversial no-interference call made by plate umpire Larry Barnett on Ed Armbrister.

Game Six was the game that turned this series into one for the ages. Trailing 6–3 and facing elimination in the bottom of the eighth inning, Fred Lynn singled and took second on a walk to Rico Petrocelli. Righthander Rawly Eastwick entered the game in relief of Pedro Borbon. Eastwick struck out Dwight Evans and got Rick Burleson to line out to left. Carbo was sent up to hit for Roger Moret. Sparky Anderson, a stickler for playing the percentages, failed to bring in the left-handed Will McEnaney, suspecting that Red Sox manager Darrell Johnson would counter with the right-handed bat of Juan Beniquez. With two strikes on him, Carbo was fooled by what Peter Gammons reported as a "fastball that befuddled Bernardo as if it were the Pythagorean theorem." Carbo believed that the pitch was a slider, coming in a spot in the count where he expected the fastball. Carbo barely managed to get a piece of the ball, fouling it off in what was later described by Carlton Fisk as possibly "the worst swing in the history of baseball." Carbo related to Peter Golenbock what happened next: "I stepped out of the box. I figured, 'He's going to be thinking I'm going to be looking slider, so instead I'm going to be looking fastball.' Eastwick got the fastball

up and away, where I was looking. I knew I would be swinging. I wasn't going to be taking. I knew I would commit myself to where it would be difficult to stop my swing. I got the pitch, and I hit it. When I started running to first base, I didn't know if the ball was going to go out of the park, because I knew that center field was a long ways. I figured it might be off the wall, and I ran to first and started for second, and I could see Geronimo turn his back, and that's when I knew the ball was gone. The game was tied."

"Bernie," Bill Lee wrote in Gammons' book *Beyond the Sixth Game*, "is the only man I know who turned fall into summer with one wave of his magic wand."

After striking out in the 10th inning of Game Six, having gone into the field for the first time in the Series, Carbo was awarded a start in left in Game Seven. Hitting in his customary 1975 leadoff position in the batting order, Carbo doubled in the first off Don Gullett. In the third, he drew a base on balls and scored the first Red Sox run on a single to right by Yastrzemski in a three-run third, the only runs the Sox would muster in a 4–3 Series clincher for the Reds. In the fourth, Carbo grounded out to second. In the sixth, he made his final Series appearance as he grounded out to first base and was replaced in the field by Rick Miller in the seventh. Carbo concluded a Series in which he hit .429 (3–7 with two big pinch-hit home runs). Carbo's sixth game heroic blast was commemorated by the Red Sox at their November 10, 2004 Hall of Fame induction as a memorable moment in Red Sox history.

The 1976 Red Sox got off to a start that was inconsistent with their status as defending American League Champions. The team lost 10 in a row from April 29 to May 11. Things got so bad that a practicing witch from Salem named Laurie Cabot appeared at Fenway with two goals in mind: getting Carbo out of a slump and stopping the Red Sox losing streak. "I unhexed Bernie Carbo's bat to end a ten-game losing streak," she said, as reported by Bill Nowlin and Jim Prime in their book *Blood Feud*. On June 2, the team's record stood at 19–23. After an 0-for-4 day against the Yankees, Carbo and his then .236 average (13-for-55 in 17 games) were traded to the Milwaukee Brewers for pitcher Tom Murphy and outfielder–DH Bobby Darwin on June 3. He spent the rest of the1976 season with the Brewers, hitting .235 over the full season.

Carbo's former minor league manager Don Zimmer took over the Red Sox during the 1976 season and was instrumental in getting Carbo included in a December 6, 1976 trade back to the Red Sox along with former Red Sox fan favorite George Scott in exchange for

Cecil Cooper. Carbo became a member of the "Crunch Bunch," a loaded 1977 Red Sox offensive line-up that hit a then-team-record 213 dingers (the 2003 club is the current record-holder with 238). Five players hit more than 25 homers. Butch Hobson, who hit mostly in the seventh and eighth spots in the line-up, swatted 30. The club hit 33 homers over one 10-game stretch and 16 in three games against the Yankees. They hit eight homers against Toronto on July 4, setting a Red Sox record for most homers in a game which still stands and a major league record seven solo shots, and hit five or more homers in a game eight times. Carbo contributed 15 of the team's then-record total and hit .289 with a .409 OBP in 86 games. Three of his homers came in pinch-hitting roles, further solidifying his reputation in the clutch. One came in the July 4 home run derby. A two-run pinch-hit homer off the Angels' Dyar Miller tied up an August 10 game won by the Red Sox. His third pinch-hit homer came at the end of the season against the Orioles. Carbo also homered in consecutive at-bats on June 18 against the Yankees' Mike Torrez in a 10–4 Red Sox win that is better known for a dugout brawl between Reggie Jackson and Billy Martin broadcast on NBC television.

Carbo's ability to come in cold off the bench and deliver a key hit and his ability to do so without thinking too much about the game situation served him well. Bill Lee, in Peter Golenbock's *Red Sox Nation*, shared the following memory: "I remember in the Hall of Fame game at Cooperstown, Bernie was out behind the fence sleeping . . . during the game because it didn't mean anything and he was getting some rest. Don Zimmer got really mad at him and tried to show him up. He woke him up and had him bat, figuring he'd do bad. Bernie walked up, hit a home run, ran around the bases, and went back to sleep. Managers hated that."

Bill Nowlin and Jim Prime, in *Tales from the Red Sox Dugout*, describe an interview Carbo gave after hitting a grand slam against Mariners lefty Mike Kekich. Carbo, upon being asked about the grand slam, replied that he had not been aware that the bases had been loaded. When served with a follow-up question as to the last time he had homered off a lefthander, Carbo thought that the reporters had been playing with him. "Now I know you're pulling my leg, because he was a right-handed pitcher. Zimmer would never let me hit against a left-hander with the bases loaded," he declared.

Carbo was a member of an informal fraternity of fun-loving players called the "Buffalo Heads," that annoyed Zimmer, and also included Lee, Rick Wise, Ferguson Jenkins, and Jim Willoughby. The name had arisen from Jenkins' unflattering nickname for Zimmer. In 1978, Carbo's recurring pattern of arriving late to the ballpark, behavior often triggered by a slump and the resulting lack of playing time, according to Zimmer, was the reason he was sold to the Cleveland Indians on June 15. Carbo hit .261 in 17 games for Boston in his final 1978 stint in a Red Sox uniform. His sale to the Indians precipitated a one-day walkout by friend Bill Lee. Upon returning the following day, Lee was fined $500.00 by general manager Haywood Sullivan. Lee's response? "Fine me fifteen hundred and give me the weekend off."

Carbo hit .287 in 60 games with the Indians in 1978. On March 10, 1979, Carbo signed as a free agent with the Cardinals, returning to the National League for the balance of his career. He batted .281 in 64 at-bats over 52 games for the Cards in 1979. His major league career came to a close in 1980, playing in 14 games with the Cardinals and seven with the Pittsburgh Pirates. Carbo finished his 12-year major league career with a .264 average and .387 OBP with 96 homers and 358 RBI.

Following the end of his baseball career, Carbo went to cosmetology school and operated a hair salon for eight years. However, his long-standing substance abuse problems led to a downward spiral which got so bad, as he related to Doug Hornig in *The Boys of October*, that he began to deal as well as consume the controlled substances. He reportedly hit bottom in 1993 after his mother had committed suicide, his father passed away, and his first marriage dissolved. His ex-teammates and fellow "Buffalo Heads" Lee and Jenkins helped him find the Baseball Assistance Team (BAT), an organization that helps needy former players and was instrumental in getting him into recovery from his addictions. Since 1980, he has run a baseball school for high school, college and pro players. He formed the "Diamond Club Ministry" in which he travels around the country speaking to primarily young adults about religion, baseball and the dangers of substance abuse. He has also served as a substitute teacher. He has remarried and has one son from his current marriage and three grown daughters from his first marriage. He currently is the field manager of the Pensacola Pelicans of the independent Central Baseball League.

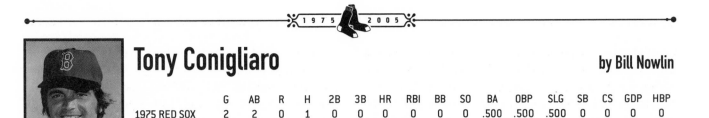

Tony Conigliaro

by Bill Nowlin

	G	AB	R	H	2B	3B	HR	RBI	BB	SO	BA	OBP	SLG	SB	CS	GDP	HBP
1975 RED SOX	2	2	0	1	0	0	0	0	0	0	.500	.500	.500	0	0	0	0

No matter how you measure it, Tony Conigliaro's career got off to a terrific start, but tragedy repeatedly intervened and the great promise of his early years remained unfulfilled. A local boy made good, Tony was born and raised in the Boston area, signed with the hometown team, and made his major league debut in 1964 soon after he turned 19 years old. In his very first at-bat at Fenway Park, Tony turned on the very first pitch he saw, and pounded it out of the park for a home run. By hitting 24 home runs in his rookie season, he set a record for the most home runs ever hit by a teenager. When he led the league in homers with 32 the following year, he became the youngest player ever to take the home run crown. When he hit home run number 100, during the first game of a doubleheader on July 23, 1967, he was only 22—the youngest AL player to reach the 100 homer plateau. He hit number 101 in the day's second game.

As if that wasn't enough, Tony Conigliaro was a bona fide celebrity and singer with a couple of regional hit records to his credit.

Tony C was born on January 7, 1945 in Revere, Massachusetts, and grew up both there and in East Boston, where he first played Little League ball at age nine. Tony and his younger brother Billy (born 1947) were obsessed with baseball, playing it at every possible opportunity, usually with the support and guidance of their uncle Vinnie Martelli. "He used to pitch batting practice to me for hours, till my hands bled," wrote Conigliaro in his autobiography *Seeing It Through*. In his very first at-bat for the Orient Park Sparks Little League team, Tony hit a home run over the center-field fence. He credits coach Ben Campbell for giving him tremendous encouragement in youth baseball.

At a very early age, Tony confessed, "I discovered how much I hated to lose." His teams didn't lose that often. By the time he was 13 and in Pony League, they were traveling out of state for tournament play. Tony went to high school at St. Mary's, in Lynn, where his father Sal was working at Triangle Tool and Die. Sal and Tony's mother Teresa were supportive of Tony's athletic endeavors and were a fixture at Tony's ballgames.

Playing both shortstop and pitching, Tony had already come to the attention of scouts like Lennie

Merullo and Milt Bolling and by the time he graduated claims to have had as many as 14 scouts tracking him. In his final couple of years, he recalls batting over .600 and having won 16 games as well as his team winning the Catholic Conference Championship. He played American Legion ball in the summertime, with the same .600 batting average. The Red Sox asked him to come to a 1962 workout at Fenway Park, and both he and Tony Horton showed their stuff. When the Legion season ended and Mr. Conigliaro courted bids, Boston's Milt Bolling and Red Sox farm director Neil Mahoney made the best bid at $20,000 and Tony signed with the Red Sox.[4] He was sent to Bradenton for the Florida Instructional League.

It was his first time far from home, and he didn't excel in winter ball. In the spring of 1963, he was invited to the Red Sox minor league camp at Ocala. He did well there, and was assigned to Wellsville in the New York–Penn League. Before reporting, he went home to see his girlfriend, got in a fight with a local boy, broke his thumb, and couldn't report to Wellsville until the end of May. That was the end of his pitching career, but the scouts were looking at his hitting more than his pitching, anyway. Tony did well at Wellsville, batting .363, hitting 24 homers, and winning the league's Rookie of the Year and MVP awards. He played winter ball in Sarasota and was added to the Red Sox 40-man roster. The next spring, 1964, he was brought to the big league spring training facility in Scottsdale, Arizona.

Boston's manager was Johnny Pesky who, as it happened, lived on the same street in Swampscott to which the Conigliaro family had recently moved: Parsons Street. Pesky saw the fire in Tony Conigliaro and played him that spring; Tony hit a monster home run off Cleveland's Gary Bell on March 22, the first day his parents came to visit him in Scottsdale. Ted Williams admired Conigliaro's style and told him, whatever he did, "Don't change that solid stance of yours, no matter what you're told." Ted told reporters, though, "He's just a kid; he's two years away."

Johnny Pesky saw otherwise. Tony C was 19, only in his second year in organized ball, but he made the big league club as the center fielder for the Red Sox. Pesky was taking a chance on a relatively-untested player, but the 1964 Sox, frankly, didn't have a great deal of talent.

Conigliaro's first major league game was in Yankee Stadium on April 16. In his first major league at-bat, he stepped into the box with men on first and second, and grounded into a double play. His third time up, he singled and finished the day 1-for-5. The next day, April 17, was Opening Day at Fenway Park. Tony was batting seventh in the order, facing Joe Horlen of the White Sox. He swung at Horlen's first pitch and hit it over the Green Monster in left field, and even over the net that hung above the Wall. Tony Conigliaro, wearing number 25, took his first home run trot. Tony told writers afterward that he always swung at the first good pitch he saw. "I don't like to give the pitcher any kind of edge," he said.

In that same spirit, Conigliaro crowded the plate. And pitchers, quite naturally, tried to back him off the plate. He was often hit by pitches, and suffered his first injury on May 24 when Moe Drabowsky hit him in the left wrist, causing a hairline fracture. Fortunately, Tony missed only four games.

Back in the lineup, back pounding out homers, Tony hit number 20 in the first game of the July 26 doubleheader against Cleveland. In the second game, he got hit for the fifth time in the season, by Pedro Ramos. It broke his arm. This time he missed a month, out until September 4. Conigliaro finished the season with 24 homers and a .290 average.

In 1965, under manager Billy Herman, Tony played in 138 games and hit 32 more homers, enough to lead the league, though his average dipped to .269. During the June free agent draft, there was more good news in the Conigliaro family: the Red Sox used their first pick to select Tony's younger brother Billy. Tony was struck yet again by another ball on July 28, when a Wes Stock pitch broke his left wrist. It was the third broken bone Tony had suffered in just over 14 months. He simply refused to back off the plate. Orioles executive Frank Lane intimated that Red Sox pitchers could defend Tony a bit better by retaliating.

Suffering no serious injuries in 1966, Tony got in a very full season, seeing action in 150 games. He banged out 28 homers and drove in 93 runs, leading the league in sacrifice flies with seven. His average was .265 and the Boston writers voted him Red Sox MVP. The Red Sox as a team, though, played poorly in these years. In 1966, they were spared the ignomy of last place only because the Yankees played even worse. Boston ended the year in ninth place, 26 games out of first, and the Yankees ended in tenth, 26 ½ games behind the Orioles. In his first three years in the majors, the highest that one of Tony's teams finished was eighth place in 1964.

Tony C's brilliant play shone all the more because of the colorless team around him. The local boy made good was a teenage heartthrob and the handsome 6'3" star attracted a lot of attention from local girls, and girls on the road. Assigning older players as roommates to provide a stabilizing presence didn't do the trick. Dick Williams wrote in his autobiography: "I never saw him. Not late at night, not first thing in the morning, never. I was providing veteran influence to a suitcase." In the early part of 1965, Tony Conigliaro the pop star released his first recording.

Billy Conigliaro joined his brother as the two traveled together to spring training in 1967. Tony got hit by a fastball in early workouts and he hurt his back as well. Billy was sent out for more seasoning; he first made the big league club in 1969. Tony got off to a slow start, batting well enough but without much power. He didn't hit his third home run until June 11. And he still crowded the plate. Johnny Pesky told author David Cataneo, "He was fearless of the ball. He would just move his head, like Williams did. A ball up and in, Tony would just move his head. He thought the ball would never hit him."

The Red Sox surprised everyone with their play in 1967. Tony contributed as well. One game that stood out was an extra-inning affair at Fenway. Boston was hosting the White Sox and the game was scoreless for 10 full innings. Chicago took a 1–0 lead in the top of the 11th, but Joe Foy singled and Conigliaro hit a two-run homer off John Buzhardt for a walkoff win. The win moved the Red Sox up by percentage points to take third place, just four games out of first, and the next day's *Boston Globe* referred to the "Impossible Dream" season the Red Sox team was having for itself.

It was on July 23 that Tony hit the 100th and 101st home runs of his major league career. The Red Sox were just one-half game out of first place. It was a tight race, with the Red Sox hanging just behind, but never quite making it on top. As late as August 14, the Red Sox were in fifth place—but only three games out.

On the 17th, Tony's partner in the music business, Ed Penney, was visiting his sons at the Ted Williams Baseball Camp in Lakeville, Massachusetts. Ted warned Penney, "Tony is crowding the plate. He's much too close. Tell him to back off. It's serious time now. The pitchers are going to get serious." As Penney was leaving the camp later that evening, Williams shouted to Penney, "Tell Tony what I said. Don't forget to tell Tony what I told you." Penney did tell him, before the game the very next night. Tony was in a slump at the time, and told brother Billy he couldn't back off the plate or pitchers

wouldn't take him seriously. If anything, he was going to dig in a little closer.

The Red Sox faced the California Angels the next day—August 18—and Jack Hamilton's fourth-inning fastball came in and struck Tony in the face, just missing his temple but hitting him in the left eye and cheekbone. Tony later wrote that he jerked his head back "so hard that my helmet flipped off just before impact." He never lost consciousness, but as he lay on the ground, David Cataneo wrote, Tony prayed, "God, please, please don't let me die right here in the dirt at home plate at Fenway Park." Tony was fortunate to escape with his life, but his season—and quite possibly his career—was over. Conigliaro had been very badly injured.

The 1967 Red Sox made it to Game Seven of the World Series before the bubble burst. It had nonetheless been a tremendous year for the team, and reignited the passion for the Sox in the city of Boston. Since 1967, tickets for Fenway Park have been hard to come by. Tony, however, felt he'd let the team down. He was down on himself and downplayed his contribution in the drive to the pennant. His teammates were the first to reassure him that they never would have reached the postseason had it not been for his contributions early on. There is little doubt, though, that Conigliaro was missed in the World Series itself. George Scott was unambiguous in his assessment: "I've said it a million times, if Tony had been in the lineup, we would have won. He was one of those guys. Reggie Jackson was a big-game player. Tony was that kind of player."

There was concern he might lose the sight in his left eye. He tried to come back in spring training, but there was just no way. His vision was inadequate, and his doctor told him, "I don't want to be cruel, and there's no way of telling you this in a nice way, but it's not safe for you to play ball anymore." Tony C wouldn't quit, though, and against all odds, his vision slowly began to improve. By late May, he was told he could begin to work out again. Tony also learned new ways to see the ball. When he looked straight on at the pitcher, he couldn't see the ball, but he learned to use his peripheral vision to pick up the ball and was able to see well enough by looking a couple of inches to the left. Tony wanted badly to get back into baseball, and he spent a good amount of time in the late summer of 1968 trying to learn to become a pitcher, and started several games in the Winter Instructional League for the Sarasota Red Sox, but he rolled up a record of 0–3, giving up 15 runs in one game, and developed a sore arm as well. He played in the outfield on the days he wasn't pitching and he began to connect for a few solid hits. He gave up the idea of pitching, emboldened to try to come back as a hitter in spring training 1969.

Not only did Tony make the team in 1969, but he broke back in with a bang, hitting a two-run homer in the top of the 10th during Opening Day in Baltimore on April 8. The O's re-tied the game, but Tony led off in the 12th and worked a walk, eventually coming home to score on Dalton Jones' sacrifice fly to right. Tony hit the game-winning hit in the fourth inning of the home opener at Fenway Park on April 14, though admittedly it wasn't much of a hit. Tony came up with the bases loaded and wanted to break the game open. Instead, he sent a 15-foot dribbler toward Brooks Robinson at third, and beat it out as Ray Culp scored from third. Tony C was back. It was never easy, and the various books on Conig's struggle document how hard he had to work at what once seemed so effortless, but Tony played in 141 games, hit 20 home runs, and drove in 82 runs. Tony won the Comeback Player of the Year Award. There wasn't any question who would win it.

1970 was Tony's best year at the plate, with a full 36 homers and 116 RBI. He also scored a career-high 89 runs. Brother Billy also made the Red Sox in 1969, getting himself 80 at-bats and acquitting himself well. Billy became a regular in 1970, appearing in 114 games and batting .271. Add his 18 homers to Tony's 36, and the resulting total of 54 set a record for the most home runs by two brothers on the same major league club. On July 4 and September 19, they each homered in the same game.

In October, the Red Sox traded Tony Conigliaro. Stats aside, they knew that he was playing on guts and native talent, but may have sensed that his vision was still questionable. His trade value was as high as it would likely ever be. Not even waiting for Baltimore and Cincinnati to finish the World Series, they packaged Conigliaro with Ray Jarvis and Jerry Moses and swapped him to the California Angels for Ken Tatum, Jarvis Tatum, and Doug Griffin. Even years later, Red Sox executives neither explained nor took credit (or responsibility) for the trade. The news stunned the baseball world—and Red Sox fans in particular. As Herb Crehan wrote in *Red Sox Heroes of Yesteryear*, naming Boston's current mayor, "it was as if Mayor Menino were to trade the *USS Constitution* to Baltimore for the *USS Constellation*." Ken Tatum may have been the key to the trade; the Sox were after a strong reliever and he'd done very well for California.

Tony was crushed, and as Crehan noted, he "never adjusted to life as a California Angel." David Cataneo writes, "Tony C and southern California just didn't happen." Conigliaro batted just .222 in 1971, with only four homers and 15 RBI just before the All-Star break. Tony had headaches coming back. He wasn't feeling well. Cataneo mentions a string of ailments, from a bad leg to a pinched nerve. He even put himself in traction for an hour before every game. Some of the Angels lost patience with him and began to mock him. Finally, fed up enough, he packed his bags and left the team after the July 9 game, announcing his retirement. He also told reporters that he simply couldn't see well enough, but took the Red Sox off the hook for having dealt tarnished goods. "My eyesight never came back to normal . . . I pick up the spin on the ball late, by looking away to the side. I don't know how I do it. I kept it away from the Red Sox. . . . I had a lot of headaches because of the strain to see . . . my search for that damn baseball."

When he heard the news that Tony had left the Angels, Bill Conigliaro exploded in the Red Sox clubhouse, telling reporters that the reason for the trade to California in the first place had been Carl Yastrzemski, that Yaz had all the influence on the ballclub. "Tony was traded because of one guy—over there," he charged, indicating Yastrzemski. Yaz "got rid of Pesky, Ken Harrelson, and Tony. I know I'm next. Yaz and Reggie [Smith] are being babied, and the club better do something about it."

Billy was part of a 10-player trade with Milwaukee, but the trade was not made until October. Billy never rejoined the Red Sox—but Tony did. It took a while.

An eye exam Tony underwent after returning to Boston showed that the blind spot in his vision had grown considerably; his vision was deteriorating once more. Tony hadn't given up yet and in October 1973 talked about wanting to mount another comeback with the Angels in 1974. It appears that the Angels wanted him to play for their Salt Lake City affiliate, to see how he worked out, but Tony was past wanting to play for a minor league team and so seems to have stayed on the voluntarily retired list. Late in 1974, he wrote to the Red Sox asking for another shot at a comeback and GM Dick O'Connell said he could come to spring training, but not at financial cost to the Red Sox. If he was willing to pay his own way, he was welcome to give it a try. The Angels graciously granted him his outright release in November 1974. The Red Sox offered him a contract with the Pawtucket Red Sox, which he signed on March 5, 1975.

Tony took up the challenge, and had an exceptional spring. On April 4, he got word that he had made the big league team. Opening Day 1975 was four days later, at Fenway Park on April 8, and Tony was the designated hitter, batting cleanup. With two outs and Yaz on first, Tony singled and Yaz took third. The crowd gave Tony C a three-minute standing ovation. Perhaps Milwaukee pitcher Jim Slaton and his batterymate Darrell Porter were caught off guard; the Red Sox scored a run when Tony and Yaz pulled off a double steal.

Tony's first home run came three days later, off Mike Cuellar in Baltimore. With a first-inning single the following day, he drove in another run, but his .200 average after the April 12 game was the highest he posted for the rest of the season. Tony appeared only in 21 games, for 57 at-bats, and was batting just .123 after the game on June 12. He was hampered by a couple of injuries; it just wasn't working out. The Red Sox needed to make room on the 25-man roster for infielder Denny Doyle and they asked Tony to go to Pawtucket. After thinking it over for a week, he agreed to and reported, traveling with the Pawsox, but not getting playing time. Manager Joe Morgan said, "He had lost those real good reflexes," and teammate Buddy Hunter told David Cataneo, "Any guy who threw real hard, he had trouble with." Hunter added, "He was dropping easy fly balls in the outfield." In August, Tony Conigliaro finally called it a day, and retired once again, this time for good. "My body is falling apart," he explained.

Before too long, Tony found work as a broadcaster, first in Providence and then in the San Francisco area. He lost a nice gig in the Bay Area in early 1980, but filled in with other stations. In a life full of setbacks, even the health food store Tony owned in California was lost to mudslides in December 1981.

In early 1982, though, Tony learned that Ken Harrelson was leaving his job as color commentator with Channel 38 in Boston, the Red Sox station. Now there was a job with appeal! He interviewed for the position on the day he turned 37, January 7, 1982. The audition went very well, and he was told he'd got the job. Tony had a couple of other stops to make, then planned to return to the Bay Area to pack up his gear for the move back to Boston.

On January 9, 1982, Billy Conigliaro was driving Tony to Logan Airport and Tony suffered a heart attack in the car. Though rushed to the hospital, Tony suffered irreversible brain damage and was hospitalized for two months before being discharged into the care of Billy and the Conigliaro family. He lived another eight years before succumbing at age 45 on February 24, 1990.

Steve Dillard

by Bill Nowlin

	G	AB	R	H	2B	3B	HR	RBI	BB	SO	BA	OBP	SLG	SB	CS	GDP	HBP
1975 RED SOX	1	5	2	2	0	0	0	0	0	0	.400	.400	.400	1	0	0	0

Infielder Steve Dillard was born in Memphis on February 8, 1951 but was raised—and still resides—in Saltillo, Mississippi, a town of around 3,400 people some 100 miles to the southeast of Memphis. Steve's parents were working in Memphis at the time, his mother for a catering cafeteria supply company named Vend-Foods and his father did a number of things, but eventually became tax collector for Lee County, Mississippi. Stephen Bradley Dillard was the oldest of four boys in the family.

Steve's father loved baseball and had played some in school, and played a little softball, but he really sparked his son's interest in it and encouraged him any way he could. His youngest three sons all played high school ball, but Steve was the only one to move into professional ball. "I started to play from the time I could walk, I guess," Steve remembers.

Dillard did well in high school, always playing shortstop, and Saltillo High won the state title his senior year. The summer before, the American Legion team from Tupelo, Mississippi on which Steve played won the Legion championship as well. Playing on a couple of standout teams like that, he got scouted a bit and attracted the attention of a bird dog scout in Tupelo, who recommended him to the San Diego Padres. His memory is that he hit around .520 for Saltillo High and he was drafted right out of high school by San Diego in the 13th round of the June 1970 draft, but had been granted a full scholarship to the University of Mississippi and elected to go to college instead.

After his sophomore year at Ole Miss, though, the Red Sox drafted him in the second round of the June 1972 free-agent draft. Milt Bolling was the Red Sox scout. "He had this area and he signed me and Butch Hobson, Jack Baker, Sam Bowen, Andy Merchant, and I'm sure a lot of others, but those guys eventually got in the big leagues for at least a little bit of time. . . . I think with the signing bonus and incentive bonuses they gave back then, it was probably worth about $35,000."

After signing with the Sox, Dillard was assigned to Winston-Salem, North Carolina in the Carolina League. "They had a team in Winter Haven, then, in the Florida State League and I guess they considered Winston–Salem the higher Class A team at that time.

Of course, now both those leagues are high A or advanced A leagues, but I think back then the Carolina League was considered a little but better than the Florida State League." He played at Winston-Salem for a month and a half or so, finishing out the season, and played there again for a full year in 1973. Both years, he went to instructional league after the season, but after the '73 season, he needed shoulder surgery, so missed the first month or two of 1974. That year saw some real progress. Dillard started in June in Double A Bristol but after only 28 at-bats was advanced to Triple A in Pawtucket and finished up the season there. Again, he played in instructional league ball.

In 1975, he started with Pawtucket, but there was another shoulder repair and he went down to Bristol to finish up the season there. When Bristol's schedule ended, he was called up for the last week of the big league season, joining the Boston Red Sox, and sitting on the bench taking it all in. The Red Sox clinched the pennant on the next-to-last day of the year, a Saturday, and both Dillard and Andy Merchant made their major league debuts on Sunday. Coming in a few weeks ahead of them had been Butch Hobson and Rick Kreuger, who also played that final game.

Dillard batted second and had a 2-for-5 game, scoring two runs and even stealing a base. He was flawless in the field, with eight chances. He enjoyed a .400 batting average his first year in the majors. "Everything was downhill there after that," he jokes.

In 1976, he made the team out of spring training, and got into 57 games. By year's end, he'd hit a very good .275, and also claimed his first major league home run off Dave Roberts in Tiger Stadium. After his couple of surgeries, he wasn't able to throw as well as before, and the Red Sox thought they might be able to convert him from a utility player to a second baseman. For a period of time in August he was sent down to try and better learn second base, a position he'd played for a few games back in eighth grade and occasionally in the minors. Shortstop was a position that was pretty well set for the Sox with Rick Burleson. Second base seemed like a good position to learn.

Between 1976 and 1977, there had been an interlude where Steve had played winter ball for Valencia Magallanes in Venezuela. Most of the position players

were in the Pirates organization, but Steve was able to go in and played second base for a couple of months. The experience was "OK," but he did say at the time he'd never go back. He wasn't sure if it really helped him to develop in any way. Most of the players were American at that time, and Steve remembers the crowds as sometimes passionate. "When Magallanes and Caracas played in Caracas, that was a big rivalry, I guess like the Red Sox and Yankees, so when they played, you might have 30,000 or so. Some big crowds there."

At second base, he was behind Doug Griffin and Denny Doyle, but in 1977 he platooned with Doyle, batting against left handers while Doyle played against righties. "I didn't get to play a lot, because most teams didn't want to start a lefthander in Fenway, so more of my playing I guess was really on the road than it was at home." He got more starts than the year before, and more at-bats. In 1977, Dillard's average dipped to .241.

Early in December 1977, the Red Sox acquired second baseman Jerry Remy from the California Angels. "I knew it was going to be pretty crowded and I asked Haywood Sullivan, I called him and told him I wouldn't mind getting traded if the opportunity was there." The Red Sox accommodated him and on January 30, 1978, Dillard was traded to Detroit for two minor league prospects and some money. "They just tried to help me out, give me a chance. He was optimistic about his chance to get more playing time with the Tigers, but that's not how it worked out. "It looked like I was going to get a real good opportunity over there because they had a couple of young infielders and they didn't know how much they were going to play or how well they were going to do, and that was Alan Trammell and Lou Whitaker." Dillard platooned with Whitaker for the first month or so, but Lou "was just wearing it out, so I didn't play very much after that."

After a full year with the Tigers, near the end of spring training 1979, Dillard was traded to the Chicago Cubs. "I spent three years with them. That was a good time. I enjoyed playing with them. The Red Sox, to me, were the greatest place to play in the American League and I thought the Chicago Cubs, that was the greatest place to play in the National League." In part, it was the old ballparks that appealed to him, but more so the fans, and how devoted and "crazy about their teams" they were. Dillard hit .283 his first year with the Cubs, but tailed off to just .225 his second year. The strike came in 1981, curtailing play for everyone, and Dillard's average dropped a to .218 in more limited action, though he still amassed 119 at-bats. "We came back and played after the strike. We were out about six weeks

that year, and then came back and played. I don't think I played hardly at all after the strike, and that was when the Cubs brought in Dallas Green from the Phillies to run their major league operation, and he released a bunch of guys." Dillard was released in December 1981, but hooked on pretty quickly with the White Sox.

He'd met White Sox GM Roland Hemond, so gave him a call and was invited to spring training. Hemond asked him if he didn't make the big league club, would he be willing to go to their Triple A team in Edmonton. Dillard said he would, and spent nearly the whole season with Edmonton. There were a couple of injuries on the big league club and he came up at the end of the season and played under Tony LaRussa from mid-September on with the White Sox, but hit a disappointing .171.

The White Sox saw other potential in Steve Dillard, though. "They wanted me to manage in the minor leagues at the end of that season, but they released me to give me an opportunity to try to find a team to sign me in the major leagues. I really couldn't find anybody. Everybody wanted the younger players, so I told them I would go to work and manage for them in the minor leagues. I started calling other teams, trying to find a job as a player. I didn't have any luck, so I called the White Sox back and said I'll manage. I started managing with them in '83. I spent two years in the Gulf Coast League with Sarasota. At that time, we had moved down to that area, too, so it was pretty nice being at home all the time. I managed Double A the next year, and we had a big changeover in general manager, farm director and all that. I went back down to the Gulf Coast and managed two more years there, I think. Then I went to the Midwest League, the last year I was with them. I was with them six years managing in the minor leagues. I was with the Astros after that for six years. I was infield instructor a couple of years and then I managed four years, I guess. Then I went with the Cubs in '95. I was a hitting coach with Rockford in the Midwest League. After that season, my kids were all getting high school age and I wanted to see them play so I got out of affiliated ball after the '95 season."

Since that time, Steve kept his hand in, even around home. He helped run an independent league team in Tupelo for a year, but the team folded in its second year. He served as hitting coach with Glens Falls, New York with Les Lancaster. "He was the manager, and he'd been the pitching coach with me with the Tupelo team. He called me up there wanted to know if I'd come up there with him. I went to Lafayette, Louisiana and managed a team, and Ron Guidry was the pitching coach down there. That's where he's from. He was king down there.

That was a good time with him. Last couple of years, I've been . . . in our old town here we started a Park and Rec. I've been director of that. We've got baseball, softball, soccer and so on."

Now Steve is actively following his son Tim, a real prospect pitching for the Brevard County team in the Florida State League. Tim Dillard signed with Milwaukee a couple of years ago. "We're hoping one day we'll have him in the big leagues." His oldest son is an engineer with the Air Force, and his second son just earned his master's degree in Business Administration.

Tim is the only one who's seeking a career in organized baseball. A right-handed pitcher, in 2005 he finished the season 12–10, with a 2.48 ERA, leading the league in starts (28), complete games (5), and innings pitched (185⅓). Tim tied for second in the league for the number of wins, and tied for first with two shutouts.

Steve still follows the Cubs and the Red Sox, and keeps up with the Cardinals and Braves as well. His father's a big Braves fan. "Now he's got a grandson, so hopefully he'll get to see him play one of these days."

Bob Heise

by Bill Nowlin

	G	AB	R	H	2B	3B	HR	RBI	BB	SO	BA	OBP	SLG	SB	CS	GDP	HBP
1975 RED SOX	63	126	12	27	3	0	0	21	4	6	.214	.246	.238	0	0	1	2

Robert Lowell Heise was born in San Antonio, but doesn't remember a thing about the place. His father, William Heise, was an officer in the military and he and the family moved around. Bob remembers more of Lompoc and Vacaville, in California. Bob's father had a degree in sociology and criminology and, after his military career, served in corrections work, ending up at the California Medical Facility in Vacaville. Bob's mother stayed at home to look after Bob, his younger brother Ben, and their sister. After Bob graduated from high school, she got her master's degree and became a schoolteacher. Ben Heise played in the Cleveland Indians organization, making it as high as Triple A; his team won a gold medal in the Pan Am Games. Ben was an infielder like his brother but wasn't able to climb the final rung of the ladder.

Baseball appealed to Bob early on. William Heise played fast-pitch softball and football in college. It was in Lompoc that Bob first remembers becoming interested in baseball at the age of five. "I knew that's what I wanted to do. It was embedded in me. And I just took it very serious. I wanted to play ball, all my life." His dad was supportive, but the drive came from within: "He played catch with me and encouraged me to, but most of the encouragement came that I wanted to do it on my own. It was my love. That's what I wanted to do." When the family moved to Vacaville, Bob was nine and Little League was starting up, fielding four teams. Bob played infield. After Little League, it was American Legion, Babe Ruth, and high school ball. At Vacaville High, he helped spark the Bulldogs to the 1964 Golden

Empire League championship. Bob's American Legion Post 165 team, coached by his father, won the league championship in 1965. "Bob was a very intense ball player, but that was one of the things that was so great about him," remarked Vacaville High's athletic director Tom Zunino. Heise graduated in 1965.

Following Bobby Heise's development was scout Roy Partee, who signed him for the Mets at age 18 in February 1966. In the winter of 1965, Heise had played in the Peninsula League just for fun—it wasn't semipro—and Bud Harrelson of the Mets was at one of the games, keeping an eye out on behalf of Partee. "You would play a doubleheader on Saturday and a single game on Sunday. I was playing second base, and Buddy Harrelson, I think, told Roy Partee, 'This kid has a little talent.'" Partee offered Heise a contract. There was a bonus, but it was, in Heise's words, "Very little. Very little. I'll leave it at that."

Heise was assigned to a Mets farm team in Jacksonville, Florida, for extended spring training in 1966 and then to Greenville, South Carolina. With the Class A Greenville team in the Western Carolinas League, Heise played in 122 games, batting .283 with six homers, 50 RBI, and 90 runs scored. He was named to the league's All-Star team. In 1967, he played in Durham, another Class A team in the Carolina League. He hit for a higher average, .298, but with just one home run and 37 RBI. In 1967, Heise joined the Mets after a stretch in the Marine Reserve, getting into his first game on September 12 as the starting second baseman against the Atlanta Braves. Heise was 1-for-4 that day, singling with two outs in the ninth. He was caught

stealing to end the inning, and the Braves scored twice in the bottom of the ninth to win the game, 4–3. By season's end, Heise played in 16 games and hit for a .323 average. It was his first of 11 major league seasons.

Heise saw only limited action each of the next two years, September call-ups both in '68 and '69. In 1968, he was a regular for Jacksonville in the International League, as he was in 1969 for Tidewater. Both seasons were solid, if not spectacular. He got in four games (hitting 3-for-10) for the historic 1969 Mets, although he was not on the postseason roster.

In 1970, Heise made the big league club out of spring training—but it was for the San Francisco Giants. The Mets had traded him and Jim Gosger to the Giants for Ray Sadecki and Dave Marshall on December 12, 1969. With San Francisco, Heise more or less split his time between backup roles at shortstop and second base, getting into 67 games, but batting only .234. Before his time in the majors was up, Heise accumulated 1,144 at-bats but he hit his one and only major league home run on June 30, 1970, off Danny Combs. The Giants were hosting the San Diego Padres at Candlestick Park.

Does Heise remember it? "Yeah! They made a [phonograph] record of it, and I played it for my grandson just recently. He found it in a drawer. So we played it for him." It's not the sort of thing one forgets. He had some good people around him in the lineup that day—Bobby Bonds was leading off, Heise was batting second, Willie Mays was in the three hole, and Willie McCovey was batting cleanup. In the third inning, Coombs made a mistake and Heise hit one out. The Padres won the game nevertheless, 3–2.

Heise had flashes of real success. He was traded to the Brewers on the first day of June in 1971 and during one stretch of 10 games for Milwaukee, there were three games when Heise went 3-for-4. They were the exceptions, though. Heise batted .234 in 1970, and hadn't had a hit his first 11 at-bats for San Francisco in 1971 prior to the trade to Milwaukee. He hit .254 for the Brewers that year, improving to .266 in 1972 when he had a career-high 271 at-bats. In 1973, he hit just .204 and was traded to the Cardinals for Tom Murphy in December. In mid-1974, St. Louis traded him to the Angels at the July 31 deadline for a player to be named later. After the season was over, the Cardinals got Doug Howard. "I loved the Angels," Heise says today. "They gave me the opportunity to play. I was having a great year with Tulsa, hitting .340 or something like that, playing for Kenny Boyer." Heise improved while playing more regularly for California, hitting .267 in the second half of the 1974 season.

In one of the first trades of the off-season, Boston sent Tommy Harper to the Angels in December 1974 and Heise became a member of the Red Sox, just in time to be on the pennant-winning 1975 Red Sox team. Heise batted just .214, but knocked in 21 runs, making key contributions. His best day was during a July 6 doubleheader in Cleveland, where he went 4-for-7 with five RBI. He pretty much won the first game, driving in three runs in a 5–3 Red Sox win. Heise's RBI were sometimes vital ones; he recalls having five game-winning hits in 1975. Come the playoffs and the World Series, though, all the regular infielders were healthy—Carl Yastrzemski, Denny Doyle, Rick Burleson, and Rico Petrocelli. "I was there, and my whole family was there. All the regulars played. The regulars played and hit .300. You got to realize the position that you're in, and what your job is. And you don't bitch about it. I did not bitch about it. The Red Sox treated me great. Tom Yawkey treated me really well. I really didn't expect to be treated that well. I had always been treated like Frank Lane would treat you in Milwaukee: 'If you're not under contract . . .' or 'I'll bury your ass in the minor leagues.' That's how I got treated in my time."

Heise was with Boston for the full 1976 season, but saw much more limited action: just 56 at-bats (though he hit .268). After the season, the Sox sold Bobby Heise to the Kansas City Royals in early December. He put in a full year playing under Whitey Herzog with the Royals, typically a late-inning sub in 54 games and accumulating only 62 at-bats. Kansas City made it into the playoffs, losing in five games to the Yankees. Once again, Bob hugged the bench as the regulars saw all the action. Again, he doesn't voice dissent. "I think the baseball person I had the most respect for of this whole game while I was playing, was Whitey Herzog. They let me go, then I knew it was over. Maybe I'd been losing a step here, a step there. If it was Whitey Herzog who let me go, I knew it was over. I didn't bitch about it and complain. So I guess that was it."

Bob Heise took retirement philosophically. "I sort of did. I wanted to raise my kids. I wanted to be at home. And that's what I did. I became a police officer, and I did that for 26 years until a couple of years ago. I retired, and I got cancer. I had cancer for about two and one-half years and right now I've beat the cancer. At my last checkup, I was cancer-free." Heise's work in corrections saw him work at Vacaville himself, as well as San Quentin and a couple of other facilities. He also worked fighting fires for 16 years.

Heise has two children and two stepchildren. One son, Heise says, was "very good in baseball, but he did

not have the drive I had." Heise himself gets offers to join some of the card and memorabilia shows, but hasn't taken up the offers, recognizing that there, too, he'd be playing the role of a utility man. He's content to stay home in his small two-stoplight town and play golf several times each week.

Did he feel happy when the Red Sox finally won it all in 2004? "I did. I did, for one person—Tom Yawkey. He treated everybody really great. He ripped up my contract twice in that '75 [season]. Before I came over for Tommy Harper, I kind of wrote a letter and said that I, you know, I signed this for California and the Angels. Going to Boston will cost a little more. They ripped it

up. One time after I drove in some big important RBI and we were going to get into the playoffs, he ripped [it] up again. And then after that, he gave me another raise. We're talking about little [amounts], but back in those times, they were big." [laughs] Mr. Yawkey was "One of the best owners in baseball, ever. So wherever he's at, you know, you know, in his grave or whatever, that was really great to see Boston win it last year.

"I have an American League Championship ring, and it says Boston Red Sox on it. And it's a thing that I'll get to pass down to my son, Bobby Jr. And now he just had a son, that's Robert Lowell Heise III, and he'll pass it down to his kid."

Butch Hobson

by Andrew Blume

	G	AB	R	H	2B	3B	HR	RBI	BB	SO	BA	OBP	SLG	SB	CS	GDP	HBP
1975 RED SOX	2	4	0	1	0	0	0	0	0	2	.250	.250	.250	0	0	0	0

Before Curt Schilling and the bloody sock in 2004, the player who came to mind as the personification of toughness in a Red Sox uniform was Butch Hobson. Hobson, seen briefly as a September call-up in 1975, did not impact the 1975 American League champs. His legacy is that of a power-hitting third baseman who brought a football mentality to the diamond in the way he played through pain and gave every ounce of effort that his body could muster.

Clell Lavern (Butch) Hobson Jr. was born on August 17, 1951, in Tuscaloosa, Alabama. An American Legion and Bessemer (Alabama) High School MVP, he followed in his father's footsteps to play football and baseball at the University of Alabama. His dad, a three-year letterman at quarterback for Alabama, was Hobson's football coach at Bessemer, where Butch was named to the All-Jefferson County team as a quarterback. Hobson was a safety and backup quarterback at Alabama playing on the gridiron for legendary coach Paul "Bear" Bryant. In the 1972 Orange Bowl national championship game won by Nebraska over Alabama by a 38–6 score, Hobson ran the "wishbone" offense for the Crimson Tide after starting quarterback Terry Davis was injured in the fourth quarter. Alabama's most successful offensive options in that game were the option running and draw plays executed by their quarterback tandem. According to Herb Crehan in *Red Sox Heroes of Yesteryear,* Hobson carried the ball 15 times, rushing for 59 yards in the Orange Bowl.

Entering his senior year at Alabama, Hobson decided to concentrate solely on baseball. As reported to *Baseball Digest*'s Kevin Glew, "I told Coach Bryant my decision and he told me, 'Well, Butch from what I've seen of you on the baseball field, you'll be playing football for me next year'" Hobson's choice proved to be a wise one. In 1973, he was the team leader in hits (38), home runs (13), and RBI (37), and tied for the team lead in runs (20), set a Southeastern Conference home run record, was named to the ABCA All-South Region Team, and was a First Team All-SEC selection. Hobson lettered in baseball at Alabama in 1970, 1972, and 1973, playing for coaches Joe Sewell and Hayden Riley. He hit .250 in his collegiate career (80-for-320) with 18 homers and 54 RBI. In 1993, Hobson was named to Alabama's All-Century baseball team in commemoration of the school's 100th anniversary of baseball.

Hobson was selected by the Red Sox in the eighth round (185th overall) of the 1973 amateur draft and was signed to a contract by Red Sox scout Milt Bolling on August 1, 1973. He was assigned to Winston-Salem where he hit a mere .179 in seventeen games. His numbers improved over a full season at Winston-Salem as he hit .284 with 14 homers and 74 RBI in 1974 and they earned him a promotion to Eastern League Bristol. His 15 homers, 73 RBI, and .265 batting average at Bristol in 1975 helped secure him a call-up to Boston that September.

Hobson made his major league debut on September 7, 1975 in the second game of a doubleheader against

the Brewers at Milwaukee's County Stadium, pinch-running for Cecil Cooper in the fifth inning. In his only other 1975 appearance in the Red Sox lineup, he started at third base at Fenway on September 28 in an 11–4 loss to the Cleveland Indians. Hitting eighth in the order, he struck out twice and flied out to center field before getting his first major league hit, a single off lefthander Jim Strickland in the eighth inning.

After beginning the 1976 season at Triple A Pawtucket (in an attempt to appeal to a broader audience, the club was briefly named the Rhode Island Red Sox, but changed back to the Pawtucket Red Sox in 1977), Hobson made his 1976 debut at Fenway on June 28 in a 12–8 victory over the Orioles. Getting the start at third base in the two spot in the batting order, Hobson went 2-for-5, doubling off Jim Palmer and hitting his first major league homer in the sixth off Rudy May. Centerfielder Paul Blair missed catching Hobson's drive to center, allowing Hobson to circle the bases with Cecil Cooper ahead of him for the inside-the-park home run.

Hobson would play 76 games at third base in 1976 for the Red Sox as the successor at the hot corner to Rico Petrocelli. Petrocelli was winding down a 13-year career with the Red Sox, hitting only .213 in 85 games his final season. Hobson, made the new everyday third baseman by new manager Don Zimmer (who replaced Darrell Johnson after the All-Star break), hit .234 in 1976, contributing eight homers and 34 RBI.

1977 was both Hobson's breakout year and also his finest as a major leaguer. Hobson smashed 30 round-trippers, establishing a Red Sox record for third basemen. It has often been printed that Hobson set the standard for Red Sox third basemen while hitting in the ninth spot in the batting order. In fact, Hobson, in 159 games in 1977, hit third in five games, sixth in 12 games, seventh in 47 games, eighth in 89 games and ninth in only six games. He hit no homers in the nine spot. Twenty-eight of his 30 homers were hit in the seventh or eighth spots in the batting order. The 1977 Red Sox offensive juggernaut, affectionately known as the "Crunch Bunch," hit a then team-record 213 home runs, 21 more than the White Sox, who were second in the major leagues. Five Red Sox hit more than 25 homers apiece, with Jim Rice leading the American League with 39. They hit five or more homers in eight games. They slugged 33 home runs in one 10-game stretch from June 14 through June 24 (establishing a major league record) and 16 in three games against the Yankees from June 17 through June 19 (also a major league record). On July 4, the Red Sox hit a then-record

eight home runs (still a Red Sox team game high), including seven solo shots (still a single game record) in a 9–6 pounding of the Blue Jays in Boston. Hobson's free-swinging ways combined to produce a career-best .265 batting average, 30 homers, 33 doubles, 112 RBI and 162 strikeouts (still a Red Sox record for a right-handed batter) in 159 games at third base. Hobson put together an 18-game hitting streak. Hobson was named the BoSox Club Man of the Year for 1977 for his contributions to the success of the team and for his cooperation in community projects.

Old football injuries sustained on the artificial turf at Alabama contributed to a nightmarish 1978 season defensively for Hobson. Bone chips floating around in his right elbow made every throw from third base an adventure. His impairment would often cause his arm to lock up, thereby disrupting his throws. A familiar sight in 1978 was Hobson making a play and then rearranging the bone chips in his elbow. In addition to his sore arm, Hobson was hobbled by cartilage damage in both knees and a torn hamstring muscle. Hobson would play 133 games at third base in 1978 (he would also serve as the DH in 14 games), and he did drive in 21 runs in a 10-game stretch from April 14 through April 23. His 43 errors yielded a fielding percentage of .899, the first time since 1916 a regular player's defensive average registered below .900 for the season.

Manager Don Zimmer, accurately characterizing Hobson as a "gamer," refused to pull him out of the lineup. While his defense suffered, he would manage to be a productive hitter, hitting 17 homers and driving in 80 runs. He would finally ask out of the lineup on September 22 in preparation for postseason elbow surgery. Jack Brohamer filled in for him at third, Hobson still serving as a DH. In the heart-breaking 5–4 playoff loss to the Yankees on October 2, Hobson was 1–4 (a single) in the number seven spot in the order.

Hobson came back in 1979 to play 142 games at third base. He slugged a career-high .496, batting .261 with 28 homers and 93 RBI. Shoulder problems in 1980 prompted Zimmer to replace Hobson at third with rookie Glenn Hoffman who hit .285 in 110 games, while Hobson's batting average dropped to .228 (with 11 homers and 39 RBI) in 93 games, 57 of them at third base. On May 31, the Red Sox hit six home runs, including a back-to-back-to-back trio of homers by Tony Perez, Carlton Fisk, and Hobson in a 19–8 loss to the Brewers. On June 12, 1980, Hobson had the only multi-homer game of his career, swatting a pair of home runs in a 13–2 win over the Angels in Anaheim.

On December 10, 1980, Hobson was traded with

Rick Burleson to the California Angels in exchange for future 1981 batting champion Carney Lansford, Rick Miller and Mark Clear. He was limited to 85 games with the Angels in the strike-shortened 1981 season as a result of elbow injuries and a separated shoulder, hitting .235 with four homers and 36 RBI. On March 24, 1982, Hobson was traded to the Yankees for Bill Castro. He hit only .172 in 30 games with New York, his final major league stop as a player. In eight years as a player in the majors, Hobson had a career average of .248 with 98 home runs and 397 RBI. He drove in four runs in a game seven times in his career with Boston and once with Anaheim. Among Red Sox third basemen defensively, entering the 2005 season, Hobson was seventh in career games played for the Red Sox, eighth in putouts (473), seventh in assists (1,042), and eighth in double plays (85).

The way Hobson threw his body around on the field for the good of the team contributed to a shortened major league career. It also helped make him a fan favorite. In a 2002 interview with Mike Petraglia of MLB.com, Hobson explained his popularity: "Boston Red Sox fans are supportive. . . . Whether a guy goes 0-for-20, as long as you are out there and giving 110 percent every day, that's all they care about. They're rooting for that blue-collar guy that runs through walls. They want that guy who will dive into the stands for a ball because they know, in the long run, it's going to be what helps them come out on top. As long as you can continue that when you play [in Boston], you're going to be very well accepted."

After playing three seasons in Columbus, the Yankees Triple A farm club and finally leaving the game as a player, Hobson returned in a manager's role. In 1987 and 1988, Hobson managed the New York Mets' Class A team in Columbia in the South Atlantic League. He joined the Red Sox system in 1989, managing Double A New Britain of the Eastern League. His 1990 squad advanced to the final round of the Eastern League Playoffs. Around this time, Hobson also served a stint as manager of the Winter Haven Super Sox in the short-lived Senior Professional Baseball League. In his fifth season as a minor league manager in 1991, Hobson guided the Triple A Pawtucket Red Sox to a 79–64 record and a first-place finish in the International League East Division. His PawSox lost in the Governor's Cup Championship, swept 3–0 by the last minor league team he had played for, the Columbus Clippers under manager Rick Down. Hobson was honored by *Baseball America* as its Minor League Manager of the Year and by the International League as its Manager of the Year.

Hobson was viewed by Red Sox management as a rising star as a manager.

On October 8, 1991, the Red Sox fired manager Joe Morgan and named Hobson as his replacement. "We couldn't risk losing such a talent in our organization," said general manager Lou Gorman. The Sox hoped they would be getting a managerial version of the tough player Hobson had been. Unfortunately, Hobson's toughness as a player was not evident in his performance as a manager as perceived by the media (Boston Globe columnist Dan Shaughnessy often referred to manager Hobson as "Daddy Butch"). This did not bode well during a three-year period during which the Red Sox seriously underachieved.

Hobson lost his first two games as manager in 1992 in New York. The season opener on April 7 was lost by a 4–3 score with Roger Clemens on the mound for the Red Sox. His first win followed, a 19-inning 7–5 decision over the Indians at Cleveland Municipal Stadium on April 11. The Sox would go on to record a 73–89 record, good for seventh place in the American League East, their worst finish since 1966 and their first last place finish since 1932. After Roger Clemens (18–11), Frank Viola (13–12) was the only pitcher with a winning percentage over .500. Offensively, the team hit .246, 13th out of 14 American League teams. Jack Clark, after hitting 28 homers in 1991 hit only five in 1992 and hit .210 in the final season of his career. Wade Boggs hit a career-low .259 and left for the Yankees after the season. Mike Greenwell hit .233. Tom Brunansky led the team with 15 homers and 74 RBI.

The 1993 season saw the batting average improve to .264 with the emergence of Mo Vaughn (29 homers, 101 RBI). However, Roger Clemens had his worst season as a professional (11–14, 4.46 ERA, a season in which he had been bitten on the pitching hand by his dog) and the team was again mired in the second division, finishing fifth in the AL East with a mediocre 80–82 record.

1994 was the year of the strike-shortened season and the Red Sox compiled a 54–61 record and finished fourth in the AL East. Clemens led the staff with a 9–7 record. The offense, led by Vaughn and John Valentin, hit a combined .263 (12th in the league) while the team ERA of 4.93 (ninth in the league) is the only other fact one needs to figure out what happened with this team. New general manager Dan Duquette shipped players in and out all year trying to light a fire under the Sox. Following the season, he decided to ship out his manager as well, firing Hobson and bringing in Kevin Kennedy to manage the team.

Don Zimmer was Hobson's bench coach in 1992, and theorizes in his book *Zim* that substance abuse, alcohol in particular, played a role in Hobson's failure as a Red Sox manager. Following his dismissal from the Red Sox, Hobson became the manager of the Triple A Scranton/Wilkes-Barre Red Barons. On May 4, 1996, his team was in Pawtucket to play the PawSox. Hobson was arrested at his hotel on a felony charge of cocaine possession. Approximately 2.6 grams of cocaine (worth roughly $120.00) were alleged to have been found in Hobson's shaving kit, the drugs having been sent to Butch in a package inside of a magazine from a former friend from Alabama named Jerry Poe. Poe owed Hobson money, and allegedly sent unsolicited drugs to him as payment of that debt. On August 8, 1996, he was fired by the Phillies, Scranton's parent club. He resolved the drug charge without a guilty finding in exchange for entering a first-offender program and performing community service. He denied ever using cocaine while managing the Red Sox or the Red Barons, and acknowledged a history with the drug beginning when he was a player. "I came up in an era when that (using drugs) was what you were supposed to do. As a good old boy from Alabama, I thought that was the way to fit in. It probably cost me three or four years of baseball", he told Kevin Glew of *Baseball Digest*.

Following his termination from the Red Barons, it was the Red Sox who gave Hobson another chance in baseball. In February 1997, he was hired as a special assignment scout. In 1998, he continued his comeback as manager of the Class A Sarasota Red Sox team in the Florida State League. Finally, on December 2, 1999, Hobson returned to New England as the manager of the independent Atlantic League Nashua (New Hampshire) Pride. As the third manager in the team's history, Hobson would lead the Pride to the Atlantic League title in his first season at the managerial helm in 2000. The championship was New Hampshire's first professional sports title in over 50 years. His 2001 squad was eliminated in the first round of the playoffs. In 2003, the Pride returned to the championship series before they lost in five games to the Somerset Patriots, the same team they had swept in three games for the 2000 title. Entering the 2005 season, his sixth with the Pride, Hobson's teams have compiled an overall record of 340–303. His 2005 deal with the team reportedly gives him some ownership interest in the team.

Hobson is married for the second time. He has three grown daughters, Allene, Libby and Polly, from his first marriage to wife Allene and three boys, K.C., Hank and Noah, and a daughter Olivia, from his present marriage to wife Krystine.

Buddy Hunter

by Bill Nowlin

	G	AB	R	H	2B	3B	HR	RBI	BB	SO	BA	OBP	SLG	SB	CS	GDP	HBP
1975 RED SOX	1	1	0	0	0	0	0	0	0	0	.000	.000	.000	0	0	0	0

Buddy Hunter describes himself as an S.O.B.—a South Omaha boy. Harold James Hunter was born in Omaha on August 9, 1947 and attended South High in the Nebraska city. He still lives about 20 miles south of downtown Omaha.

Hunter's parents were both involved with cattle. His father was a cattle salesman in the stockyards and his mother was a cattle hide saleswoman. There was a little bit of baseball ancestry. Buddy's uncle Don Hunter played ball for nine years in the Dodgers system, making it as far as Triple A, playing for the Sacramento Solons in 1955 and 1958. This was before expansion, when there 16 major league clubs instead of 30. He might well have made the majors in today's baseball. And Buddy's father played ball, too. He signed a contract

with the Pittsburgh Pirates and was assigned to a farm team in Sheboygan, Wisconsin. Sheboygan was in the Class D Wisconsin State League. It was a career that washed out pretty early, though. When he arrived in Sheboygan, it rained for 10 days and he never played a game. Frustrated, he said, "If it rains tomorrow, I'm going home." It rained the next day, so he hopped a freight train and got back to Omaha three days before a letter he'd mailed to his wife arrived.

Buddy's brother, Jeff, was signed by the Red Sox. Jeff was 10 years younger than Buddy, but signed with the Sox and found himself assigned to the Winston-Salem Red Sox. And found that his brother Buddy was the manager of the team. "He played three years and that was it," says Buddy. "He was a home run hitter that struck out a lot. He didn't put the bat on the ball

enough. He'd seen the handwriting on the wall and left. He had a job in the offseason and they said if you go off to play, don't come back here anymore." He stuck with the job.

Buddy's father got him started, taking Buddy out into the yard when Buddy was about four. "He used to hit me ground balls, hit me fly balls. Hit, hit, hit, hit. That's why I was a pretty good infielder and not a very good hitter; we practiced on me catching the ball all the time." Evidently, dad liked to hit too much himself and didn't let Buddy get in enough cuts at the plate. Buddy played Little League, but credits the time he spent playing pickup games with friends on city parks and sandlots as more important to his own development. "If there wasn't nine players on each team and there was nobody in right field, you hit to right field, you're out. And then you had to go get the ball. That's where I really learned how to play the game. You don't see sandlot baseball anymore. It's all organized. We patrolled ourselves. We didn't have any parents around."

Buddy played ball for South High in Omaha and made all-conference and all-state. He also won himself a full ride scholarship to the University of Nebraska. "I did well in sports, not too well in academics." That was an understatement when it came to university. He lasted only one year. Hunter transferred to Pershing College, a small college in Beatrice, Nebraska. Pershing had an excellent baseball program, and Hunter recalls that in one two-year stretch there were seven Pershing players drafted by organized baseball. "There were more scouts in the stands than there were fans! If you had 24 major league teams, there were 24 scouts there."

Hunter was signed by Red Sox scout Danny Doyle, but it was a visit by Sox farm director Neil Mahoney that probably sealed the deal. Mahoney, Hunter recalls, asked a lot of questions about family. He apparently liked what he learned; Buddy Hunter was drafted by the Red Sox on June 5, 1969, in the third round of the amateur draft, 61st pick overall. Rick Miller was picked in the second round that year, and Dwight Evans was picked in the fifth round. (The first-round pick was Noel Jenke, who was drafted by three pro sports teams—the Minnesota Vikings, the Chicago Black Hawks, and the Boston Red Sox. He signed with Boston, and played 2½ years in the system, but didn't do as well as hoped. He did make the pros in football, though; Jenke played four seasons in the NFL.)

Hunter got a $15,000 bonus. "Bought a half a house with that," Hunter recalls. He was assigned to Double A Pittsfield in the Eastern League, and played at historic Waconah Park. It was unusual to start in Double A right

after being drafted, but there were a number of injuries and they felt he could fill in one of their holes. It may have been an unfortunate decision, because Hunter found himself in a tough pitching league. "I should have gone to A ball," he thinks today. But roving Red Sox coach Sam Mele was pleased that the youngster could hit .242 in a tough league. The next year, 1970, Hunter was assigned to Pawtucket.

Pawtucket in 1970 was still a Double A team. Hunter played in Pawtucket in 1970, then moved up to Triple A Louisville in 1971 and 1972. In '72, Louisville won the pennant, thanks to the play of Dwight Evans and a number of other talented players. In the winter of '72, though, the park in Louisville was knocked down and made into a football stadium. The Red Sox transferred their Triple A club to Pawtucket, where it has been ever since. For Buddy, it was like going from the big leagues back to the minors, because Louisville was "a great town" and then he was sent back to Pawtucket, which had been a Double A town. (Ben Mondor took over the franchise in 1977, though, and made all the difference in Pawtucket.)

Hunter's first year with the big league club in spring training was actually 1970, though there was never any thought that he would make the major league team. He was on the 40-man roster, though, on a major league contract. Hunter made his first visit to the majors in 1971, debuting on July 1, 1971. Second baseman Doug Griffin hurt his back, and the Red Sox wanted a little more depth behind veteran utility men John Kennedy and Phil Gagliano. He didn't get to play much, and still feels that it was four or five weeks wasted sitting on the bench. But he did experience something that thousands of minor leaguers never have: the chance to get in a major league game.

Buddy Hunter appeared in eight games in 1971, with a total of nine at-bats. He collected a single and a double, for a .222 average. And he got a taste of major league ball. There are a couple of interesting side stories about Hunter's first visit to The Show.

In Hunter's first game, he pinch-ran for Luis Aparicio in the top of the ninth in Tiger Stadium, after Aparicio had been hit by a pitch. He moved to second on Reggie Smith's single, but was able to trot home when Rico Petrocelli hit a three-run homer lifting the Sox from a 7–5 deficit to an 8–7 score that held up for the game's final score.

It was in his second appearance that he got his first major league at-bat. Back in high school, playing for Omaha's South High, the first pitcher Hunter ever faced was a kid from the Council Bluffs, Iowa high school team named Stan Bahnsen. Hunter was a freshman and Bahnsen was a senior. He got a hit up the middle. When he entered the game on July 2 at Fenway Park, the starting pitcher for the Yankees was none other than Stan Bahnsen. Hunter came in to sub for Aparicio to start the seventh inning, and got his first at-bat leading off the bottom of the eighth. Bahnsen "threw me a fastball right down the can. And I popped it up. And I was looking for a fastball! I swing big-time. Major league popup. It could just as easily have been a home run, but . . ." It was in only his fourth game that Hunter collected his first hit, in the eighth inning of a game in which he'd already worked two walks. He singled to Cleveland Stadium's right field off Ed Farmer.

When Hunter first arrived in Boston, he checked into the Fenway Motor Lodge (now the Howard Johnson's on Boylston Street) and went to the ballpark three hours before he was due to report, just to meet the batboys and clubhouse kids. "So I go over there and I meet them, and there's this old guy and he picked up this towel. He's got this white shirt on and it's a real thin white shirt, and in his pocket he's got this card that's a yellow card. You could see the yellow color through . . . that's how thin his shirt was. The next day, same old man, picking up the towels. I went to the clubhouse kid and I went, 'Hey, who's the old man over there, picking up the towels?' He says, 'That's Mr. Yawkey. He owns the team.' So I went up to Mr. Yawkey, and he had the same white shirt on. The same yellow card in his pocket. I couldn't believe it. I said, 'Mr. Yawkey, I heard so many nice things about you. I just want to introduce myself. I'm Buddy Hunter from South Omaha, Nebraska.' He said, 'Well, Buddy, congratulations on making the Boston Red Sox. I hope you have a great career.' Two months later, I get called down to Louisville, and Dick O'Connell—he was the general manager, Dick O'Connell—he calls me in the office and he says, 'Buddy, we've got to send you down. Doug Griffin's coming off the disabled list. We've got to send you down to Louisville, and I don't know what you said to Mr. Yawkey, but he wanted you to keep your major league money and send you back to the minor leagues.' And he said, 'That's the first time this has ever been done.' I was making more than the managers were down there. It was only like $20,000 a year but still . . . playing minor league baseball. Those guys were only making around $1,200 a month, you know, at the most."

That was in 1971, when Hunter played in Louisville in 1972 and the team won the pennant. Starting the season with Pawtucket in '73, Buddy got another call up to the Red Sox, asked to join the team in Kansas City

in late May. He took over defensively for Rico Petrocelli in the seventh inning of the May 27 game, and came up to bat in the top of the eighth. He hit a long single to left field, scoring Yaz from first base for his first RBI—albeit it in a game the Sox would lose 13–3.

Hunter appeared in 13 games in 1973, but got only seven at-bats. He did have one big game, on July 8 in the second game of a doubleheader in Chicago. The White Sox had won the first game, 6–1, and were tied 2–2 in the second game after nine innings. Before the game, outside the park, the Wilson Sporting Goods sales rep was there meeting some of the players who were signed to Wilson. As Buddy recounts the story, "There's about five guys, and myself, that were on Wilson contracts. Yaz goes up and he gets about three pairs of shoes and a glove. Aparicio goes up and gets about three gloves and a pair of spikes or two. After all of them were done, I went up to the guy and tell him, 'Buddy Hunter.' 'And can I help you?' I go, 'Yeah, I'm on a contract, too.' He looks me up and he goes, 'Oh yeah, Buddy, yeah, yeah, yeah. You're on the contract. What do you need?' I said, 'I need one pair of shoes. Size 10.' And he looked, and he goes, 'Out of them. I'll send you a pair.'"

Dwight Evans led off the Boston 10th with a double, and Hunter singled him in with the go-ahead run. That was all it took, as the White Sox failed to score in the bottom of the 10th, but as it happened, Boston scored nine times in the top of the inning. Hunter doubled his second time up. So, back to the Wilson rep. Hunter picks up the story: "I'm in the game. I win the game. I turn two double plays that game. I had a great game. After the game, he comes up to me. After I get the game-winning hit and turn two double plays in nine innings . . . . I get the game-winning hit, and he comes in the locker room. He goes, 'Buddy . . . uh . . . I found two pairs of size 10s.'"

Buddy was up for about six weeks, then sent back down, but meanwhile had gone 3-for-7 at the plate. His .429 average led the team in 1973.

In late 1973, though, on December 10, Hunter was sold to the Kansas City Royals. He played out the year in Omaha, of all places, for the Omaha Royals. It was his hometown, but as it happened, it was the worst year of his career. George Brett was on the team. So was Dennis Leonard, very briefly. It was a great team on paper, but too many players were called up to the parent club. And Buddy had a bad year, batting just .216.

A funny thing happened on the way to the 1975 season. "In the spring, like in February when your contract comes out, all of a sudden I get a contract from Boston instead of the Royals. And I'm going,

Wait a minute? Who am I? Royals or Red Sox? Well, anyway, I got this contract so I called Boston. They said, 'We bought you back.' It was a scam deal. They just protected me." What really happened, he pieced together later: the Red Sox had acquired Juan Marichal in December 1973, but had no room for him on the 40-man roster, but as it turned out, Kansas City only had 39 players on its roster. So a deal was done, and Hunter played 1974 in the Royals system only to find himself back with the Red Sox when he was, in the words of Baseball-reference.com transaction data, "sent from the Kansas City Royals to the Boston Red Sox in an unknown transaction." Later still, Hunter also learned that a couple of years after that Mike Easler had sued and won a lawsuit over the same practice. Essentially, the Red Sox had stored Hunter on the K.C. roster for a year, then retrieved him in time for the 1975 season.

Hunter started the season in Pawtucket with the Rhode Island Red Sox and was called up, again at midseason, again due to injury. "They always sent me up in the middle of the year. That's why I don't have a baseball card," he said. Baseball card photos were typically taken in spring training. He got in just one game, the June 1 game against the Twins. He got up once—his last major league at-bat—and grounded out to end the seventh. He'd been up every other year—1971, 1973, and 1975. He would never come up again, though he didn't know that at the time. "Darrell Johnson said 'the guy at second base is not doing good for me, Buddy. I'm going to work you in the tail end of games, get you some experience. You're going to be my starting second baseman.' So I sat on the bench for about a week and never got in a game. I got in one game, and all of a sudden, he calls me in his office and he says, 'We're going to send you back to Pawtucket. We have three doubleheaders in five games. I need to call up a pitcher. We're going to send you down and then we're going to call you right back up after these doubleheaders. I still want you to be my second baseman.' I went down to Pawtucket. They're playing in Rochester. First game in, broke my wrist. So I don't know if I would have been called back up again. I wasn't, because I was injured. That's when they purchased the contract of Denny Doyle. He did one hell of a job for the Red Sox and I never returned to the big leagues."

Buddy played with Pawtucket in '75, but watched on television as the Red Sox competed in the World Series.

He got a $250 share, less than the batboy, $186.12 after taxes. It paid the rent the month it arrived, though.

Hunter had a very good 1976 in Pawtucket . In 1977, the team won the International League pennant and Hunter says he was named co-MVP of the League, with third base teammate Ted Cox. Hunter has nothing but good things to say about Pawtucket manager Joe Morgan. He still keeps in touch with Morgan every two or three weeks. In 1978 and 1979, he played with Pawtucket, but never got a call up, even late in the season. Denny Doyle was the regular second baseman for the Red Sox through 1977, and Jerry Remy took over in 1978. Hunter was already working with the PawSox as a player-coach, in effect getting training to become a manager after he was finished playing. He was getting older, and "that last year, I think I collected my check with a gun and a mask. I wasn't very good." Starting in 1980, Hunter managed in Winston-Salem for two years. As we have seen, one of the players he managed for the Winston-Salem Red Sox was his younger brother.

At that point, he decided to leave baseball. What happened was that Sox farm director Ed Kenney called him up and offered him a job taking over for a scout who had just retired in California. Buddy and his wife visited the area to look for a home, but found the cost of living such that even with the small raise the Red Sox offered, "We would have went broke out there. We would have had to live in the slums." He went into sales instead, and has worked for 25 years now quite successfully for a company selling material handling products—from school and employee lockers to warehouse shelving and racking, conveyers, carts, and dollies.

Meanwhile, some other Hunters carry on the family tradition of athletic achievement. Jeff Hunter's daughter Lindsey was second-team all-American in volleyball with the University of Missouri in 2004–2005, her junior year. Buddy's nephew Jason Parker, his sister's son, Staff Sergeant Jason A. Parker won the Gold Medal in air rifle shooting World's Cup in 2003, setting a new world's record in the process with a score of 702.5 out of a possible 709. Buddy Hunter's daughter played some softball, and his oldest son earned a full scholarship to the University of Nebraska at Omaha, but his engineering curriculum prevented him from pursuing the game further. Their youngest son is a professional golf instructor. Buddy Hunter remains a Red Sox fan to this day.

Deron Johnson

by John Vorperian

	G	AB	R	H	2B	3B	HR	RBI	BB	SO	BA	OBP	SLG	SB	CS	GDP	HBP
1975 RED SOX	3	10	2	6	0	0	1	3	2	0	.600	.667	.900	0	0	0	0

Deron Roger Johnson, labeled the "next Mickey Mantle," spent 16 seasons as a major league slugger. His finest year was not as a Bronx Bomber but as a Cincinnati Red. A dual-football and baseball-interscholastic sports star, the San Diego native excelled on the gridiron. Johnson played end, linebacker, kicker, and punter for San Diego High School. In 1955, Johnson scored 15 touchdowns for the Cavers as the team went on to capture the Southern California championship. His football coach Duane Maley said Johnson "would have been a great college player and a pro player. . . . I saw him punt one 72 yards in the air." Maley further declared, "Deron was a coach's dream. He never missed a practice. He was never late." His baseball coach Les Cassie confirmed such and added the All-American end was among the top athletes ever to come out of San Diego High.

Pursued by several colleges, he was offered numerous football scholarships including one from the Fighting Irish but Johnson turned down Notre Dame and the other schools. Upon graduation in 1956, having been also sought by the Yanks, Braves, Red Sox, Tribe, and Bucs, Johnson inked a pact with the New York Yankees. Yankee scout Gordon "Deacon" Jones signed Johnson to a Class D contract for $1,000 a month.

Why wasn't Johnson authorized to be a Bonus Baby? A "Bonus Baby" was an individual who signed a contract for more than $4,000 and, by rule, had to be kept on the major league roster for two years. Brent P. Kelley in his book *They Too Wore Pinstripes* showed that New York skipper Casey Stengel simply did not play 1954's Frank Leja nor 1955 signee Tommy Carroll. So by mid-1956 the Yankees front office opted out of the "Bonus Baby" game. Additionally, Kelley reports that Johnson had determined he would rather be in the minor leagues playing every day. The D-level Kearney club of the Nebraska State League played only 63 games over two months. Thus, the net deal "was essentially the major league minimum ($6,000 a year)" and with a good season Johnson could be given a raise. Johnson figured correctly.

The 17-year-old "flycatcher" was assigned to Kearney, where he led the Nebraska State League in total bases (167), runs scored (70), RBI (78), and home

runs (24). Named to the circuit's All-Star team he also tied the NSL lead in double plays by outfielders with four. The next year, the young phenom was promoted to Class A, Binghamton. Again the outfielder made his conference's All-Star team, and led the Eastern League with 279 total bases, 103 runs scored, and 26 home runs. In 1958, Johnson moved up to Triple A Richmond (International League), where he clubbed 27 doubles, five triples, 27 homers, and was selected as an IL All-Star. In addition to the outfield, the Californian was called upon to handle the "hot corner." The year also brought the first of national family, i.e. Uncle Sam, duties that would occasionally interrupt his ball playing career. From 1958 to 1959, Johnson served in the US Army for six months in the Reserve Training Program. His 1959 and 1960 seasons were spent with Richmond.

Then on September 20, 1960 Johnson made his major league debut. The 22-year-old was called upon to pinch hit in the ninth inning of a 1–1 knot between New York and Washington. In the Bronx sandlot he faced Senators southpaw Hal Woodeshick. Mantle flied out to right and Skowron doubled. Johnson advanced Skowron to third with a fly to center. The Yankees won 2–1 in the 11th.

Overall, Johnson donned the pinstripes for 19 games. As he swiftly moved through the organization, the Big Apple sports media tagged him as a Mantle replacement. But there were others being bantered about as Commerce Comet Comers. So on June 14, 1961, he joined numerous other would-be Bombers in being sucked into the NY-KC trade pipeline. The Athletics swapped lefty Bud Daley for righthander Art Ditmar and Johnson.

At Kansas City, Johnson batted .216. In October '61, he was recalled to active duty in the military and discharged in August 1962. The remainder of the 1962 season he batted a paltry .105. That October, he wed Lucille DeMaria. They would have three children, two sons, Deron Jr. and Dominick, and a daughter, Dena. In April 1963, Kansas City sold him to the Cincinnati Reds organization.

1963 was a honeymoon of a year. Johnson returned to his native California and was golden. With San Diego he topped the Pacific Coast League with 33

home runs, tied for fifth with 91 RBI, and was picked as first baseman on the PCL All-Star team. This stellar performance pushed him onto the parent club's 1964 roster where he remained for four seasons. In *They Too Wore Pinstripes*, Johnson said of his full major league season in '64, "That was my first year. That was a hell of a pennant race. There was five teams right there: us, the Cardinals, the Phillies, the Braves, and the Giants. There was so many damned teams there, if you won one day you'd go from fourth to first. It was really fun. Once we were tied for first. Every day you go you know it means something." Cincinnati did not capture the NL Flag, but, Johnson proceeded into a super second season with the Reds.

Johnson had a banner year in 1965. He headed the Senior Circuit with 130 RBI, shared top rank in sacrifice flies with 10, batted a career high .287, made *The Sporting News* and the Associated Press All-Star teams as a third baseman, and came in fourth for the NL MVP award. In commenting about that fantastic term Johnson told Brent P. Kelley, "I had a good year. I was on a good ballclub. We had some good hitters. We had Pete Rose and Vada Pinson. I had Frank Robinson hitting in front of me. I had a hell of a year, really."

Two years later, he batted less than a deuce and a quarter, .224, and on October 10, 1967 the Reds dealt him to the Atlanta Braves for outfielder Mack Jones, pitcher Jay Ritchie, and first baseman Jim Beauchamp. Johnson barely swatted .208 with MLB's Dixie outpost and lasted just a season. On December 3, 1968, the Braves sold him to the Philadelphia Phillies.

The move above the Mason-Dixon Line to the City of Brotherly Love revived the slugger in Johnson. From 1969 to 1973, he clubbed 88 homers, 304 RBI, and 82 doubles for the Fightin' Phillies, despite only playing 12 games with them in 1973. 1971 was his most productive year; Johnson batted .265, garnered 95 RBI, and hit 34 home runs. In fact, Johnson went yard 22 times at home and broke Del Ennis' 1950 Philadelphia record. Further proof of his long ball skill happened July 10 & 11, 1971 as he belted four consecutive home runs against the Montreal Expos, three of them coming on the 11th.

On May 2, 1973, after nearly a decade of playing in the National League, Johnson found himself back in the American League, as the Phils traded him to the Oakland A's for third baseman/outfielder Jack Bastable. He clocked 19 homers, 81 RBI, and 14 doubles for Charlie Finley's Athletics. The switch got him into the American League Championship Series, and a World Series ring as the A's bested the NY Mets in the '73 Fall Classic. He also made another record, entering baseball history as the first player to net 20 home runs in a season divided between both circuits.

He opened 1974 with the A's, yet was on the supplemental disabled list for 15 days in April. On June 24, 1974, he was released on waivers to the Milwaukee Brewers. The Brew Crew later assigned hurler Bill Parsons to complete the transaction. On September 7, 1974, Johnson was sold to the Boston Red Sox. A month later, on October 25, 1974 he was released. On April 5, 1975, as a free agent, he signed with the Windy City's Pale Hose. To the sports press, Chicago's GM Roland Hemond stated that the Red Sox did not need Johnson because Tony Conigliaro had a successful spring comeback and that Boston did not want to stand in the way of Johnson. The 36-year-old veteran joined the ChiSox for opening day in Oakland.

In 148 games for Bill Veeck's club, Johnson hit 18 home runs, and drove in 72 RBI. On September 21, 1975, after Jim Rice had been injured earlier in the day, the "Other Sox" needed some supplemental power and so called and swapped to reacquire Johnson, sending cash and a player to be named later. Later in 1975, catcher Chuck Erickson was sent to the White Sox to seal the deal. Johnson's Red Sox role was to play first base and serve as designated hitter. He got into three games, ten at bats, in 1975, and hit .132 in fifteen games in 1976. On June 4, 1976, Boston released him and he retired.

Over his playing career, Deron Johnson participated in 1,765 games, netted 245 home runs, 1,447 hits, 923 RBI and batted .244.

A Poway, California resident, Johnson owned a construction company in San Diego and operated a 40-acre cattle ranch. Nevertheless he still maintained his contact with the Diamond Game.

In 1978, he returned to the Pacific Coast League and piloted Salt Lake City to a 72–65 win–loss profile for a second place finish. The club lost in the playoff semi-finals to Albuquerque, three games to none.

With the advent of the 1979 season, he became a coach for the California Angels. In addition to the Halos (1979–1980, 1989–1991), Johnson coached for the Mets (1981), Phillies (1982–1984), Mariners (1985–1986), and White Sox (1987).

In June 1991, Johnson was diagnosed with lung cancer. After a long fight with the illness, he succumbed to the disease on April 23, 1992. He is buried at Dearborn Memorial Park, Poway, CA. Over his 28-year baseball life he did tell Cooperstown staff his greatest game thrills were having played in the 1973 World Series and hitting four home runs in a row.

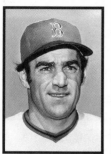

Dick McAuliffe

by John Cizik

	G	AB	R	H	2B	3B	HR	RBI	BB	SO	BA	OBP	SLG	SB	CS	GDP	HBP
1975 RED SOX	7	15	0	2	0	0	0	1	1	2	.133	.188	.133	0	0	1	0

Richard John McAuliffe was born in Hartford, Connecticut on November 29, 1939. He grew up in the tiny town of Unionville, a burg "not exactly a breeding spot for major league athletes," according to *Los Angeles Times* columnist Jim Murray, another Connecticut native. "Chickens are more along its line.. .. Unionville has about nine months of winter," Murray recalled. "And summer is apt to be three months of thunder showers." McAuliffe played baseball at Farmington High School under legendary coach Leo Pinsky, whose teams won 411 games and three State Championships. "He was an excellent baseball coach," McAuliffe recalls. "A very tough individual. When you didn't show up for practice, when you didn't run hard, when you didn't hustle, he'd take you right out of the ballgame and sit you right down. I thought those were good rules he had, and I think that gave me a lot of desire and hustle." At 5' 10" and 140 pounds, Dick was also the fullback on Farmington's football team, and a star basketball player.

Dick caught the attention of Red Sox scout Joe Dugan during a tryout camp at Bristol's Muzzy Field during his junior year in high school. McAuliffe was 16 years old. Dugan told him to come back around the next year when he turned 17. Unfortunately, the McAuliffe family was a victim of the 1955 flood that damaged many houses in Collinsville and the Farmington River valley, and Dick spent the year helping restore housing instead of returning to Farmington High. He did finish school a year later, leading the Indians baseball team to the state tournament at Muzzy Field as a pitcher and third baseman. "I was pitching a game in the State Championships.... I always had a good arm in high school," Dick says. "My first eleven pitches I threw were all balls. And we had two guys on and a 3–0 count on the next hitter, so Leo Pinsky took me out. [H]e put me at third base . . . and I made a couple of good plays . . . and got a couple of hits. Detroit Tigers scout Lew Cassell was in the stands during that tournament, and McAuliffe recalls their conversation after that game. "'You're not a pitcher, by the way, are you?'" Dick remembers Cassell asking. "I think he already knew that, but he was pulling my leg. Then he gave me an application to fill out . . . and about two weeks

later he was in the area, and he called my parents on a Sunday afternoon and he asked if I wanted to sign professionally... and I said 'yes, I do.'" McAuliffe signed shortly after the class of 1957 graduated, guaranteeing a $500 bonus and an opportunity to play professional ball immediately.

The June 22, 1957, *New York Times* reported the signing of the "infielder-outfielder from Hartford, Conn." He would report to the Class D New York–Penn League Erie (Pennsylvania) Sailors, one of nine Detroit farm teams in 1957. "I flew from Bradley Field in Hartford to Erie," McAuliffe remembers. "I go to the ballpark . . . and the team had just left to go on the road to Jamestown, which was a couple hour bus ride, but they would return that evening." The cab driver took him downtown to the general manager's office. The GM told Dick to go across the street and check into the team hotel, and come back for dinner. "I had my only suit and tie on, thinking he's going to take me out to a fancy restaurant," Dick says. "I get there, and he takes me to the corner drugstore and buys me a 69-cent macaroni and cheese dinner! And then we drive over to Jamestown . . . we watched the ballgame and the first thing that came to my mind after I watched was yes, I can handle this." The 17-year-old played 60 games, mostly at shortstop, had 175 AB, 36 hits, 9 doubles, 16 RBI, and a .206 batting average. "Don't they throw curves in Unionville, sonny?" he was asked. Charles Kress was the Erie manager, and the team led the league in attendance with a total of 54,923. The Sailors won the Eastern League championship, beating the Batavia Indians three games to one. .

"My first year in pro ball, the velocity that the pitchers threw compared to high school was a lot more," lefty McAuliffe remembers. "I was hitting everything to left field. I wasn't getting around on pitches." Tigers hitting instructor Wayne Blackburn had a fix. "They were flooding me to the left side, and it was difficult, there weren't any holes out there to get hits," Dick says. "So [Wayne] got me to open up, get my hip out of the way, and pretty much develop the stance that I had, and I was pretty successful with it. I stayed with it that whole spring training and after six or seven weeks of spring training I got familiar with it, and I was hitting the ball to right field, left field, and up the middle. By

the time I left spring training I was very comfortable with it." Many compared the new McAuliffe "foot in the bucket" stance to that of Mel Ott, the former New York Giants star. Bill James, who ranked McAuliffe 22nd all-time among second baseman in his *Historical Baseball Abstract*, described it this way:

"[H]e tucked his right wrist under his chin and held his bat over his head, so it looked as if he were dodging the sword of Damocles in mid-descent. He pointed his left knee at the catcher and his right knee at the pitcher and spread the two as far apart as humanly possible, his right foot balanced on the toes, so that to have lowered his heel two inches would have pulled his knee inward by a foot. He whipped the bat in a sort of violent pinwheel which produced line drives, strikeouts, and fly balls, few ground balls, and not a lot of pop outs."

It was back to Class D and the Valdosta franchise in the Georgia-Florida League in 1958. The now 5' 11" shortstop made the All-Star team, hitting .286 with 17 doubles, 5 triples, 8 home runs, and 62 RBI. "I just started progressing," Dick says. "Started hitting for average, hitting with power. Making less mental mistakes and physical mistakes." His fielding left much to be desired, as he tallied 45 errors in 93 games. Valdosta, under manager Stubby Overmire, won the league title over Albany in the playoffs. McAuliffe wasn't around for the postseason, however, having been sent to the Class A Augusta Tigers in the South Atlantic League for the end of the 1958 season. Now 18, he played 41 games with Augusta, hitting .241 with no home runs and 13 RBI. The Tigers finished the season in first place, but lost in the first round of the Sally League playoffs to the eventual champion Macon Dodgers.

1959 began for McAuliffe with the Durham Bulls of the Class B Carolina League. He was again an All-Star shortstop, despite 35 errors in 94 games at Durham. (The All-Star second baseman and league MVP from the pennant-winning Raleigh Capitals was Carl Yastrzemski—who would become McAuliffe's teammate 15 years later.) Dick hit .267 for the Bulls, driving in 43 runs on 84 hits, 20 doubles, 4 triples, and 4 home runs. He finished up the '59 season back in the Sally League with the Class A Knoxville Smokies, managed by former Red Sox great Johnny Pesky. "I liked Johnny, his brand of baseball," Dick says. "He was a tough man to play for. You know, a real red-ass." He played only 11 games for Pesky that year, getting four hits in 26 at-bats for a .154 average.

Back to Knoxville in 1960, this time under manager Frank Skaff. Dick was again an All-Star, backing up starter Chico Ruiz. McAuliffe's 109 runs scored led the

league. He batted .301, hit 27 doubles, a career-best (and league leading) 21 triples, 7 homers, and drove in 54 runs. It was a season that earned him a promotion to the big club at the end of the year. On September 15, 1960, the Tigers purchased the contract of the 20-year-old shortstop from the Smokies.

The 1960 Detroit Tigers were on their way to a 71–83 record, good for a sixth-place finish in the American League, 26 games behind the pennant-winning Yankees. Rocky Colavito slugged 35 homers for Detroit. Al Kaline was fourth in the league in stolen bases with 19. Jim Bunning led the league in strikeouts with 201 and had a 2.79 ERA. Frank Lary topped the junior circuit in complete games with 15. McAuliffe remembers his first major league appearance:

"[It] was in Detroit, in a game that I pinch-hit for the pitcher, and we were way behind. [The pitcher] walked me on four straight pitches, and there was one out at the time, and we were behind by a lot of runs, and [had] no chance of winning the ballgame. So I get on first base, and there's one out, and all I want to do is don't make any mistakes out on the base paths. So Coot Veal got up, and hits a real soft line drive to shortstop, and I don't know what made me do it—I guess the excitement that I was in the big leagues and all the people there and everything combined—and I just broke for second base . . . and I got doubled off first base. So it wasn't a very good impression."

His first official at-bat came against the Indians. "Jim Perry was pitching for Cleveland, in Cleveland, and the first three times up I got two singles, and a triple," McAuliffe remembers. "And then [Dick Stigman] came in, and [he] was just throwing balloons up there, and he threw one down the middle of the plate and I popped it up. And that was my first big-league out." (McAuliffe would even the score with Stigman in 1961, hitting his first major league home run off the Indian hurler on June 23rd at Cleveland Stadium.) McAuliffe's defense was still a work in progress in 1960—in seven games at shortstop, Dick committed five errors.

At the end of the season, manager Joe Gordon wanted his young shortstop to come to California. "[He] wanted to take me to Sacramento, where he lived," says McAuliffe. "He wanted to tutor me while I was out there, and he would get me a job at one of the big factories. . . . They have great baseball, semi-pro baseball out there. He wanted me to hook up with one of the teams and play, get in shape . . . while I was out there. And at the end of the season they fired Joe Gordon, so I never did get to go." Bob Scheffing would be brought in for the 1961 season. "The best manager

I played for was Joe Gordon." Dick recalls. "He was tough, he was fair. He treated the player like a man."

McAuliffe stared 1961 in the rarefied air of Colorado, playing for manager Charlie Metro and the Triple A Denver Bears. After 64 games with Denver, the 22-year-old shortstop was hitting .353, with 95 hits, 14 doubles, 14 triples, 5 home runs, and 31 RBI. He made 24 errors, but his hitting earned him a call to the Motor City. Joining the team for a game against the Washington Senators on June 22, 1961, shortstop Dick McAuliffe was a Tiger to stay. In July, there was some concern that President Kennedy would expand the military draft—leaving McAuliffe vulnerable. Fortunately, it didn't come to pass. (He finished a six-month stint in the Air Force prior to spring training in 1962.) The 1961 Tigers had an excellent campaign, posting a 101–61 record. Norm Cash led the league in hitting, and Al Kaline led in doubles. Frank Lary's 22 complete games topped the AL as he went 23-9 for the year. But this was 1961, and the New York Yankees were a dominant 109–53. McAuliffe played 55 games at short and 22 at third in '61, spelling regulars Chico Fernandez and Steve Boros.

Dick added a wife and second base to his repertoire in 1962. He married JoAnne Lee Cromack on March 3. Dick played 71 games at second, 49 at third, and 16 at short. He committed 30 errors, but more than made up for them with his bat—hitting 20 doubles, 12 home runs, 63 RBI, and compiling a .263 average hitting predominantly sixth and seventh in the order. He had his first career four-hit game against the Red Sox at Tiger Stadium on May 11. His first child, Mary Elizabeth, was born in the offseason.

The Tigers regular shortstop in the early 1960's was journeyman Chico Fernandez, a native of Havana, Cuba. They had no other shortstops in their system capable of replacing him. With his average at .143 in early May of 1963, it was time for the Tigers to make a change. Fernandez was traded to the Milwaukee Braves for Lou Johnson (who would never play for Detroit) and cash. McAuliffe took over as the regular shortstop, starting 133 games there and committing 22 errors. The '63 Tigers finished tied for fifth in the American League, 25½ games behind the Yankees.

1964 was a breakout season for McAuliffe. He played in 162 games, 160 of them at shortstop and two as a pinch-hitter. His career-high 32 errors were tied for third most in baseball. But his offensive output—for a 1960's shortstop—was remarkable. The 25-year-old led the Tigers and set a team record for shortstops with 24 home runs. His 77 walks were good for ninth in the

American League. He drove in 66 runs batting mostly in the bottom third of the order. The '64 Tigers had a decent season, finishing 85–77, good for fourth in the AL, 14 games behind the pennant-winning Yankees.

In 1965, Dick became an All-Star. Voted the American League starter at short, he led off the bottom of the first against NL starter Juan Marichal at Metropolitan Stadium in Bloomington. He popped out to shortstop Maury Wills in foul territory. Jim Maloney came in for the Nationals in the fourth, and McAuliffe singled and later scored on a Rocky Colavito hit. Cincinnati Red Jim Maloney was still in the game in the fifth, and Dick faced him again. "He threw me a high fastball, and in fact it was a funny thing, because Bill Freehan, our catcher was out in the bullpen," McAuliffe remembers. "And Bill was talking to one of the catchers in the NL, and he was saying, 'How the hell does a guy like McAuliffe hit with that type of stance?' And no sooner was it out of his mouth than I hit the ball over his head . . . [a]nd Freehan just turned to him and said, 'Just like that!'" The National League went on to win the game 6–5. "I played in three All-Star games," says Dick. "And . . . we lost by one run each and every time. The theory of the AL was the starters who were voted in to start the game were probably the best players of that given year. The NL, the same thing, except that the AL would always play everybody that's on the squad. The NL always played their starters, and maybe substituted a couple of guys, but they were always out to really win the ballgame, more so than the AL."

McAuliffe's numbers fell off a bit in '65, due in part to a broken hand that limited him to 113 games. Still, he hit .260, slugged 15 home runs, and drove in 54. He began a transition into the leadoff spot that year, batting first in 48 games. "I was the type of guy who had a pretty good eye at the plate and got a fair amount of walks," McAuliffe says of his leadoff hitting. "My on-base percentage was always good, so therefore if I'm on base quite often it gives a chance for the number two, three and four hitters to drive me in." He hit quite a few leadoff home runs in his time as well. "I think it's great for a ball club," Dick says. "Because if you have the power to hit the ball out of the ballpark before the other team comes up, that's a plus. Not that I'd do it that often, but it is a big plus and it gives an incentive to the rest of the [team,] especially the starting pitcher that day. It gives him a little incentive that before he goes to the mound he's going to be ahead one to nothing at least." Dick gave his pitcher a leadoff home run 19 times in his career.

Dick and JoAnne's second child, John Michael, was

born in February 1966. That season, illness and injury again affected Dick. He was limited to 124 games, but made only 17 errors at short. He spent some time at third base, and was again voted the starting shortstop in the All-Star Game. He went hitless, and struck out against Juan Marichal. His season was outstanding, as he connected for 23 home runs, drove in 56, and brought his average up to a career-best .274.

By 1966, it was clear to the Tigers that second baseman Jerry Lumpe was near the end of the line. The starter at the keystone since 1964, the Missouri native's batting average had declined every year since 1963, and his career-high in home runs (10) had come in 1962. To solve the problem, for the 1967 season Detroit moved their All-Star shortstop to second, and installed defensive whiz Ray Oyler at short. "The Tigers had no illusions about Oyler's lack of ability with the bat," says Brad Smith in his article "A History of Detroit Tigers Shortstops." "[T]hanks to McAuliffe's injuries, he had batted 400 times over the course of the 1965–1966 seasons, hitting .178."

1967's All-Star starters were chosen by the players, coaches, and managers, and Rod Carew was tapped to start at second. Dick came in as a defensive replacement in the seventh. He flied to right in the eighth, again in the 11th and once again in the 14th inning—his final career All-Star at-bat. And yes, the AL lost by one run, 2–1, on a Tony Perez dinger in the top of the 15th.

Dick had another fine offensive year in '67, hitting in the top third of the order. Twenty-three home runs, a career-high 105 walks, and 65 RBI helped the Tigers to a 91–71 record and an epic battle down to the final out of the season with the "Impossible Dream" Boston Red Sox. In fact, it was McAuliffe's 4-6-3 double play grounder in Detroit, against the California Angels in the season's finale, that kicked off a pennant celebration in Boston. It was only the second GIDP for McAuliffe that season, both in the last five games. He would set a major league record the next season when he didn't ground into a double play all season. "I wasn't quick. I wasn't fast," Dick told interviewer Peter Zanardi in the early 1990's. "I could get down to first base, being left-handed and had a quick start at home plate. But one thing that helped me was leading off so many times with nobody on base."

The 1968 Detroit Tigers ran away with the American League, finishing 103–59, 12 games ahead of runner-up Baltimore. "[We were] absolutely phenomenal for that particular year," McAuliffe remembers. "I mean, when you think a guy like Denny McLain won 31 ballgames, but it was more than that. We averaged five plus runs

for Denny throughout that year. Mickey Lolich was a great pitcher for our team, won [17] ballgames, but the key factor I think is that everybody contributed at the right time. I'd have to say that 1968 was the highlight of my life."

Al Kaline was in the outfield, "The best right fielder you'd ever want to see," Dick says. "Never a mistake in the outfield, never drop a ball, always throw to the right base. Quick release, not only a strong arm, but very accurate." Norm Cash was "the comic of our ball club," says McAuliffe, and "Stormin' Norman" slugged 25 home runs. Big Willie Horton led the team with 36, and outfielder Jim Northrup drove in 90 runs. Bill Freehan was "a good catcher, excellent with knowing how to pitch teams," recalls McAuliffe. "[A] good, solid man behind the plate. Knew how to call a ballgame, knew the pitchers that he had [.]"

When asked about manager Mayo Smith, Dick says "I don't call him a great manager, but I think the biggest plus that he asserted to the club was that he would have everybody moving on the bases. No matter who was on base. If a guy was on first and second and the count was 3-1 or 3-2, you'd be running. We were so successful with it that it was unbelievable. We'd stay out of double plays, we'd put the bat on the ball, we got base hits, and it really created a spark."

Some sparks flew at Tiger Stadium with the Chicago White Sox in town on the night of August 22, 1968. "[Al Lopez] was managing the White Sox," McAuliffe remembers, though Lopez was recuperating from an appendectomy at the time. "And they were not that far out of the race at the time. I was sort of the spark plug of the Tigers, scoring a lot of runs and playing good defense." Mickey Lolich was on the mound for Motown, Tommy John started for the Sox. McAuliffe played second, and led off the bottom of the first with a single. He scored on a Willie Horton single. "So [they must have] felt, if they were minus me, maybe John could hit me in the kneecap and I'd be out for two or three weeks, and they could catch up," Dick speculated, though in reality they were 28 games out with just 37 to play at the time.

The Tigers still led 1–0 when McAuliffe came up with one out in the bottom of the third. He remembers what happened next this way:

"[T]he first pitch at me was right at my head, and I mean right at my head. The catcher never laid any leather on it, and it hit the backstop. And I didn't think too much of it. . . . Tommy John has got some of the best control you'll ever see, and he's a lowball, sinker-slider type of pitcher with great control [and] not a

great deal of velocity, but he was throwing the ball hard at me that day. So he threw the next pitch, he spun me down, threw it behind me. And I turned around to the umpire, Al Salerno, and I said, "Boy, if that thing hit me it would really put me away.' Al didn't say anything, and I've got a glare in my eye then but I didn't say anything. The count worked to 3–2, so I dug in, and there's no way that John is going to throw at me again. The next pitch . . . hit the backstop again. And now I'm mad. But not mad enough to go out and charge him. So I take about two steps, and I'm glaring out at the mound at him, and he starts popping off at me [saying] 'What the hell are you looking at, you . . .' or something like that. And all I saw were stars after that, and I just rushed out at him, and both benches emptied."

John remembers the incident differently. "I was 10–5 with a 1.98 ERA and pitching against the Tigers in August. A 3–2 pitch slipped out of my hand and sailed over Dick McAuliffe's head. I didn't throw at him, but McAuliffe was yelling at me as he went to first, and he charged the mound. McAuliffe drove his knee into my left shoulder and separated it." John was out for the year; McAuliffe was suspended for five games and fined $250 by league president Joe Cronin. "John hit us four times in Chicago in June," said manager Smith. "They hit eight of our guys in the series there and we didn't hit any of theirs." Tigers GM Jim Campbell said, "Cronin used bad judgment."

McAuliffe had another sterling season in 1968. Most significantly, he reduced his error total from 28 in 1967 to nine in 1968. (He was shocked that he didn't win the Gold Glove that year—Bobby Knoop, who made 15 errors, did.) He hit 24 doubles, 10 triples, and 16 home runs, drove in 56 runs, and hit .249. His 95 runs scored led the American League. Dick would play in his first World Series, against the St. Louis Cardinals. His offensive stats weren't impressive, but he didn't commit an error in the seven-game Tigers Series win. And he added a home run in a losing effort in Game Three against the Cards' Ray Washburn. "It was a high fastball," Dick remembers.

A knee injury and subsequent surgery derailed the 1969 season, limiting the 29-year-old McAuliffe to 74 games. He still managed 11 homers and 33 RBI. He matched 1968's error total with nine. He would play four more years with Detroit, never reaching the heights of the 1960s.

Dick made one more postseason appearance, back at short for four games and second for one in the 1972 ALCS. He hit only .200 for the series, but hit a big home run off Catfish Hunter in Detroit's Game Four win. The

A's would go on to win the series in Game Five.

By 1973, he was a platoon player, sharing time at second with Cuban journeyman Tony Taylor. On July 15, 1973, the Tigers hosted Nolan Ryan and the California Angels. "Ryan was tough," McAuliffe says. "You couldn't dig in against him back then as you could [later in his career]. That [day] was the best stuff I've seen from a pitcher in my whole career." So good that Ryan fanned Dick three times in three at-bats. Not that the rest of the Tigers fared better—Ryan threw his second no-hitter of the season that day.

Dick had a decent season for the Tigers in 1973, playing in 106 games, batting .274, and 12 homers. But at age 33, he knew the end was near. "I wanted to move back East—I told them I wasn't coming back," McAuliffe says. "I wasn't pressuring [the Tigers] into trading me to Boston, but I knew my career was near the end, and I wanted to maybe make a connection and get into business of some sort, and Detroit obliged me."

On October 23, 1973, the Red Sox announced that they had acquired the veteran infielder for young outfielder Ben Oglivie. According to an article about Oglivie in the December 13, 1975 *Sporting News*, Oglivie was the "only body Boston was willing to give up to get [McAuliffe]." Manager Darrell Johnson expected Dick to challenge Doug Griffin for the second base job at best, and at worst, back up Rico Petrocelli at third. McAuliffe would wear number 3 for Boston, a number worn by another Connecticut-born player—Moosup's Walt Dropo—from 1949 to 1952. Dick was excited about playing at Fenway. "[It's] a great stadium to play in, because the fans are close to you. Just has that aroma in the air." As for the Boston fans, "[they] are very, very critical, very tough," McAuliffe says. "But they know the game. They really do."

Things didn't work out exactly as manager Johnson had planned. McAuliffe played a utility role in 1974, playing 53 games at second, 40 at third, three at short, and three as the Bosox designated hitter. He had only 272 at-bats, and hit .210 with 5 home runs. It was clear that at age 34, the end had come. Dick retired at the end of the season, and accepted the Red Sox offer to manage in their minor league system.

Muzzy Field in Bristol, Connecticut was a 20-minute commute from McAuliffe's home in Simsbury, and home to the Double A Eastern League Bristol Red Sox. In 1975, Dick would manage the B-Sox. Bristol went 81–57 on the year, behind young hitting star Butch Hobson. They swept the Reading Phillies 3–0 to capture the Eastern League championship. McAuliffe wasn't around to taste the champagne, however.

In August, Red Sox third baseman Rico Petrocelli was suffering from headaches, inner ear trouble, and vertigo, possibly the result of a 1974 beaning. The 32-year-old Petrocelli left the Sox in Chicago on August 17, at the time hitting .241, with four home runs and 44 RBI. Some wondered if his career, much less the 1975 season, were over. "I just don't see certain pitches well at all," Petrocelli told *The Sporting News*. Rico was placed on the disabled list, Bob Heise was installed as the regular third baseman, and Dick McAuliffe was pulled from his managerial job in Bristol. "I'm in good shape," McAuliffe told Peter Gammons of *The Sporting News*. "I'm seven pounds lighter than I was. I've been throwing in batting practice every day so my arm's strong, my legs are in good condition, and I've been hitting off and on."

When Petrocelli went down, the Sox inquired about the readiness of Butch Hobson. "Butch had a pretty good bat for me all year long," McAuliffe says. "But in the field he'd make an awful lot of mistakes. Especially throwing mistakes. And I didn't think he was ready right then. [A]nd they asked, 'would you be interested in coming up?'" There were about six weeks left in the season, and the Sox had a big lead in the AL East. "I really didn't think about it, and I said, 'Well, yeah, I would be.' Six weeks or so, you know, it's not long." But the veteran hadn't been completely honest with the parent club or the press. "[T]he only bad thing about it was I wasn't in shape," Dick says some 15 years later. "I hadn't picked up a bat all year. I threw batting practice—the only thing that was in shape was my arm."

McAuliffe played in seven games, all at third base, making his first appearance as a defensive replacement on August 23. He batted 15 times, with only two singles. His batting average was .133. His career ended on a sour note on September 1. The Red Sox were hosting the rival Yankees, and McAuliffe started the game at third, batting eighth. With one out in the second, Yankee DH Walt Williams hit a pop-up between third and home. McAuliffe dropped the ball for an error. With one run in, Bomber shortstop Fred Stanley tapped a ball to third, and McAuliffe's throw pulled first baseman Carl Yastrzemski off the bag. It was scored a single, and another run came in. Dick drove in his only run of the season in the contest, but the Sox lost the game 4–2, and Dick McAuliffe's major league career was over. "I never, ever remember being booed in the big leagues," Dick remembers. "But that one game everything stood out, and the fans in Boston were tough. And I really felt bad after that and that was the only time after making an error that I felt really bad about losing a ballgame. And I said, 'Well, I guess I am over the hill.'" The Red Sox obviously agreed—McAuliffe was left off the postseason roster. In the classic 1975 World Series, Rico Petrocelli was back at third base.

The Sox wanted McAuliffe to manage in their farm system in 1976, but Dick had had enough. "You know, the salary wasn't very big," McAuliffe explains. "I enjoyed doing what I did, but it was tough being on the road once again after 20 years of playing [baseball.] Leaving your family . . . and I said that's enough." Would he have changed anything about his career? "I think the only mistake I made was I should have stayed back in Detroit, where I felt more comfortable, and finished up there," Dick says. "[T]hey would have given me a job in the minor leagues either as a hitting instructor—or in the big leagues—or managing in the minor leagues, which would have been fine. And gave me a decent salary."

McAuliffe went into the private sector, running a couple of baseball schools and teaching kids how to play the game. "If you've got the desire, you don't need to have superstar skills," Dick told author Chris Stern in 1979. Shortly after retiring, he bought a business that repaired and installed coin-operated washers and dryers. "I did quite well with it," says McAuliffe. "I was in the laundry business over 10 years, and then got tired of doing it." He sold the business after 10 years, and is now semi-retired, playing golf, appearing occasionally at minor league games, and at autograph tables at county fairs and card shows.

"The game was very important to me," McAuliffe says. "I took it to heart. I played as hard as I could. I always thought I gave 100 percent, and was proud of the feats I'd done. I thought overall I should have done better. That's just my personal feeling. I think I've been successful."

Tim McCarver

by Dave Williams

	G	AB	R	H	2B	3B	HR	RBI	BB	SO	BA	OBP	SLG	SB	CS	GDP	HBP
1975 RED SOX	12	21	1	8	2	1	0	3	1	3	.381	.409	.571	0	0	0	0

For those who saw Tim McCarver break in with the St. Louis Cardinals more than 40 years ago, it is probably a surprise that he is now better known for his broadcasting career than for his days as a catcher. Not that he wasn't always articulate and glib, and that finding a home in the broadcast booth is a shock, it's just that he was a pretty good ball player who was a major contributor on championship teams.

James Timothy McCarver was born October 16, 1941 in Memphis, Tennessee. A police officer's son, he had three brothers and one sister. Surprisingly, it is his sister Marilyn that he gave much of the credit to for his early development. She turned him into a left-handed hitter and worked with young Tim on his fielding. By the time he graduated from Christian Brothers High School in 1959 he was a three-sport athlete, shining in football and baseball. He was all-state in both sports as well as captain of both squads. His football team was a powerhouse that won 20 straight games. Tim was a standout at linebacker and was recruited by both Tennessee and Notre Dame. He played American Legion ball for Tony Gagliano, uncle of Phil Gagliano, who also later played with Tim in St. Louis.

McCarver was signed by Cardinals scout Buddy Lewis for $80,000. The New York Yankees were also interested in him. His first assignment was at Keokuk of the Midwest League, where Brent Musburger served as home plate umpire in Tim's first professional game. One can only imagine the in-game chatter between those two future broadcast legends. He hit .360 in 275 at-bats and then was promoted to Rochester of the International League, where he hit .357 in 70 at-bats. This earned Tim a late-season promotion to the majors and his first look at big league pitching: he had four hits in 24 at-bats (.167).

In 1960, McCarver had a big year at Memphis of the Southern Association. He batted .347, good for second in the league. This earned him another late-season call-up to the big leagues. He appeared in 10 games for the Cards and batted .200 with two hits in 10 at-bats. 1961 would not be so kind, however. He stumbled to a .229 average while playing for San Juan/Charleston of the International League. Another promotion to the Cards saw him get his first significant playing time in

the majors. Tim appeared in 22 games and had 67 at-bats. The results weren't overwhelming as he batted just .239, but did hit his first home run, a shot off Tony Cloninger of the Braves.

1962 would be the last he would see of the minor leagues. He played for the famed Atlanta Crackers in the International League and had a solid season with a .275 average, 11 homers, and 57 RBI. Because Atlanta was in the playoffs, McCarver played in the minors into early October; he had to wait until the next spring to see the majors again. When he did, he was there to stay and impressed from the start. Despite his youth, he exhibited leadership skills and St. Louis liked him enough to trade starting catcher Gene Oliver, who clubbed 14 homers for them in '62, in a trading deadline deal for Lew Burdette of the Milwaukee Braves. The trade officially anointed McCarver as the starting catcher and he responded with a .289 average, 4 homers, and 51 RBI. He also had seven triples. In 1966, his 13 triples tied him with Johnny Kling (1903) for the post-1900 record for triples by a catcher.

Showing rare speed for a man of his position, McCarver displayed some in a June game against the Mets when he hit his first career grand slam, a rare inside-the-park grand slam. McCarver hit a shot that Mets outfielder Rod Kanehl slipped going after and McCarver raced around the bases before Kanehl could recover. McCarver was also a popular player in the clubhouse. Not surprisingly, he was viewed as a cerebral player who liked to pick at the nuances of the game, but he also had a very keen sense of humor. He was noted for his dead-on impersonation of Frank Fontaine, who was the rubber-faced funny man on the very popular Jackie Gleason show.

A July 22, 1967 article in *The Sporting News* recapped some pretty heady praise McCarver inspired in his rookie season. Wally Schang, known both for his days as catcher with Connie Mack's Philadelphia Athletics and for the first three Yankees pennant-winning teams, said, "The kid reminds me of Mickey Cochrane. I don't know if McCarver will hit with Cochrane, but he's got Mickey's same aggressiveness and speed. And as a kid, McCarver's a pretty good hitter right now." The legendary Branch Rickey was quoted in the same article as comparing McCarver to Bill

DeLancey, catcher from the 1934 Cardinals Gas House Gang: "DeLancey had the stronger throwing arm, but Tim's arm is strong enough. McCarver's a solid .280 hitter. He could hit .300 and he can run faster than DeLancey could. He has the same aggressiveness and baseball intelligence."

Success did not go to his head and 1964 would prove to be a big year for Tim and the St. Louis Cardinals. He followed his strong rookie campaign with another good season as he batted .288 with 9 homers and 52 RBI. He hit three triples, a fall-off from seven the year before. The Cards found themselves in a tight pennant race in September 1964, a season that is known for the collapse of the Philadelphia Phillies. Philadelphia blew a substantial August lead by losing 10 games in a row in late September. On September 21, with a 6½-game lead and World Series tickets already printed, the Phils dropped 10 consecutive games and found themselves in a four-way race along with St. Louis, San Francisco, and Cincinnati. Despite losing two straight games to the lowly Mets on the final weekend of the season, the Cards pulled out the pennant when they finally beat the Mets in the last game while the Reds, with manager Fred Hutchinson dying of cancer, lost to the Phils.

St. Louis would head off to the World Series to play the New York Yankees. McCarver was a standout. In the critical Game Five, with the Series squared at two games apiece, Bob Gibson had the Yankees shut out until Tom Tresh hit a two-run homer in the bottom of the ninth inning to knot the score, 2–2. McCarver then hit a three-run homer in the top of the 10th inning and the Cards held on for a 5–2 victory and the Series lead. St. Louis won the series in the seventh game and had its first World Championship since 1946. McCarver batted .478 with 11 hits in 23 at-bats, knocking in five runs and scoring four. He also tied a Series record by hitting safely in all seven games. It was quite a year for a young man who turned 23 the day after the Series ended. He capped the year by marrying his high school sweetheart, Anne McDaniel, on December 29, 1964. The McCarvers would eventually have two daughters, Kelly and Kathy.

1965 began inauspiciously as he broke a finger in spring training and missed the first week of the regular season. Battling injuries all season that limited him to 113 games, he was still productive at the plate finishing with 11 homers, 48 RBI, and a .276 average. The Cardinals slumped to a seventh-place finish as several key players—most notably Ken Boyer, Ray Sadecki, and Curt Simmons—had significant drop-offs in performance. The club improved only slightly to a

sixth-place finish in 1966, but McCarver had another fine season at the plate. He improved to 12 home runs, 68 RBI, and had a .274 average, and set a major league record for catchers with 13 triples. He stayed injury-free and was a workhorse behind the plate, catching in 148 games.

The 1966 All-Star Game was held in St. Louis and McCarver was selected for the first time to represent the National League. On a very hot day, McCarver began a game-winning rally in the bottom of the 10th with a single. He was sacrificed to second by Ron Hunt and scored on a single by Maury Wills, beating Tony Oliva's throw to the plate.

There was an interesting incident in April, 1966, which sheds light on the pre-Marvin Miller relationship between players and management. McCarver and veteran pitcher Bob Purkey were representing the players in a meeting with management, in a dispute over compensation for appearances on pre- and post-game shows. The players felt they were not being fairly compensated, and wanted more for these appearances ($25 for radio, and $50 for television). Management pointed to a section in the standard player contract that explained that players would "cooperate with the club and participate in any and all promotional activities of the club and league." That was the end of that.

1967 was a big year for McCarver and the Cardinals. Buoyed by an MVP season from first baseman Orlando Cepeda, St. Louis won the pennant by a comfortable 10½-game margin over the San Francisco Giants. McCarver was batting .348 at the All-Star break and earned a second, and final, trip to the midseason classic. His average tailed off to .295, but he still finished with career highs in home runs, 14, and RBI, 69. The Cardinals went into the 1967 World Series to face the "Impossible Dream" Boston Red Sox. Boston, which had finished ninth the season before, was led by Triple Crown winner Carl Yastrzemski and pitcher Jim Lonborg, who won 22 games. The Series was hard fought and finally the Cardinals rode the strong arm of pitcher Bob Gibson to a seven game victory. McCarver did not have the same outstanding performance as he did in the 1964 Series, batting only .125 with 3 hits in 24 at-bats.

1968 marked the last year in the great run for the St. Louis Cardinals. They captured their third pennant in five years, again finishing comfortably ahead of the San Francisco Giants. 1968 was also known as the Year of the Pitcher and St. Louis was carried by Bob Gibson's historic 1.12 ERA and 22 victories. McCarver saw his average dip to .253, but he atoned for his poor

performance in the 1967 Series with a very good 1968 Series. He batted .333 and among his nine hits was a three-run home run in the fifth inning of Game Three off Pat Dobson that put the Cards ahead and spurred them on to a 7–3 victory. Alas, things did not turn out as well for the Cards as it had in '64 and '67. St. Louis stormed out to a three-games-to-one lead before the Tigers mounted a comeback and took three games in a row to win the World Championship.

McCarver ended his first tour of duty with the Cardinals in 1969 with another solid season; 7 homers, 51 RBI, .260. The club slumped to fourth place, 13 games behind the first-place "Miracle Mets." In a historic trade, McCarver was sent off to the Philadelphia Phillies along with Curt Flood in a six-player deal that also saw enigmatic Dick Allen go to St. Louis. Flood refused to report to the Phillies and took his case all the way to the Supreme Court. This was the precursor to all the player/management labor disputes in the 1970s that changed the baseball landscape forever.

This also was the beginning of the vagabond era of McCarver's career. He began the 1970 season as the Phillies starting catcher, but in a microcosm of all the troubles that befell the Phillies in those days, McCarver broke his finger on a foul ball off the bat of Willie Mays in early May. In the very same inning, backup catcher Mike Ryan suffered a similar injury and both were shelved for a good part of the season. McCarver already possesses a less-than-powerful arm, the broken finger did not heal straight. The effect was that his throws moved like a cut fastball.

McCarver returned to form with the Phillies in 1971. He appeared in 134 games and again produced solid offensive numbers with a .278 average to go along with 8 round-trippers and 46 RBI. An interesting incident with his former Cardinal teammates took place in September. It began when McCarver dropped a popup near the St. Louis dugout. Cardinal players began riding him and really got under his skin when they began yelling "There he goes!" from the dugout when the slow-footed Joe Torre was on first base—the implication being that McCarver's throwing problems would not even allow him to catch a pedestrian Torre on a stolen base attempt. When Lou Brock was at the plate he was brushed back by pitcher Manny Muniz on two consecutive pitches. Brock made a comment and the two former teammates (and current friends) began to scuffle. Umpire Al Barlick ejected McCarver.

The two teams met again the following week. Brock was on third when Torre lifted a shallow fly ball to right field. Brock tried to score and Willie Montanez's throw

easily beat him to the plate and he was left no choice but to bowl over McCarver. There was a brief moment when it appeared that the previous week's fight would resume, but Brock picked up McCarver's hat and handed it to him which put an end to the hostility.

McCarver's first stint with the Phils ended in 1972 with a deadline trade to the Montreal Expos. Of the trade, McCarver said, "Being traded is something I'm acclimated to, but it would be easier to accept if the people being traded and their families were treated with respect." Two things bothered him; one is that he never heard from general manager Paul Owens who traded him and the other was that he just put $1,100 down on an apartment in Philadelphia.

His time in Montreal was brief, but for the first time in his big league career he played positions other than catcher. He appeared in six games as a third baseman and 14 as an outfielder. The 1973 season saw McCarver return to his baseball roots in St. Louis. He appeared in 130 games—77 of those at first base—and he hit a respectable .266. The 1974 season saw another move: the Boston Red Sox bought McCarver in a stretch-drive move aimed at strengthening the bench for their pennant battle with the Baltimore Orioles. He was not much help; he batted only .250 with one RBI and the Red Sox fell short in their bid to unseat Baltimore as American League Eastern Division champions.

It was expected that Boston would release him after the season but they did not. A spring training talk with manager Darrell Johnson convinced him that his chances of making the team were good and he would be counted on to contribute. He was quoted in the *Boston Globe* on March 15, 1975: "I'm not here to be a fill in. . . . I have a little pride with the good years I have had behind me." Unfortunately, things did not work out so well for McCarver. He appeared in four May games but didn't start in June; he was released despite a .381 batting average when Carlton Fisk was reactivated.

Thinking his playing days were over, McCarver did some audition tapes at various Philadelphia television stations. Before anything came of it, the Phillies signed him to a contract and his career continued. There would prove to be some productive times ahead. With Phillies ace Steve Carlton struggling, manager Danny Ozark began having McCarver catch Carlton on his turn through the rotation with good results. In 1976, with Carlton off to a slow start, Ozark paired the two again and Lefty won four starts in a row with McCarver behind the dish. He became Carlton's personal catcher and the Phillies won the Eastern Division, making the postseason for the first time since 1950. McCarver

showed he could still hit, as he batted .277. Philadelphia lost the NLCS to the Cincinnati Reds.

An unfortunate McCarver incident occurred on July 4, as the nation celebrated its bicentennial. He hit a grand slam into the right-field seats in Pittsburgh's Three Rivers Stadium, and on his tour of the bases he passed teammate Garry Maddox. He was called out for passing a base runner and received credit for a single.

1977 was another good year for the McCarver-Carlton tandem and the Phillies. Carlton went 23–10 en route to his second Cy Young award while McCarver batted .320. The Phillies won their second consecutive division title, but again lost in the NLCS, this time to the Los Angeles Dodgers.

McCarver's playing days wound down in 1978 and 1979. He still caught Carlton regularly, but some of his starts were handled by Bob Boone. He retired at the end of the 1979 season and was hired into the broadcast booth by the Phillies. He immediately took to the job and a second career was born. His playing days were not quite finished, as he returned to the playing field in September of 1980 to become one of

the few players—and the first 20th century catcher—to play in four decades. He moved over to the New York Mets broadcast booth in 1983 and would soon receive national recognition as an insightful analyst.

Just days before the 1985 World Series, ABC fired Howard Cosell and McCarver was invited to share the booth with Al Michaels and Jim Palmer. He was an instant success on the national stage. In an October 19, 2003 *Boston Globe* article McCarver said, "I was nervous, very nervous. Broadcasting a World Series was not even close to playing in one. As a player, you have a chance to do something about the outcome.... From a player's standpoint you think you know about 85 percent of the game. Then you go upstairs and find out you're wrong about that."

If that is the case, then McCarver has certainly proved that he has learned about the game. Opinionated, studious, and witty, McCarver has survived in the booth for longer than he was a player. As a testament to his longevity as the top analyst in the sport, McCarver has now done more World Series telecasts than any other announcer in baseball history.

Andy Merchant

by Bill Nowlin

	G	AB	R	H	2B	3B	HR	RBI	BB	SO	BA	OBP	SLG	SB	CS	GDP	HBP
1975 RED SOX	1	4	1	2	0	0	0	0	1	0	.500	.600	.500	0	0	0	0

When the Red Sox season ended on September 28, 1975, Andy Merchant trotted off the field and the Red Sox had only their third American League postseason berth since 1918. The Sox had clinched the division title the day before, thanks to the New York Yankees, who had swept a doubleheader from the second-place Orioles. So the 28th was a bit of a rest day for the Red Sox. Merchant debuted behind the plate, catching starter Dick Pole and batting third in the order. Also making his major league debut in the day's game was second baseman Steve Dillard.

Merchant was tested immediately. The Indians' leadoff batter was John Lowenstein, who singled. He tried to steal second, but Merchant's throw to second base cut him down.

First time up, Merchant flied deep to center off Cleveland's Fred Beene; Dillard, who had singled and stolen second, took third on the fly out. The game proved to be Beene's last after seven years in the majors. Bernie Carbo singled Dillard home. Merchant came up

again in the bottom of the third. Dillard singled to lead off, and Merchant singled, moving Dillard to second. Three batters later, Merchant scored on Rick Miller's single. Before the inning was over, the Sox had a 4–2 lead. It didn't last; as the Indians scored six times in the top of the fifth.

Merchant batted a third time in the bottom of the fifth and reached on an error by third baseman Alan Ashby, moved up to second on a wild pitch and to third on a groundout, but was left stranded there when Bob Montgomery made an out to shortstop. He walked in the seventh but was stranded on second. With the score 11–4 in favor of the Indians, Merchant came up again with two outs in the bottom of the ninth. He singled to the pitcher, but was left at first base when Carbo made the regular season's final out.

His major league stats for 1975 thus showed four at-bats, with two hits and a walk—an average of .500 with an on-base percentage of .600. He'd scored one run, and was flawless in the field—two putouts (on strikeouts by Jim Willoughby in the eighth inning) and

the one first-inning assist in three chances. The *Boston Globe* story was headlined "Red Sox scrubs bite dust, 11–4" but Andy thoroughly enjoyed the day. "I had the best time of my life," he recalled in a 2005 interview.

James Anderson Merchant was born in Mobile, Alabama, on Ted Williams' birthday, August 30, in the year 1950. His father worked for the Alabama Power Company, and both father and mother were supportive as he began to play ball from a fairly early age. Merchant attributes his initial interest in baseball to a local man named Merle Mason: "He put a catcher's mitt on my hand and he's the one who taught me in the very, very beginning." Andy was 10 or 11 at the time, and he progressed through Little League, on into Babe Ruth League and then on to what was called at the time Advanced Babe Ruth. Andy's dad was very active during his youth baseball years and served as vice president of the Babe Ruth League. "They always followed me everywhere I went," he remembers. "I still question Mom, where they got the money. She said, we always borrowed it—and paid it back." Andy had siblings, but none played baseball for long.

Merchant was always a catcher, every step along the way. In high school, he was the team MVP. After high school, he attended Auburn University and graduated from there in four years, majoring in business administration. The first year he had been given a "books and board" scholarship, but he got a chance to break into the lineup on the baseball team and as of his sophomore year, he was on a full scholarship. It paid off for Auburn, too. For three years, Andy was all-Southeastern Conference. He won the SEC batting title with a .400 average. He still holds one record in the conference, making six hits in one game.

Boston Red Sox scout Milt Bolling pursued him and signed him with an $8,000 bonus after the Red Sox selected Merchant in the 10th round of the 1972 amateur draft. He laughs about the bonus today: "I went and bought myself a [brand-new] Monte Carlo and hit the road!" Before too long, he drove to Winston-Salem, North Carolina, where he played Class A ball in the Red Sox farm system. In 121 at-bats, Merchant hit for a .339 average with four homers and 21 RBI.

He got married the following year, and progressed up the ladder to the Double A Bristol (Connecticut) Red Sox, where he roomed for a good while with Fred Lynn. In his 1973 season, he saw some action as an outfielder as well, accumulating 171 at-bats in all, with 24 RBI but a dip in average to .269.

A groin injury at Bristol, diving back into third, reduced his playing time. 1974 saw him back in the

Carolina League with Winston-Salem where he got a lot more experience, 366 at-bats in 113 games, and an average of .292, with 62 RBI.

The 1974 year earned him a promotion to Triple A Pawtucket for the following year, and he spent most of his professional career with the Pawtucket team, both before and after his brief stints with the big league club in 1975 and again in 1976. His 1975 year with Pawtucket gave him 375 at-bats in 119 games, and a solid .281 average and made him a candidate for the late-season call-up.

He appeared in 68 games with Pawtucket (renamed the Rhode Island Red Sox this year). He hit .296 in 1976, and was up and down a bit with Boston during the course of the season, though only appearing in two games with the big league club. "I'd gone up several times, in fact. They'd call when someone got an injury. They'd call me up for a little while. I was kind of the next catcher in line. I was back and forth." The Sox system had several good catchers ahead of Merchant—Carlton Fisk, Bob Montgomery, and Tim Blackwell.

Of course, in 1975, as the Red Sox faced Oakland in the American League Championship Series and then the Reds in the World Series, Merchant was not on the playoff roster. "I just went home and watched old Carlton on TV like everybody else." He'd made at least some small contribution, though. He threw a lot of batting practice while he was up and recalls throwing BP to players like Carl Yastrzemski as something he will always remember. Though Merchant was a left-handed hitting batter, he threw right-handed.

Merchant was pleased to receive a partial World Series share later in the year.

In 1976, Merchant was up and down a bit again, and got in two games in June. On June 2 at Fenway Park, he pinch-hit against Ed Figueroa of the Yankees, batting for Bob Montgomery in the bottom of the eighth, and was called out on strikes for the second out of the inning. Andy stayed in the game for the ninth, recording another putout on a Reggie Cleveland strikeout of Chris Chambliss. The Yankees won the game 7–2 on the strength of a five-run top of the second. Eight days later, Merchant got into another game, also in Boston, against the Oakland A's. With two outs and nobody on in the bottom of the ninth, he pinch-hit for Doug Griffin, facing future Hall of Famer Rollie Fingers. Oakland was leading the game, 8–5, after scoring six runs in the top of the eighth. Fingers fooled him on a pitch, and once again Merchant struck out looking. As it would turn out, that was his last appearance in the major leagues. After batting .500 in 1975, he'd struck

out twice in two at-bats in '76 and been sent back to Pawtucket. "I was terrible then. I was sitting on the bench too long and I lost all my timing."

Back with the Pawsox, though, Merchant did quite well. And he did earn a ring playing baseball; he is a proud member of the 1977 Pawtucket Red Sox, which finished first in the International League regular season. He gladly attended a reunion in Pawtucket in recent years and told writer Joe Kuras how much things had changed from the old chicken-wire cages they used as lockers back then. But, he added, "I was always one who came early to the ballpark. I used to help them on the field. I used to come and work out. I just loved being around the ballpark. It was my life. I loved it."

The next couple of years, 1978 and 1979, Andy played for Joe Morgan in Pawtucket, never playing full-time and never truly outstanding (.263 with 14 RBI in 1978, but declining to .152 and 10 RBI in 1979). In 1978, oddly, he switched positions in the battery and threw from the mound during one game—just for an inning, in which he gave up three hits and two earned runs. In 2005, he didn't have a distinct memory of the occasion—though he did recall pitching a no-hitter back in Little League.

Merchant had it in mind to become a bullpen coach after his playing days were over and felt he'd been in line for a position along those lines, serving as "sort of a player-coach". But things went awry and it didn't work out that way. Despite the depth the Sox had in catching, Merchant was a lefthanded-hitting catcher and those were rare so the Sox were reluctant to let him go. "I never was in the trade picture, I guess you might say." The way it all ended, though, was a bit bizarre. In 1980, he'd received a letter inviting him to spring training and directing him to report to the minor league camp. "I didn't show up and I didn't plan on coming back, but then I had a phone call. Sam Bowen called me up [from the big league camp]. He said, 'Your uniform's in your locker. Everybody's wondering where you're at.' I said, I didn't get a letter, I didn't hear from Boston or anybody.' I didn't know I was supposed to report back to the big league team that particular year." So he called up Red Sox executive Ed Kenney. "He wanted to know if I could

catch the next flight out to report to spring training. I said I'd be glad to. I done missed about a week. And I said, `Well, would y'all pay me for that week if I come?' And you're not going to believe this, but the connection on the phone, we faded out. We lost connection." It wasn't as though Kenney hung up on Merchant. "No, it went fuzzy and we lost connection. I didn't call him back and he didn't call me back and that's the way my career ended right there."

Merchant took up working for Alabama Power as a line-clearing specialist. He noted further, "I never have to this day got a release from Boston." When the interviewer suggested that perhaps he should report for duty, even though it was more than a quarter-century later, Merchant said that some people had told him, "You ought to sue them for retroactive. You never got your release."

Andy Merchant worked 20 years for Alabama Power and took his retirement in the year 2000. He currently works as a caregiver, helping take care of a man in his neighborhood who is wheelchair-bound with rheumatoid arthritis.

"The type people that were ahead of me, I feel like I never got the opportunity to show what I could do. You get called up from Triple A, and you sit around. You lose your timing, you lose everything sitting on the bench. Just warming up pitchers in the bullpen, you can't perform in front of 30,000 people who expect you to perform well. In '75, I got right into a game, which was all right. In '76, it felt like I just sat around a lot more. It is hard. It's very difficult to perform where you're sitting around like that."

Merchant is glad to receive alumni mailings from the Red Sox today, and has kept them informed of his changes in work, even though the team he roots for these days is the Atlanta Braves. He is clear, though, that he harbors no animosity at all toward the Red Sox. "I got overlooked a little bit. It's part of life. I enjoyed a cup of coffee and then went on about my way. I came along at the wrong time, evidently, but that's all right. I enjoyed it while I was there, I really did. I don't have no complaints or gripes about it. It was really special in my life."

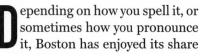

Rick Miller

by Mike Richard

	G	AB	R	H	2B	3B	HR	RBI	BB	SO	BA	OBP	SLG	SB	CS	GDP	HBP
1975 RED SOX	77	108	21	21	2	1	0	15	21	20	.194	.326	.231	3	2	3	0

Depending on how you spell it, or sometimes how you pronounce it, Boston has enjoyed its share of "Miller Time" for many seasons. The present crop of Red Sox has pitcher Wade Miller, third baseman Bill Mueller (pronounced Miller) and first baseman Kevin Millar (close enough). In past there was also outfielder Hack Miller of the 1918 World Champs, third baseman Otto Miller of the early 1930s, outfielder Bing Miller of the mid-1930s, and even Elmer Miller from 1922.

However, there's no question that for longevity purposes and overall production, the best known of the bunch has been a fleet-footed left-handed batting outfielder by the name of Rick Miller.

Richard Alan Miller was born on April 19, 1948, in Grand Rapids, Michigan to Irving and Marguerite Miller. Irving Miller was an outstanding center for the Union High School football team in Grand Rapids in the late 1920s, in his day playing opposite Gerald Ford while the future president was a student at South High School in Grand Rapids.

Rick Miller began playing baseball at the age of nine in the Grand Rapids Little League program. While he acknowledged that both parents were very supportive of his athletic endeavors, his dad was also his biggest critic. "He'd say things like 'Don't get a big head; if you go four-for-five, what happened the fifth time,'" he recalled.

The Millers had withstood a family tragedy before Rick was born, as a brother Arlan died of leukemia at the age of 5. While Miller's sports idols while growing up were Tigers Hall of Fame outfielder Al Kaline and Detroit hockey great Gordie Howe, Rick's brother Irving II provided the yardstick by which the younger Miller would be measured. In 1956, Irving—a three-sport standout at Union High—was named Most Valuable Athlete out of the 10 Class A high schools that comprised Grand Rapids. Exactly 10 years later, Rick—a football, basketball and baseball star—was recipient of the same award. "It was quite an achievement, probably something that I'm most proud of through all the things I did in sports," he said, noting that he was a pitcher and outfielder at Union, where he had the most wins and lowest ERA in the city in 1966.

Miller was invited to a pre-game workout with the Detroit Tigers in the summer of 1966 along with a fellow Michigan high school standout Ted Simmons, where he had the chance to meet his boyhood hero Kaline. "I even hit a few home runs there," Miller admitted. "I was amazed at how easy it was to hit home runs at Tiger Stadium," he added, commenting on the old short porch in right field.

After high school, Miller won a baseball scholarship to Michigan State, where he also played one year as a walk-on with the basketball team, winning a starting guard position. However, an ankle injury forced him to curtail basketball to concentrate on baseball. An All-American at Michigan State, Miller was converted from a pitcher to an outfielder, under coach Danny Litwhiler. (Litwhiler had spent 11 years in the majors, an outfielder with several teams including the world champion St. Louis Cardinals of 1944.) "They wanted me to pitch, but I wanted to play every day," he said. "In fall ball as a freshman I went out and laid it in against the varsity and got killed, so (Litwhiler) made me a centerfielder."

Miller won the Big Ten batting title with a .429 average in 1969, his junior year, and became the number two selection of the Boston Red Sox in the June 1969 draft. Boston's number one choice that year, Noel Jenke of the University of Minnesota, finished second to Miller in Big Ten batting, but instead opted for a football career. He went on to become a linebacker with Minnesota, Atlanta and Green Bay in the NFL. Miller was signed to a Red Sox contract on June 19, 1969, by scout Maurice DeLoof, the same man who signed Dick Radatz.

A six-foot, 180-pounder, Miller then reported to Boston's Double A Pittsfield squad and played in 77 games, batting .262 with six home runs and 32 RBI. The following year, when the Pittsfield Eastern League affiliate was moved to Pawtucket, Miller joined many players who would one day become his Red Sox teammates including Carlton Fisk, Ben Oglivie, Buddy Hunter, John Curtis, and Roger Moret. In 113 games that season, he hit .247 with 12 homers and 56 RBI.

Then in 1971, while in Triple A Louisville, he hit a career-high 15 home runs and drove in 58 while again batting .247. He led the league in walks with 106, while also coming in third with 117 strikeouts.

"I was taking a lot of pitches, but I was actually swinging for the fences," Miller admitted. "To hit 15 home runs, I'm not that big a guy. I was using a big bat, 33 ounces, way too big for me. I was getting in a bad position to hit."

Miller claimed he was "an afterthought to be brought up (to the Red Sox in late 1971)," he said. "I was a very good defensive outfielder. They took Fisk because they needed catchers late in the season, but after our last game they said, 'Tell Miller to come up too,'" he recalled. "They were a little weak in the outfield at the time and they knew what I could do defensively."

Eddie Kasko was the manager of the Red Sox at the time. Miller said Kasko was "the best manager I had in baseball. He knew the game very well. He let you play, just go do your thing. He was a very good tactician."

In the final 15 games with the Red Sox that season, he played reserve roles in an outfield that was comprised of Carl Yastrzemski, Reggie Smith, Billy Conigliaro, and Joe Lahoud. He wound up going 11-for-33 with a home run, batting .333 after August.

In his first game, on September 4, 1971, Miller came into the game as a pinch-runner, but got his first at-bat in the ninth inning and swung at the first pitch he saw from Cleveland hurler Phil Hennigan. "I was really nervous. It was a high fast ball, first swing and it went for a double off the Green Monster," he said. Miller also recalled that his first home run that season was off another Cleveland pitcher, Rich Hand.

In 1972, sharing time in an outfield of Yastrzemski, Smith and Tommy Harper, Miller played in 89 games, but usually as a late-game defensive replacement for Harper in center field. He hit three home runs with a .214 batting average.

Miller was also named Red Sox "Unsung Hero of 1972" by the Boston chapter of the Baseball Writers Association of America.

By 1973, Yastrzemski had shifted to first base and Harper played left field. The outfield was intended to be Harper in left, Smith in center, and Dwight Evans in right. Miller played center when Smith got hurt, and served as defensive replacement. He played 60 games in right when Evans didn't hit. Rick's batting average rose to .261 with major league career-highs of six home runs and 43 RBI in 143 games. In addition, his 12 stolen bases were third on the team to Aparicio (13) and to Harper, who set a Red Sox record that season with 54.

In a June 20 game against Milwaukee that season, Miller led off the game with a home run, while Smith followed back-to-back off Bill Parsons, helping lefty Bill Lee to a 3–2 win.

According to the 1974 Red Sox yearbook, his "emergence as a dependable hitter to go along with his outstanding defensive skills in center field made it possible for Red Sox to trade Reggie Smith for pitching help." The Sox would acquire Rick Wise and Bernie Carbo, both major cogs in their 1975 American League pennant-winning season, in the trade with St. Louis for Smith and Ken Tatum.

"I got great jumps, I knew how to play players, I would cheat, I knew the counts, I always moved on each pitch according to the count," he said, describing his forte as a defensive specialist in Fenway's tough center field. "Thurman Munson just hated me, because I would play him perfect. I took more hits away from him. He'd be all over me from the catcher's position when I came up to bat. I'd just step out and say 'Are you done yet?'"

In the off season that year, Miller married teammate Carlton Fisk's sister Janet Marie, whom he had first met while the two ballplayers were teammates in Pawtucket in 1970. The couple has a son Joshua, who is currently 25 and a skier and mountain biker.

In 1974, Miller played 77 games in center field, while Juan Beniquez played 91. Darrell Johnson used all his players, and Miller played the outfield with Harper, Carbo, Evans, and Beniquez—and even Yaz during one stretch when Harper wasn't hitting. Miller again batted .261. Fred Lynn was called up in September and took the center field slot.

At the conclusion of the 1974 season, the BoSox Club named Miller its "Man of the Year" due to his many visits to hospitalized children in the Boston area. He admitted that his parents' experience losing a son to leukemia before he was born was an underlying factor in his willingness to join in the Red Sox charity work with the Jimmy Fund, among other charities.

"It's something you do as a player. They would ask us to go to Children's Hospital to meet with some kids and I'd say 'sure.' It was easy for me," he said. "Thinking about my brother, we didn't really talk about it, but that death really changed my parents."

Miller felt he was forecast as the leadoff hitter for the 1975 season, but the day before the team broke training camp manager Darrell Johnson opted to go with Beniquez, so that he could get Fred Lynn into the lineup on a regular basis. Jim Rice was the DH for most of the first half, but then took over the left field slot. Miller was a valued backup outfielder who played when one of the others struggled or when someone got hurt.

"I had been groomed by Johnny Pesky to hit the ball on the ground, get on base, so I had to change my

swing a lot to be a contact hitter," Miller said. "The rest is history, and Freddy never came out of the lineup."

With the emergence of Boston's renowned "gold dust twins," Fred Lynn and Jim Rice in center and left, and Dwight Evans solidifying his job in right, Miller saw his starting time begin to dwindle. Lynn posted numbers (21 homers, 105 RBI, and a .331 average) that led to his becoming baseball's first Most Valuable Player and Rookie of the Year in the same season. Meanwhile, Rice was becoming one of the game's most feared sluggers with 22 home runs, 102 RBI, and a .309 average.

Despite Boston's remarkable charge to the pennant and World Series 1975, Miller recalled it as "the absolute worst year I ever had," he said. "Fred (Lynn) played all the time, Jim Rice played all the time. If it hadn't been for the World Series, it would have been really bad for me that year, mentally and as a player."

Nonetheless, there were a few bright spots that season for Miller. On April 12, he came into the game as a pinch-runner in the 13th inning, and scored on a Doug Griffin single to beat Baltimore, 3–2. On June 4, again as pinch-runner, he scored the game-winner on a Rick Burleson single as the Red Sox rallied from a three-run deficit to score four in the ninth and beat Chicago at Fenway 7–6.

"Even as exciting as that World Series was, it was terrible because it rained so much," he said. "We didn't have any time to go out and practice, just to go out in the outfield and have some fun shagging flies and taking batting practice. It was terrible," he added, noting that his fondest memory of the World Series was playing cards during all the rain delays.

Miller had two at-bats in the 1975 World Series against the Reds, and recalled one in Cincinnati where he thought he had a base hit with a ball up the middle. "As I was running to first base I looked up and Joe Morgan was standing there. They were pitching me away and playing me away," he said. "They had done their scouting but I hadn't played much, so I don't know how they scouted me."

In 1976, due to injuries to Lynn, Miller played in 105 games and had a good season hitting for Boston at .283, and played all three outfield positions. He was 5-for-17 in pinch-hitting roles.

The 1977 season marked the final year of Miller's first stint with the team. He broke his left thumb when he was hit by a pitch thrown by Seattle's John Montague, and was on the disabled list from May 3 to May 30. He still managed to hit .254 and made only one error in 86 games in the outfield.

That season he played without a contract because he was going to become a free agent the following year. If he had signed a contract, the Red Sox would have been able to get compensation from whatever team Miller signed with. Since he was an unsigned free agent, should he go to another team it would not have to give up any players.

After the season, in December, Miller signed with the California Angels following a re-entry draft, becoming the first free agent to leave the Red Sox. "I'm sure the Red Sox had ample opportunities to trade me before that, but I think they felt I was too valuable to trade because of the way I played defense," Miller said.

With the Angels, Miller became their everyday right fielder (he played 93 games in CF and 36 games in RF) and won a Gold Glove with a fielding percentage of .989, collecting 353 outfield putouts and only four errors. He also added nine assists and was involved in five double plays. The 1979 season allowed Miller to play in the American League championship series as the Western Division champion Angels lost to Baltimore three games to one. That season, primarily serving as leadoff hitter, he batted a career-high .293, and shared the outfield with Dan Ford, Don Baylor, and Joe Rudi.

After the 1980 season, when he batted .274, Miller was dealt back to the Red Sox on December 10, in a trade that also brought third baseman Carney Lansford and pitcher Mark Clear for Rick Burleson and Butch Hobson.

"It was good for me, I was happy to go back. Boston is a great place to play baseball," he said. "California was a little more laid back, and not as exciting."

Upon his return to the Red Sox, Miller became the regular center fielder for the strike-interrupted 1981 season. That year he responded with his Red Sox high .291 average, and on May 11, he went 5-for-5 in a game in Toronto, including a record-tying four doubles. He was again named the "Red Sox Unsung Hero" at the conclusion of the season. He followed this up with another solid year in 1982, playing in the outfield between Rice and Evans, hitting .254 in 135 games.

In 1983, the Red Sox traded for Tony Armas, who took over in centerfield, and Miller's playing time began to wane. He played a little first base and also had a few games as a designated hitter, but his playing time dropped way off to only 41 appearances as a result of a hip injury during his final season, 1985. Miller was highly regarded for his extraordinary pinch-hitting. In 1983, he was 17-for-36 (.472), and then in 1984 was 14-for-53 (.264). What is remarkable is how often he pinch hit. He was the best in the league and known for it.

In his first years away from baseball Miller worked

with his financial advisor, then developed a promotional business dealing in autograph shows. However, he says that he had a serendipitous moment following the death of his father that brought him back to baseball. "I was watching *Field of Dreams* and I had this revelation that my dad wanted me back in the game of baseball, teaching and coaching," he said. "As I was watching that movie, I could almost hear my dad talking to me."

Upon moving to his current home in New London, New Hampshire, he began an association with Colby–Sawyer College as a volunteer assistant coach with the

baseball team there. He also runs baseball clinics for youth sports programs throughout New England, as well as doing charity work in baseball.

When looking back at a career punctuated by his reputation as a solid left-handed batter and an exceptional defensive outfielder, Miller knows exactly how he'd like to be remembered.

"I'd like to be known as somebody who gave everything, all the time, and was a complete player who did every phase of the game well," he said. "I came in as a defensive specialist and left as an offensive specialist."

Bob Montgomery

by Bill Nowlin

	G	AB	R	H	2B	3B	HR	RBI	BB	SO	BA	OBP	SLG	SB	CS	GDP	HBP
1975 RED SOX	62	195	16	44	10	1	2	26	4	37	.226	.241	.318	1	1	3	1

Nashville native and Boston Red Sox catcher Bob Montgomery was born Robert Edward Montgomery on April 16, 1944. He played his entire career with one major league team—the Boston Red Sox—a career that encompassed the 1970s, from his debut on September 6, 1970 to his final game on September 9, 1979.

It took a while for Monty to make the majors, initially signed as an amateur free agent by the Red Sox on June 9, 1962. Baseball ran in the family. His father played sandlot ball and was apparently pretty good. Bob's brother Gerald was also in the Red Sox farm system for a while. Bob himself played several sports for Central High School in the Tennessee capital, and was all-state in three sports, but it was always baseball that held the greatest appeal. For Central, he pitched, played first base, and played outfield. It wasn't until he was playing professionally that he made the move to behind the plate.

After high school graduation, Red Sox scout George Digby got Bob Montgomery's signature on a contract and the 18-year-old was assigned to the Olean, New York team in Boston's farm system. There he played both outfield and third base and batted .273, earning him a step up in the system in 1963. The new year saw Montgomery playing in Waterloo, Iowa under manager Len Okrie. Monty explained to author Herb Crehan that Okrie suggested he become a catcher. Okrie told him, "If you want to make it to the majors, you're going to have to make yourself into a catcher. You don't have the power to make it at the corner positions in the majors,

but you could make it as a catcher." Monty got in a little backstop work late in '63, but the following year served as the full-time catcher for Waterloo and even made the league's All-Star team. He told Crehan that he found the transition a relatively easy one.

Although it was a long slog to make it to the majors, Monty says he never got discouraged. "I never thought about quitting. I had one goal in mind: to play baseball at the big league level. I stayed focused on that goal and just moved a little closer every year." He continued to rise in the system, if slowly, and by 1968 was playing for Triple A Louisville, the top club in Boston's system before Pawtucket assumed that honor. Montgomery played in over 100 games and batted a very strong .292. In 1970, Montgomery put in another year at Triple A (.324 in 131 games, and showing some power with 14 homers), and earned himself a call up to the big league club once Louisville's season was over.

Bob Montgomery made his major league debut, subbing for catcher Tom Satriano in a game the Sox were losing 6–1 to the Orioles. He was called out on strikes in his first at-bat, but came up again in the Sox sixth with Dave McNally on the mound and runners on first and second. His single to right field moved up both Rico Petrocelli and Billy Conigliaro and loaded the bases. Two runs scored on a hit-by-pitch and a sacrifice fly, and the score was 6–4. The Red Sox went on to win the game in the bottom of the 11th when reliever Pete Richert loaded the bases and then threw a wild pitch as Billy Conigliaro stood in the batter's box and Montgomery waited in the on-deck circle. Monty took over as the regular catcher for the rest of the season.

The first of his 23 career home runs came a few days later, a September 11 solo homer in the fifth inning off future Hall of Famer Jim Palmer. Montgomery saw a lot of action in September, appearing in 22 games and performing well (three errors, with 143 putouts and 13 assists), though hitting a little anemically at .179. He enjoyed the winter months, with 14 major league hits in the record books and what looked to be a steady job in the majors in 1971.

The Red Sox acquired Duane Josephson over the winter to be the regular catcher, but a series of nagging injuries provided plenty of playing opportunities for an able backup, and Bob Montgomery shared catching duties in 1971. Josephson appeared in 91 games and hit .245 with 10 homers while Montgomery got into 67 games, hitting .239 with a couple of homers. But then Carlton Fisk was called up in September and began to make himself a catcher who would not be denied. His .313 average and great defense, and an injury to Josephson, helped ensure Fisk would take center stage starting in 1972.

Montgomery understandably played the backup to Fisk, and appeared in just 24 games. He upped his average appreciably to .286, however, taking full advantage of his at-bats. The Red Sox missed the pennant by only half a game in the season that opened late due to an ongoing player strike that was not resolved until several days into the regular season schedule.

1973 provided Monty a little more action—34 games, 128 at-bats, and an improved batting average: .320. To work as a backup catcher isn't the easiest of tasks, he told Herb Crehan. He had to be ready to step in and perform at any minute. "I focused on every single pitch, even if I hadn't played in a week." The attention to detail so key in a catcher was reflected in his climbing batting average and probably served him well in his later career as a broadcaster with the Red Sox.

When Carlton Fisk suffered a season-ending injury on June 28, 1974, Montgomery stepped in and appeared in 88 games, with Tim Blackwell serving as his backup. Monty's average dropped to .252 but he filled in capably and the team continued to contend, in first place until shortly after Labor Day.

Fisk was still unable to return as the 1975 season opened, due to a second injury—a broken arm suffered in spring training—and Montgomery was the main man strapping on the mask and chest protector and calling pitches for the 1975 team until Fisk was able to come back on June 23. Though his average slipped yet again, to .226, Monty appeared in 62 games and did his share to keep the Sox in the hunt. At the season's start,

Montgomery was responsible for the game-winning RBI in four of the first 11 wins. Fisk hurt his finger in August and Monty got some more playing time. He also started a couple of games at first base, filling in at first six times before season's end.

In postseason play, Montgomery saw no action at all in the three-game series with Oakland, and almost missed out on any action in the World Series. He finally got his moment at almost the last possible moment, appearing as a pinch hitter in the bottom of the ninth inning in Game Seven. Will McEnaney was in for Cincinnati to protect a slim 4–3 lead, and there was one out, Juan Beniquez having flied out to right. Monty could have become an instant hero with a home run, tying the game and setting the stage for Yaz to come up with a winning back-to-back blow. Alas, it was not to be. Monty grounded out to the shortstop. Yastrzemski flied out to center field and the Series was over.

There was every hope that the Red Sox could come back and contend again in 1976, but they never got on track. Ownership even fired manager Darrell Johnson in the middle of the season, handing the reins to Don Zimmer. With Fisk healthy the full year, Monty got into only 31 games but did boost his average to a more respectable .247.

Montgomery got even less playing time in '77, but batted an even .300 in 40 at-bats, with a couple of homers in the mix.

1978 was another exceptional year in Red Sox history. Monty saw action in only 10 games; he hit .241 on the strength of just seven hits in 29 at-bats—and more than half of those hits all came in one game, the second game of a May 21 doubleheader in Tiger Stadium. Montgomery was 4-for-5 that day, with an RBI triple in the ninth inning off Fernando Arroyo. The last game he was in, as the pennant drive was on in earnest, came against the Yankees on September 7 at Fenway, a 15–3 blowout for New York. Monty had two plate appearances, striking out the first time and drawing a walk the second.

The last year of the 1970s was the last year for Bob Montgomery as a major league ballplayer. He went out with his head held high, appearing in 32 games and batting a career-best .349 in 86 at-bats. When he played his final game (September 9, 1979), he was 1-for-2 and scored a run, but also earned the distinction of being the last major leaguer to ever bat without a protective batting helmet on his head.

Though he tried to make the team in spring training 1980, he suffered recurring elbow problems and just couldn't continue to compete at the major league level.

In April, he turned 36 and the Sox were going with Fisk and Gary Allenson (Allenson had seen a lot of work in 1979, though with distinctly lower production at the plate. He was only 25 years old in 1980 and the Red Sox elected to look to him to spell Fisk.) In 1980 and 1981, Monty worked a little in sports radio and did some Red Sox games on radio as a backup guy. For the 1982 season, Channel 38 was looking to hire a new color commentator and interviewed Tony Conigliaro for the position. Tony's stroke removed him from consideration and Montgomery was hired to do the color on Red Sox telecasts. Monty worked as Ned Martin's partner doing TV for the Red Sox for 17 years, right up through the 1995 season when Channel 38's run with the Red Sox came to a close.

For several years now, Montgomery has worked in sales and marketing for Unison, a company based in Boston which specializes in signage work. He is married with one daughter.

Herb Crehan ends his *Red Sox Heroes of Yesteryear* profile of Bob Montgomery quoting Monty as saying of himself, "I was what they call a 50/50 player. I didn't help you an awful lot, but I didn't hurt you either." Crehan protests the modesty, opining that Monty was "probably the premier backup catcher in the major leagues throughout the seventies."

THE BULLPEN: Notes

1. Langworthy, Dave. "Tim Blackwell: He Used To Collect Autographs, Now His Own is In Big Demand." *Christian Science Monitor* August 29, 1974: 9.

2. Ibid.

3. Goddard, Joe. "Blackwell Fits In Foote Shoes." *The Sporting News* August 30, 1980: 39.

4. Conigliaro with Zanger, *Seeing It Through*, pp. 145, 146. Some contemporary press reports put the figure at $25,000.

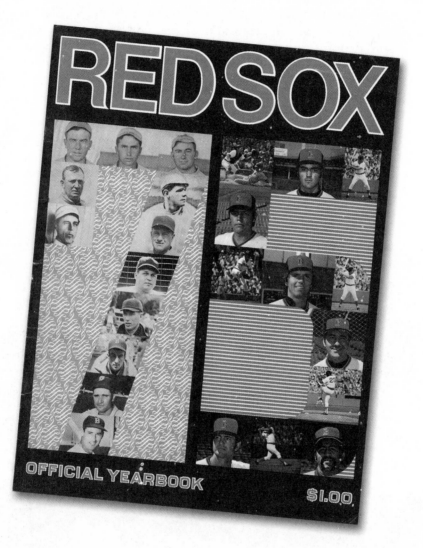

RED SOX

OFFICIAL YEARBOOK

$1.00

THE COACHES

Photograph overleaf, L to R: Don Bryant, John Pesky, Darrell Johnson, Stan Williams, Eddie Popowski, and Don Zimmer.

Darrell Johnson, Manager

by Bill Nowlin

	G	W	L	WP
1975 RED SOX	160	95	65	.594

Darrell Dean Johnson was born in the small community of Horace, Nebraska on August 25, 1927. At age 22, after playing in the California state amateur tourney in 1949, Johnson was signed by St. Louis Browns scout Tony Robello.

With the St. Louis Browns organization, Johnson compiled the following statistics:

1949   Redding Browns, Class D Far West League: 88 games, 9 HR, 58 RBI, .276 average

1950   Marshall Browns, Class C East Texas League: 131 games, .329, 13 HR, 105 RBI. Johnson tied for the league lead with 36 doubles; led league's catcher in fielding average (.979).

1951   San Antonio Missions, Double-A Texas League: 49 games, .266, 3 HR, 24 RBI

1951   Wichita Falls Spudders, Class B Big State League: 71 games, .309, 2 HR, 38 RBI

Johnson was named to the South team for Texas League All-Star game in '51, but could not play, because just a few hours before the team was announced, Johnson had been sent down to Wichita Falls.

Johnson was not on the Browns' 1952 spring roster, but he elected to participate in advanced spring training. New manager Rogers Hornsby liked his work and kept him on the Opening Day roster. (At the time, teams often started the season with extended rosters and did not have to pare down to 25 men until 30 days after the season started.) He had his major league debut on April 20, 1952. He singled and scored in his one at-bat, against Chicago's Billy Pierce.

When fellow rookie Clint Courtney emerged as the regular catcher for the Browns in May, Johnson was sent down to get more playing time with the San Antonio Missions. With the Missions, he got in 24 games, batting .325 with three home runs and 15 RBI. In June, Johnson was brought back up to the Browns. In all, Johnson appeared in 29 games with the Browns, batting .282 and driving in nine runs. On July 28, the Browns traded Johnson and Jim Rivera to the Chicago

White Sox in exchange for Jay Porter and Ray Coleman.

With the White Sox, Johnson served as backup catcher behind Sherm Lollar, getting into 22 games but only for 37 at-bats. He hit .108 and drove in one run.

Johnson spent the next four years playing minor league ball. In 1953, he spent the entire season with the Memphis Chickasaws of the Double A Southern Association, playing in 113 games, batting .249 with four home runs and 44 RBI. He was traded back to the Browns on June 13, sent with Lou Kretlow and $75,000 to St. Louis for Virgil Trucks and Bob Elliott. Under the terms of the deal, he was to remain with Memphis for the balance of the season.

But there was no St. Louis Browns team after 1953, as the franchise moved to Baltimore and became the Baltimore Orioles. In 1954, Clint Courtney was still the regular catcher and even though Johnson was on the major league roster early in 1954, he was optioned to Richmond without appearing in a major league game.

1954 Richmond Virginians, Triple A International League—90 games, 6 HR, 37 RBI, .261 average.

On November 4, Johnson was recalled by Baltimore and packaged in a huge 18-player trade sending him to New York Yankees, who in turn assigned him to their Denver Bears Triple A club. The Yankees were set at catcher with Yogi Berra and Charlie Silvera, and there wasn't much room for Johnson. Silvera was traded after 1955, but both Elston Howard and Johnny Blanchard were emerging prospects. Darrell was odd man out.

An interesting note found in an October 19, 1955 article in *The Sporting News* states that Johnson never had an injury to his throwing hand in seven years of professional catching. The reason cited was his double-jointed thumbs. "Most of the time a foul tip knocks the thumb into the other joint and I can just snap it right back in." He was reported to have a peculiar throwing motion; he would curve his thumb outward. Nonetheless, he had an outstanding throwing arm.

1955   Denver Bears, Triple A American Association: 52 games, .306, 4 HR and 49 RBI

1956   Denver Bears, Triple A American Association: 107 games, .319, 7 HR and 48 RBI

In 1957, he made it to the big league club and spent both 1957 and 1958 with the New York Yankees, but saw very little action.

1957 Yankees: 21 games, .217, 1 HR and 8 RBI

1958 Yankees: Five games, .250, without any home runs or a RBI. In both years, he was in the World Series and received a full share, but did not play.

In 1959, Johnson began the season with the Yankees but never appeared in even one game. He was sent to the Richmond Virginians of the Triple A International League, which had become a Yankee farm club. There he played in 94 games and hit for a .306 average, with 4 homers and 28 RBI. He was selected the best-throwing catcher in a poll of managers in the league.

Johnson was selected by the St. Louis Cardinals in the Rule 5 draft at the 1959 winter meetings. He was one of five catchers competing for a spot during spring training 1960, a group that included a young Tim McCarver. Since Johnson had spent most of his major league career in the bullpen, he was kept on the team as a catcher-coach. McCarver was sent to the minors, but when McCarver was recalled on July 31, Johnson was released as a player, and then signed to a new contract as just a coach. He played just eight games with the Cardinals in 1960, going hitless in two at-bats, again without driving in a run.

Darrell Johnson was named manager of the Cardinals entry in the Peninsula Winter League. This was apparently his first formal coaching job.

Johnson began the 1961 season as a coach with the Cardinals, but he was let go when manager Solly Hemus was fired on July 8. The very next day, the Philadelphia Phillies signed him as a player. Manager Gene Mauch was unhappy with the work of Jimmy Coker's catching, and Mauch was hoping Johnson's handling of pitchers would improve his pitching staff. Darrell played 21 games with the Phillies in July and early August, batting .230. On August 14, however, he was sold to the Cincinnati Reds. The Reds had two rookies sharing catching duties, Johnny Edwards and Jerry Zimmerman, and were looking for a veteran catcher for the pennant run. Johnson, a right-handed batter like Zimmerman, platooned with the lefty Edwards down the stretch as the Reds won the pennant.

Johnson appeared in 20 games for the Reds, batting .315 with one homer and six RBI in 54 at-bats, and finally got his chance to play in the World Series—

this time against the New York Yankees. He played in the two games started by New York lefty Whitey Ford—Games One and Four—and he went 2-for-4 off the Yankee ace. Despite his contributions, the Yankees won both games, and the Series. Meanwhile, Browns fans still had not forgotten Johnson, and he was named "Brownie of 1961," an award given by the St. Louis Browns Fan Club of Chicago to perpetuate the memory of the Browns. Johnson was one of 11 former Browns still in major league baseball.

In Spring, 1962, the Reds moved him to Baltimore for catcher Hank Foiles, though it was an unusual deal which saw Cincinnati releasing him on April 24 and Baltimore signing him on the very same day.

Johnson was acquired to be a coach. O's executive Lee MacPhail said he had always admired Johnson's work while both were with Yankees and thought he would be good choice to manage the bullpen. In a pinch, he could always be reactivated.

Indeed he was activated on May 22, when Gus Triandos broke a finger. Johnson caught six games, batting .182, but resumed coaching after the Orioles acquired catcher Hobie Landrith. Other than a brief appearance made while managing Rochester in 1965, that was the end of Darrell Johnson's playing career.

Following the 1962 season, the Orioles named him manager of Rochester, the club's top farm club, where he spent the next three seasons, winning the International League championship in 1964. After a disappointing fifth-place finish in 1965, the Orioles promoted Earl Weaver from Double A Elmira and gave Johnson the Elmira job.

In 1967, Johnson scouted for Yankees, but beginning in 1968 he worked with the Boston Red Sox. He served as a Red Sox coach in '68 and '69, and as an instructor and special assignment scout in 1970. In 1971 and 1972, Johnson managed Triple A Louisville for the Sox and the team finished first in 1972 but lost in the International League playoff finals.

In 1973, Johnson managed the Pawtucket Red Sox (Louisville had moved to Pawtucket); the team finished second during the season, but won the playoffs.

Johnson was named manager of the Boston Red Sox for the 1974 season. The team finished seven games out of first place that year, but as we know won the pennant in 1975. Darrell Johnson was back in the World Series, this time at the helm of the Red Sox. Though the Sox lost the Series, Johnson was named Major League Manager of the Year by *The Sporting News*.

Despite the accolades, he didn't last long as manager after that. Less than two weeks after owner

Tom Yawkey died, Johnson was fired, on July 19, 1976. When the American League expanded for the 1977 season, adding two franchises, Johnson was named the first manager of the Seattle team. He managed the Mariners into the 1980 season, when he was replaced by Maury Wills.

From 1983 to 1993, Johnson served as a special assignment scout for the New York Mets. It was during this tenure that Johnson finally tasted World Series champagne, when the Mets beat the Red Sox in 1986 and Johnson joined in the clubhouse celebration. For a season in 1993, he was a coach with the Mets and then he became a special assistant to the Mets' general manager from 1993 through 1999, which was his last year in baseball.

Darrell Johnson died of leukemia on May 3, 2004, in Fairfield, California.

Don Bryant, Bullpen Coach

Don Bryant was a 6'5", 200-pound catcher, with a career batting average of .220 in 109 at-bats over three seasons with the Cubs and Astros. He hit one home run, and drove in 13 runs.

Bryant was signed by Detroit Tigers scout Bill Pierre in 1959, and was in the Tigers system through 1965. After the '65 season, he was sold to the Chicago Cubs in early December. He appeared in 13 games with the Cubs in 1966, batting .308 with four RBIs.

The following spring, Chicago traded Bryant to the Giants on April 3 for Dick Bertell. Bryant spent '67 and '68 in the minors for the Giants, then was selected by the Astros in the Rule 5 draft in December 1968.

Bryant was up and down with the Astros in 1969, playing in 31 games, but batting only .186 in 59 at-bats. He did hit his only major league home run, a two-run homer in the Astrodome off Bobby Bolin on May 3, in a 4–3 win over the Giants. Bryant finished the season with just six RBIs. After the season was over, the short-lived Seattle Pilots selected him—again in December—in the Rule 5 draft. As the Seattle franchise then changed city, Bryant became a Milwaukee player.

Milwaukee, though, elected not to keep Bryant and he was thus returned to the Astros in April 1970. In 1970, Houston used him in 15 games for 24 at-bats. He hit .208, with three RBIs. In another December transaction, the Astros sold Don to the Boston Red Sox on December 3, 1970.

Bryant had actually been purchased by Louisville, the Red Sox Triple A farm club at the time, and he played in Louisville both in 1971 and 1972, and then served as player-coach under Pawtucket Red Sox manager Darrell Johnson in 1973, after the Louisville team had been relocated to Rhode Island. Bryant ended his playing career in 1973, and when Johnson was named manager of the Boston Red Sox, he brought Bryant with him to serve as bullpen coach with the Red Sox from 1974 to 1976.

Johnson was released mid-season in 1976 and Bryant was kept on, but not retained by Red Sox manager Don Zimmer following the '76 season.

Darrell Johnson managed the Seattle Mariners in 1977 and he added Bryant as his bullpen coach; when Johnson was fired in August 1980, so was Bryant.

Johnny Pesky, First Base Coach

Born John Michael Paveskovich, he joined the Red Sox in 1942 after hitting .325 and leading the league in hits each of his two minor league seasons. He would also lead in hits in each of his first three American League seasons, 1942, and 1946–1947 (missing 1943 and 1945 due to World War II). Pesky was second only to Ted Williams in the batting race in 1942 and third in the MVP voting—clearly rookie of the year, had there been such a category at the time.

A shortstop–third baseman, he was a regular with the Red Sox until a mid-season trade sent him to the Tigers in 1952. He played two seasons with the Tigers before going to Senators in the middle of the 1954 season. Released after the season, he was signed by the Orioles but released during the first week of the 1955 season without appearing in a game. Pesky compiled a career .307 batting average in 10 seasons of major league ball. He drove in 404 runs, with 17 home runs, but was primarily noted as an excellent "table-setter" for Ted Williams. Johnny scored over 100 runs in each of his first six seasons in the majors.

In 1955, Johnny was hired by Ralph Houk as a

player–coach with the Denver Bears, the Yankees' top farm club. Darrell Johnson was Denver's catcher.

Pesky managed in the Tigers system, making five stops in five years (Durham, 1956; Birmingham, 1957; Lancaster, 1958; Knoxville, 1959; and Victoria, 1960).

Johnny rejoined Red Sox organization as manager of the Seattle Rainiers in 1961–1962, and became manager of the big league Boston Red Sox for the 1963 and 1964 seasons, before being replaced for the final two games of the '64 season.

After serving as a coach with the Pirates from 1965 to 1968, he became a Red Sox broadcaster (1969–1974), but was back on the field as Darrell Johnson's first base coach in 1975—and glad to congratulate both Bernie Carbo and Carlton Fisk for their key home runs in Game Six of the World Series.

Pesky served 10 seasons as a coach with the Red Sox, and even took over as manager once more in the final week of the 1980 season, when the team fired Don Zimmer a few days before the season was over.

Eddie Popowski, Special Assignment Coach

Eddie Popowski started his career in an uncommon fashion, playing for the House of David touring baseball team from 1934 to 1937 until he was signed by the Red Sox.

With the exception of the 1942 season, which he missed due to military service, Pop was part of the Red Sox organization every season from 1937 until his death in 2001. A small second baseman (5' 4½", 145 lbs), Popowski never made it to the big leagues as a player, reaching only as high as Double A with the 1943 Louisville club. Though a light hitter with only six career home runs, he led the league in fielding average in each of his six full seasons in the minor leagues.

Pop began his managing career in 1944, though he continued playing through 1948. He managed in 14 cities in the Red Sox system through 1966 with the exception of 1951 and 1952 when he was a coach

with Louisville. When Dick Williams became Red Sox manager in 1967, he selected Popowski as one of his coaches. Pop managed the final nine games of the 1969 season when Williams was fired. He also took the helm for the final day of the 1973 season when Eddie Kasko was let go.

Pop remained a Red Sox coach through 1975, and he would get a rise from the crowd when fielding a foul ball in the coach's box. Using an old House of David trick, he'd return the ball to the pitcher with a behind-the-back toss.

He began the 1976 season as a minor league instructor, but was added to the coaching staff to coach third base when Don Zimmer took over as manager. He was not retained by Zimmer after that one season.

Eddie Popowski died on December 4, 2001 at his Sayreville, New Jersey home at age 88.

Stan Williams, Pitching Coach

A hard-throwing, 6'4", 225-pound right hander, Williams was signed to the Brooklyn Dodgers by scouts Bert Wells and Manuel Boody in 1954. He debuted in the majors in 1958 with the Dodgers, who had moved to Los Angeles by then. Williams was 9–7, with a 4.01 ERA in his rookie year. He won 57 games for the Dodgers in five seasons, but was traded to the Yankees for Bill Skowron in November 1962. He started 31 games with the Yankees over the 1963 and 1964 seasons with the Yankees, but had a 10–13 record despite decent ERAs each year.

Right at the end of spring training 1965, the Yankees sold him to the Cleveland Indians. He pitched just three games with the Indians and was sent to the

minors, returning in mid-1967 to get in 16 games with a 2.62 ERA. Swapped with Luis Tiant to Minnesota after the 1969 season, Williams was used almost exclusively as a reliever by the Twins.

Traded to the Cardinals in September 1971, he quickly posted a 3–0 mark in the final month of the season with an excellent 1.42 ERA, but was released the following April. Oddly, one of the wins Williams is credited with was the completion of the August 1 suspended game. Stan pitched the last two innings, the 12th and 13th, and St. Louis won the game. The win actually occurred on September 7, but Williams is credited with a win of a game of an August 1 game—when he was actually on the roster of another team and

in the other league.

After his release, he quickly hooked on with the Angels farm club in Salt Lake City in April 1972, but was released in June. Stan was signed by the Boston Red Sox to a Louisville contract and brought up to the parent club in July. He was released in September after appearing in just three games and throwing just 4⅓ innings. That was his final work as a major league pitcher.

Out of baseball in 1973, Williams was named the 1974 manager of Bristol, the Red Sox Double A farm club. After losing a couple of pitchers to injuries,

Williams activated himself and pitched five games, going 2–0 including a seven-inning no-hitter over Quebec City.

He served as pitching coach for the Red Sox under Darrell Johnson in 1975 and 1976, but was not retained after the 1976 season, when Don Zimmer put together his own staff.

Since that time, Stan Williams has been active in a number of roles with a number of organizations. In his major league career, Stan had a won-loss record of 109–94 with 43 saves, and a lifetime 3.48 ERA in 482 games, spanning 14 seasons of work.

Don Zimmer, Third Base Coach

Don Zimmer was signed as a shortstop to the Brooklyn Dodgers in 1949 by scouts Cliff Alexander and George Sisler. He was leading the American Association in 1954 in both home runs (23) and RBIs (63) when a beaning ended his season. He came back and made the parent Dodgers in mid-season, debuting in July 1954. He was a member of the only Brooklyn Dodgers club to win a World Series, in 1955, batting .239 with 50 RBIs. The Dodgers were also in the Series in 1956, but Zimmer's season had ended in June when a pitch fractured his cheekbone.

Zimmer played six seasons with the Dodgers, the first four in Brooklyn and then the 1958 and 1959 seasons in Los Angeles. Zimmer appeared in the 1959 World Series for the Dodgers, but only for one at-bat. He was traded to the Chicago Cubs in April 1960 for three players and $25,000 and played two years with Cubs, playing in the 1961 All-Star Game. But the Cubs did not protect him during the October 1961 expansion draft and he was selected by the New York Mets.

Don was the starting third baseman in the first game the Mets ever played. Less than a month later,

though, he was traded to Cincinnati and, in turn, Cincinnati traded him back to his original team—the Dodgers—prior to the 1963 season. He stayed with the Dodgers until being sold to the Washington Senators in June 1963. The Senators released him after the 1965 season.

As a major leaguer, Don appeared in 1,095 games over 12 seasons, with a career .235 average. He hit 91 homers and drove in 352 runs.

Zimmer played in Japan in 1966, batting just .182 with the Toei Flyers.

He began coaching and managerial work in the 1967 season, serving as player-manager of Knoxville in the Reds farm system. With both Knoxville and Buffalo in last place in their leagues in July, the Reds decided to swap the managers with Lou Fitzgerald taking over Knoxville and Zimmer taking over Buffalo.

Since then, Zimmer has had a long career coaching in the major and minor leagues. From 2004 to the present, Don Zimmer has served as assistant to general manager of the Tampa Bay Devil Rays.

Coach biographies written by Wayne McElreavy and Bill Nowlin, with thanks to Maxwell Kates.

⚒ BIBLIOGRAPHY ⚒

GENERAL REFERENCES

Books

Adelman, Tom. *The Long Ball*. Boston, MA: Back Bay Books/ Little, Brown, 2003.

The Baseball Encyclopedia, various editions. The most recent edition is: Gillette, Gary and Pete Palmer, *The 2005 ESPN Baseball Encyclopedia*. New York: Sterling, 2005.

Crehan, Herb. *Red Sox Heroes of Yesterday*. Cambridge MA: Rounder Books, 2005.

Boston Red Sox Official Yearbooks, 1968–1981.

Boston Red Sox media guides, past and present.

Boston Red Sox 1976 Press–TV–Radio Guide.

Gammons, Peter. *Beyond the Sixth Game*. Boston: Houghton Mifflin Company, 1985.

Gillette, Gary, and Pete Palmer, eds. *The 2005 ESPN Baseball Encyclopedia*. New York: Sterling, 2005.

Golenbock, Peter. *Red Sox Nation*. Chicago: Triumph Books, 2005.

Hornig, Doug, *The Boys of October*. Chicago: Contemporary Books, 2003.

Johnson, Lloyd and Miles Wolff, eds. *The Encyclopedia of Minor League Baseball*, 2nd ed., Baseball America, 1997.

Neft, David S., Richard M. Cohen and Michael L. Neft. *The Sports Encyclopedia: Baseball 2004, 24th Edition*. New York: St. Martin's Griffin, 2004.

The Sporting News Baseball Guide, 1963–1979.

The Sporting News Baseball Guide and Register, various years.

Stout, Glenn and Richard Johnson. *Red Sox Century: The Definitive History of Baseball's Most Storied Franchise*. Boston, MA: Houghton Mifflin, 2004.

Tiant, Luis and Joe Fitzgerald. *El Tiante*. Garden City, NY: Doubleday, 1976.

Total Baseball, various editions. The most recent edition is: Thorn, John, Phil Birnbaum, and Bill Deane, *Total Baseball*, 8th edition. Toronto, ON: Sport Classic Books, 2004.

Archives

Player files at the National Baseball Hall of Fame.

Periodicals

Boston Globe
Boston Herald
Boston Record American
Chicago Tribune
Manchester Union Leader
New York Times
The Sporting News
Washington Post

Web Sites

www.baseball-almanac.com
TheBaseballCube.com
BaseballLibrary.com
Baseball-Reference.com
MinorLeagueBaseball.com
Nationmaster.com
Retrosheet.org
SABR.org
Sports123.com
Travs.com

✕ BIBLIOGRAPHY ✕

SPECIAL REFERENCES

Andrew, Kim
Interview with Kim Andrew, July 24, 2005.

Blackwell, Tim
Interview with Cecil Cooper, June 8, 2005, Queens, NY.
Interview with John Kennedy, June 24, 2005, New Haven, CT.
www.mwlguide.com

Burleson, Rick
Lee, Bill and Dick Lally. *The Wrong Stuff.* New York: Viking, 1984.

Burton, Jim
Morgan, Joe. *Joe Morgan: A Life in Baseball.* New York: W. W. Norton, 1993.

Carbo, Bernie
Clendennen, Andy. "Where Have You Gone Bernie Carbo?" *The Sporting News* October 26, 2001.
Complete Baseball Record Book 2004 Edition. St. Louis, MO: The Sporting News, 2004.
James, Bill. *The New Bill James Historical Baseball Abstract,* New York: The Free Press, 2001.
Nowlin, Bill and Jim Prime. *Blood Feud.* Cambridge MA: Rounder Books, 2005.
Prime, Jim with Bill Nowlin, *Tales From the Red Sox Dugout.* Champaign IL: Sports Publishing Inc., 2001.
Smith, Curt. *Our House.* Chicago: Masters Press, 1999.

Conigliaro, Tony
Cataneo, David. *Tony C.* Nashville TN: Rutledge Hill, 1997.
Conigliaro, Tony with Jack Zanger,. *Seeing It Through.* NY: Macmillan, 1970.
Williams, Dick with Bill Plaschke. *No More Mr. Nice Guy.* San Diego: Harcourt Brace Jovanovich, 1990.
Thanks to Wayne McElreavy for considerable assistance with this profile.

Cooper, Cecil
Guiliotti, Joe. "Cecil Cooper: He Would Rather Be No. 1!" *Baseball Digest* June, 1981.

Gammons, Peter. "Cooper Groggy, But In One Piece." *Boston Globe* September 8, 1975.
"What Cecil Cooper Can Do." *New York Times* June 27, 1982.
Christian Science Monitor. October 7, 1980.
"Harvey's Wallbangers." *Newsweek* August 2, 1982.
Hoffmann, Gregg. *Down in the Valley: The History of Milwaukee County Stadium.* Milwaukee, WI: Milwaukee Brewers Baseball Club and *Milwaukee Journal-Sentinel,* 2000: 97.
Fimrite, Ron. "I'm the Lou Gehrig of My Time." *Sports Illustrated* September 19, 1983.
Flaherty, Tom. "Cooper Earns Clemente Prize." *The Sporting News* February 28, 1983.
www.milwaukeebrewers.com
www.astros.com

Cleveland, Reggie
Ambassador World Atlas. Hammond, Inc. Maplewood, NJ: Hammond, 1988.
Interview with Reggie Cleveland on August 4, 1990 by Dan Dinardo. The interview was transcribed by Joseph Hetrick.
Interview with Reggie Cleveland by author on August 5, 2005.
MacLean, Norman, ed. *1982 Who's Who in Baseball.* New York: Baseball Magazine Co., 1982.
Marcin, Joe, Chris Roewe, Larry Wigge, and Larry Vickrey, eds. *Official Baseball Guide-—1976.* St. Louis, MO: The Sporting News, 1976.
Shearon, Jim. *Canada's Baseball Legends.* Kanata, ON: Malin Head Press, 1994.
Shury, Dave, ed. *Saskatchewan Historical Baseball Review.* Battleford, SK: The Saskatchewan Baseball Hall of Fame and Museum Association. 1984, 1986, 1990.
Turner, Dan. *Heroes, Bums and Ordinary Men.* Toronto, ON: Doubleday Canada Limited, 1988.

Doyle, Denny
Interview with Denny Doyle, July 15, 2005.

Fisk, Carlton
Correspondence with Mac McElreavy, September, 2005.
Interviews with Cecil and Leona Fisk, May, 1999.
Interviews with Ralph Silva, May, 1999.

Griffin, Doug

Bjarkman, Peter C. *The Baseball Scrapbook*. Barnes & Noble/ Brompton, 1995, 164.

Cole, Milton and Jim Kaplan. *The Boston Red Sox*. JG Press, 2005: 41, 47.

Neft, David S. and Richard M. Cohen. *The World Series*, New York: St. Martin's Press, 1990.

Heise, Bob

Interview with Bob Heise, August 23, 2005.

The Reporter, Vacaville, CA.

Hobson, Butch

Ashmore, Mike, "Ten Questions with Butch." www. AtlanticLeagueBaseball.com, September 14, 2004.

Brooks, Scott. "Hobson's Choice: Pride Boss Staying in Nashua." *New Hampshire Union-Leader* November 23, 2004.

Comey, Jonathan. "Hobson finally back where he belongs," *South Coast Today*, February 8, 1997.

Complete Baseball Record Book, 2004 Edition. St. Louis, MO: The Sporting News, 2004.

Courtney, Will. "The Fall and Rise of Butch." www.EagleTribune. com August 10, 2000.

Dewey, Donald and Nicholas Acocella. *The New Biographical History of Baseball*. Chicago: Triumph Books, 2002.

Glew, Kevin. "Former Third Baseman Butch Hobson: Players Who Left the Game on Their Own Terms." *Baseball Digest* December, 2004.

Halvatgis, Jenna. "Hobson's Hope." *South Coast Today* May 11, 1998.

Hickling, Dan. "Hobson's Choice." www.MinorLeagueNews.com May 6, 2005.

Kahn, Roger. *October Men*. San Diego, CA: Harcourt, 2003.

Linn, Ed. *The Great Rivalry*. New York: Ticknor & Fields, 1991.

Malinowski, W. Zachary, and John Castellucci, New England Sports Service. "Butch Gets Busted." *South Coast Today* May 9, 1996.

McDonald, Joe. "The Independent Interview: Butch Hobson." www. ALIndependent.com July 9, 2004.

Nashua Pride.com.

Petraglia, Mike. "Where Have You Gone, Butch Hobson?" www. MLB.com February 19, 2002.

RollTide.com.

Smith, Curt. *Our House*. Chicago: Masters Press, 1999.

Hunter, Buddy

Interview with Buddy Hunter, August 24, 2005.

Johnson, Deron

Kelley, Brent P. *They Too Wore Pinstripes*. Jefferson, NC: McFarland, 1998.

New York Times obituary April 25, 1992.

Pietrusza, David, Matthew Silverman, and Michael Gershman, eds. *Baseball: The Biographical Encyclopedia*. Kingston, NY: Total Sports, 2000.

Porter, David L., ed. *Biographical Dictionary of American Sports: Baseball*. Westport, CT: Greenwood Press, 2000.

San Diego Union-Tribune April 24, 1992.

Kreuger, Rick

Interviews with Rick Kreuger, August 22 and September 23, 2005. Transcript provided by Dan Desrochers.

Lee, Bill

Interviews with Bill Lee, various dates.

Lee, Bill with Jim Prime. *The Little Red (Sox) Book*. Chicago: Triumph Books, 2004.

Lynn, Fred

Allen, Maury. *Baseball's 100*, New York: Galahad Books, 1981.

Ballew, Bill. *The Pastime in the Seventies*. Jefferson, NC: McFarland, 2002.

Correspondence with Fred Lynn.

Dolan, Edward F. and Richard B. Lyttle. *Fred Lynn: The Hero from Boston, 1976*. Garden City, NY: Doubleday, 1978.

Frommer, Harvey, and Frederic J. Frommer. *Growing Up Baseball*. Dallas, TX: Taylor Trade, 2001.

Goode, Jon. "Catching Up with Fred Lynn." Boston.com August 27, 2004.

Hollander, Zander. *The Complete Handbook of Baseball 1976*. New York: Signet, 1976.

James, Bill, John Dewan, Neil Munro, and Don Zminda. *STATS All-Time Major League Handbook*. Chicago, IL: Stats, Inc., 1998.

www.FredLynn.net.

www.usctrojans.com.

McAuliffe, Dick

Chass, Murray. "Yanks Use Munson at 3d and Win." *New York Times* September 2, 1975.

Detroit Tigers 1969 Press Guide.

Detroit Tigers 1972 Yearbook.

Doyle, Al. "Tommy John: The Game I'll Never Forget." *Baseball Digest* May 2004.

Gammons, Peter. "McAuliffe Back as Bosox Lose Rico." *The Sporting News* September 6, 1975.

Green, Jerry. "Time Hasn't Taken Fight out of Tigers Franchise." *Detroit News* August 20, 2001.

Hawkins, Jim. "Tigers Tabbing Oglivie as a Regular." *The Sporting News* December 13, 1975.

"Majors Fear Loss of Players From a Possible Military Draft." *New York Times* July 23, 1961.

McConnell, Bob, and David Vincent, eds., *SABR Home Run Encyclopedia*. New York: Macmillan, 1996.

Murray, Jim. "Sticks to Riches." *Los Angeles Times* June 9, 1965.

O'Gara, Roger. "Eastern's Openers Hit Fouls in Bad Weather." *The Sporting News* 1975.

"Ryan Hurls His 2nd No-Hitter of Year." *New York Times* July 16, 1973.

Smith, Brad. "A History of Detroit Tigers Shortstops." www. people.virginia.edu/~pw7e/tigershistory/shortstops.html, January 27, 1999.

Spoelstra, Watson. "Kaline Marks 27th Birthday." *The Sporting News* January 3, 1962.

Stern, Chris. *Where Have They Gone?* New York: Tempo Books, 1979: 118.

"Tigers Buy McAuliffe." *New York Times* September 16, 1960.

"Tigers Sign Two Schoolboys." *New York Times* June 22, 1957.

www.hphshall.com/PINSKYHOF.htm

Zanardi, Peter. "An Interview With Dick McAuliffe." *Oldtyme Baseball News*, Volume 5, Issue 2, 1993.

Zanardi, Peter. Interview with Dick McAuliffe (cassette), 1990/1991.

McCarver, Tim

St. Louis Post-Dispatch.

Merchant, Andy

Interviews with Andy Merchant on October 12, 2001, August 10, 2005, and September 24, 2005.

webpages.charter.net/joekuras/psox07b.htm.

Miller, Rick

Diary Of A Winner—1975, Play By Play and Day By Day. Shamrock, 1975.

Interview with Rick Miller, August 9, 2005.

Walton, Ed. *Red Sox Triumphs and Tragedies.* New York: Stein and Day, 1980.

Walton, Ed, *This Day In Boston Red Sox History.* New York: Stein and Day, 1978.

Moret, Roger

Grossman, Leigh. *The Red Sox Fan Handbook.* Cambridge, MA: Rounder Books, 2005.

Petrocelli, Rico

Interviews with Rico Petrocelli, 1994–2005.

Segui, Diego

Bergman, Ron. "Reliever Segui Saving A's With Slick Starting Jobs." *The Sporting News* August 15, 1970.

Gammons, Peter. "Bosox Feel Secure With Segui in Relief." *The Sporting News* March 16, 1974.

Gammons, Peter. "Segui, Garagiola in Heated Exchange." *Boston Globe* October 19, 1975.

Box Score, Game Five, World Series. *Boston Globe* October 19, 1975.

Interview with Luis Tiant, July 15, 2005.

Kachline, Clifford. "Cuban Standouts Shun Own Land, Play Elsewhere." *The Sporting News* November 29, 1961.

Keane, Clif. "Wise, Segui Ponder Reasons for Trade." *Boston Evening Globe* March 6, 1974.

Keane, Clif. "Red Sox, you ask?" *Boston Sunday Globe* March 17, 1974.

McCoy, Bob. "Baseball Trivia in Space." *The Sporting News* September 17, 1984.

Red Sox Notebook. "Tiant's Sore Shoulder Gave Segui the Start." *Boston Globe* July 30, 1975.

The Sporting News December 13, 1961.

The Sporting News September 7, 1968.

"Roster Packing Hassle Big Jolt to Merged Loop." *The Sporting News* January 24, 1962.

"Can Bolin Polish Pilot Swap Image?" *The Sporting News* January 3, 1970.

"Reliever Segui Saving A's With Slick Starting Jobs." *The Sporting News* August 15, 1970.

Zimmerman, Hy. "Can Bolin Polish Pilot Swap Image?" *The Sporting News* January 3, 1970.

Zimmerman, Hy. "So Long to Ancient Mariner." *The Sporting News* November 19, 1977.

Tiant, Luis

Angell, Roger, *Late Innings.* New York: Simon and Schuster, 1977.

Claflin, Larry. "He Smokes in Shower, Sizzles on Hill." *The Sporting News* October 14, 1972.

Clark, Dick and Larry Lester, eds., *The Negro Leagues Book.* Cleveland, OH: SABR, 1994.

Fitzgerald, Joe. "Nothing Dull About El Tiante." *Boston Herald* June 7, 1984.

Fitzgerald, Joe. "Luis Tiant Can Tell You the Real Story of Cuba." *Boston Herald* November 6, 1983.

Fitzpatrick, Thomas. "The Most Popular Indian." *Sport* September, 1968.

Gammons, Peter. *Baseball's Finest.* Ed. Danny Peary. North Dighton, MA: World, 1996.

Horgan, Tim. "El Tiante: Pitcher, Philosopher." *Boston Herald* February 3, 1985.

Kirchheimer, Anne. *Boston Globe* August 22, 1975.

Leggett, William. "Funny Kind of a Race." *Sports Illustrated* September 25, 1972.

The Oregonian (newspaper), April through July, 1964.

Schneider, Russell. "'I'm Skinny, Lucky,' Says Winner Luis." *The Sporting News* May 28, 1966.

Schneider, Russell. "Lucky Luis? Modest Hurler Tiant Thinks So." *The Sporting News* August 3, 1968.

Schneider, Russell. "Shutout Ace Tiant Sees Homer Wreck His Dream." *The Sporting News* June 1, 1968.

Willoughby, Jim

Lee, Bill with Dick Lally. *The Wrong Stuff.* New York: Penguin, 1988.

Interview with Jim Willoughby, July 11, 2004.

www.jimwilloughby.com

Wise, Rick

Interview with Rick Wise, September 1, 2005.

Yastrzemski, Carl

Interviews with Carl Yastrzemski, May 1999.

Yastrzemski, Carl and Gerald Eskenazi. *Yaz: Baseball, the Wall, and Me.* New York: Doubleday, 1990.

Yastrzemski, Carl with Al Hirshberg. *Yaz.* New York: Viking, 1968.

RON ANDERSON grew up in the Boston area and is a consummate Red Sox and baseball fan. His zeal for the Sox began with the Ted Williams era in the 1950s. He suffered along with the rest of Beantown through many hapless years, then experienced delirious joy in 2004 upon winning a long-delayed championship. Ron attributes his love for the game to his father who played ball in the Boston City Park League, and who got him started in a life of baseball. His writing credentials include document and speech writing among duties for his employer in the insurance industry. He is now retired and lives with his wife in Plymouth, Massachusetts.

MARK ARMOUR grew up in Connecticut but now writes baseball from his home in Oregon. He is the co-author of *Paths to Glory*, the director of SABR's Baseball Biography Project, a contributor to many websites and SABR journals, and, most importantly, Maya and Drew's father.

JONATHAN ARNOLD finally returned to his family's New England roots as an 11-year-old, after his dad finished up a world tour in the Air Force, and overcame a brief Cardinal romance to become a Red Sox fanatic, which he has been ever since. Living in a Boston suburb, he's raising two daughters to be lifelong natives of Red Sox Nation—while working as a software engineer.

ERIC ARON is a native New Yorker who admits to taking great joy in the outcome of Game Six of the 1986 World Series. He has never been a Yankee fan. Eric holds a Master's degree in public history from Northeastern University. This is his first SABR biography.

RAY BIRCH lives in North Kingstown, Rhode Island. He is a retired middle school teacher from Narragansett, Rhode Island where he co-taught a class on baseball. He has been a member of SABR since 2000. Ray is a lifelong Red Sox fan who attended Game Seven of the 1975 World Series between the Red Sox and the Reds.

ANDREW BLUME has long been obsessed with all things baseball and Red Sox. A SABR member since 2001, he lives in Natick, Massachusetts with his wife Nancy, daughters Emily and Abigail, and feline Tigger. In his spare time, he practices law. This is his first attempt at baseball research.

MAURICE BOUCHARD, lives in Shrewsbury, Massachusetts with his wife Kim, and has been a baseball fan since Sandy Koufax struck out Bob Allison for the final out of the 1965 World Series. Bouchard, who grew up in upstate New York, was originally a Yankees fan but George Steinbrenner cured him of that. Since 1987, he has rooted for the Old Towne Team. He has two children, Ian and Gina, both of whom are inveterate Red Sox fans. Bouchard has been a member of SABR since 1999.

BOB BRADY grew up as a fan of the Boston Braves and Boston Red Sox and remains true to both to this day. In his free time, you can find him seated either in Section 26 at Fenway Park or working on the next newsletter for the Boston Braves Historical Association. Bob has been a SABR member since 1991.

JOHN CIZIK grew up a Yankee fan in Wilton, Connecticut living next door to a Red Sox fan. Something must have rubbed off, because he married Jenny, a Sox fan, in 1990. A lawyer practicing in Waterbury, Connecticut (the hometown of Roger Connor, Jimmy Piersall, Dave Wallace, and Ron Diorio), he has always had an interest in doing research on and collecting memorabilia of Connecticut-born players.

HERB CREHAN is in his 10th season with *Red Sox Magazine*, the official program of the Boston Red Sox. He is the author of *Lightning In A Bottle: The Sox of '67* and a contributing writer to *Boston Red Sox *100 Years* The Official Retrospective*. His new book, *Red Sox Heroes of Yesteryear* (Rounder), is available in bookstores and online. Crehan has been a SABR member since 1992.

JON DALY is a lifelong resident of the Greater Hartford area. His father introduced him to baseball and the Red Sox during the 1975 season. Because he was a young lad at the time, he expected the Red Sox to play in the World Series every year. Boy, was he wrong! In his free time, he works in the financial service industry. Jon has been a SABR member since 2001.

DAN DESROCHERS' noted ventures to Fenway Park began in 1967 as a 12-year-old who had a passionate desire to attend a Red Sox game. Unbeknownst to his parents, he schemed and plotted his "Impossible Dream" Maine-to-Boston venture that combined bicycling, hiking, and bus and train rides to catch his first Red Sox game. He successfully completed the 200-mile trip and managed to get home before dark. He now lives in Rollinsford, New Hampshire though he still considers himself a Mainer—and he continues to organize trips to Red Sox games today without his mom's permission. He was in St. Louis when the Red Sox won it all in 2004.

BOB DONALDSON is a lifelong Red Sox fan, born a few months after Yaz completed his rookie season. In 1970 he attended his first game and saw his hero Yaz hit a first inning home run. In 1975 he spent many afternoons at Fenway including Game Two of the World Series. Bob is a bit of a pack rat and still has the first baseball cards he pulled from a pack in 1967 (threw out the gum though). 1975 being a special season, Bob kept a lot of stuff, some of which is used to illustrate this book. Bob lives in Lincoln with his wife Cristine, teenage step children Liz and Wil, and daughter Sara (3 years old, favorite player Johnny Damon).

ALEX EDELMAN lives in Brookline, Massachusetts where he attends high school and obsesses over the Red Sox. He spends most of his spare time at Fenway and playing ice hockey for the Brookline Warriors. His essay, "Paradise Found," about the 2004 American League Championship Series was a recipient of the New England Sports Museum's Will McDonough Writing Award.

TOM HARKINS is two days older than Dick Drago and although he has been a Red Sox season ticketholder in the bleachers since 1985, he missed the 2004 World Series games in Fenway because he was at a Notre Dame football game (a greater love than the Red Sox). A SABR member since 1988 he is a retired school librarian who lives in Needham, Massachusetts.

JOANNE HULBERT resides in Mudville, a venerable, old neighborhood of Holliston, Massachusetts, a town rich in early baseball history. Although Diego Segui had been her random choice from the list of players, he turned out to be a poetic subject most fitting for the co-chair of SABR's Music and Poetry Committee.

MARK KANTER grew up in Bristol, Pennsylvania, where he became a lifelong Phillies fan. He got the itch while watching the last few outs of Jim Bunning's perfect game on Father's Day in 1964. He has written several articles for SABR's *Baseball Research Journal* and was the editor for Boston SABR 2002 Convention Publication. He has won a number of National SABR trivia contests since 1997. He and his wife, Lynne, who is also a great baseball fan in her own right, live in the idyllic seaside community of Portsmouth, Rhode Island.

SEAMUS KEARNEY is the Chair for SABRBoston. He works in social services as a Certified Information & Referral Specialist but has had previous careers, most notably as a chef and as a window cleaner (a *long* time ago). At social gatherings he introduces himself as a baseball scholar. He has a BA in History from Boston University and a MA in History from Harvard. He lives in Malden with his wife Joan Lukas but currently resides on Cloud 9 with the Sox victory in the 2004 World Series.

LEN LEVIN has been a SABR member since 1977. He has been a Red Sox fan more than twice as long, and fondly remembers the first major league game he attended, Dave Ferriss' shutout of the Yankees in his first appearance at Fenway Park (1945). He has been an officer of SABR twice, and currently is the custodian of the SABR Research Library. In his spare time he works as a copy editor at *The Patriot Ledger* in Quincy, Massachusetts.

R. R. MARSHALL has been a writer on the Boston sports scene for over a decade. His articles on the Red Sox, Patriots, and Boston College Eagles appear in both the print and electronic media year round. He also serves as a consultant to the Sports Museum of New England.

LES MASTERSON is a Malden, Massachusetts resident and editor of *The Arlington Advocate* newspaper in Arlington, Massachusetts. He has won numerous awards for his newspaper writing and editing from the New England Press Association and Massachusetts Press Association. He is also a rarity—a New York Mets fan who was born and raised in the shadows of Boston.

WAYNE McELREAVY is a lifelong Red Sox fan who began following baseball with the 1975 Red Sox. A baseball researcher who has contributed to numerous books, he has a special interest in baseball records and players with New Hampshire connections. He lives in Claremont, New Hampshire with son Ryan and daughter Christine where he occasionally daydreams of swatting one over the Green Monster.

TOM NAHIGIAN has been a Red Sox fan for as long as he can remember. He recently moved to the Chicago area, but still loves his Red Sox. A longtime Strat-O-Matic player and a fan of baseball analyst Bill James, a SABR member since 1983 and a 1984 graduate of Boston University, Tom attended 32 games in 1982. Fenway Park is walking distance from Boston University.

BILL NOWLIN is national Vice President of SABR and the author of a dozen books on the Red Sox. Standing in line for about 18 hours got him tickets for every game of the 1975 World Series and his standing room ticket let him watch Game Six from the aisle between Fenway's grandstand sections 17 and 18. Bill is also co-founder of Rounder Records of Cambridge, Massachusetts. He's traveled to more than 100 countries, but says there's no place like Fenway Park.

MARK PATTISON, a Detroit native now living in Washington, DC is treasurer of the Mayo Smith Society, a nationwide organization of Detroit Tigers fans, and editor of its "Tigers Stripes" and "E-Mayo Flash" publications. He also co-authored *Detroit Tigers Lists and More: Runs, Hits and Eras,* and is an editor for the Society for American Baseball Research's BioProject. When not playing with his toddler daughter, he does baseball research—or is it the other way around?

JIM PRIME is the author of several baseball books, including *The Little Red (Sox) Book,* co-authored with Bill Lee, and *Blood Feud,* co-authored with Bill Nowlin. He lives in Nova Scotia.

MIKE RICHARD spent the "Summer of Love"—1967—falling in love with the Impossible Dream Red Sox. He attended Opening Day in 1975 and when the first pitch was thrown a strike, he proclaimed from the center-field bleachers: "Pennant Fever!" He may go down as the first true prophet of the '75 Sox. He taught high school English for 26 years, and is now a guidance counselor at Gardner (Massachusetts) High School. He is the author of two books *Glory To Gardner: 100 Years of Football in the Chair City* and *Super Saturdays: The Complete History of the Massachusetts High School Super Bowl, 1972–2002.* He lives in Gardner with his wife Peggy and two college-aged children Casey and Lindsey.

DAVID SOUTHWICK has been a SABR member since 2000, but a Red Sox fan longer than that. He serves the Boston Chapter as Publicity Director. When he's not petitioning the Giants to retire Johnnie LeMaster's No. 10, he can be found outside Fenway Park selling *Boston Baseball* and *SIX43* magazines. David currently lives in South Boston, Massachusetts.

BRIAN STEVENS is a devout Red Sox fan whose faith in the game (and life in general) was renewed in October 2004. The CFO of Smugglers' Notch Management Co. and a CPA, Brian lives with his wife, Cathie, in Jericho, Vermont.

CECILIA TAN is a freelance writer and editor living in Cambridge, Massachusetts. She co-edited *The Fenway Project* with Bill Nowlin and has been active in the Boston chapter of SABR since 2001. Her baseball writing has appeared in *Fenway Fiction, Baseball Ink,* and many places on the Internet. She is the author of *The 50 Greatest Yankees Games* (Wiley, 2005) and co-author with Bill Nowlin of *The 50 Greatest Red Sox Games* (Wiley, 2006).

JOHN VORPERIAN spent his childhood summers at Fenway Park and Plum Island, Massachusetts. Those halcyon days led to an incurable Red Sox obsession. A SABR member since 2000, John hosts "Beyond the Game" on White Plains Cable Television. When not producing the sports history program or writing for johnnyvsports.fws1.com, he daydreams about surfcasting with Ted Williams.

DAVE WILLIAMS is a lifelong Mets fan. He is currently a Territory Manager with Wilson Sporting Goods in Glastonbury, Connecticut where he resides with his wife and daughter. They do not understand how he can agonize over the Mets lack of offense year after year.